The World of the Ancient Maya

THE WORLD OF THE ANCIENT MAYA

SECOND EDITION

JOHN S. HENDERSON

Cornell University Press
Ithaca and London

First edition first published 1981 by Cornell University Press.
First printing, Cornell Paperbacks, 1983.
Second edition first published 1997.
First printing, Cornell Paperbacks, 1997.

Design and composition: Wilsted & Taylor Publishing Services
Printed in the United States of America

Library of Congress Cataloging-in-Publication Data
Henderson, John S.
The world of the ancient Maya / John S. Henderson. — 2nd ed.
p. cm.
Includes bibliographical references (p.) and index.
ISBN 0-8014-3183-2 (cloth : alk. paper). — ISBN 0-8014-8284-4 (paper : alk. paper)
1. Mayas. I. Title.
F1435.H6 1997
972.81'016—dc21 97-14353

Cornell University Press strives to utilize environmentally responsible suppliers and materials to the fullest extent possible in the publishing of its books. Such materials include vegetable-based, low-VOC inks and acid-free papers that are also either recycled, totally chlorine-free, or partly composed of nonwood fibers.

Cloth printing 10 9 8 7 6 5 4 3 2 1
Paperback printing 10 9 8 7 6 5 4 3 2 1

For Jeanne

Contents

Maps

The color plates follow page 140.

Here we shall write then,
    We shall start out then, the former words,
The beginnings,
    And the taproots . . .

So this is what we shall collect then,
    The decipherment,
The clarification,
    And the explanation
Of the mysteries
    and the illumination . . .

We shall save it
    Because there is no longer
A sight of the Book of Counsel,
    A sight of the bright things come from beside the sea,
The description of our shadows,
    A sight of the bright life, as it is called.
There was once the manuscript of it,
    And it was written long ago,
Only hiding his face is the reader of it,
    The mediator of it.
Great was its account
    And its description
Of when there was finished
    The birth
Of all heaven
    and earth . . .

—from Munro S. Edmonson, *The Book of Counsel: The Popol Vuh of the Quiché Maya of Guatemala*

Preface

The second edition of *The World of the Ancient Maya* has been reorganized as well as revised. Archaeologists and ethnohistorians have produced vast quantities of new data about the Maya in the 1980s and 1990s. Epigraphers have put forward an avalanche of new interpretations of glyphs and readings of texts that provide a rich source of information for reconstructing the politics of Classic Maya cities. The pace of development in the study of Maya texts and symbols is so rapid that it is difficult for epigraphers to present their new readings with all of the appropriate supporting arguments; it is even more difficult for them to retract or reassess all of the older (but still quite recent) interpretations that are superseded by each new reading. It is more difficult still for Mayanists with other specializations to keep up. No book can present all or most of the latest textual interpretations; this one does not pretend to.

In some ways the new information has brought about a shift in our basic perspectives on the Maya cultural tradition. To take a single example: investigations in the northern lowlands—especially the syntheses of the last centuries of the prehispanic period produced by Anthony Andrews and his colleagues—have laid the foundation for a new appreciation of the history of Chichén Itzá, its relationships with Uxmal, Cobá, and other northern cities, and the continuities and changes from the Classic Maya world to the successor states of the Postclassic period.

As in the first edition, the Introduction situates the ancient Maya and my approach to them in the context of larger themes in archaeological thought. Chapter 1 provides an overview of the Spanish invasion of the Maya world and traces the development of modern Maya studies. Chapter 2 introduces the environments and peoples of the Maya world and places them on the broader Mesoamerican stage. Its capsule histories of the various regions provide a preview of the fuller discussions in Chapters 4 through 9. Chapter 3 presents an overview of the Maya societies that the Spaniards encountered in the sixteenth century, including a summary of the insights that early documents provide into Maya philosophy and religion, especially in relation to the elaborate Maya calendars.

Chapters 4 through 9 comprise a chronological summary of the history of the Maya world. Discussions of early seminomadic bands and of the evolution of farming and settled life in Chapter 4 inevitably rely heavily on information from the better documented areas of western Mesoamerica; the brief summary of Olmec civilization emphasizes the Gulf Coast. With the appearance of complex Maya societies in the Late Preclassic period, our focus narrows to concentrate on the elaboration of societies in the Maya world proper, although relationships with the rest of Mesoamerica are not ignored. Chapter 10 returns to the broader issues and theoretical concerns raised in the Introduction in light of the information summarized in the intervening pages.

Entries in the Bibliography provide a good indication of my intellectual debts to other students of the Maya. Several colleagues have been particularly generous with ideas and encouragement. To name but a few: Anthony Andrews, E. Wyllys Andrews V, Katherine Emery, Julia Hendon, Stephen Houston, Rosemary Joyce, Richard Leventhal, Joyce Marcus, Don Rice, Pru Rice, Barbara Stark, Jeremy Sabloff, and Barbara Voorhies. Bev. Phillips cheerfully helped produce draft after draft and handled a thousand other matters, small and large, relating to the manuscript. As always, Jeanne Henderson has given me wonderful advice and moral support. I am deeply grateful to them all. Their efforts have improved the book immensely.

JOHN S. HENDERSON

Ithaca, New York

Guide to Pronunciation

Vowels are pronounced as they are in Spanish:

a as in *father*

e as in *grey*

i as *ee* in *knee*

o as in *most*

u as *oo* in *fool*

When *u* precedes another vowel, it is pronounced as English *w* (except that it is silent after *q*). A quick closing of the glottis occurs between doubled vowels, producing a short, sharp sound.

Consonants are pronounced as in Spanish, except that

c is always hard

x is pronounced as English *sh*

k is glottalized *c*

q' is a glottalized consonant similar to *k*, but produced in the back of the mouth (in Quiché words)

ch' is glottalized *ch*

dz is glottalized *tz*

h is gently aspirated (in Mayan words; silent in Spanish)

tl is voiceless—almost silent, with no buzzing of the vocal cords (at the ends of Nahuatl words)

In Mayan languages, the stress is generally on the final syllable. In Nahuatl, it is often on the penultimate, although Spanish influence has shifted the stress to the final syllable in many cases.

Examples

MAYAN	Chichén Itzá	chee-*chain* ee-*tsah*
	Holmul	hohl-*mool*
	Iximché	ee-sheem-*chay*
	Uaxactún	wah-shahk-*toon*
	Yaxchilán	yahsh-chee-*lahn*
NAHUATL	Quetzalcoatl	kay-tsahl-*koh*-ahtl
	Teotihuacan	properly, tay-oh-tee-*wah*-kahn (now usually tay-oh-tee-wah-*kahn*, spelled Teotihuacán)
SPANISH	Palenque	pah-*lain*-kay

The spelling conventions used for Mayan words are those which are commonest in the archaeological literature, sacrificing linguistic accuracy for the sake of clarity. Because the names of Mesoamerican places and peoples have entered our language through the tongue of the first Europeans to learn of their existence, such names are customarily written with the accents that are used in Spanish. That practice is followed here. Accents that normally do not appear in English-language contexts (as in "Mexico" and "Yucatan") are omitted.

Chronological Chart

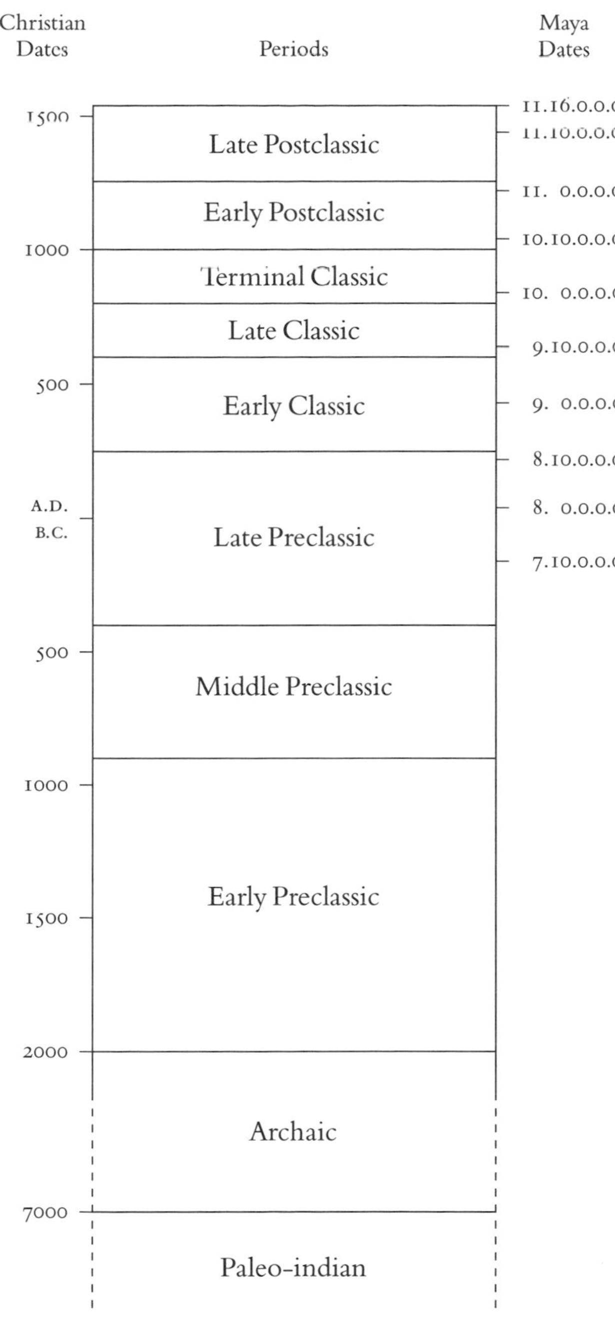

Christian era dates offered here and in the text represent calendar years. Radiocarbon dates have been converted to calendar dates by means of the CALIB program (Ver. 3.0.3 [Stuiver and Reimer 1993]). This conversion places some events, particularly in the Early and Middle Preclassic periods, at earlier dates than in traditional chronologies. Evidence of the emergence of kingdoms with monumental architecture, political art, and hieroglyphic texts in the Maya world during the centuries just before and after the beginning of the Christian era continues to accumulate, blurring the distinction between the Late Preclassic and Early Classic periods. In many regions, changes from the Middle Preclassic to the Late Preclassic are more striking, but the traditional Preclassic/Classic boundary is so embedded in the literature that it is retained here. Some chronologies recognize a distinct Middle Classic period, typically defined so as to embrace the time during which Teotihuacán was interacting most intensely with Maya polities, from about A.D. 400 to 700. In fact, the nature and intensity of Teotihuacán's impact was quite variable from region to region, and a discrete Middle Classic period is not very useful. The chronology of the Classic and Postclassic periods depends heavily on the Maya Long Count. The Maya dates at the right of the chart reflect the 11.16, or Goodman-Martínez-Thompson, correlation of the Long Count with the Gregorian calendar (see Chapter 5).

The World of the Ancient Maya

Introduction

All remnants of the distant past are romantic, but ancient Maya civilization has a special fascination. It is a "lost" civilization, whose secrets lie deep in the mysterious tropical forest. The style of Maya architecture and sculpture seems alien and bizarre. A writing system, partly deciphered but still the repository of so many tantalizing secrets of the past, completes the effect. John Lloyd Stephens, a nineteenth-century visitor to the Maya area, was particularly sensitive to the aura of mystery clinging to the monuments of the ancient Maya:

> Of the moral effect of the monuments themselves, standing as they do in the depths of a tropical forest, silent and solemn, strange in design, excellent in sculpture, rich in ornament, different from the works of any other people, their uses and purposes and whole history so entirely unknown with hieroglyphics explaining all, but being perfectly unintelligible, I shall not pretend to convey any idea. Often the imagination was pained in gazing at them.[1]

Stephens was enchanted by Copán, a ruined Maya center in Honduras (Color Plate 3). He called it "a valley of romance and wonder where . . . the genii who attended on King Solomon seem to have been the artists,"[2] and bought the site for $50.

In some ways modern archaeology—with its endless catalogs of artifacts, meticulous descriptions of excavated buildings, prosaic discussions of environmental resources, and brash reconstructions of ancient ways of life—has dispelled this romantic aura. In other respects archaeology has deepened the mystery surrounding the Maya, posing the profound puzzle of the so-called Maya collapse which preoccupied Maya studies for decades. New evidence has replaced the old idea of a sudden and total societal failure with a view of the "collapse" as a long-term process with multiple causes that transformed the political and economic order of the various regions of the Maya world in different ways at slightly different times. Nonetheless, there was a sweeping transformation, especially dramatic in the southern part of Yucatan where Maya societies were in many ways at the pinnacle of their development, and the causes of that transformation are still not well understood.

In a deeper sense, the fuller our understanding of the ancient Maya becomes, the more we can appreciate the enormous gulf that separates their culture from any in the European tradition. Nowhere are these differences more apparent than in Maya philosophy and world view, in which time and space, the physical world and the supernatural universe, are continuous: interconnected facets of a single, seamless reality. Maya reality is not ours. It would be difficult to invent a belief system more profoundly different from our own. Similar contrasts appear, less strikingly perhaps, in every other facet of Maya civilization.

If something beyond romantic fascination were required to give Maya civilization a claim on our attention, these differences provide a powerful intellectual stimulus. If most of us today are familiar with any aspect of the ancient world, it is with the cultural heritage of European civilization, stretching back through the Classical world to the ancient Near East. Our implicit feeling is that these cultures are the norm, perhaps even the highest possible stage of development, for early civilization. A proper appreciation of their nature and their achievement can come only with the perspective provided by familiarity with a different tradition of civilization. Maya civilization, with its totally different styles, institutions, organizations, and developmental history, offers just such a perspective. Even the briefest examination of Maya civilization and its history cannot fail to improve our understanding of other early civilizations.

The problems of defining civilization and explaining its rise have preoccupied some of the best minds in archaeology. Maya civilization, unusual in its setting and its form, makes a crucial contribution to our understanding of the general processes involved in the origins of civilization. The general public and theorists alike almost universally view civilizations as urban phenomena and focus on cities as their most prominent feature.[3] Theories that purport to account for the origins of civilization are often in fact explanations for the beginnings of urban life. Maya civilization was organized around great civic centers that were seats of power and hubs of social, religious, economic, and political affairs, but those centers were noticeably different from cities as they are usually defined. Only a few Maya cities ever approached the density of population usually associated with urbanism, and even that growth occurred centuries after the essential features of Maya civilization had emerged. No theory that focuses on demographic aspects of the rise of cities can account for Maya development.

With few exceptions, the earliest civilizations arose and flourished in great temperate or semiarid river valleys and in environmentally varied highland regions. Only in Mesoamerica and Southeast Asia were lowland tropical forests their cradle. Most explanations for the rise of civilization are tailored to fit very different environmental circumstances and are of dubious relevance to the Maya case. The ideas of Karl Wittfogel illustrate the problem well.[4] Wittfogel, among the most influential of the theorists to consider the beginnings of civilization, was most familiar with the river-valley civilizations of China and the Near East. Reduced to its most simplistic form, his argument places the stimulus for civilization in the development of large-scale irrigation facilities needed to feed expanding populations. Such facilities, he claims, have heavy and continuous managerial requirements that can be met only by a highly organized bureaucracy. In effect, the need for complex hydraulic works calls centralized, often despotic, states into existence. Without substantial modification, the theory of hydraulic civilization[5] cannot account for the appearance and florescence of civilization in the tropical lowlands of Mesoamerica, where irrigation makes little sense as a farming strategy. The theory is also open to criticism when it is applied to the areas from which Wittfogel derived the data for its initial formulation, but it has been extremely influential.

Similar ideas have been invoked to explain the rise of civilization in the highlands of central Mexico.[6] Here theorists have also sought to tie civilization to cities, and much of their discussion has been directed toward the beginnings of urbanism. Some scholars are inclined to play down the complexity of lowland Mesoamerican societies, particularly the Olmec; a related view treats the Maya as a derivative civilization, whose complexity was a result of heavy influence from highland urban civilizations. The most extreme solution to the problems posed by lowland Mesoamerican civilizations must be credited to V. Gordon Childe, probably the most influential of all archaeological theorists. Childe simply eliminated the entire New World as an arena of interesting ancient cultural development, remarking, "Never been there—peripheral and highly suspect."[7]

For reasons that should become increasingly evident as we explore the problem, these approaches are not satisfactory. In many ways Maya culture is the most complex ever to arise in the New World. The Maya are, for example, the only Native American people to develop a full-fledged writing system, and their complex of astronomical, mathematical, and calendrical thought is sophisticated from any perspective.

The question of an appropriate definition of civilization might easily occupy an entire volume. A simple working definition recognizes civilization as a complex variety of culture, with considerable elaboration in many areas; civilizations exhibit a great deal of economic specialization and support many kinds of full-time specialists. Civilizations occupy substantial geographic areas, and their political organizations are especially complex, reaching the state level. Institutionalized specialist leadership positions exercise effective control over substantial numbers of people. But this definition leaves much unspecified: What kinds of cultural elaboration? How many specialists, of what sorts? How large an area? What kinds of political offices, controlling how many people? The strength of such a definition lies in its generality, which makes for flexibility, inclusiveness, and adaptability to archaeological data. Because early civilizations and the processes by which they came into being are not uniform, trait-list definitions do not work well. The more specific the traits, the more quickly the definition breaks down, so that exceptions are required to include obviously relevant cultures. The Olmec and the Maya lacked "true" cities; the Inca of Peru had no writing system; early Sumer had no single political state. Quantitative criteria fare even worse in the face of archaeological evidence, from which it is extraordinarily difficult to wring reliable estimates of population or of the geographic limits of political units.

Specifics are most profitably left for empirical determination and description. The best criteria are the most general, simply pointing to the most important dimensions of civilizations. Within these parameters considerable variation must be accommodated. Cultural elaboration may be found in any or all of a variety of cultural realms: technology, subsistence, economics, commerce, religion, politics. The lack of a particular development, such as bronze metallurgy, is interesting but has no effect on the status of a culture as a civilization. Civilizations are regional, not local, in scale, but the cultural ties that bind localities together may be economic or religious or social as well as political. State-level political organization must embrace a substantial population—considerably more people than would normally engage in face-to-face interaction—but they may be widely dispersed across the landscape rather than packed densely into cities. The definition is elastic enough to embrace the enormous empires of the Inca and ancient Egypt, the city-states of early Mesopotamia, and the regional states of the Maya.

All indications are that Maya civilization is a primary civilization: there is no convincing evidence that its development depended to a significant degree on influence from the highland civilizations of central Mexico. The tropical-forest setting of Maya civilization and the unusual character of its cities make it especially interesting. Maya civilization also makes a fascinating case study in culture-historical reconstruction on other grounds. A multifaceted and multidisciplinary approach is appropriate for any investigation of culture history, particularly for a complex prehistoric culture. Because of the variety of types and sources of information, Maya civilization lends itself exceptionally well to such an approach.

The creators of Maya civilization did not disappear without issue. Their descendants today occupy vast areas of Guatemala and eastern Mexico.[8] In the face of heavy pressures toward change, now in their fifth century, they cling tenaciously to their own ways. The Maya have accommodated themselves to the dominant Spanish American culture in a variety of ways that permit the preservation of distinctive ways of life. Millions of people still grow up speaking Mayan languages as their first tongues and wrest a living from the land principally by means of the ancient methods of slash-and-burn farming. Christianity is tempered with a strong admixture of native beliefs and practices.

Careful study of the Maya of today can be a priceless source of information about the Maya of precolumbian times. A simple projection of modern Maya culture into the past, though, is useless, for no culture is static (Color Plate 11). Cultures exist in a dynamic equilibrium with their environments, both natural and cultural. No modern Maya group is a living relic of its ancestry. Such a view ignores one of the most striking aspects of postconquest Maya history: the remarkable flexibility that has allowed Maya cultures to adapt to European domination without losing their distinctiveness. Other bars to a simple backward projection are equally obvious. Which modern Maya society should be the model for ancient Maya culture? Even the briefest survey of the dozens of Maya groups produces one impression above all: that of a cultural kaleidoscope, in which variations of the same elements are combined and recombined to produce an array of related groups whose cultural patterns represent complex variations on the same basic themes. This variation reflects differences in the ways Maya groups have adapted to the European conquest as well as a complex cultural heritage from precolumbian times.[9] It is not even a simple matter to sort out borrowings from Spanish culture, so subtle are the ways in which they are altered, recombined, and reworked into the fabric of the native tradition.

So many and complex are the contrasts among the Maya of today that it is in some ways difficult to recognize what all groups hold in common, to specify the essential features of a Maya culture. The only really obvious common denominator is language: all Maya groups speak related tongues. That is in fact how they are defined: in an ethnographic context, that is what one means by a Maya group. Yet in the realm of language, too, Maya groups vary strikingly.

Some linguists recognize more than two dozen distinct languages, many of them mutually unintelligible, within the Mayan family.[10] The precise relationships among them are a matter of some dispute among linguists. All are recognizably Mayan, though, either because a language reflects cultural relationships particularly clearly or, more likely, because linguists are more adept at detecting relationships among languages than other cultural anthropologists are at assessing connections among economic systems, political institutions, social organizations, religious beliefs, or art styles.

A vast assortment of written documents, from snippets to treatises, records information about the Maya between the arrival of Europeans and the present day. The works of early historians, both Europeans and natives interested in recording aspects of their own tradition, preserve not only Maya history but also literature, poetry, song, myth, and ritual. Precious nuggets of information may be gleaned from *conquistadores'* memoirs and from travelers' journals. Administrative records of state and church complete the list. These records range from general summary descriptions of regions and people for the information of distant officials to accounts of court proceedings, dispute settlements, investigations of officials, and all of the minutiae with which bureaucracies concern themselves. Together these documents constitute a rich fund of information about the Maya. Having been accumulated through such a diversity of intents, this is not a particularly coherent body of information, and much of it remains scattered in dusty archives, unpublished and even unexamined. Still, taken together, these sources can be used, along with reconstructions of the history of Mayan languages, to extend the ethnographic record backward in time. The historical ethnography of the conquest period, sketchy though it is, shows no less variation than the modern Maya scene. Sixteenth-century Maya, of course, were no more fossilized representatives of their precolumbian ancestors than are their modern descendants.

Working back into the preconquest period, for which no eyewitness accounts exist, is still more difficult. For the late prehispanic period in northern Yucatan and the central Maya highlands, native histories recorded after the Spanish invasion are primary sources. They must be used with extreme caution, for they are not free from bias; nor do they pretend to be objective accounts. Like all histories, they adopt particular points of view, serving particular political ends. Those ends may be apparent, as in the case of Spanish churchmen who were describing the history of a people whose pagan religion was to be obliterated. Native Maya biases are much less transparent, and much more misleading. Though recorded in European script, sometimes by Spaniards and sometimes by reeducated Mayas, the early colonial sources reflect, at least in part, Maya concepts of history. Maya history has its own set of goals and assumptions, which give it an entirely different character from European history.[11] Later ethnographic observations and historical linguistics may also contribute to general reconstructions of the precolumbian Maya, but inferences based on these sources seldom provide specific insights.

The deeper into preconquest Maya history we try to penetrate, the more our reconstructions depend on archaeological evidence. Archaeologists draw inferences about people from patterns in the material traces they have left behind: tools and utensils, food remains, remnants of buildings, layouts of settlements, distributions of settlements across the landscape. Such traces are in many areas the only available evidence for reconstructing prehistory. There are other lines of evidence for the Maya, notably hieroglyphic texts. Since writing was in use in only some parts of the Maya world and in some time periods, and since the vast majority of the texts that were produced do not survive, archaeology will remain the principal source of information, even when decipherment has advanced to the point of capturing the nuances as well as the gists of ancient texts.

The archaeological record of the Maya area is by no means uniform. The vagaries of preservation and accessibility of archaeological remains ensure that some regions and time periods are less well represented than others. Large zones are virtually untouched. Even in the most thoroughly investigated regions, research has emphasized certain sites, usually the largest, richest, and most impressive, to the neglect or even exclusion of others. Archaeologists have investigated relatively few small settlements without major public architecture or sculpture. Within the cities, excavations have usually focused on impressive buildings and monuments. Few projects have set out to discover the full range of variation in house types, or subsistence strategies, or artifact inventories within a given community. Not even the most intensively excavated Maya city is fully understood either in terms of its internal structure or in terms of its relationships with other settlements within the region.

Nevertheless, enough data have accumulated from various regions and time periods to indicate a very great deal of regional variation among the preconquest Maya. Such variations existed in every period for which data are available. They tended to increase through time, and they were especially pronounced in some periods.

The most productive approach to understanding Maya culture history, then, demands the use of all available sources of information: archaeology, history, linguistics, and ethnography. Few other ancient civilizations have such a wealth of available material. The value and the potential of this approach is particularly apparent in the investigation of ancient Maya thought and symbols. An approach to the Maya hieroglyphic texts in isolation, in terms of their own pattern and structure, yields minimal understanding. Broadening the scope of inquiry to include insights into Maya religion from ethnography, modern analyses of Mayan languages, and documents of the colonial period touching on Maya writing, ritual, and belief sets the stage for a multifaceted approach that can lead to a reasonably full understanding of at least some texts and some aspects of Maya thought. Ultimately there is a tremendously exciting potential for actually entering, albeit partially and hesitantly, the symbolic world of the precolumbian Maya. This is a rare opportunity in any area and unique for the preconquest Americas. It adds considerably to the interest and importance of the Maya as a case study in culture-historical reconstruction.

The chapters that follow examine the history of Maya culture from the earliest archaeological traces of settlement in the Maya region through the great florescence of the first millennium of the Christian era down to the period of the Spanish conquest. The enormous amount of cultural variation within the Maya world at any given time certainly does not lighten the task of understanding the complex processes through which Maya societies evolved. Yet this regional diversity is itself a crucial fact of Maya culture history. It can hardly be ignored. The Classic Maya "collapse" is a case in point: the process brought sweeping changes to virtually every part of the Maya world, but it took a different form, and had a different timing, in each region.

To consider the growth and development of the Maya world and its internal variation at many time levels is a complex task. To examine such regional and developmental complexity through the lens of archaeological evidence, with its all too apparent biases and lacunae, compounds the difficulties. Whenever possible, the evidence of linguistics, ethnography, and history will be brought to bear on the problems at hand, but archaeology is the principal source of data. Too often it is the only source.

It is important to try to examine the great Maya cities as varied functional entities, not simply as collections of monuments and buildings. Insofar as the data permit, each city must be placed in its regional context, as a part of a functioning system. This approach dictates a concern with the relationships among contemporary settlements as well as with their similarities and contrasts. At a higher level, the focus shifts to the discovery of contrasts among the many regions of the Maya area and to an identification of the relationships that linked them.

Although it is interesting to point to some of the crucial factors and processes involved in the growth and development of the Maya cultural tradition, I do not attempt to isolate governing causal factors. It would be naive to expect to understand the evolution of a phenomenon as complex and multifaceted as Maya civilization by reference to one or a few causal factors. An understanding of the evolution of Maya culture is more readily achieved, with much less distortion, through a detailed culture history: that is to say, through the most precise reconstruction of the regional variants of Maya culture and their functional interrelations during as many periods as possible. When these factors are woven into a descriptive historical narrative of a set of related cultures within a single tradition, it may be possible to recognize the cultural processes that connect the stages. If not, at least no violence will have been done to the rich historical complexity of the Maya world.

Myriad threads intertwine in the tapestry of the Maya cultural tradition; their colors blend subtly to represent many themes. We cannot achieve a full understanding of the processes by which Maya civilization came into being by pulling out a few bright threads. True insight depends on the laborious unraveling of many historical strands.

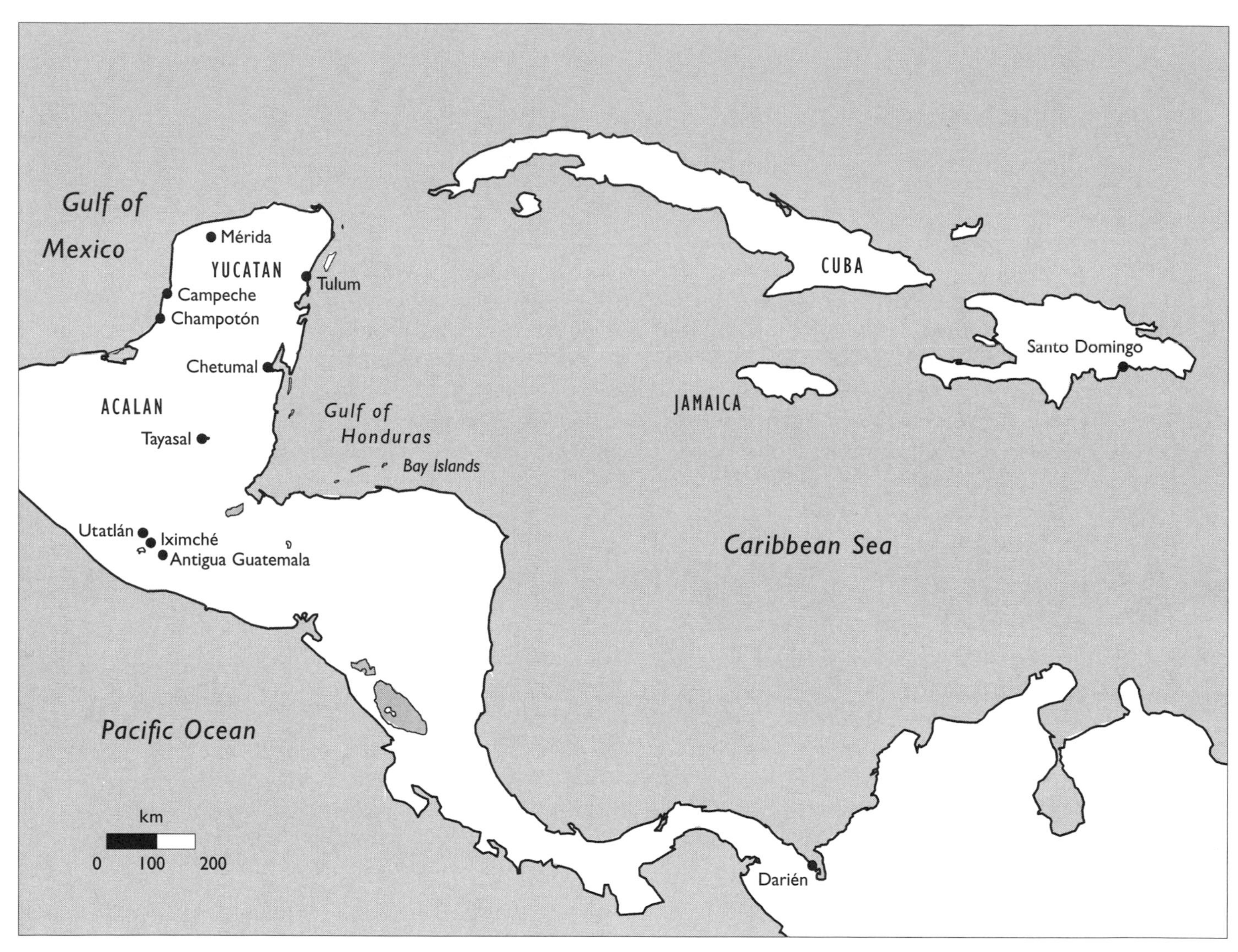

MAP 1. The Spanish Main: the Maya world and the Caribbean.

ONE

The Discovery of the Maya

Spanish voyages to the Americas beginning at the end of the fifteenth century resulted in what was, for most Europeans, the discovery of a "New World" and of peoples whose existence was unsuspected. In fact, Europeans had probably been fishing off the coast of North America for centuries, and the Norse had settled Vinland and parts of coastal North America before A.D. 1000.[1] Fishermen seldom advertise the location of rich waters to potential competitors; the Norse colonies did not last long, and the peoples they met were not rich by European standards. So it was only in the aftermath of Columbus's expeditions that the Americas came to the attention of Europeans hungry for land, labor, and gold.[2] From the point of view of native peoples, of course, this episode was not so much a discovery as an invasion.

Europeans began to encounter Maya societies almost as soon as they became aware of the mainland, and Spaniards began to establish permanent settlements among conquered Maya peoples right away. Many of the first few generations of Spanish invaders understood that the remains of precolumbian Maya civilization represented the ancestors of the contemporary subjugated Maya, but their successors soon lost sight of the linkage, and of the ruins themselves, so that the existence of one of the great ancient civilizations of the world in the forests of Yucatan was astonishing to Europeans and North Americans. The intellectual rediscovery of the grandeur of the Maya past is the achievement of Maya archaeology.

The Spanish Invasion

In 1502, during his final voyage of discovery, Columbus met an impressive vessel in the Gulf of Honduras, near the Bay Islands (Map 1). This was the first encounter between Europeans and the Maya.[3] Commanded by a merchant from the "province called Maia," the canoe bore his entourage and a rich and varied cargo of trade goods: metal tools and ornaments, metalworking paraphernalia, clubs edged with stone blades, pottery, cotton garments with multicolored designs, and a wealth of other items. No one, apparently, attached particular interest to this episode, later cataloged without emphasis among the events of the voyage. Nor was there a special reason to do otherwise. Though plainly prosperous, these traders did not seem to differ much from other native groups the Spaniards had met. Certainly they did not display the anticipated wealth and splendor of the Orient. In any case, the encounter produced no immediate impulse to locate the homeland of the traders. Even when more intensive and sustained contact with the Maya came about during the following decades, it occasioned no special comment, for the impressive achievements of Maya civilization were then centuries and more in the past. No sixteenth-century Maya settlement could compare with Tenochtitlan, the splendid island capital of the Aztecs, and the size and wealth of the Aztec state were unmatched north of Peru. Naturally, the Maya attracted correspondingly less attention from early chroniclers and historians, so that innumerable aspects of their native tradition passed quickly into oblivion following the conquest.

The greater part of the coast of Yucatan was officially discovered in 1508, although again no immediate attempt was made to explore or conquer it.[4] In 1511 a caravel bound from Darién in Panama to Santo Domingo went aground on the shoals off Jamaica. The dozen survivors who drifted ashore on the east coast of Yucatan two weeks later became the first Europeans to have extended contact with the Maya. Juan de Valdivia, the commander, and four companions met quick deaths on the sacrificial altar; their bodies were consumed in a cannibalistic ritual. Gerónimo de Aguilar, one of the two castaways still living when Spanish exploration of Yucatan began in earnest, recalled: "I, together with six others, remained in a coop, in order that for another festival that was approaching, being fatter, we might solemnize their banquet with our flesh. Understanding that the end of our days was drawing near, we decided to venture our lives in another way, so we broke the cage in which we had been placed, and [fled] through the bush."[5] The European diseases that they and the Spaniards who came after them carried, notably measles and smallpox, quickly touched off virulent epidemics which took a devastating toll of Maya populations that had had no opportunity to develop immunity.[6]

Aguilar eventually rejoined his countrymen, bringing valuable reports about Maya culture as well as a knowledge of one of the Mayan languages. Gonzalo Guerrero, the other survivor, refused to be repatriated, preferring to remain with his Maya wife and children among her people in Chetumal.[7] Guerrero maintained his position as a prominent military commander in the service of the lord of Chetumal for some twenty years. He died in 1536 in Honduras, in command of a flotilla of war canoes, defending the commercial interests of Chetumal against the Spaniards. After the battle, his horrified countrymen found him among the slain—hair worn long, body tattooed, nose, lips, and ears pierced for jewels.

Juan Ponce de León paused briefly along the coast of Yucatan on his return from Florida in 1513.[8] The first protracted exploration came in 1517, when a vessel commanded by Francisco Hernández de Córdoba skirted the coast of Yucatan.[9] His first landfall was Isla Mujeres (Isle of Women), named after the many statues of Maya goddesses found in a local shrine. Taking with them several gold objects, the Spaniards continued westward along the coast and then south to the native town of Campeche. Farther south, at Champotón, Hernández's luck ran out. Wounded dozens of times in a skirmish with the fierce local Maya, he "sadly returned to Cuba."[10] Within two weeks Hernández was dead, but his exaggerated reports of the golden wealth of Yucatan aroused the cupidity of several adventurous countrymen. Thus began the tradition of misunderstanding and violence that the Spaniards, bent on exploration, conquest, and colonization, brought to their interaction with the Maya.

The following year, Juan de Grijalva made a similar voyage along the coast of Yucatan, making note of substantial native settlements.[11] Grijalva landed first at Cozumel, a Maya pilgrimage center off the east coast. He claimed the island in the name of the crown and proceeded south. The Spaniards were particularly taken with Tulum, overlooking the sea (Color Plate 7). "Towards sunset," wrote the expedition chaplain, "we saw from afar off a town or village so large that the city of Seville could not appear greater or better; and in it was seen a very great tower."[12] Doubling back around Yucatan, Grijalva continued west and north as far as what is now Tampico. From these northern lands, dominions of the Aztec empire, Grijalva brought back gold and silver along with precious stones, colorful textiles, and exotic ornaments of all kinds.

Word of these discoveries came quickly to the ears of Hernán Cortés in Cuba, then nursing his ambitions for conquest, power, wealth, and glory.[13] In 1519 he was at last able to mount the expedition that would result in the conquest of the Aztec empire and the destruction of the civilizations of central Mexico. His first landfall was Cozumel, where he found deserted villages and shrines. There Gerónimo de Aguilar, one of the surviving castaways, joined Cortés, providing the Spaniards their first real intelligence about Maya culture.

Leaving Cozumel, Cortés followed the coast, landing again near the Río Grijalva, on the western edge of the Maya area. Here he acquired the invaluable Doña Marina, the daughter of a high-ranking native merchant, who spoke both Mayan and Nahuatl (the language of the Aztecs). Through Marina and Aguilar, who spoke both Mayan and Spanish, Cortés was now able to communicate more easily with the native groups he encountered. He moved north along the coast and shortly began the march inland that culminated in the conquest of Tenochtitlan, island capital of the Aztecs.

The following decades brought repeated forays into northern Yucatan and the western fringe of the Maya region along the base of the Gulf of Mexico. Although exploration and attempts at settlements were practically continuous, conquest and colonization proceeded very slowly. The Spaniards now found themselves in a very different situation from the one in central Mexico. Yucatan had no single, extensive, highly centralized state that could be toppled at a blow. Political organization was fragmented, and each local polity had to be dealt with separately. Even when a town had been defeated, its inhabitants were likely to melt into the forest rather than remain to serve European masters. In 1542, with the founding of Mérida, the Spaniards finally established a permanent base in Yucatan, but full, effective control of the peninsula was still many years in the future.

Europeans found it very difficult to establish effective transportation and communication facilities in the forested lowlands of the Maya area, and many zones remain isolated today. Although the Spaniards achieved formal sovereignty over Yucatan with relative ease, many local Maya groups successfully resisted effective domination and assimilation for centuries. Indeed, substantial numbers of Maya in eastern Yucatan still refused to acknowledge the authority of the Mexican government in the 1920s.

The southern sector of the Maya lowlands, at the

base of the Yucatan peninsula, was even more resistant to Spanish domination than the northern zone. With its heavier rainfall and high, lush tropical forest, the environment seemed particularly forbidding to European eyes. Accounts of Cortes's march across the heart of the Yucatan peninsula to Honduras in 1524–25 dwell at length on the suffering occasioned by the Spaniards' inability to cope with the environment. Cortes's description of the approach to the province of Acalán conveys something of his growing distaste for the Maya lowlands:

After having marched for three days through dense forest along a very narrow track, we reached a great lagoon more than five hundred paces wide, and though I searched up and down for a way across I could find none. Moreover, the guides told me that it was a useless search unless I marched for twenty days toward the mountain. . . . To turn back was . . . impossible, for it meant certain death for all, not only because of the bad roads we would have to travel, and the great rains which had fallen, swelling the rivers . . . but also because we had consumed all our provisions and could find nothing else to eat. . . . I determined, therefore, that as there was no other solution I would build a bridge, and at once set about having some timbers cut, from nine to ten fathoms in length. . . . No one believed that such a task could ever be accomplished, and some even whispered that it would be better to return before everyone was too exhausted and weak with hunger to be able to. . . . When I saw how discouraged they were, and truly they had cause to be, for . . . they were demoralized and lethargic, having eaten nothing but the roots of plants, I told them that . . . I would complete it with the Indians alone. . . . So hard did they work, and so skillfully, that in four days they had finished the bridge. . . . When all the men and horses had finally crossed this lagoon, we came upon a great marsh which lasted for two crossbowshots, the most frightful thing the men had ever seen, where the unsaddled horses sank in up to their girths until nothing else could be seen; and in struggling to get out they only sank in deeper, so that we lost all hope of being able to bring a single horse out safely. But still we determined to attempt it, and by placing bundles of reeds and twigs beneath them to support them and prevent them from sinking, they were somewhat better off. . . . Thus it pleased our Lord that they should all emerge without loss, though so exhausted they could barely stand up.[14]

These accounts also provide the first picture, albeit a confused one, of the native peoples of the region. Settlement was relatively sparse and ethnic variation considerable. Complex economic, political, and social ties formed links across a mosaic of small, independent political units.

After Cortés's march, this interior sector of the Yucatan peninsula remained very isolated for centuries, though not entirely untouched by Spanish culture. The Itzá of Tayasal were unsubjugated until 1697, although Cortés's brief sojourn did result in a remarkable episode of acculturation. An ailing horse, abandoned by Cortés, achieved lasting fame among the people of Tayasal.[15] Missionaries who arrived there at the end of the seventeenth century found them making offerings of flowers and turkeys to the horse's image, which they called Tizimin Chac. The horse had become a minor deity associated with thunder and lightning.

The central sector of the Maya highlands succumbed to the Spaniards much more rapidly than the lowland zones.[16] Pedro de Alvarado and his cohorts arrived from Mexico in 1524. His conquest of the most prominent of the native states, the Quiché and the Cakchiquel, along with most of their neighbors, was swift and brutal. The traditional history of the Cakchiquel, transcribed shortly after the conquest, paints a terrifying portrait of the blond Alvarado, called Tonatiuh or Tunatiuh, after the sun god:

On the day 1 Ganel [February 20, 1524] the Quichés were destroyed by the Spaniards. Their chief, he who was called Tunatiuh Avilantaro, conquered all the people. . . . Then [the Spaniards] went forth to the city of Gumarcaah [Utatlán, the Quiché capital], where they were received by the kings, the Ahpop and the Ahpop Qamahay, and the Quichés paid them tribute. Soon the kings were tortured by Tunatiuh. On the day 4 Qat [March 7, 1524] the kings Ahpop and Ahpop Qamahay were burned by Tunatiuh. The heart of Tunatiuh was without compassion for the people. . . . On the day 1 Hunahpu [April 12, 1524] the Spaniards came to the city of Yximché; . . . Tunatiuh then asked for one of the daughters of the king and the lords gave her to Tunatiuh. Then Tunatiuh asked the kings for money. He wished them to give him piles of metal, their vessels and crowns. And as they did not bring them to him immediately, Tunatiuh became angry with the kings and said to them: "Why have you not brought me the metal? If you do not bring with you all of the money of the tribes, I will burn you and I will hang you," he said to the lords. Next Tunatiuh ordered them to pay twelve hundred pesos of gold. The kings tried to have the amount reduced and they began to weep, but Tunatiuh did not consent, and he said to them: "Get the metal and bring it within five days. Woe to you if you do not bring it! I know my heart!" Thus he said to the lords. . . . Then we abandoned the city of Yximché. . . . Ten days after we fled from the city, Tunatiuh began to make war upon us. On the day 4 Camey [September 5, 1524] they began to make us suffer. We scattered ourselves under the trees, under the vines, oh, my sons![17]

A functioning colonial capital, established almost at once near Iximché (Color Plate 8) and later transferred to the site now known as Antigua Guatemala, provided a base for the conquest of the highlands and of the adjacent piedmont and Pacific Coast. Surprisingly, cultural assimilation did not automatically follow in the wake of the early conquest and rapid establishment of Spanish administrative control. On the contrary, Maya groups in the highlands still retain their languages and much of the native cultural tradition.

Northern and western sectors of the highlands and the slopes descending to the southern Maya lowlands were not so easily brought within the colonial orbit. Spanish penetration of these areas was haphazard and retarded. Like the southern lowlands of Yucatan, these zones remained beyond effective Spanish administrative control for a considerable time, and many sectors are still remote and difficult to reach.

The conquest of the eastern fringe of the Maya area, at the base of the Gulf of Honduras, began early and was contested by a variety of Spanish parties that proceeded independently from Mexico, lower Central America, the Caribbean islands and, later, Guatemala and Yucatan. Full administrative control was achieved relatively quickly, under the jurisdiction of Guatemala. Here the native cultural tradition was almost entirely obliterated at an early stage under the combined effects of ferocious competition among Spanish factions and the subsequent single-minded exploitation of native labor in mining operations.

The Maya writing system did not long survive the conquest. The Spaniards quickly recognized that the writing of the Maya was inseparable from the fabric of their belief and symbol systems. It became a prime target for extirpation. Whether or not the Maya came to believe that these hieroglyphs endangered their souls, the possession of ritual books and other repositories of visual symbols certainly put their bodies in deadly peril at the hands of the churchmen. A great portion of Maya thought perished with the native books (Color Plate 9), most of which the Spaniards destroyed. Diego de Landa, a sixteenth-century bishop of Yucatan, presided over the purge: "We found a large number of books in these characters and, as they contained nothing in which there were not to be seen superstition and lies of the devil, we burned them all, which they regretted to an amazing degree, and which caused them much affliction."[18] Of the thousands of native books—genealogies, biographies, collections of songs, books of science, history, prophecy, astrology, ritual—only four remain.[19] Like the books themselves, knowledge of Maya writing went underground after the conquest, ultimately to be lost. Mayas continued to produce documents recording aspects of the native tradition, but now with Spanish characters. There are no bilingual texts in Maya hieroglyphs and Spanish. The closest thing to a Maya Rosetta stone comes from the pen of the bibliophobic Bishop Landa. His encyclopedic account of native life in Yucatan includes a discussion of the Maya calendar and writing. Although he misunderstood the system, his remarks would eventually provide important leads in the decipherment of the script.

Rediscovery

Dazzled by the architectural grandeur of Tenochtitlan and by the material wealth and power of its Aztec rulers, Spaniards found the sixteenth-century Maya unimpressive. They had little reason to suppose that the Maya past was more spectacular, particularly when even the historical traditions of the Maya traced the ancestry of the elite, ruling groups to the Toltecs of central Mexico. Only in northern Yucatan, where native tradition emphasized the historical continuity from the heyday of Chichén Itzá to the Spanish conquest, could the sixteenth-century Maya be linked with impressive archaeological remains. Even here the connection was quickly forgotten. Bishop Landa's encyclopedic treatise on the Maya of Yucatan—so fascinating to the modern reader—attracted little attention.[20] It was unearthed and published only in the nineteenth century.

The achievements of the Classic period of Maya civilization were more than half a millennium in the past when Spaniards first came to Mesoamerica. Most of its greatest architectural and sculptural monuments were lost in the remote forests of southern Yucatan, and they remained so for centuries. Small wonder, then, that the Maya were so long in claiming their rightful place among the great civilizations of antiquity. In the eighteenth and early nineteenth centuries, occasional explorers came across the ruins of the great Maya centers.[21] Almost without exception, they attributed the monuments to ancient migrants from the Mediterranean—Egyptians, Chaldeans, Israelites, anyone but the Maya. Fortunately, perhaps, their reports received scant notice.

EXPLORATION

Between 1839 and 1842, John Lloyd Stephens, an American traveler, lawyer, and sometime diplomat, visited the Maya area in the company of the English artist Frederick Catherwood.[22] Stephens's descriptions of Maya archaeological monuments, magnificently illustrated by Catherwood, became immensely popular. The absorbing accounts of their journeys first brought the remnants of a vanished civilization to the attention of Europeans and North Americans. Fortunately, Stephens brought caution and reason to interpretation and was a careful observer. He rightly concluded that the ancestors of the Maya—not wandering Near Easterners—were responsible for the monuments. Stephens's careful approach largely set the tone for Maya archaeology during the following century. Such pioneer Maya archaeologists as Alfred P. Maudslay and Teobert Maler concerned themselves mainly with discovery and careful description.[23] They preferred to augment the scanty corpus of information on Maya civilization rather than to indulge in fanciful interpretation.

Meanwhile, of course, the old tradition of untrammeled speculation had not died without issue. The most bizarre interpretations of the ancient Maya came from the pen of Augustus Le Plongeon, an adventurer of epic stature who turned to Maya archaeology late in the nineteenth century. Among the tamest of his beliefs was the notion that Maya civilization had been imported to Mesoamerica fully formed from Atlantis. His conclusions about the subsequent spread of Maya culture to the Mediterranean neatly reversed the common diffusionist position, and had the added advantage of making possible startling new interpretations of familiar events. Jesus, on the cross, had spoken Maya, not Hebrew, saying, "Now, now, sinking black ink over nose."[24] Surely a classic in the annals of revisionist history. Neither Le Plongeon's extravagant theories nor his genuinely interesting discoveries attracted much attention in the emergent field of Maya studies, an outcome that embittered him terribly.[25]

EARLY EXCAVATIONS IN ANCIENT MAYA CITIES

Near the end of the nineteenth century, major excavations of ancient Maya cities began with the work of the Peabody Museum of Harvard at Copán (Map 9, Color Plate 3).[26] Location of new cities, documentation of ruins with maps, drawings, and photographs, and occasional excavation programs continued in the early decades of the twentieth century. Large-scale excavations of Maya cities, sponsored by the Carnegie Institution of Washington during the 1920s, 1930s, and 1940s, set the tone for Maya archaeology until the 1960s.[27] Projects were data-oriented, seeking information that could be used for ever more detailed characterizations of Maya societies and their history in terms of their greatest achievements in monumental art and architecture. Large-scale excavations at Copán, Uaxactún, Kaminaljuyú, Chichén Itzá (Maps 8, 9, Color Plate 6), and Mayapán were meant to explore the prehistory of all parts of the Maya world and the full chronological span of Maya civilization, from its emergence to the Spanish invasion.

These excavations produced wonderfully detailed descriptions of temples and palaces, monumental stone sculpture, painted pottery, carved jade jewelry, and other fine craft products. This information provided the chronological outline for Maya archaeology and also created the conceptual framework within which archaeologists tried to reconstruct the nature of ancient Maya societies. Insights into social relations, however, based on buildings and the imagery associated with them, pertained almost exclusively to aristocratic segments of Maya societies. In the same way, patterns inferred from the distributions of imported materials and craft items were those of the economies of aristocracies, especially of royal courts. The styles, organizational patterns, and developmental trajectories of these cities were taken to define the "norms" of a Maya civilization that was thought to be quite uniform. Variability from region to region was of little interest, except as a way of defining the geographic limits of the Maya world. Nonelite facets of ancient Maya civilization—houses of ordinary farmers and craftsmen in the cities and in outlying villages—generally got short shrift. Even towns and smaller cities within the orbits of the powerful capitals attracted little attention. Problems of explanation—accounting for the rise of Maya civilization or for its developmental trajectory—were secondary in importance, subjects suitable for speculation only when sufficient information had been amassed. Maya archaeologists were not much concerned with trying to understand the Maya in the context of anthropological thought about the nature of complex societies. Mayanists, inclined to celebrate the aesthetic and intellectual achievements of the ancient Maya and to emphasize the distinctive aspects of Maya civilization, were not deeply engaged in a detailed comparison of Maya societies with other early states.

EARLY STUDIES OF MAYA SYMBOLS AND WRITING

Late in the nineteenth century, a second major avenue of research into ancient Maya civilization opened with investigations of Maya imagery and hieroglyphic writing.[28] Graphic images—painted in murals, in books, or on pots; carved in stone; incised on portable objects—range from straightforward pictorial representation to extremely conventionalized sets of abstract symbols. Maya art, like that of other Mesoamerican peoples, involves well-defined and widely understood pictorial conventions and symbols that enhance its information content. A forearm held across the breast, the fingers outstretched toward the opposite shoulder (Fig. 7-36), is a standard gesture of friendship or submission. Buildings, especially temples, are represented in stylized cross section (Figs. 3-1, 7-29). Particular items of dress and ornamentation, as well as distinctive physical features, distinguish portraits that may represent individual deities (Fig. 3-8).[29] Such pictorial symbols often accompany more abstract symbols, especially in the books, and provide important clues for decipherment. Symbols for numbers and time periods (Figs. 3-2, 3-3, 3-4, 5-3, 7-17) are the most straightforward of the more abstract symbols. Other signs, associated with the distinctive portraits, seem to function as names of supernatural beings. Maya calendar signs and deity emblems are comparable to the symbols developed by other Mesoamerican peoples. They are limited, special-purpose systems, not capable of automatic extension to other realms of meaning. In addition to the signs that represent concepts—"seven," "twentieth day," "sun god"—or the particular words for them in the language recorded by the writing system, Maya scribes used other kinds of symbols, including signs that represent specific words and units of sound. Like ancient Egyptian writing, the system is mixed, including phonetic as well as nonphonetic signs.

A principal bar to full decipherment (in the sense of producing readings of texts in Mayan) has been uncertainty about the languages recorded by the hieroglyphic texts. No modern Mayan language is identical to the language of the texts. Mayan languages, along with other facets of Maya culture, have undergone considerable change since the sixteenth century. More than fifteen hundred years elapsed between the period of the earliest inscriptions and the conquest. During this period the six main branches of the Mayan family split into thirty-one distinct languages (Fig. 2-4). All texts deciphered so far are in Yucatec or one of the Cholan languages, but they reflect a great deal of change within those languages over the centuries.

Charles-Etienne Brasseur de Bourbourg's rediscovery of Bishop Landa's lost *History of the Things of Yucatan* in 1863 added a concern with Maya writing to the general reawakening of interest in the Maya.[30] Landa understood the Maya calendar reasonably well, and his manuscript provides a lucid account of the system, along with illustrations of many calendrical glyphs. Landa's comprehension of other aspects of Maya writing, however, was less than perfect. A series of brilliant early studies—above all the work of Ernst Förstemann—clarified much of the calendrical and mathematical portion of the Maya script. This basic understanding of the Maya system of time reckoning laid the groundwork for a realistic chronological framework for Maya civilization. Real progress in the decipherment of other aspects of Maya writing took much longer, although early work on mathematical and calendrical notation did provide clues to the language recorded by the glyphs (Fig. 1-1).

Following Förstemann's lead, Mayanists continued to emphasize the numerical and calendrical aspects of the script until well after the middle of the twentieth century. Such a focus was logical, since the pervasive importance of time in Maya thought and religion was apparent in historical sources of the colonial period and among the modern Maya. Because the reckoning of time occupies such a prominent place in most Maya texts, this approach was productive. Sylvanus Morley epitomized the intellectual thrust of the period, devoting his energy to documenting inscriptions and interpreting their calen-

FIG. 1-1. One way of writing Maya numbers. Each number from 1 to 12 is represented by the head of a different deity, while the glyphs for 13 through 19 are composites formed by adding part of the sign for 10 (the fleshless jaw of a skull) to the heads for 3 through 9. Some, but not all, Mayan languages form the words for these numbers in just this way, with unique words for "eleven" and "twelve" but with "thirteen" through "nineteen" combining elements of the words for "three" through "nine" with that for "ten."

drical references in order to provide a chronological framework for his descriptive synthesis of Maya civilization. The ubiquitous dates in the carved inscriptions yielded a precise chronological framework for the great cities of the Classic period. It was not unreasonable to infer, as most Mayanists did, that the undeciphered portions of these texts, like the painted manuscripts, dealt with matters religious and ritual. In fact, the subject matter of most inscriptions is quite different: dynastic history.

Despite the stubborn resistance of most noncalendrical glyphs to decipherment, the content of the few surviving painted books was plain: astronomy, astrology, divination, and other ritual matters predominated. Maya books, or codices (Color Plate 9), are made of paper manufactured from the bark of the fig tree. Each book consists of a single long strip folded like a screen. A thin coating of white plaster on both sides provides finished surfaces for pictorial representations and glyphs. The four surviving books were painted in late prehispanic times, probably in the northern lowlands, although they may incorporate earlier material. All four deal with religious and scientific matters. Most of their content is given over to divinatory almanacs setting out the auguries for various time periods (Figs. 3-1, 3-6). Astronomy is represented by a table of the movements of Venus (Color Plate 9), an eclipse table, and a zodiac, and possibly by references to other planets.[31] Here, too, the slant is astrological with emphasis on the gods and omens associated with heavenly cycles. Other sections contain fairly explicit cosmological statements specifying relations among time, space, and deities. The calendrical structure of these sections was clear, and images of gods were identified and correlated with particular glyphs quite early. Precise meanings, however, remained elusive.

Although some early epigraphers[32] attempted to read texts in terms of the way that glyphs reflect Mayan language, most of the early successes in decipherment resulted from attempts to deduce basic meanings (not linguistic equivalences) from patterns in glyph occurrences, especially in their associations with pictorial images. These nonlinguistic approaches to decipherment resulted in the identification of glyphs for the directions, the colors, several animals, several gods, and a few other nouns ("burden," "capture," "sky") (Figs. 1-3, 3-6, 3-8). Brasseur, however, described the system as though it included a simple modified alphabet; he was the first of many to go badly astray by using Landa's description of Maya writing in this way to produce a translation of the codices. He "discovered" what he wished to find: an account of the lost civilization of Atlantis.

By the beginning of the twentieth century, linguistic decipherment was in low repute, while nonlinguistic glyph identification had enjoyed notable success. The topic of phoneticism became almost taboo for the next half century, and epigraphers renewed their emphasis on nonlinguistic identification, particularly of calendrical and astronomical glyphs. Such glyphs are now quite well understood. This approach, along with the view that phoneticism was not an important principle of Maya writing, held sway until the 1950s. J. Eric S. Thompson was the foremost practitioner of the nonlinguistic approach. He identified an astounding number of glyphs, and his work constitutes a monumental contribution to the understanding of Maya texts.[33] Actually, Thompson proposed a few linguistic readings himself. Most were of the rebus type, in which signs that stand for words (such as *tee*, "wood" or "tree") were extended to represent homonyms (such as *te*, a numerical classifier). More often, he marshaled evidence against the occasional exponent of phoneticism in the Maya script, and his devastating arguments substantially delayed a general appreciation of the true nature of Maya writing.

MAYA ARCHAEOLOGY TODAY

Excavation. The perspectives of Maya archaeologists have broadened substantially since 1970, partly in response to developments in anthropological archaeology at large.[34] Beginning in the 1960s, what is now often called "processual archaeology"[35] brought about a radical transformation in the way archaeologists approach the past. Processual archaeology called for investigations that are explicitly theoretical and problem-oriented, with excavations designed to answer particular questions about the past which are phrased in such a way as to be of general interest (i.e., relevant to archaeologists concerned with comparable issues in other parts of the world). Maya archaeologists, like their colleagues working in western Mesoamerica, initially resisted much of the agenda of processual archaeology, especially its emphasis on uncovering laws of human behavior, as well as its inclination to favor abstract theoretical jargon. The strengths of processual archaeology—especially with respect to reconstructing the ecology of ancient societies—did eventually have an impact, though, contributing to the increasing attention of Maya archaeologists to subsistence, demography, economic organization, and the nature and distribution of Maya settlements.[36] These shifts in emphasis reflect the growing interest of Mayanists in nonelite aspects of Maya civilization and in geographic variation beyond the core area of major cities. Maya civilization represents a wonderful laboratory for exploring an array of questions of anthropological interest—processes of agricultural intensification, the emergence and dissolution of state-level political systems, the organization of large-scale and long-distance exchange, the nature of kingship, native concepts of time and history—and today's Maya archaeologists tend to be more interested than their predecessors in these issues. Nonetheless, large-scale excavation projects continued, often with a traditional "elite-monumental" orientation, and since the 1980s a renewed focus on aristocratic concerns and state institutions (perhaps in part a response to high-profile developments in the interpretation of Maya art and writing) has counterbalanced the processual orientation of the previous decades.

Decipherment. One key advance in Maya studies has come about through investigations of the writing system. Tatiana Proskouriakoff, with her brilliant demonstration that the monumental inscriptions record mainly historical matters, led the way in 1960 to a radically new understanding of those texts.[37] Subsequent investigations in this vein have opened a new pathway to understanding ancient Maya civilization and have yielded a wealth of new insights: information concerning the relationships among cities and the careers of individual rulers has been gleaned from references to genealogical ties, marriages, conquests, and alliances (Figs. 7-31, 7-32). At roughly the same time, Yurii Knorozov revived the moribund theory that Maya writing was partly phonetic.[38] Investigations following his leads have made giant strides in deciphering ancient Maya texts.

FIG. 1-2. Bishop Landa's "alphabet." Adapted from D. Kelley 1976:fig. 60.

Since 1950, following the Russian Knorozov, Maya epigraphers have returned to the linguistic approach and to the phonetic hypothesis.[39] Knorozov suggested a syllabic rather than an alphabetic phonetic principle: that some Maya glyphs would stand for consonant-plus-vowel combinations. On close inspection, Landa's alphabet (Fig. 1-2) does look like a misunderstood syllabary. Several signs are plainly labeled as syllables, and several Spanish letters have more than one corresponding Maya character. Asking his informant for Mayan equivalents of Spanish letters, Landa did not realize that he was recording signs corresponding to the *names* of the letters.[40] His first B, a footprint,[41] stands for the syllable *be*, "road" or "travel" in Yucatec, and the Spanish name for the letter B. When Landa's alphabet is used as a starting point, a series of plausible readings can be made (Fig. 1-3). Internal confirmations in this chain of interlocking readings lend weight to the particular readings and also establish that Maya writing makes use of signs that directly represent not units of meaning, but the sounds of language. With these signs, Maya scribes could write any message that could be spoken. Using phonetic signs, the Maya carried the elaboration of graphic symbols to heights unmatched elsewhere in the Americas. Maya hieroglyphic writing is just that: a true writing system, capable of expressing an unlimited range of information.

Maya writing is not exclusively syllabic: there are far too many glyphs for a simple syllabary. Most signs stand for concepts or words. At the present stage of decipherment, it is often difficult to distinguish the

FIG. 1-3. Syllabic glyphs used in the prehispanic painted books. The glyph under discussion appears in bold line. (a) *ku-k(u)*, "quetzal"; (b) *cu-tz(u)*, "turkey"; (c) *tzu-l(u)*, "dog"; (d) *u-cu-ch(u)*, "her burden"; (e) *chu-ca-h(a)*, "captured" (note that Chac has his arms bound behind his back). Adapted from Codex Dresdensis 1975:7, 16, 17, 37 and Codex Tro-Cortesianus 1967:91.

two. Nonphonetic glyphs may stand alone, or they may be combined with phonetic signs, and this sort of compound "glyph group" appears to be common in Maya writing. In practice, distinctions between the types of symbols are blurred. A single sign may represent a word or concept in one context, a sound in another, adding enormously to the difficulties of decipherment. Glyphs, or elements of glyphs, are used emblematically in pictorial representations as well as in texts.[42]

The two main sources of Maya texts, painted manuscripts and inscriptions on stone monuments, contrast sharply in date, style, and subject matter. Most known monumental inscriptions come from lowland cities of the Classic period and deal mainly with historical and political matters. Recognition of the subject matter of these inscriptions is the greatest achievement of the nonlinguistic approach to Maya writing, although initially that interpretation was as heretical as Knorozov's phonetic hypothesis. Until 1960, conventional wisdom held that the inscriptions, like the codices, dealt with religious matters. Most epigraphers interpreted the ubiquitous Long Count dates as esoteric astrological and mythological references.

The first departure from orthodoxy was Heinrich Berlin's identification of a class of glyphs designating specific ancient centers (Figs. 7-31, 7-32).[43] The standard prefixes of these "emblem glyphs"—a sign that may translate as "holy" followed by a pair of glyphs signifying "lord" (*ahpo* or *ahau*) that also appears in the sun god's name glyph (Fig. 3-8c)—marks them as titles. Although emblem glyphs technically may refer to the ruler or ruling group, rather than to the city as an abstract entity, for most purposes they function as if they actually name cities.

A similar recognition of internal patterns in the texts and associated pictorial representations at Piedras Negras led Proskouriakoff to identify references to historical individuals and their careers.[44]

She noted that the monuments formed sets; within each set, texts emphasize the same names and titles, and dates cover a period that might reasonably represent an individual's life span. The earliest monument of each series shows the accession of a ruler to power: a young figure appears in a raised niche, and the fancifully named "toothache" glyph (Fig. 7-31c) accompanies the contemporary date. A date some years in the past, marked by the "upended frog" glyph (Fig. 7-31b), refers to his birth, or perhaps to a ceremony corresponding to baptism. Later monuments in the series refer to these and other important events in the ruler's life. After his death, a new set of monuments was raised to record the career of his successor.

Proskouriakoff's insights have been extended to other cities[45] and broadened to shed light on many aspects of ancient Maya societies. When Proskouriakoff identified female names and titles in the texts, figures that had often been taken for pudgy priests became immediately recognizable as women.[46] The importance of women in the inscriptions profoundly altered the accepted view of the role of women in Maya aristocracies. Politics was not divorced from religion, and rulers often sought to establish supernatural charters for their reigns. Several texts connect living rulers with divine ancestors and mythical events far in the past. Kings at Naranjo and elsewhere reckoned their positions in dynastic sequences that begin with deities rather than with human ancestors.[47]

A new generation of epigraphers, building on Berlin's and Proskouriakoff's analyses of the structure and content of monumental texts and on Knorozov's insights into the way the glyphs convey information, has produced an avalanche of new readings of glyphs and texts, new references to births, accessions, marriages, offspring, alliances, conquests, and deaths. Analyses of the imagery that typically accompanies hieroglyphic texts have burgeoned as well, extending new interpretations into virtually every domain of aristocratic life, including religion.[48]

So active are the students of Maya art and writing, so interesting and creative are their interpretations, that it sometimes seems as if Maya archaeology has been revolutionized and our approach to reconstructing ancient Maya societies set on a new footing. Recent interpretations of Maya texts and images have, of course, enriched our understanding immensely, but they have not changed our view of the ancient Maya in truly fundamental ways.[49] For these textual references which accompany the images of lords arrayed in their finery and laden with the emblems of status and power in Maya political art—rich though they may be in biographical detail, and precise though they may be in terms of the Long Count—must be subjected to skeptical assessment.[50] These texts are the raw material of history, but we cannot assume that they consist of simple factual statements, even when they refer to contemporary persons and events, and certainly not when they deal with earlier times. Monumental inscriptions, like all political documents, incorporate biases that are difficult to understand clearly. No Maya inscription is an objective historical report. Hieroglyphic texts reflect the perspectives and agendas of the aristocrats who commissioned them, as well as other aspects of the social milieu in which they were produced.

At the simplest level, these texts have a propaganda dimension, presenting current situations and recent events in the perspective that best serves the authors' ends. The appearance of the Tikal emblem glyph, a personal title meaning, roughly, "Tikal lord," as part of names of lords on Tikal's early stelae might signify that they had actually been formally invested with that title as part of their accession to office (although very little is known of the nature of political institutions or of their relationship to glyphic titles). Sometimes, however, the use of such titles may well have been a claim to status that had not actually been achieved, corresponding to strategies of self-aggrandizement by the nobles who commissioned the monuments. In the same way, texts that imply dominance of one lord or city over another may sometimes reflect goals rather than accomplishments. Statements about the past must always be treated as interpretations rather than objective history; they inevitably recast the past in the light that would be most favorable in terms of the agenda of the author of the later text. Thus, a text that designates its protagonist as *n*th in the succession of kings beginning with a particular ancestral figure may reflect uncontested fact or may be a fictive claim of kinship or succession. A text recounting the accession of a king on a given Long Count date may be a record of an event that actually took place on that date, but it might also be a revisionist account, redating the accession to gain some rhetorical advantage or legitimizing a power seizure with a fictive prior ceremony that would imply adherence to orthodox rules of succession.

Maya notions of history complicate the interpretation of ancient historical accounts even further. There is every reason to believe that the Classic Maya, like their descendants and all of their Mesoamerican relatives, held a cyclical concept of time that did not lend itself to drawing sharp distinctions between the past, the present, and the future. History, current events, and prophecy all reflected the operation of the same fundamental principles, forces, and relationships; not only was the past a guide to the present, and both a preview of the future, but current situations provided insight about prior events since structural patterns were repetitive. Thus, if current events seemed inconsistent in terms of orthodox history, reinterpreting the past in a way that made the present explicable—that is, rewriting history—was a likely response.

Further complicating the use of texts to reconstruct Classic Maya political history is the problem of survival of early inscriptions. Most of the extant texts reflect the perspectives of lords who lived rather late in the histories of Maya cities, partly because the monuments commissioned by these late lords were less likely to be destroyed during subsequent episodes of remodeling. More problematic is the fact that many preserved early texts survived only because later lords found them useful. Conversely, monuments whose texts were inconsistent with the perspectives of those who succeeded their authors were suppressed. Many early texts are from monuments that had been buried, incorporated into construction fill, or thrown into the garbage. The monuments are typically broken and the texts are fragmentary. Early monuments do sometimes seem to confirm later historical accounts, but the reason may often be simply that the later texts were written to be consistent with certain selectively preserved ancient texts. Not only did the winners produce their own versions of history, they also suppressed earlier records not to their liking. Thus the competing claims of rival factions are barely detectable in the surviving texts, although there are a few instances of texts that give alternative versions of sequences of rulers and that count successions from different ancestors. It is also important to emphasize that social factions without the means to produce texts (especially those carved on monuments, by far the most likely to survive) have no voice at all. It is not appropriate to attempt to fit all the biographical and historical statements from the surviving texts of a given city into a consistent synthetic history. Treated as reflections of the perspectives and political strategies of the lords who commissioned them, however, these texts do provide fascinating, if limited, insights into the complex social and political milieu of the Classic Maya world.

For all these reasons, inscriptions cannot provide the primary framework for reconstructing Maya civilization. Writing appeared relatively late in Maya history; some Maya societies remained entirely nonliterate long after others were producing texts; almost exclusively, texts reflect aristocratic aspects of Maya societies; and only a tiny unrepresentative fraction of these aristocratic texts survives in the archaeological record. To privilege texts would create an artificial gulf between those periods, regions, and social groups which produced surviving texts and those which did not. Texts do shed light on ancient Maya societies, but the material record of artifacts and architecture provides a much more inclusive basic framework for Maya history. Texts, used as one among many kinds of archaeological data, are a priceless complement to the material record.

The Maya have always been interested in their own history and have maintained distinctively Maya perspectives on history.[51] In recent years, the Maya have begun to explore their own historical heritage using the tools and findings of Maya studies, even adopting some of the perspectives of non-Maya students of the Maya.[52] This process will have a profound impact on the Mayas' sense of cultural identity and therefore on their place in the national life of the republics of Mexico and Central America in which they live. These developments add immensely to the scholarly obligation to do justice to the history one of the world's great cultural traditions.

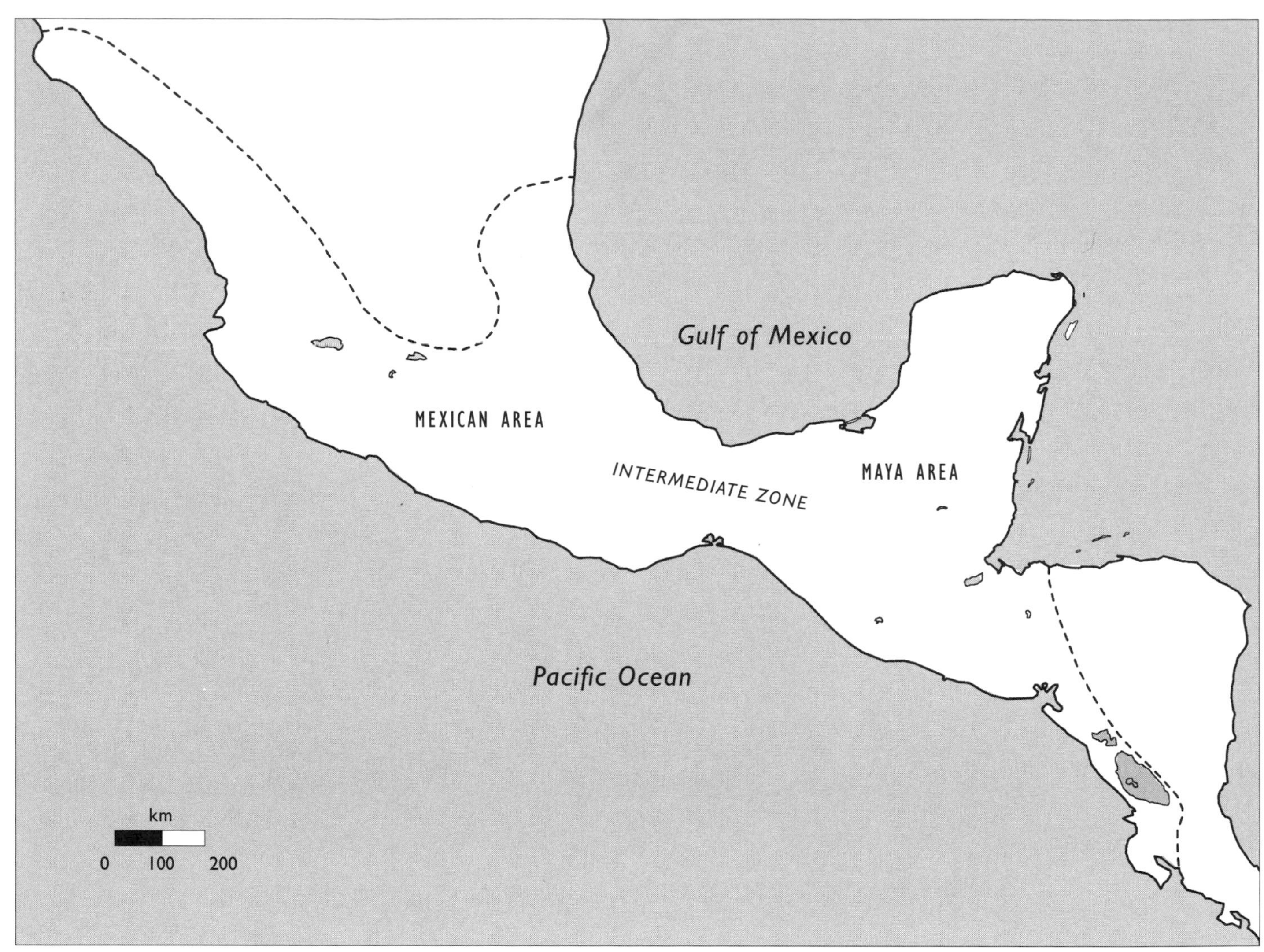

MAP 2. Mesoamerica.

TWO

The Maya World

The Maya and Their Neighbors

The descendants of the ancient Maya today occupy the lowland expanse of the Yucatan peninsula and the mountain valleys of the great highland massif along its southern flank. Here much of the Maya cultural tradition, including several distinct Mayan languages, still persists after nearly half a millennium of European dominance.[1] In the sixteenth century the area was almost solidly Mayan-speaking. The archaeological remains dotting the area are the remnants of the ancient Maya: a material record of the cultural tradition created by Maya peoples over the course of three millennia and more. Mayan speakers were probably the first settlers of the area, occupants of the earliest small farming villages. All indications—from archaeology, history, ethnography, and linguistic reconstructions alike—point to essential cultural continuity. There is no evidence that any other people was ever dominant in the Maya area.

Beyond the eastern frontiers of the Maya area, native cultures have not resisted the impact of European culture so successfully. In prehispanic times this zone of upper Central America was the home of peoples whose languages and cultural traditions were very different from those of the Maya. The Maya also differ from the cultures to their west and north, although here the contrasts are much less prominent and shared cultural features are more evident. Stretching from north-central Mexico to upper Central America, Mesoamerica (Map 2) embraces these related peoples along with the Maya. Their cultural commonality has considerable time depth, stretching back centuries before the Christian era. Collectively, these peoples and their ancestors represent a cultural tradition as well as a culture area.[2]

The features shared by Mesoamerican cultures are varied. Some are distinctively Mesoamerican, setting these peoples clearly apart from their non-Mesoamerican neighbors. Ceramic lip plugs, wooden swords edged with stone flakes, quilted cotton armor, sandals with heels. These things are distinctive indeed, but they reveal little of the character of Mesoamerican cultures. Some of the most basic Mesoamerican cultural traits, in contrast, occur widely in the Americas. Farming systems featuring *milpa* or slash-and-burn cultivation of maize, along with beans, squash, and chile peppers, are by no means peculiar to Mesoamerican peoples.

The most interesting features of the Mesoamerican culture pattern are those which are both basic and distinctive. Perhaps the most fundamental is the constellation of traits involved in the production and preparation of food. Equally important and far more distinctive are Mesoamerican religion and cosmology. The gods of rain and maize, the death deity, the gods of the sun, moon, and morning star, though they bear various names and titles, appear in similar guises in pantheons all across Mesoamerica. Color-coded cardinal directions are the foci of the Mesoamerican universe, which is also layered, with many-tiered heavens and hells. Elaborate calendars kept track of the passage of time and the changing astrological omens. Details vary—the east was red or yellow or blue-green for Mesoamericans in different regions at different times—but all Mesoamerican peoples shared a cosmology in which the universe and the calendar had the same basic structure. Whatever its ultimate origins, this shared world view demonstrates the fundamental unity of the diverse peoples of Mesoamerica and the reality of a Mesoamerican cultural tradition.

A ball game played with a solid rubber ball in a formal court was a ceremonial event, a political tool, and a form of recreation throughout Mesoamerica.[3] Ball courts were magnets for people in the hinterlands of towns and cities, and their very presence marked the communities that built and maintained them as important nodes in the political landscape. The game was often played as a divinatory act, to determine the shape of the future, and losers frequently met death on the sacrificial altar. On other occasions it was simply a spectator sport, with avid wagering on the outcome. Some ball courts have rings on the side walls, through which players had to propel the ball in order to score; others have markers along the sides or along the center of the court floor; others still are perfectly plain.

Specifying precise geographic limits for Mesoamerica is as fruitless a task as trying to pinpoint the time of its emergence as a distinct culture area. Even for the conquest period, information is not uniform for all regions, and coverage of some of the frontier areas is especially poor. For earlier prehispanic periods the difficulties are much greater, because many distinctive Mesoamerican cultural features that are clearly reflected in historical documents, including some of the key traits, are not easily detected in the archaeological evidence. In any case, Mesoamerica never had the sharply defined boundaries of a modern political state. The frontiers of Mesoamerica are better conceptualized as regions where Mesoamerican and non-Mesoamerican peoples mingled at many levels, from individual households to entire communities. The transitions of frontier zones were gradual but not uniform, resulting in complex mosaics of groups with contrasting cultural affiliations.[4] Nor is there any reason to suppose that Mesoamerica's frontiers were static. On the contrary, every indication is that they underwent constant, often considerable, shifts through time as political, economic, social, and even climatic and environmental patterns changed.

A distinctive Mesoamerican sphere of interaction had certainly emerged before 1000 B.C., for the Olmec civilization is recognizably Mesoamerican. The Mesoamerican cultural tradition presumably did not spring into existence fully formed with the appearance of the Olmec. Rather, it must have emerged as a coherent cultural pattern gradually, over the course of many preceding centuries which are almost unrepresented in the archaeological record.

Beneath the unity of Mesoamerican culture lies a wealth of diversity—in language, social organization, economics, politics, religion, art, and every other facet of culture. Basic Mesoamerican patterns are expressed in many ways among its various peoples. A focus on this variation dissolves the area into regions with contrasting cultural patterns. Some regions are very homogeneous, with long, stable cultural traditions; others are diverse and experienced considerable cultural change through time. All can be subdivided on the basis of still finer cultural variation.

Regions can also be combined. Cultural and environmental contrasts between southeastern and northwestern Mesoamerica are easily recognized. The Maya area, largely lowland tropical forest, comprises most of the southeastern zone. The drier highlands of central Mexico form the heart of the northwestern area. These regions can be viewed as the hearths of the distinct Maya and Mexican cultural traditions, although both are fundamentally Mesoamerican and their histories are linked at many points. The differences are better conceived as a continuum of variation. An Intermediate Zone stretching from the Gulf Coast plain south across the Isthmus of Tehuantepec and east along the Pacific coast and piedmont (Map 2) forms an environmental and cultural bridge between idealized Mexican and Maya poles of contrast.[5] These differences are especially clear with respect to political organization and settlement pattern. Central Mexico was the seat of large political states, even empires, with great urban capitals. In the Maya area, political units were normally much smaller and populations were not densely packed into urban cores, but dispersed in the hinterlands surrounding cities.

Until the middle of the first millennium B.C., a single cultural pattern, the Olmec, dominated Mesoamerica. The northwest/southeast contrast developed after the decline of Olmec civilization. In the last centuries before the Christian era, Teotihuacán, in the heart of the central Mexican highlands, was emerging as Mesoamerica's first urban civilization. At the same time, Maya societies began to take on the complexity that would culminate in Classic Maya civilization. The existence of a Maya/Mexican polarity and the interaction of cultures representing the two patterns would be important factors in Mesoamerican culture history from this time on. Maya culture history, as the story of the development of one end of a continuum, cannot be written without continual reference to Mexican Mesoamerica.

The Maya Area

The Maya area (Map 3) is by no means uniform, environmentally or culturally. With environments ranging from steamy lowland tropical forest to near-desert interior valleys to cool, pine-clad highlands, Maya country is remarkably varied. Even the vast tracts of lowland forest, seemingly unbroken and homogeneous, dissolve on closer inspection into a patchwork of regions differing in climate, topography, flora, and fauna.[6]

A massive chain of volcanic mountains, flanked by metamorphic highlands to the north, curves south and east from southern Mexico to form the spine of Central America. From its base the Yucatan peninsula juts into the Caribbean like a great limestone shelf. From the coast to the foothills of the cordillera, only the low Puuc hills in the northwest and the Maya Mountains in the east interrupt the expanse of tropical lowlands that is Yucatan (Color Plates 6, 7). The major river systems—the Grijalva and Usumacinta in the west and the Motagua and Ulúa in the east—rise in the highlands and flow generally northward along the flanks of the Maya world.

Northern Yucatan is much like central and southern Florida. Rainfall is not heavy, and the thin soil supports a low, thorny forest of palms, scrub pine, live oak, and palmetto. Surface water is rare except where the limestone crust has fallen through to expose the water table, forming *cenotes* (sinkholes). To the south, rainfall becomes heavier, exceeding 3,000 millimeters per year along the southern fringe of the lowlands. Soils are deeper, and vegetation grows progressively more lush and less familiar.

The high, canopied rain forest of the southern lowlands boasts mahogany, wild fig, and ceiba trees that soar 50 meters and more (Color Plate 1). Sapodilla, cedar, logwood, palms, avocado, mamey, and *ramón* (breadnut), along with many other trees and vines, provide a wide range of useful products, including edible fruits and nuts. The high forest is closed above. Little sunlight reaches the forest floor, which remains relatively open, except where a great tree has fallen or where people have cleared the forest. Wherever the canopy is broken, ferocious secondary growth forms a temporary niche of very different aspect: dense, tangled, almost impenetrable. Patches of savannah-like grassland with only occasional stunted trees form open oases throughout the forest. Animal life in the lowlands is rich and varied as well. There are few large mammals: deer, peccary, tapir, and jaguar. Exotic smaller mammals abound, particularly in the higher forests of the south. Agouti and coatimundi roam the forest along with rabbits, foxes, and spider and howler monkeys. The boa joins the rattlesnake, coral snake, fer-de-lance, and a host of less spectacular snakes, lizards, toads, and frogs to fill out the roster of reptiles and amphibians. In the air are hundreds of species of birds, from the curassow, guan, gaudy parrots, and toucans to the more familiar wild turkey and quail. Everywhere insects abound.

Terrain is more varied in the southern lowlands than in the north, with as much as 60 meters of relief between ridges and intervening lower stretches, which support rather different plant communities, The low-lying areas become swamps during the rainy months, so that well-drained slopes and relatively level ridge tops are best for habitation. The heart of the Maya lowlands has no surface streams. Some clay-lined water holes hold collected rain throughout the year, and in a few areas shallow lakes provide fresh water and fish. Along the western edge of the lowlands flow the great Usumacinta and its tributaries. These rivers are major arteries of communication, and they provide hundreds of kilometers of riverine environment where fresh water, fish, and other aquatic resources are available. To the east, the pine-clad slopes of the Maya Mountains rise to elevations of some 1,000 meters. The streams that flow east, emptying into the Caribbean, create another series of riverine niches in the forest. To the southeast are the great inland gulf of Lake Izabal and the lower course of the Río Motagua, which drains much of the central highland region. Beyond, the Ulúa drains the highlands at the southeastern edge of the Maya world. This diversity adds up to a remarkable array of distinct local environments within the seemingly uniform tropical forest.

Stretching in a great arc along the western and southern flank of the lowlands, the foothills of the cordillera mark the transition to a region of steep slopes and broken terrain. This is a land of numberless pocket valleys, ravines, steep gorges, and chasms amid mountain peaks (Fig. 2-1). Millennia of erosion have left little level land in the mountain massif, except in a few great basins. With the highest volcanic peaks reaching elevations above 4,000 meters, the highlands generally are clothed in pine and oak forest, with occasional grassy alpine meadows. Dense cloud forests dominated by oak and laurel, draped with moss and mixed with tree ferns, occupy the highest slopes (above 2,000 meters). In a few regions of intermediate elevation—in the Grijalva

FIG. 2-1. Hilly terrain with terraced farm plots in the western Maya highlands.

FIG. 2-2. Making milpa. In the cleared and burned fields, farmers drop maize seeds, carried in the pouches at their belts, into individual holes made with pointed digging sticks.

basin along the western edge of the highlands and along the middle course of the Río Motagua—are stretches of very dry country. Animal life is much less abundant here than in the lowlands, in part because of today's much denser highland population. Numerous mountain streams feed the two great highland lakes, or join the Usumacinta, Motagua, and Ulúa river systems to empty ultimately into the Gulf of Mexico and the Gulf of Honduras. South of the continental divide, the rivers of the slopes drain into the Pacific. Descending, the piedmont becomes progressively more tropical. Thorn forest gives way along the coast to tidal lagoons, estuaries, and mangrove swamp rich in fish, mollusks, crabs, caymans, and other marine animals.

Throughout the area, the alternation of wet and dry seasons dominates weather patterns and the farming cycle. In May the rains begin, continuing almost daily until October or November. In some years the rains slacken during the midsummer dog days, but not always. During the dry season, beginning in November or December, there is little or no rain, and milpa farmers turn to clearing new fields. By April the cut vegetation is dry. Now is the time for burning, to release nutrients into the soil, and for planting. The traditional slash-and-burn or swidden farmer has only to poke holes in the ash with his digging stick, drop in the seeds—commonly maize, along with beans, squash, and chile peppers—and wait for the rain (Fig. 2-2). Timing is important, for burning and planting should be completed before the rains set in. At the same time, too early a start courts disaster: the nutrients in the ashes may be scattered by the wind, and the seeds may die before moisture reaches them. There is some margin for error, though; if the rains are delayed, it is often possible to make a second planting and salvage a crop. Slash-mulch (or *tapado*) farming, in which a crop, typically beans, is planted beneath the cut vegetation which is left unburned as a protective mulch, offers the advantage of inhibiting a variety of plant pests.[7] Harvesttime is in the autumn, although in favored areas two crops are possible. Fallowing varies greatly with local soil, moisture, and vegetation conditions. In some highland regions with deep fertile soils, plots may be cultivated for a decade or longer, requiring only a few years to regain fertility. In many lowland zones, in contrast, a plot may produce reasonable yields for only two seasons, after which it must lie fallow for as long as a generation. Native domestic animals are few: dogs are ubiquitous, turkeys common, and in some regions bees are kept for honey and wax.

In much of the Maya world, milpa farming is still the cornerstone of local economies and maize the staff of life, as it has been for three thousand years and more. The Tzotzil *milperos* of Zinacantán are not fossilized prehistoric Maya farmers, but their techniques for wresting a living from the land do draw heavily on their precolumbian Maya heritage.[8] Prehispanic Maya farming systems were not utterly different.

Zinacantecos cultivate milpas locally in the highlands and also journey into adjacent lowland regions to work rented lands. The best highland plots may be cultivated continuously for many years. In the lowlands, the agricultural cycle is shorter and fields must be prepared more often. Here the farmer must fell trees in December to allow sufficient time for drying. Brush and other secondary growth can be cut at any time before March, and the dried vegetation is burned in April. Planting takes place in May (earlier in the highlands), following ceremonies designed to placate the Earth Owner, who controls the clouds, the rains, and the wind. A man knowledgeable in ritual matters, often with a special relationship to the Earth Owner and other gods, will join his kinsmen in a special meal and lead them in a ritual procession to shrines set up at the corners and in the center of their fields. Here the farmers will offer prayers, candles, flowers, and pine boughs in the hope of steady rains and a fine crop.

A pointed digging stick and an armadillo shell or net bag to carry the carefully selected seeds are the only planting tools. The milpero moves through his plot row by row. Into the small hole made with his digging stick he drops several seeds of maize, covers them over with his sandal, and moves on. Especially in highland plots, bean and squash seeds may be planted in the same hole with the maize. Here the milpero's wife usually follows along the rows, adding the complementary seeds to each hole. Squash is more often planted on the fringe of the milpa.

Every milpa must be weeded at least once, after another ceremony to propitiate the Earth Owner. Fields in use for a few years require two or more weedings, usually in mid-June and mid-July. The maize ripens by September. The farmer again moves through his milpa, bending each stalk double, allowing the maize to dry and harden without being ruined by the rain. Now the milpero sows another bean crop between the bent rows of maize in lowland plots. October is harvesttime in the highlands, but the drying lowland maize can be left on the dead stalks until December or January.

Most farmers plant chiles, chayotes, gourds, and other minor crops separately. They cultivate a variety of fruit trees, mainly in or near their house compounds. Hunting is now a casual activity for Zinacantecos, although it was surely more important before dense populations decimated the local fauna. Today beans are the chief source of protein; meat provides only a minor dietary supplement. Zinacantecos still occasionally shoot deer and rabbits. They trap birds, rats, and mice and collect wasp larvae, other insects, river snails, and some land snails. Chicken, the principal meat for ceremonial occasions, has supplanted the indigenous turkey. Today as in the past, iguanas sometimes replace fowl for ritual use.

Wild plants, in contrast, are very important. Zinacantecos collect more than a dozen varieties of edible mushrooms, several plants cooked as greens, coriander and other condiments, a special plant to chew in order to reduce thirst when one is working, and many plants for medicinal and ritual use. This sketch barely indicates the importance of noncrop plants to Zinacantecos, for it is all too easy for outside observers to overlook interactions with plants that do not conform with familiar agricultural patterns.

The Lacandón Maya, occupying the remote forests west of the Río Usumacinta and least affected by European cultural patterns, make extensive use of the exuberant natural flora. Alfred Tozzer, who lived among the Lacandón in 1901 and 1903, remarked that "the native makes use of practically every tree, plant, and shrub for food, medicine, or in the practice of some of his arts."[9] Table 1 lists some of these plants and their uses.

Lacandón farmers cultivate several fruit trees, along with maize, beans, chiles, tomato, manioc, sweet potato, chayote, gourds, cotton, and tobacco. Deer, peccary, armadillo, monkey, agouti, iguana, wild turkey, curassow, partridge, quail, and snails are only the most important of the many animals Lacandones hunt, trap, and collect. They take fish with lines, nets, and arrows. Beekeeping—involving hollow logs placed in temples—is primarily a ceremonial activity.

The distribution of natural resources is far from uniform, and the exchange of commodities among the diverse regions has always been important. The Maya area has never been without networks of exchange linking its parts. Limestone is readily available for construction throughout the lowlands. In many areas it contains deposits of chert that can be fashioned into durable cutting tools, although highland obsidian is much sharper. Hard volcanic stone, used for grinding tools, and volcanic mineral pigments occur only in the Maya Mountains and in the highlands. Jade, the most precious of all materials, can be found only in the Motagua Valley and in the adjacent metamorphic highlands. Salt is readily available in the coastal regions of Yucatan, along the Pacific Coast, and from deposits along the northern fringes of the highlands, but it is not to be found in the central lowlands. Tropical-forest products include resins from various trees (used as incense), hardwoods, and the plumage of brightly feathered birds, as well as drug and spice plants. A variety of marine products is vital to Maya ritual: shell, coral, pearls, stingray spines. Add to this array a thriving trade in local agricultural specialties and manufactured products—cacao, honey, wax, pottery, textiles, lapidary work, and the like—and exchange emerges as a major force in Maya culture history, balancing regional diversification with elaborate networks of communication and interaction.

Maya Peoples

Culturally the Maya world is less varied than the natural environment. In the sixteenth century, the central part of the Maya world was solidly Mayan-speaking, although speakers of other languages occupied parts of the northwest along the Gulf of Mexico, the western highlands, the Pacific piedmont, and the Ulúa drainage in the southeast. Today, of course, the Spanish American national cultures of Mexico, Guatemala, Belize, Honduras, and El Salvador are dominant. Those groups which have not lost their native heritage entirely are increasingly reduced to the status of marginal peasant subcultures

TABLE 1. Plants and plant products of southeastern Mexico and uses to which they are put by the Lacandón Maya

PLANT OR PLANT PRODUCT	USE
Mahogany	Canoes
Logwood	Arrow shafts, dye
Lignum vitae	Bows
Protium heptaphyllum resin (*pom*, copal)	Incense
Rubber tree sap	Incense
Pitch pine	Torches
Lonchocarpus longistylus bark	*Balché*, a fermented intoxicating beverage for ceremonial occasions
Vines, many varieties	Tying thatch and house frames; wickerwork house doors; baskets; source of water for travelers; general use as rope or twine
Palm leaves	Thatch
Guava (*guayaba, Psidium guajava*)	Food
Tamarind (*Tamarindus indica*)	Food
Avocado (*Persea gratissima*)	Food
Mango (*Mangifera indica*)	Food
Coconut (*Cocos nucifera*)	Food
Papaya (*Papaya carica*)	Food
Sweetsop (*Anona squamosa*)	Food
Soursop (*guanabana, Anona muricata*)	Food
Chicosapote (*Achras sapota*)	Food
Mamey (*Lucuma mammosa*)	Food
Coyol palm (*Acrocomia mexicana*)	Food
Cacao	Chocolate, ceremonial drink (important source of fat; conquest-period Yucatecs extracted from it "a grease which resembles butter," used to make another drink)

FIG. 2-3. Thatched house in the lower Ulúa Valley. The walls are made of adobe over a pole framework.

(Fig. 2-3). They face an often hostile society that surrounds and threatens to overwhelm them. Even allowing for the homogenizing pressures of modern Latin American societies, Maya groups are by no means uniform. On the contrary, no two have ever been exactly alike, and the overall picture is one of nearly endless variation on the same fundamental themes.

The distribution of Maya peoples follows the main lines of natural regions (Map 3), although the patterns of interaction that produced cultural regions often cut across environmental zones. Copán, for example, on the northeast fringe of the highlands, shared most of its cultural patterns with communities in the lowlands, and the same is true of Toniná in the northwest. There are no sharp boundaries; the shift from one Maya group to the next is even more gradual and complex than the transition between adjacent environmental provinces. In the same way, the external frontiers of the Maya area are zones where contrasting cultural patterns and the people who carry them mingle in complex mosaic arrangements. Reconstructions of the history of the Mayan family of languages (Fig. 2-4) call for a more or less homogeneous ancestral Mayan stock centered in the highlands.[10] Before 2000 B.C. the ancestors of

MAP 3. The Maya world.

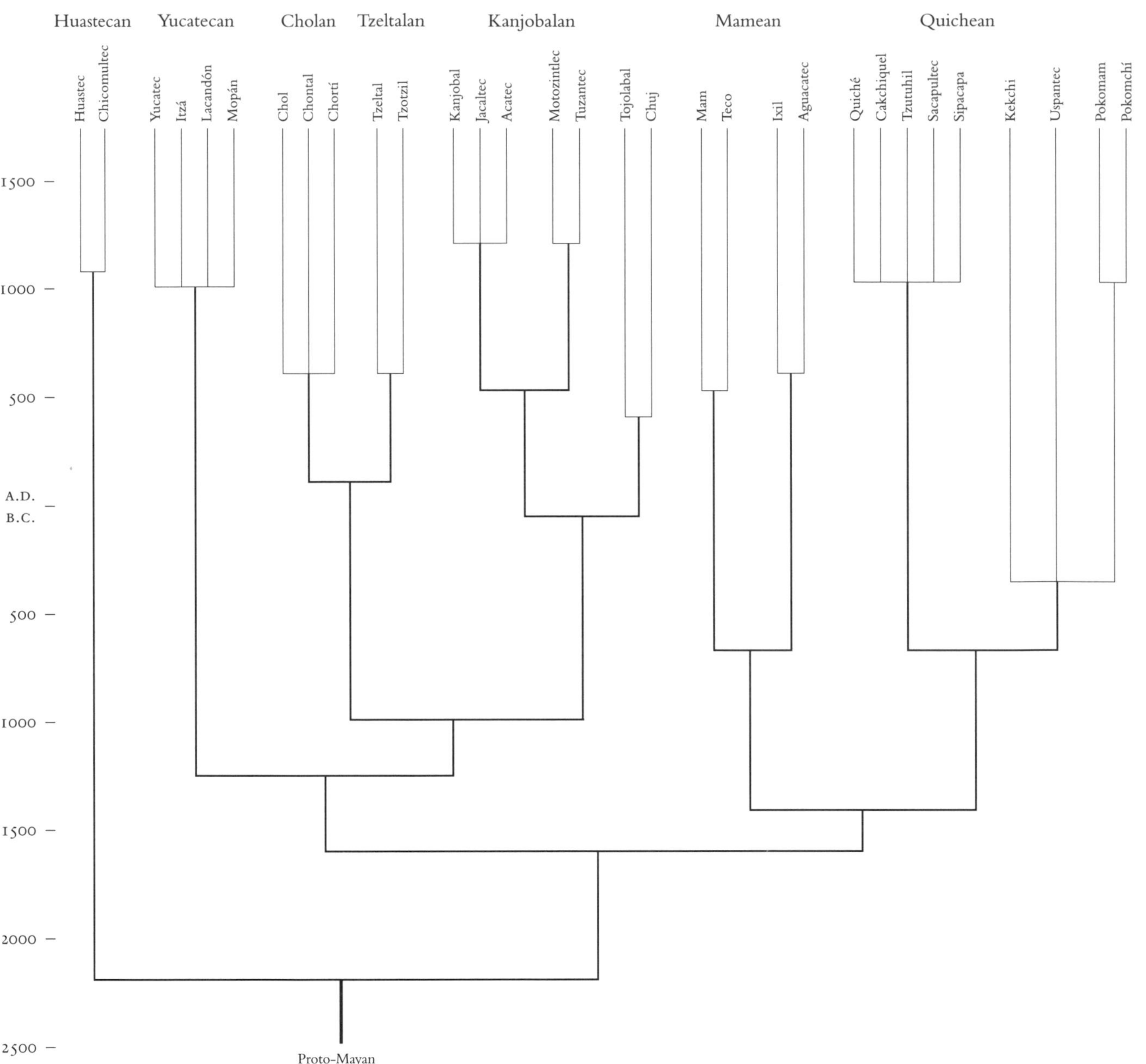

FIG. 2-4. Schematic outline of the history of the Mayan family of languages (based primarily on Kaufman 1976). The absolute time scale is a rough approximation.

today's Maya groups began a long, slow process of progressive differentiation and dispersal. The result is the present distribution of distinct Mayan tongues, comparable in their variability to the Romance languages.

THE NORTHERN LOWLANDS

Northern Yucatan is the home of the Yucatec, the most numerous and widespread modern Maya group.[11] Among the first to separate from the ancestral Maya stock, the Yucatec have occupied the northern lowlands for many centuries. There the Spaniards found them in the sixteenth century, and traditional histories linked them to ruins already hundreds of years old.

Small farming villages, composed of a few one- and two-room houses, appeared in northern Yucatan midway through the Preclassic period (2000 B.C.–A.D. 250; see Chronological Chart). These first known occupants of the region may have been the ancestral Yucatec, who had emerged as a distinct language group before 1000 B.C. During the following centuries settlements grew larger and more complex. By the beginning of the Christian era, public buildings of masonry construction graced several northern centers. The small houses and plain burials of ordinary farmers contrast with large dwellings with plaster-coated stone walls and tombs stocked with rich funerary offerings. Distinct social groups marked by differences in wealth and rank were emerging within communities. Eventually, powerful aristocratic families dominated each local society.

Growth and development continued during the Classic period (A.D. 250–1000). Dzibilchaltún, Uxmal, Edzná, Oxkintok, Río Bec, Becán, Chichén Itzá, Cobá, and many other communities became powerful cities. Elaborately decorated masonry palaces, administrative buildings, and temples on tall platforms dominated large and diverse communities. Regional differences became apparent, with related but distinctive cultural spheres along the east coast, on the northern plains, in the hilly western Puuc region, and in central Yucatan. Central Yucatan was in many ways culturally intermediate between the northern and central lowlands.

In the north, the emergence of powerful cities and the processes of change that transformed them took effect relatively late in comparison with the south. Many causal factors contributed to the transformation, and it affected each region in different ways (and at different times). In the ninth and tenth centuries, when Uxmal and Chichén Itzá reached their developmental peaks, many southern cities had been in decline for a century or more. One of the variable factors was the effect of interaction with foreign groups, especially Mexicans and Mexican-influenced Mayas from the Gulf Coast, on the western fringe of the Maya lowlands. Indications of these foreign connections are common in the art and architecture of northern cities during the period of their florescence in the Terminal Classic period, and the foreign presence was evidently not disruptive as it was in many parts of the south.

After the collapse of Chichén Itzá and the other Classic period cities, Mayapán emerged as the dominant northern city. According to traditional Maya histories recorded at the time of the Spanish invasion, a revolt brought an end to the rule of Mayapán in the mid fifteenth century. Three-quarters of a century later, the Spaniards found northern Yucatan politically fragmented, with more than a dozen petty states vying for local dominance. Long-distance trade, particularly maritime networks, linked the towns of Yucatan with the Gulf Coast and with commercial centers at the base of the Gulf of Honduras.

Today the Yucatec share the northern lowlands with Spanish-speaking Mexicans. Native Yucatec and modern Mexican culture coexist in varying blends: from urban, Mexican Mérida to very traditional rural villages. Life in the more remote hinterlands of eastern and central Yucatan has a very definite Maya character.

THE SOUTHERN LOWLANDS

Much of the southern lowland zone has been remote from colonial and modern seats of bureaucracy, and historical information is correspondingly scarce, so the region is difficult to characterize culturally and linguistically. Fundamentally, most of the southern lowlands is the homeland of the Cholan branch of the Mayan language family—the Chol, Chontal, and Chortí—although language distributions within the region changed over time, as the frontier between Yucatec speakers to the north and Chol speakers to the south shifted.[12]

Epigraphic evidence suggests a similar situation in the Classic period: hieroglyphic texts at Palenque seem to incorporate distinctive features of the Chol language and Copán's texts include Chortí words. The western margin of the southern lowlands, along the southern Gulf Coast of Mexico, is a frontier zone between the Maya area and the Mexican region stretching to the west and north. Environmentally the area is one: the tropical forest continues unbroken along the entire coastal plain; culturally, too, there is no sharp boundary. At the time of the conquest this was a complex zone where speakers of Nahuatl, the language of the Aztecs of central Mexico, mingled with Chol and Chontal Maya. Far to the north on the Gulf Coast are the Huastec, now isolated from all other Mayan speakers.[13] Linguistically and culturally very different from other Maya peoples, the Huastec were probably first to separate from the ancestral stock. At the other end of the southern lowlands, east and south of Copán, the Chortí Maya gave way to the Lenca and other non-Mayan speakers, although culturally much of this area was firmly within the Maya world.

The southern Gulf Coast just west of the Maya area was the cradle of Mesoamerica's first truly complex culture, the Olmec. Olmec civilization emerged not long after 1500 B.C. and soon spread far beyond the heartland to dominate most of Mesoamerica. In some ways the heritage of Maya civilization can be traced to the Olmec, and there are even some grounds for entertaining the possibility that the Olmec may have been Maya speakers.

The earliest known occupants of the southern Maya lowlands are village farmers of the late second millennium B.C. In some communities, especially on the northwestern and southeastern edges of the lowlands, pottery and other material goods show the impact of Olmec styles. There is almost no evidence of Olmec-style monumental art and architecture in southern lowland communities, although Los Naranjos in the southeast is an exception.[14] Farming villages were widely established by 1000 B.C.; five hundred to a thousand years of community growth and development led to the emergence of the first southern lowland cities. At Mirador, Nakbé, Tikal, Uaxactún, Lamanai, and a few other communities, large-scale construction projects were under way by the last centuries before the Christian era. Temples rose above all other buildings. Dwellings and burials of wealthy aristocrats contrast sharply with those of the bulk of the populace.

The history of the Classic period in the southern lowlands is a story of progressive growth and elaboration. Communities multiplied. Many grew into powerful cities with imposing public architecture. Monumental art and hieroglyphic inscriptions became increasingly prominent. True palaces and enormously rich burials marked widening social gaps. Occupational specialists held positions of intermediate status between small ruling groups and masses of ordinary farmers. Trade and other forms of interaction linked communities throughout the southern lowlands, but regional differences—in styles of art and architecture, in the details of social and political organization, and in developmental trajectories—were clearly marked as well.

The heart of the southern lowlands—the Petén, including much of what is now Belize, to the east—is often considered a cultural core zone. Here are some of the largest, most impressive, and most thoroughly investigated centers of the Classic period. Tikal is only the foremost of many. In consequence, this region has had an impact on conceptions of Maya civilization out of all proportion to its actual prominence. Even within the Petén region, cities reflect distinctive regional cultural spheres: Calakmul in the north; Tikal, Uaxactún, and Yaxhá in the central zone; Naranjo and Xunantunich, Caracol, Lamanai and Altun Ha in the east. These are only the most prominent among hundreds of communities. Other distinctive regions include Palenque, Toniná, Comalcalco, and the Gulf Coast frontier cities of the northwest; Piedras Negras and Yaxchilán in the middle Usumacinta region; Altar de Sacrificios, Seibal, Dos Pilas, Aguateca, and neighboring centers in the Río Pasión zone; Copán and Quiriguá in the Motagua drainage; and Travesía and the neighboring communities of the Ulúa sphere along the southeast fringe of the Maya world.

Southern lowland communities responded in a variety of ways to the Terminal Classic transformation process. First along the Usumacinta, then along the Pasión, city after city stopped constructing buildings and erecting monuments. Pressure from the culturally Mexicanized peoples of the Gulf Coast was an important part of the process and, at least in the Pasión region, warfare intensified sharply. Seibal, under heavy influence from the north, maintained a prominent position in the region for nearly a century. By the early decades of the tenth century, however, all major cities had ceased to function as capitals of regional states, although occupation did not end entirely at every site. At Tikal and most other cities in the Petén, public construction projects and other state activities decreased rapidly in the ninth century; by the tenth century most of the great cities had been abandoned, and even rural populations had apparently declined substantially.[15]

In the east, the situation was different. Xunantunich continued to function during the Terminal Classic period, well after the collapse of cities to the west. Lamanai, still a thriving community at the time of the Spanish invasion, evidently continued to prosper without serious interruption. Small farming communities dotted much of the eastern countryside through the Postclassic period.

In the southeast, the transformation process also began early. At Copán, state functions came to an end near the beginning of the ninth century, even though there was no general population decline. Aristocrats living outside the city center maintained their prosperity, and to some degree their power, for decades; rural farming hamlets persisted for centuries. In the lower Ulúa Valley, Cerro Palenque emerged as the largest city in the southeast during the Terminal Classic, as most Late Classic communities went into decline.

Along the northwestern and southeastern extremes of the southern lowlands, prosperous commercial centers flourished during the Postclassic period. Acalán, in the Chontal-speaking region near the northwestern frontier of the Maya world, boasted several mercantile centers, dominated by Itzamkanac. The traders of Acalán carried on a thriving and far-flung commerce, maintaining economic links with Maya groups far to the south and east as well as with northern Yucatan and with Mexican peoples of the Gulf Coast. Nahuatl-speaking merchants affiliated with the Aztec empire maintained a commercial outpost at Xicalango, a center on the Laguna de Términos which was rather like a free-trade zone. Acalán and Chontal culture had a decidedly international flavor.

Other trade centers grew up at Nito, near the mouth of the Río Dulce; in the lower Ulúa Valley; and at Naco, on the middle Chamelecón. These and other towns maintained active commercial links with eastern and northern Yucatan, with the great trade ports of the Gulf of Mexico, and with Central America to the east and south. The thriving international trade involved extensive maritime networks as well as overland routes. By the time of the Spanish invasion, the southeastern lowlands was an area of remarkable cultural diversity. A variety of foreign mercantile enclaves further complicated the region's heterogeneous makeup. The area of Lake Izabal and the lower Río Motagua, along with the coastal zone as far east as the Ulúa, were Chol territory. The Chortí occupied the inland region around Copán, giving way to Lenca and other non-Mayan speakers to the east and south. In the lower Ulúa Valley and adjacent frontier zones, Maya groups mingled with other Central American peoples to form a complex cultural mosaic. Southeastern Maya peoples, like their Central American neighbors to the east, suffered greatly at the hands of colonial administrations. The lower Ulúa Valley became the focus of intense slaving almost immediately after the Spaniards discovered it, and the native population was quickly exterminated. Much of the region's native cultural tradition has been destroyed. Only the Chortí retain substantial portions of their Maya heritage.

In the central Petén, Tayasal exercised hegemony over the area around Lake Petén Itzá when Cortés passed through the region. Tipú, to the east, was another prosperous, politically prominent town at the time of the Spanish invasion. Otherwise, most Postclassic communities in the central and western parts of the southern lowlands were small villages or towns. No great cities rivaled those of the Classic period.[16] Documents of the colonial period have little to say about the native cultures of the region; then, as now, they were largely isolated from the workings of government. All indications are that in colonial times Yucatecan languages were spoken in the northern and eastern sectors of the region, and Cholan languages in most of the west and south. Even today, most of the southern lowlands are only lightly populated. In the remote country south and west of the middle Usumacinta live the wild and enigmatic Lacandón.[17] Reduced to a few hundred souls by the pressure of encroaching modern Mexico, the Lacandón have retreated progressively deeper into the forest. Their ancestry is obscure, although linguistically they are closely related to the Yucatec. Almost entirely isolated from the modern world until very recently, the Lacandón differ from all other Maya peoples in their mobile lifestyle and in the corresponding simplicity of their material culture.

Elsewhere in the southern lowlands, recent immigrants, mainly of non-Maya culture, make up the bulk of the population. Individuals, families, and small groups, attracted by the wilderness and the frontier quality of life, continue to move into the underpopulated forests. The Kekchi, formerly a highland people, have been the most prominent Maya colonists. Kekchi settlers, moving down from their homeland along the northern slopes of the highlands, are progressively colonizing the sparsely inhabited southern fringe of the lowlands.[18]

THE HIGHLANDS

The mountains of the volcanic cordillera are the ancient homeland of other branches of the ancestral Maya stock. More than a dozen distinct Mayan languages are still spoken in the highlands. European cultural patterns have made fewer obvious inroads among highland Maya peoples than among most of their lowland relatives.

The western highland zone is the home of the Tzeltalan branch of the Mayan language family.[19] Tzeltalan-speaking peoples became distinct from their Cholan-speaking relatives about the beginning of the Christian era. Sometime thereafter, the Tzeltal and Tzotzil reached their present location, where the Spaniards found them in the sixteenth century.

The archaeological record for the area is sketchy indeed. Earlier periods are almost entirely blank. In the Classic period, poorly understood regional variants of Maya civilization developed in the western highlands and in the foothills descending toward the Río Usumacinta. These variants may reflect stages in the westward movement of Tzeltalan speakers after their split from the Cholan block. Ancestors of the Kanjobalan speakers, now eastern neighbors of the Tzeltal, might also have been involved in the creation of these cultures.

A village farming way of life was established in the central and eastern highlands by 1500 B.C. Not long afterward, the impact of Olmec civilization left its mark on ceramics and portable art objects. After 1000 B.C. Kaminaljuyú and a few other communities grew to great size and boasted large-scale public architecture. Dwellings and burials reflect sharp differences in wealth and social status between aristocrats and ordinary farmers. By the beginning of the Christian era, Kaminaljuyú and many other highland centers were part of the Izapan world, centered in the Intermediate Zone. Maya art and writing evolved in the highlands and piedmont during this period, with Izapan art styles and symbols forming a major component of the emergent tradition.

In subsequent centuries, the prominence of Kaminaljuyú waned, to revive again in the Classic period under the powerful stimulus of contact with the urban Mexican civilization of Teotihuacán. From a base at Kaminaljuyú, Teotihuacanos developed economic ties with cities in the southern lowlands. The end of direct Teotihuacán involvement in the Maya world before A.D. 600 ushered in a poorly understood period of regionalization in which local cultures vied for prominence. The florescence of Classic Maya civilization evidently did not include central and eastern highland societies. Communities in these areas did not produce the monumental architecture, sculpture, and hieroglyphic inscriptions that are so typical of the lowland cities. The relationships between highland Maya peoples and the better-understood lowland variants of Classic Maya civilization remain to be worked out.

In the closing centuries of the prehispanic epoch, a series of relatively small, ethnically and linguistically distinct Maya groups competed for local political hegemony in the central and eastern highlands. The most prominent were the Quiché.

At the western edge of the zone lived the Kanjobalans: Kanjobal, Jacaltec, Acatec, Motozintlec, Tuzantec, Tojolabal, and Chuj.[20] Their role in the region's history is obscure. Today they are vastly reduced in numbers, and their languages and cultural traditions are almost extinct. They cling to a precarious existence at the margins of modern Mexican and Guatemalan society.

The Mamean branch of the Mayan language family separated early from their Quichean-speaking relations, probably by 1500 B.C., not long after Eastern Mayan became distinct from the Proto-Mayan stock. Mamean languages have remained very archaic. Of all Mayan tongues, Mam, Teco, Ixil, and Aguacatec have changed least from the Proto-Mayan language. In late prehispanic times, these peoples were more numerous and more prominent than their western neighbors. The Mam dominated a substantial zone from their capital at Zaculeu. Just before the Spanish conquest they came under heavy pressure from their eastern neighbors, the Quiché. In the centuries since the conquest, Mamean speakers have expanded south into the piedmont and coastal regions.[21]

The central highland region around Lake Atitlán is the homeland of Quichean speakers (Color Plate 10).[22] Quichean underwent a late divergence, with Quiché, Cakchiquel, Tzutuhil, Sacapultec, and Sipacapa emerging as distinct languages only about A.D. 1000. In the last centuries of the prehispanic era a parallel process of cultural and political differentiation produced independent Quiché, Cakchiquel, and Tzutuhil states competing for local hegemony. The arrival of the Spaniards interrupted the Quiché people's rise to dominance.

The eastern highlands are the home of other Quichean peoples: Kekchi and Uspantec in the north and Pokom in the east.[23] Over the past century, the Kekchi have expanded into the southern fringe of the lowlands. On the northeast are the Cholan Chortí, in the foothills descending to the southeastern lowlands.[24] On the east and south, Pokom speakers occupy the frontier of the Maya world and of Mesoamerica. The Pokomam and Pokomchi separated only about A.D. 1000. Their distribution at the time of the Spanish invasion may reflect a relatively recent expansion east and south into what may formerly have been non-Maya territory. Beyond the Pokomam are non-Mesoamerican peoples: the Paya, Lenca, and Xinca.

THE PACIFIC COAST AND SLOPE

Farming villages appeared in the coast and piedmont sector of the Intermediate Zone before 1500 B.C. They evolved from an earlier tradition of settled communities that exploited the rich wild-food resources of the coast. In the centuries after 1500 B.C., the region was linked with the Olmec Gulf Coast, participating in networks of interaction which stretched across the lowland belt spanning the Isthmus of Tehuantepec and extended far to the east along the Pacific coast and piedmont.

During the final centuries of the Preclassic period, the Intermediate Zone was the home of a confusing series of related cultures. Chiapa de Corza, Izapa, Abaj Takalik, El Baúl, and Monte Alto, along with such highland communities as Kaminaljuyú and Chalchuapa, grew into prominent towns. Monumental architecture and sculpture with hieroglyphic inscriptions burgeoned. An underlying similarity in style and content cuts across the regional differences in these vigorous local cultures. This Izapan artistic tradition shows a plain heritage from Olmec civilization. Equally clear is the contribution of Izapan art and symbols to the emergence of Classic Maya art, calendar systems, and writing.

The piedmont and coastal zone had a complex history during the Classic period. In the east, relationships with lowland Maya civilization, especially its southeastern variant, were strongest. Here, along the southern end of the frontier zone bordering Central America, considerable mingling of peoples created a complicated mosaic of cultural patterns. Farther west were several poorly understood regional cultures, many of them evidently aligned more with the Mexican than with the Maya tradition. Beginning as early as A.D. 800, speakers of Pipil, a branch of the Nahua family closely related to the language of the Aztecs, filtered southward and eastward from central Mexico, settling in enclaves among local groups. These movements reflect sweeping political and cultural changes that took place in central Mexico after the collapse of Teotihuacán.

At the time of the Spanish invasion, the western Pacific coast and slope was basically Zoque country, with a substantial Pipil component. The Aztec empire had recently incorporated a large portion of the area into the coastal province of Xoconochco (Soconusco), ensuring access to its rich cacao production. To the east, Pipil enclaves were increasingly prominent among speakers of Xinca, Lenca, and other Central American languages. In recent centuries, Mayan-speaking groups have spilled down from the highlands into the piedmont and coastal plain.

The uneven quality of available data exaggerates the cultural and historical contrasts among the various regions of the Maya world. This distortion is particularly severe for the earlier periods, since evidence of early settlements, often buried under later construction or obliterated by it, is found more often by chance than by design. Vast regions remain almost unknown archaeologically, even for later periods. Much of central Yucatan, intermediate between the northern and southern lowlands, has hardly been investigated. Huge tracts of southern forest, especially in the foothills rising to the highlands, are practically unexplored. Copán, in the southeast, and Palenque, in the northwest, seem marginal to central lowland patterns mainly because the intervening territory is nearly blank on the archaeological map. Recent work in central Yucatan has uncovered intermediate forms and styles that blur the contrast between northern and southern lowlands. By the same token, when more is known about the southern margin of the lowlands, transitional variants will bridge the apparent gulf between highland and lowland Maya cultures.

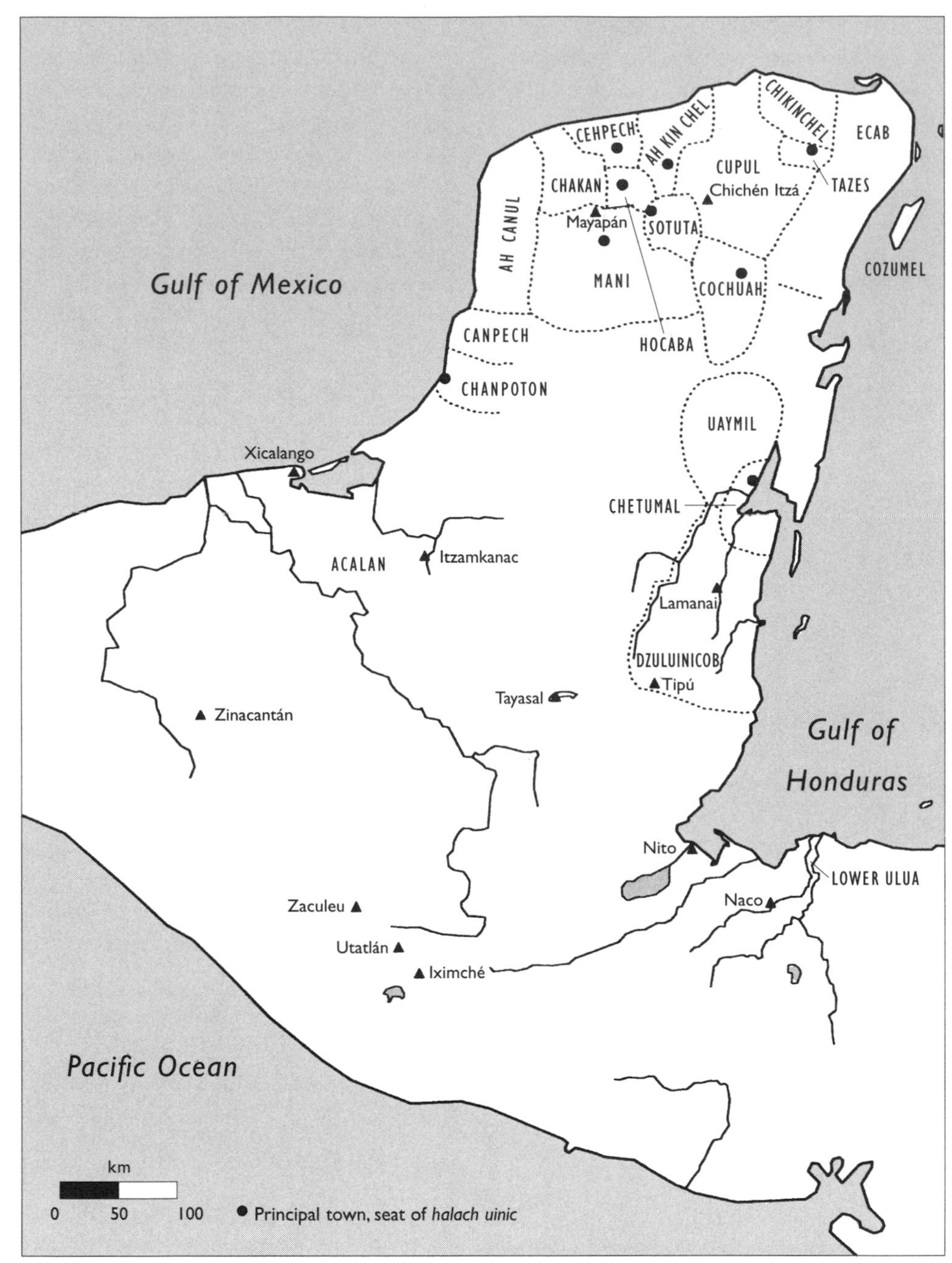

MAP 4. The Maya world on the eve of the Spanish invasion. The limits indicated for the Quiché state represent its maximum expansion, achieved in the mid fifteenth century.

THREE

The Maya World on the Eve of the Spanish Conquest

The Spaniards who conquered and colonized the Maya area were firsthand observers of Maya societies before the demise of their economic and political independence. Yet the picture of sixteenth-century Maya societies that can be pieced together from Spanish accounts is spotty. Few groups have thorough documentation, and some have none at all. The conquerors were most interested in native political geography and trade networks, of course, for political and economic institutions could most easily be adapted to Spanish ends. Such cultural spheres as religion, difficult to comprehend and slated to be stamped out, attracted much less attention. Even the best descriptions of Maya groups in early colonial documents are heavily biased toward politics and economics. Uneven and imperfect as they are, these glimpses of the Maya just after the conquest are priceless, for they often reveal facets of culture that are all but impossible to reconstruct from archaeological evidence. Although much of the Maya tradition survived to become the subject of modern observation, never again were Maya societies untouched by the political, economic, and social impact of the dominant European culture. Used cautiously, reconstructions of early colonial Maya societies can provide useful models for interpreting the precolumbian predecessors of those societies.

The States of Northern Yucatan

Several of the politically autonomous districts comprising northern Yucatan in the sixteenth century (Map 4) had been provinces under the sway of Mayapán in earlier times.[1] Much of the eastern peninsula had remained beyond the direct control of Mayapán; Dzuluinicob, south of Chetumal, had always been autonomous. Tipú, in the region's extreme southwest, was its economic and political focus, and maintained close connections with Tayasal to the west as well as with northern towns. Christian churches built at Tipú and Lamanai in the sixteenth century reflect their prominence in the eyes of the Spanish invaders.[2]

POLITICS

Although all were culturally and linguistically Yucatec, to some extent northern towns were ethnically distinct, dominated by powerful competing families. Despite the many cultural links that bound them together, relations among towns were not always harmonious. Boundaries between polities, never sharply defined, were often disputed, and disagreement occasionally erupted into armed conflict.

Some provinces had shed the old centralized organization entirely. Chakán, in the northwest, Chikinchel, along the north coast, and Ecab, in the east, scarcely constituted political units at all. Casual alliances linking the independent towns shifted frequently. Ah Canul, in the west, maintained a slightly firmer identity. Nobles of the Canul family controlled most of the main centers and generally acted in concert. A similar situation obtained in the east-central plains, where the Cupul family dominated.

Maní was the home of the Tutul Xiu, whose nobles had been at the forefront of the revolt that toppled Mayapán, while Sotuta had become the refuge of the Cocom family, deposed lords of Mayapán. Here and in Chanpotón, Cehpech, Hocaba, Ah Kin Chel, Tazes, Cochuah, and Chetumal, central political and economic hierarchies persisted. Each of these provinces was, at least nominally, under the authority of a *halach uinic* ("true man"), although his control was not always complete. In some provinces, outlying towns exercised effective local independence, while recognizing the nominal authority of the halach uinic. His functions were mainly political and military, and he was concerned especially with defense of the province and maintenance of its boundaries. At the same time, the halach uinic had important religious roles, and he could be referred to as a "bishop." The office was hereditary, often passing from the incumbent to his younger brother, then to his son. Subject towns provided for the upkeep of the halach uinic and his ménage through tribute, usually in foods.

The *batab* headed municipal organization; the halach uinic himself served as batab of provincial capitals. This office too was principally political and military, charged with general administrative and judicial oversight, particularly of farming and public construction activity. Townspeople provided the batab with food and domestic service. Each ward or municipal subdivision had its local administrative head, the *ah cuch cab*. Collectively these officials formed a sort of town council that served the batab in an advisory capacity. Most towns had, in addition, several lower ranks of municipal officers.

ECONOMY AND SOCIETY

Throughout northern Yucatan, society was organized along much the same lines. At birth each person became a member of a lineage group, comprising kinsmen related through males. Children entered the lineage of their father, taking his surname, which was also the lineage name. Persons with the same lineage surname were scattered throughout northern Yucatan. However distant the actual kinship relation, they were forbidden to marry. Common lineage names also implied at least the theoretical obligation of mutual assistance, although conflicting political loyalties often intervened. Locally, lineages constituted functioning corporate groups, with their own council chambers. Local lineages were ranked. Even though differences in social and economic status cut across lineage lines, high political offices and wealth tended to concentrate in the hands of male leaders of powerful families in high-ranking lineages. The *ah holpop*, head of the most prominent local lineage, often served as batab or filled some other powerful office.

Ownership of land, buildings, orchards, beehives (Fig. 3-1), jewels, and other real property passed mainly along male lines, from fathers to sons. Women also held property, sometimes land, in their own right, and daughters inherited from their mothers. Like men, women derived high social rank from family and lineage connections, and they sometimes held important political offices. In addition to the lineage surname, each person took a *naal* ("house name") from his or her mother.

Young men lived in community or barrio dormitories, where they underwent informal social and religious education. Those destined for the priesthood or high political office received more formal training elsewhere. On marriage, typically in late adolescence, a young man moved in with his bride's family for a period of service that might last six years or more. Thereafter, the couple went to live with the husband's family or established a new household. Multiple-family dwellings were the norm.

Men of noble or wealthy family and lineage connections gravitated toward careers in politics. Young sons of wealthy houses for whom no offices were available, or who were unsuited for political life, often turned to commerce. An alternative, probably also open to achieving sons of lesser families, was the priesthood. Assorted religious offices fell into a rough status and authority ranking, but they were not part of a single formal hierarchy. Some priests performed a wide range of ritual duties, while others specialized. *Chilams* interpreted prophecy. More numerous were specialists in heart removal and other methods of human sacrifice.

Sons of lesser families ordinarily became farmers. Agrarian methods were much the same as they

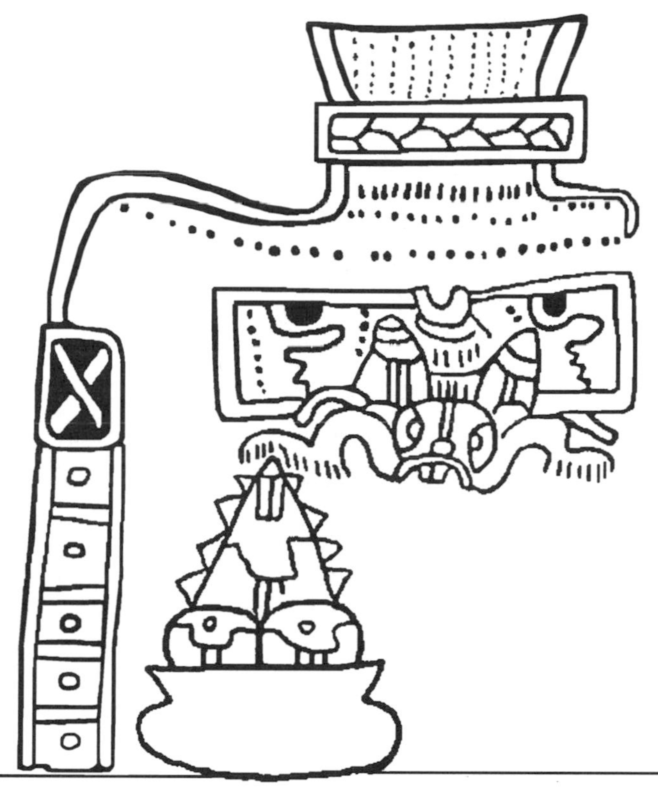

FIG. 3-1. Section of an almanac in the Madrid Codex, a Yucatec painted book of the late precolumbian period, relating calendar positions and supernatural forces of concern to beekeepers. The scene features a stylized temple, shown in cutaway view, in which a giant bee hovers over an offering consisting of corn and iguana. Adapted from Codex Tro-Cortesianus 1967:106.

are in Yucatan today, but with a much enhanced religious and ritual component. The prehispanic milpa farmer operated not in a world of fixed natural processes but in a universe filled with supernatural powers of variable disposition. He therefore had not simply to follow mechanical farming methods, but to adopt procedures designed to persuade these beings to confer a bountiful harvest by producing favorable conditions (Figs. 3-1, 3-6).[3]

Extreme contrasts in wealth and social status separated nobles from ordinary farmers, but only slaves constituted a sharply bounded social class. Craft specialists and minor merchants comprised a loosely defined middle group that ranked below the aristocracy but above the common farmers. Debtors, criminals, and prisoners of war were enslaved. Most slaves performed domestic service or agricultural labor; some became victims for the sacrificial altar.

Social, economic, and even political ties cut across the fabric of formal political divisions in northern Yucatan. The same lineages were represented everywhere, and common lineage membership promoted a feeling of solidarity that could stimulate cooperation in economic and political arenas. Economic links connected districts. Each had a diversified economy with a strong milpa-farming component, but emphases differed. A few coastal towns specialized in fishing or salt collecting. Chetumal's prosperity flowed from its exceptionally productive cacao orchards as well as from its position as an important trading center. Commerce, monopolized by noble merchants, was active and extensive. The island of Cozumel was a major commercial center in the maritime exchange network ringing the coast of Yucatan.[4] As in the days when Chichén Itzá and then Mayapán had held sway, cotton cloth, salt, honey, wax, and slaves moved south to Chetumal and on to Nito and Naco, at the base of the Gulf of Honduras. In return, cacao, precious metals, feathers, and the like were shipped north.

THE STRUCTURE OF TIME, THE UNIVERSE, AND THE SUPERNATURAL

Yucatec philosophy held that the universe is unified,[5] that the physical world is inextricably intertwined with other realms.[6] The province of the supernatural, of the incorporeal, and of extrasensory experience is a part of everyday experience, an ordinary aspect of reality. Space is not bounded by the limits of the terrestrial world, but embraces the heavens and the underworlds as well. One set of dimensions unifies the natural and supernatural worlds. Space and time are inseparable complementary components of the universe. A life force animates virtually everything, including cenotes, caves, hills, and buildings.

A host of supernatural entities inhabits the universe. Along with ordinary humans, animals, and plants, the universe harbors deities, symbolic flora and fauna, and legions of minor spirits. Each of these beings has special associations with one or more regions of the universe—with a particular cardinal direction or a specific unit of time—but they do not occupy their sectors exclusively, for all of the universe is continuous. Its denizens constantly move through the space–time continuum. In this sense, the Maya supernaturals are also dimensions of the universe, facets of time and space.[7]

Time. Beliefs about time were central to Yucatec thought.[8] They permeated every aspect of daily life. Some facets of Yucatec concepts of time are familiar: time is not static; it has a direction; it is measurable. Time can be divided into hierarchical units that can be manipulated mathematically—to calculate amounts of elapsed time, to make projections into the future, or simply to locate events at specific points in the stream of time. Other notions about time may seem bizarre: it is cyclical, not linear. Points in time and the events assigned to them are not unique; as named units of time recur, events comparable to the

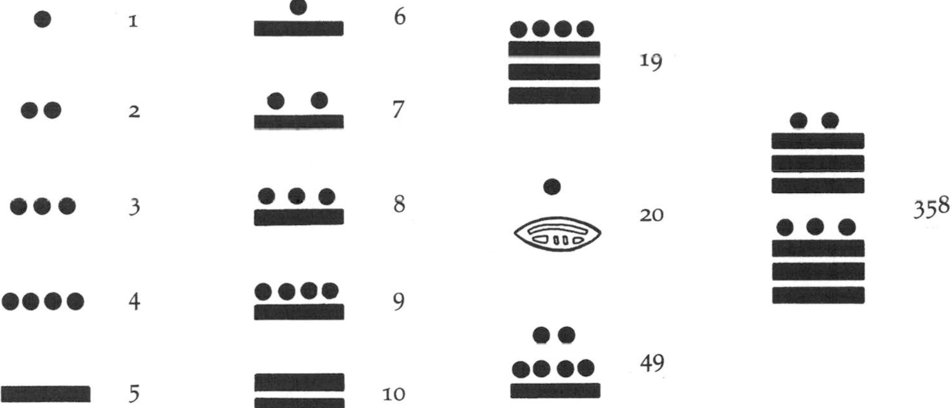

FIG. 3-2. Maya numbers. The commonest method of writing numbers features a dot for 1 and a bar for 5. For numbers greater than 19, Maya place-notation employs a stylized sign (a shell in the painted books) for 0. The place system is vigesimal, so that the value of the places increases by 20 (reading up). For time calculation, however, a special convention sets the third place equal to 360 instead of 400.

events linked to them in the past are to be expected. This follows from the nature of the universe. Supernatural beings gain special influence over events from their association with particular segments of time. The past is a clue to the present, and both past and present can be used to project the future. This cyclical perspective, along with the intimate relationship between units of time and supernatural beings (Figs. 3-1, 7-17), naturally adds a divinatory or astrological quality to the concept of time.[9]

The Yucatec calendar is a complex synthesis of many discrete parts.[10] A series of cycles, all proceeding concurrently, keeps track of the passage of time in a variety of ways. Each cycle performs unique functions, but the cycles are not separable. Overlapping associations with the same deities and quarters of the universe connect the cycles. The calendar as a whole is an intricate mechanism in which each part can influence all others. Divination—calculating the omens for a given time or determining the suitability of a particular action—becomes a marvelously complex operation.

The most basic part of the calendar is a cycle of 260 days, usually called the Ritual Almanac. Primarily religious and divinatory in function, it serves to schedule ceremonial activity and is the chief guide to the auguries.[11]

The day, *kin* in Yucatec, is the elementary unit of the Ritual Almanac and of all calendar cycles. Each day has a designation produced by the combination of two elements: a number between 1 and 13 (Fig. 3-2) and one of a set of twenty names (Fig. 3-3). The numbers and names form repeating cycles, so that the first day is 1 Imix, the second 2 Ik, the fourteenth 1 Ix, the twenty-first 8 Imix, and so on. The permutation of the two rounds creates a cycle of 260 combinations. The designation 1 Imix does not reappear until day 261.

Each of the twenty names is associated with a deity, who assumes particular importance on days

FIG. 3-3. Name glyphs of Ritual Almanac days in the style used in painted books. The names are those recorded by Bishop Diego de Landa in the sixteenth century. Maya scholars conventionally use these Yucatec names to refer to calendar glyphs.

bearing the corresponding name. Numbers are commonly written with bars and dots, but there are alternate glyphs that feature the heads of deities (Fig. 1-1), so the thirteen numbers probably also designate patrons of particular days. These deities, along with additional associations stemming from other cycles and from the assignment of days to quarters of the world, determine the omens of each day.

Attempts to explain the Ritual Almanac as a reflection of some natural phenomenon—the length of the rainy season, the period of time between zenith passages of the sun, even the term of human pregnancy—are not convincing.[12] The Ritual Almanac repeats continuously, with no breaks; the proposed models do not. The 260-day period may simply be an artifact of the permutation of its two subcycles. Thirteen and 20 are numbers of considerable ritual and symbolic importance throughout Mesoamerica. There is no compelling reason to suppose that 260 is significant in its own right.[13]

A second calendar cycle, called *haab* in Yucatec, corresponds to the solar year.[14] Eighteen months of 20 days each, along with an additional 5-day period, make up this cycle of 365 days (Fig. 3-4). Even though the solar year is actually slightly longer than 365 days, the Yucatec calendar makes no provision for added "leap" days. Each month is named, and the days are designated by numbers. The first day of the

FIG. 3-4. Name glyphs of the Solar Year calendar months in the style used in painted books. The first 18 months are of 20 days each; the final "Uayeb" period represents the remaining 5 days of the year.

first month is 0 Pop, better transcribed as "the seating of Pop"; the second day is 1 Pop, the third 2 Pop, and so on through the twentieth day, 19 Pop. The following day is the beginning of the second month, "the seating of Uo." An alternative way of writing "the seating of Uo" also designates it as the twentieth and final day of the preceding month, Pop. Although time periods may be discrete in reckoning, in another sense they overlap. This method of timekeeping may reflect a belief that the influences of a time period and its deities extend slightly beyond the official span.

Like the days of the Ritual Almanac, the months have specific patron deities, who exert influence over persons and events. For purposes of divination, the Solar Year calendar must be taken into account along with the Ritual Almanac. Although many activities scheduled with reference to the solar year are agricultural, and perhaps administrative, most of them have strong ritual dimensions.

The Ritual Almanac and the Solar Year are simultaneous cycles. Each day can be designated by reference to either system or to both (in practice, though, the Solar Year designation never appears alone). Days are referred to by Ritual Almanac designations alone or, more often, by these designations in combination with Solar Year positions. Just as the thirteen numbers and twenty names combine to produce a cycle of 260 days, so the permutation of the 260-day Ritual Almanac against the 365-day Solar Year creates a larger cycle of 18,980 days (Fig. 3-5). That is, to say, a given pair of positions—1 Ik 0 Pop, for example—recurs only on the 18,981st day. Thus, the dual designation specifies a unique day within a period of 52 solar years (18,980 ÷ 365), called the Calendar Round.[15]

Native histories of northern Yucatan at the time of the Spanish invasion use a system of time reckoning that measured the passage of time in terms of *katuns*, periods of 7,200 days. Katuns are named after the Ritual Almanac positions of the days on which they end. The final day is always Ahau, with one of the thirteen numbers as coefficient. Such reckoning creates a cycle of thirteen katuns (lasting approximately 256 years) called *u kahlay katunob*, or "count of the katuns."[16] This Short Count is more precise than the Calendar Round but still leaves room for ambiguity in the interpretation of native histories.

Space. The four cardinal directions are the foci of the flat earth.[17] Great trees support each quarter of the heavens, and each quarter has its special color, which typifies the gods assigned to it as well as its tree. Time is likewise assigned to the directions. The days of the Ritual Almanac move continuously through vividly colored space in a counterclockwise circuit: east-red, north-white, west-black, south-yellow (Fig. 3-6). In some respects the center, or the up–down dimension, with its green ceiba tree (*yaxche*, "green tree"), constitutes a fifth direction.

The heavens are layered, with specific deities and celestial bodies occupying each of its thirteen tiers. In another sense, the dominant feature of the sky is a two-headed dragon whose body bears the symbols of the sun, the moon, Venus, and other celestial bodies (Fig. 3-7). Its terrestrial counterpart is a monstrous saurian floating in a great pool, its back forming the surface of the earth. The underworld occupies the maw of this beast, whose jaws emit the gods at birth and swallow up the dead. The underworld has nine levels, each with its own lord of the night. These deities rule the days (or nights) in succession.

The Gods. The Yucatec pantheon is remarkably complex.[18] Deities appear in a host of guises, with many names and titles. Most deities are not one, but four: one aspect is associated with each cardinal direction. The appropriate colors are incorporated into their regalia, their names, or both. At the same time, a dualistic conception invests each deity with diametrically opposed qualities and roles: male/female, old/young, good/evil, celestial/underworld. It is no simple matter to sort the dozens of divine aspects into clusters corresponding to discrete deities, nor is it certain that ancient theologians and artists thought of their pantheon as a collection of easily distinguishable gods with invariable attributes. It is still more difficult to match precolumbian visual representations with the names and epithets recorded in postconquest documents. It is likely that the Yucatec concept of the supernatural envisioned a more generalized force, or array of powers and qualities, with a subset relevant to any particular occasion or ceremony. It may be that the images usually identified as deities are simply personified representations of the commonest combinations of supernatural elements.[19] In place of a massive inventory of gods of uncertain function and affiliation, a few relatively well known deities (or common combinations of attributes) can represent the richness of the pantheon.

Chief among the gods is Itzamná (Fig. 3-8a), who is both celestial and terrestrial, a creator and patron of knowledge. He has supreme importance for every facet of life. Equally powerful, but with a contrasting character, is the many-faceted death god (Fig. 3-8b), ruler of the underworld. The important celestial bodies are deities: the sun, the moon, and

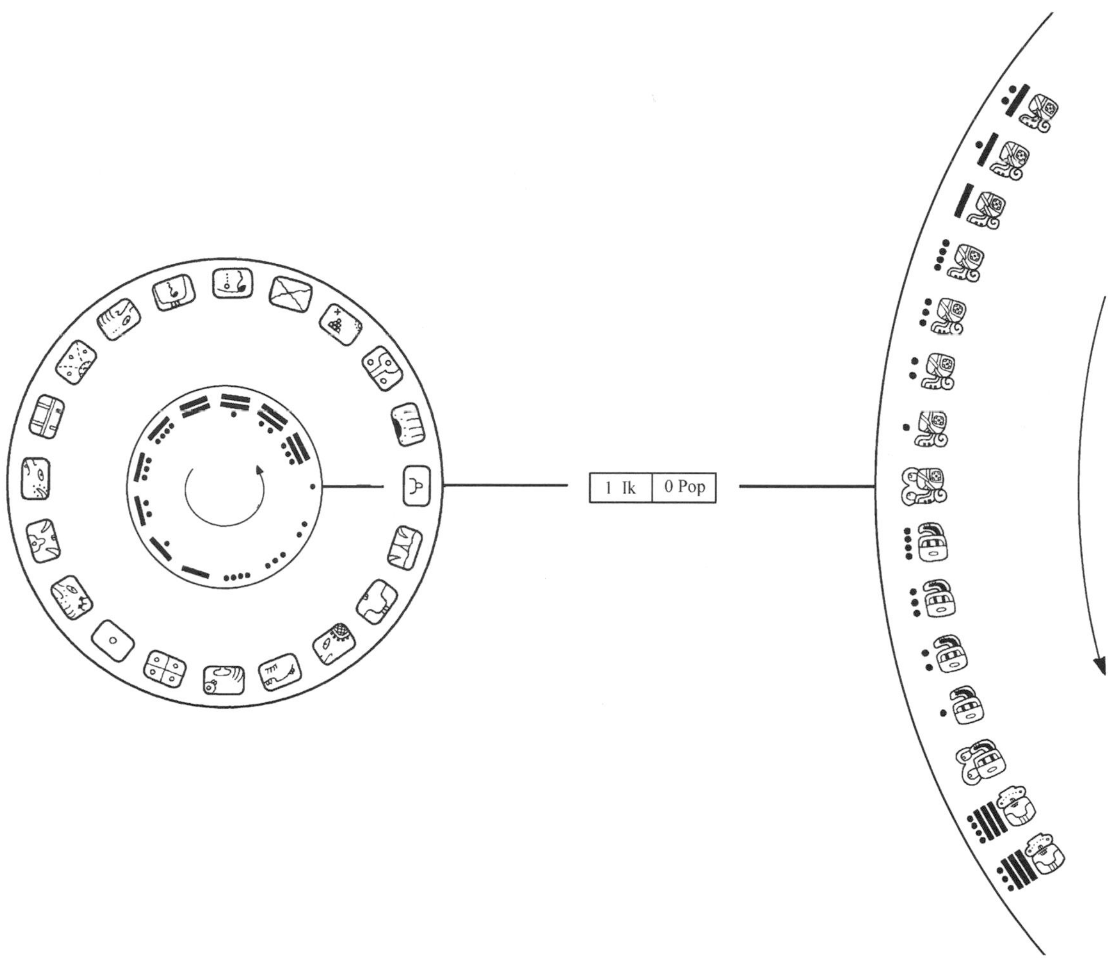

FIG. 3-5. The Calendar Round. Repeating cycles of thirteen numbers (*left, inner*) and twenty names (*left, outer*) create the 260-day Ritual Almanac. The permutation of the Ritual Almanac against the 365-day Solar Year system (*right*) creates the Calendar Round of 18,980 days, or 52 solar years.

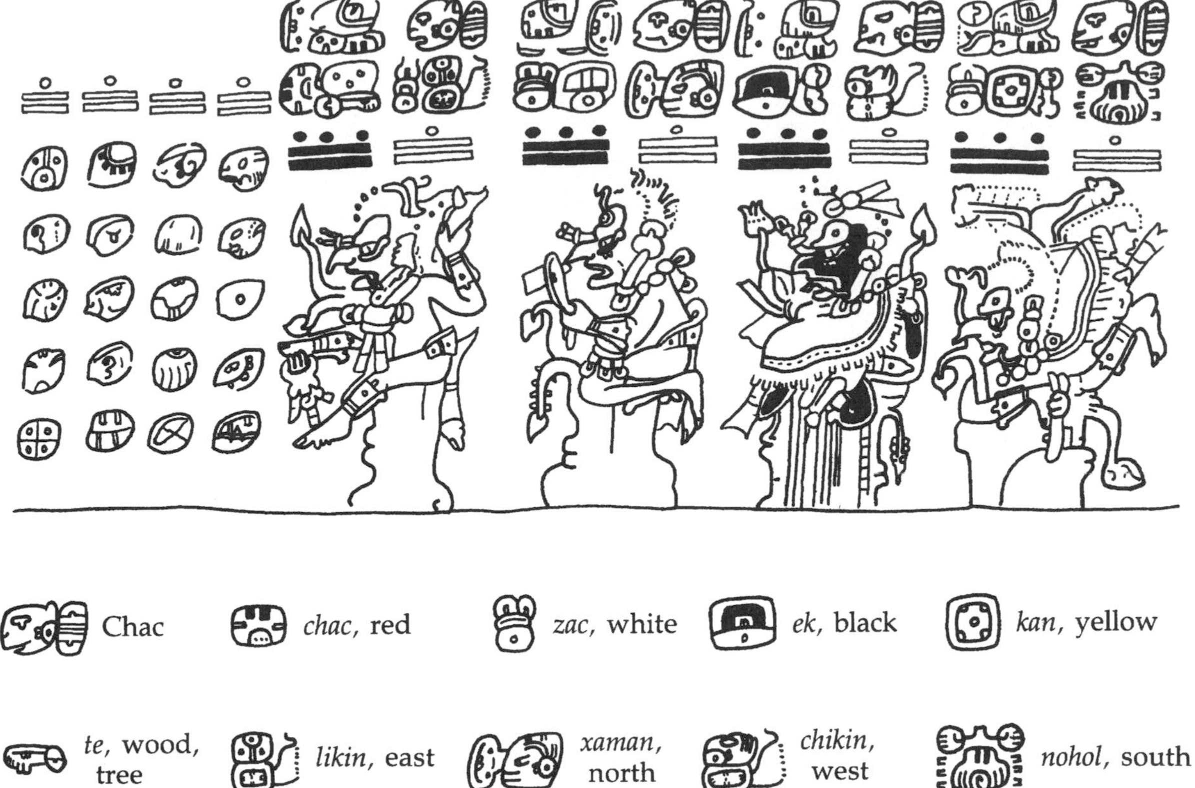

FIG. 3-6. The four quarters of the universe: a section of pages 30 and 31 of the Dresden Codex, a Yucatec painted book of the late precolumbian period. Each of the four sections shows Chac, the rain god, in the tree associated with one quarter of the universe. The text above each picture consists of four glyphs. The upper pair—an introductory glyph and Chac's name glyph—is repeated over each section. The lower pair specifies the color of the tree and the direction associated with each quarter: red tree, east; white tree, north; black tree, west; yellow tree, south. The Chacs themselves differ as well: the Chac associated with the west is himself black, like the tree of the west. This section of the codex is the beginning of a shorthand almanac. The day signs and numbers link certain days of the 260-day cycle with each section and therefore with the world quarters and their associated trees, colors, and gods. Note the "bumps" on the *te* glyph for tree and on the depictions of the tree trunks. Adapted from Codex Dresdensis 1975:30, 31.

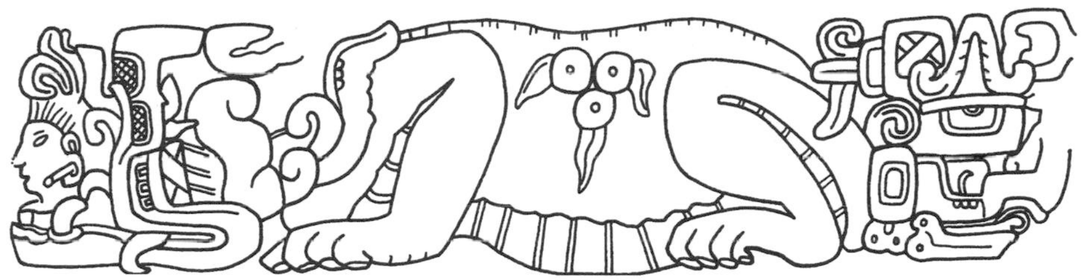

FIG. 3-7. Two-headed dragon representing the sky, with symbols of the sun and other celestial bodies. This Classic-period sculpture from Copán represents an earlier, presumably Chortí, version of the Yucatec concept of the heavens.

Venus are the most prominent. Each has numerous separately named aspects. Sometimes young but often old, the sun, Ah Kin or Kinich Ahau (Fig. 3-8c), is hard to distinguish from Itzamná, whose aspect he may be. In the sky he is the familiar sun, who may bring warmth or drought. In the underworld he becomes the night sun, with features of the jaguar. The moon goddess (Fig. 3-8d) is Ah Kin's consort. She may be an aspect of Ix Chel, a lunar goddess who presides over weaving, divination, childbirth, and medicine. Ix Chel, or another older goddess, is the consort of Itzamná. Venus (Fig. 3-8e), sometimes the sun's brother, has a plethora of named aspects. Most are malevolent and dangerous, particularly when the planet first rises as the morning star.

Terrestrial phenomena are equally represented in the pantheon. Notable among the benevolent gods in this class are the maize god (Fig. 3-8f) and the multifaceted Chacs, bringers of rain, thunder, and lightning. The Chacs are four, one associated with each world quarter (Fig. 3-6). There are also four Atlantean bacabs (Fig. 3-8g), who support the heavens at the corners of the universe.

Patrons of the various occupational and social groups form yet another class of deities. The most prominent are Ek Chuah (Fig. 3-8h), god of merchants and cacao producers, and Kukulcán, the feathered serpent, a special god of the aristocracy. The feathered serpent had many guises and many names throughout Mesoamerica.[20] In northern Yucatan, Kukulcán took on extreme importance and many new features following the Mexican incursions in the Postclassic period. At least one prominent historical personage of the epoch bore his name as a title. Yucatec histories confuse this man (or these men), who became a larger-than-life culture hero, with the god.[21]

Divination and Prophecy. Most of these deities, along with a host of others, have calendrical roles as patrons of one or another unit of time. Collectively, they hold sway over human affairs. As the cycles of the calendar are repeated, so do the gods come to prominence again and again in endless sequence. Rational action in this universe demands an assessment of which forces are in the ascendant at any given time. The omens are of crucial importance in determining the suitability and probable outcome of a proposed action, in predicting the fate of an individual according to the date of his or her birth, and as a general guide to action and a preview of destiny. Determining the omens, though, is no simple matter. The complexity of the calendar ensures that many deities reign concurrently, and there is no guarantee that their dispositions will be consistent.

The two patrons of the Ritual Almanac day (one

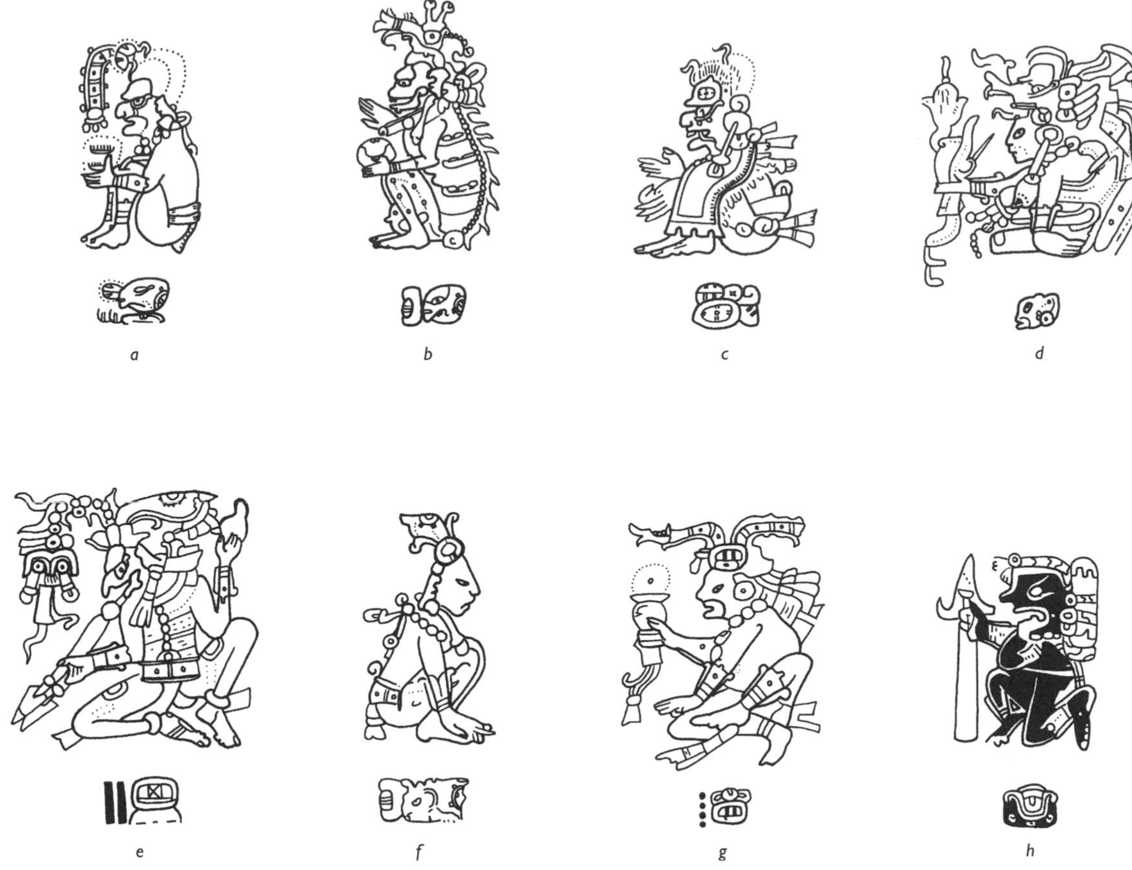

FIG. 3-8. Yucatec deities: portraits and name glyphs taken from the prehispanic painted books. Note the similarity between the name glyphs and the elements of the headdresses in a, c, and g. (a) Itzamná, celestial god; (b) death god; (c) Ah Kin or Kinich Ahau, sun god with *kin* ("day," "sun") sign on his forehead; (d) moon goddess; (e) Venus god with Venus glyph in his headdress; (f) maize god with an ear of maize in his headdress; (g) one of the four bacabs; (h) Ek Chuah, patron of merchants and cacao producers, carrying a traveler's pack with the aid of a tumpline. Adapted from Codex Dresdensis 1975:7, 9, 13, 26, 47–49 and Codex Tro-Cortesianus 1967:52.

designated by the name, one by the number) exert the preeminent influence, but they do not act alone. The patron of the Solar Year month also has a role to play, as does the lord of the night, and probably the gods of the larger units of time—the tun, the katun, and the *baktun* (20 katuns). The connections between time and space bring the associations of the cardinal directions into play as well. Venus and the other celestial bodies also wield influence, as deities in their own right and as the bases for additional cycles that associate gods with segments of time. The thrust of Maya astronomy, then, and of all Maya "science" (i.e., the determination of supernatural influences on human life), made it closer to astrology than to Western science. Careful astronomical observation and records and elaborate calculation of correlations with calendar cycles (Color Plate 9) reveal an extraordinarily intense interest in astrology.

Divination is plainly an esoteric business. For advice about optimal scheduling of important events and about the advisability of contemplated actions, lay people turned to specialists. Priests were trained in the complexities of astrological science and were conversant with the books in which the relationships among time, space, and the pantheon were recorded.[22]

The history of the universe itself is cyclical in much the same way. The world has been repeatedly created in past ages, each time to be destroyed in a great cataclysm. The present creation, too, will meet a spectacular end: the world and all its inhabitants will perish in another universal catastrophe.[23]

The same profoundly cyclical quality of time carries over into thinking about recent historical time. Parallel events should occur in time periods with the same designation. The past is a guide to present action, and the present sheds light on the events of the past; both reflect the future. History and prophecy are one. In the seventeenth century, the lords of Tayasal, still independent in the remote forests of the southern lowlands (see below), cast their deliberations about whether or not to accept Christianity and Spanish rule in the context of the political implications of the katun cycles: a katun in which major political change was to be expected was about to begin.[24]

Religion also promoted communication. Special regional shrines of wide repute became pilgrimage centers, attracting devotees in large numbers from great distances. The ruins of the old capital of Chichén Itzá retained ritual importance. People from all over northern Yucatan and beyond came to cast offerings into its cenote, sacred to the rain god. Cozumel had special importance for worshipers of Ix Chel, moon goddess and consort of the sun, patroness of weaving, divination, medicine, and childbirth. A steady stream of pilgrims came to consult the oracle at Ix Chel's shrine, on the island, where a concealed priest answered questions put to her image.

Acalán

Exchange networks stretched west and south from northern Yucatan to Gulf Coast ports and the inland trade centers of Acalán. Xicalango, on the Laguna de Términos, was a mercantile nexus of the first importance.[25] Merchants came to Xicalango from Yucatan, from Acalán, and from Mexican towns along the Gulf Coast to the west. Even *pochtecas*, men of the Aztec merchant class, came from distant Tenochtitlan. Xicalango had something of the character of a free-trade zone; this was a politically neutral town where merchants could conduct business regardless of their cultural or political affiliations. Several cultural groups maintained resident enclaves, trading and managing warehouses and other commercial facilities. Nahuatl was evidently the leading language of Xicalango.

The Candelaria basin, south and east of Xicalango, was the Chontal Maya province of Acalán

("Place of Canoes").[26] Chontal societies were organized along much the same lines as those of northern Yucatan. Noble families controlled politics, commerce, and religion. Ordinary farmers made up the largest social group. Slaves, lowest in the social hierarchy, probably provided most of the labor for Acalán's great cacao plantations, which required a constant supply of intensive labor, since cacao ripens throughout the year. Acalán was one of Mesoamerica's premier cacao-producing regions. The only notable difference from Yucatecan societies is that couples were much more likely to live permanently with the wife's family after marriage.

Itzamkanac, the capital of Acalán, was a large and prosperous town. Early Spanish visitors described hundreds of fine houses. Those of the principal families even boasted masonry walls. Cortés found Itzamkanac much more impressive than Tayasal, the dominant town in the Petén region. One administrative building in the town center was spacious enough to accommodate all of the Spaniards who accompanied Cortés, and their horses as well. Itzamkanac was divided into four quarters, each with its own administrative head. Collectively they exercised considerable power, but they were formally subordinate to a supreme ruler, or *ahau*, equivalent to the Yucatecan halach uinic. In 1525 Paxbolonacha held this office, ruling Itzamkanac and all of Acalán. There must have been many more levels of political hierarchy, both within Itzamkanac and in the subordinate towns.

Itzamkanac had many impressive temples, the principal one sacred to Cukulchán, the tutelary god of the ruler. Cukulchán is the equivalent of Yucatec Kukulcán ("quetzal bird–snake"), a god and culture hero identified with the period of Mexican influence. Each quarter had its own temple, dedicated to especially important deities, including Ix Chel and Ykchaua. The latter, called Ek Chuah in Yucatan, was the patron of merchants and cacao producers, a logical combination, since cacao was a standard of exchange and value, a form of money.

With their strong mercantile orientation, the Chontal towns had a long history of economic interaction with Mexican peoples of the Gulf Coast. Over the centuries their own culture had taken on a decided Mexican cast. Nahua personal names were widespread. Several communities or barrios within communities consisted of enclaves of Nahua-speaking Mexicans.

Acalán's prosperity depended on commerce as well as on cacao growing. Acalán's ruler was also its principal merchant. According to Francisco López de Gómara, chaplain and secretary to Cortés:

> In the land of Acalán, so they say, the people have the custom of choosing as their lord the most prosperous merchant, which is why Apoxpalón (Paxbolonacha) had been chosen, for he enjoyed a large land trade in cotton, cacao, slaves, salt, and gold (although this was not plentiful and was mixed with copper and other things); in colored shells, with which they adorn themselves and their idols; in resin and other incense for the temples; in pitch pine for lighting; in pigments and dyes with which they paint themselves for war and festivals, and stain their bodies as a defense against heat and cold; and in many other articles of merchandise, luxuries or necessities. For this purpose he held fairs in many towns, such as Nito, where he had agents and separate districts for his own vassals and traders.[27]

Acalán did not focus its commercial interests exclusively on the Gulf Coast and northern Yucatan; Chontal merchants also traded in markets to the south and east. On his march from the Gulf Coast to Honduras in 1523–25, Cortés followed some of the overland routes stretching from Acalán through the southern lowlands, at least as far as the Gulf of Honduras. Paxbolonacha, Acalán's ruler, maintained a commercial enclave at Nito, the Chol trade port on the Gulf of Honduras. His brother governed the Chontal quarter of the town.

Tayasal

Tayasal dominated the region around Lake Petén Itzá at the time of the Spanish conquest.[28] Remote from centers of colonial administration, its people remained independent until the end of the seventeenth century.

Five small islands in the lake were the heart of the Tayasal community. The principal island, only 500 meters long and half as wide, housed Tayasal's civic core, with elaborate masonry and stucco temples, palaces, and administrative halls. Clustered together on the high ground at the center of the island, the temples were surrounded by aristocratic dwellings nearer the shore. Evidently, only the highest-ranking lords and their retainers lived on the main island. One Spanish estimate put the population of this civic nucleus at 2,000 on the eve of its conquest; an earlier visitor mentioned two hundred houses. Island dwellers maintained secondary residences on the mainland for periods of heavy agricultural work. Outlying subordinate settlements on the mainland were quite small. Most ordinary farmers, the bulk of the population, lived dispersed in the surround ing countryside. Tayasal's political sphere embraced some 20,000 souls at the end of the seventeenth century.

Culturally the people of Tayasal were much like their Yucatec relatives to the north, and as the proper name of the polity—Tah Itzá—suggests, at least one segment of the dominant group identified itself with the Itzá who were so prominent in the late history of that part of the Maya world. Many of the people of Tayasal had Yucatec personal names. At the same time, the population of the region was ethnically varied, and descendants of the Classic-period peoples of the region were probably in the majority.

Lineage organization played a leading role in society and politics. Ahau Canek, the ruler of Tayasal at the time of its fall, bore the same dynastic or lineage name as his predecessor who had greeted Cortés. His first cousin, Kin Canek, was the high priest. *Ahau* and *ah kin* are Yucatec titles of political officials and priests, respectively. Politics and religion were intertwined, for Ahau Canek had religious duties and Kin Canek held political power. Priests and rulers also shared esoteric knowledge, for Ahau Canek could read the books of history and prophecy kept in his house. Officials in charge of outlying communities were often priests as well. The main temples were evidently dedicated to special aristocratic cults and tutelary deities of the nobles, for common folk worshiped elsewhere, mainly at sacred places in the forest.

Four *batabs* (another Yucatec title) ruled the quarters of Tayasal. These quarters were subdivided into smaller units that probably corresponded in part to lineage groups, for the name of the official in charge of each district could be applied to all of its inhabitants. Residences accommodated multiple or extended families. The *nacon*, a military officer, bore the same title as his Yucatec counterpart.

Most of Tayasal's gods, including the preeminent Itzamná, were also worshiped in northern Yucatan. At the top of the stair before the main entrance to Kin Canek's principal temple was an idol "squatting on its heels." Reclining chacmool figures were ubiquitous in Yucatec temples. Images of some deities spoke to worshipers, recalling the oracle at Ix Chel's shrine on Cozumel. Human sacrifice, especially by heart removal, was quite common. The music of flutes and drums accompanied the ceremonial dances performed on such occasions. A ritual meal of the victim's flesh often followed. Prisoners of war were the preferred victims, but local boys were also sacrificed and devoured. On one occasion, the men of Tayasal impaled the heads of a group of Spaniards on stakes on a low mound, evidently a rustic counterpart of the *tzompantlis* (skull racks) of northern Yucatan and central Mexico. Spanish reports that homosexuality was common recall traditional Yucatec aspersions on the "lewdness" of the Itzá.

Milpa farming, the foundation of the local economy, was exceptionally productive: in this region, milpas ordinarily produced two crops a year, sometimes three, and remained fertile for a decade or more. In addition to maize, milperos cultivated beans, squashes, chiles, maguey, manioc, sweet potatoes, and many other vegetables and root crops. They tended orchards of cacao and fruit trees and kept bees for honey. Fish, shellfish, turtles, deer, wild pigs, rabbits, dogs, turkeys, and many other birds provided protein. Tobacco was the most important of the plants cultivated for ritual and medicinal use.

Cotton was a particularly important crop, and luxury textiles were a major export. Salt, hard stone for grinding tools, obsidian for cutting tools, and other vital resources had to be imported. Tayasal depended heavily on external exchange networks and maintained enclaves in foreign territory, where needed commodities could be had. Canek told Cortés of his vassals who lived on the Caribbean coast in order to grow cacao. This outpost was probably at Nito, although Chetumal is another possible site. Both were situated in important cacao-producing regions, and both were prominent ports on the sea routes ringing Yucatan. The enclave probably had commercial as well as agricultural functions.

Naco and the Lower Ulúa Valley

The lower Ulúa Valley, just southeast of Nito, was another, perhaps even busier, mercantile zone.[29] Here Chetumal and other northern trade centers maintained commercial outposts with storage facilities. Here, in times past, the lords of Chichén Itzá and Mayapán had come to trade for gold, other metals, feathers, and particularly the cacao for which the region was famous. The Ulúa zone was a connecting link, probably a major transshipment point, between the exchange networks of the Maya world and those stretching east and south, beyond Mesoamerica, into the metal-rich regions of Central America. It was part of a frontier zone where peoples of Chortí and Chol speech mingled with Lenca and possibly Jicaque, Paya, and Care. Chontal Maya and Nahua-speaking Pipil with ties to the Pacific Coast may have formed enclaves alongside Yucatec outposts.

Naco, a prosperous town of some 10,000 souls located in the middle Chamelecón Valley (Fig. 9-6), was the most prominent center in the frontier region when the Spaniards arrived. Its economic and political sphere extended east, down the Río Chamelecón, into the lower Ulúa Valley, but craft styles also link Naco with the highlands to the south and west. Highland obsidian was a major import for local consumption and for resale. Naco was probably a Chortí or Lenca town, but as an important frontier trade center it surely had a cosmopolitan character. There are hints that a Pipil enclave may have settled there.

The Highland States

Early colonial documents have little to say of the western highland peoples. Tzotzil, Tzeltal, and Kanjobalan groups formed many small, independent political-economic spheres. Farther east, the Mam capital of Zaculeu controlled a much larger territory. Zinacantán, the Tzotzil trade center, was the most prominent western town. A Spanish conquistador remarked that Zinacantecos were "sensible people and many of them traders." Aztec merchants were vitally interested in regional products, but they regarded Zinacantán's sphere as dangerous territory and donned elaborate disguise when they traveled there; eventually the Aztecs established a permanent enclave. Salt, amber, quetzal feathers, and animal pelts were among the exports reaching central Mexico from Zinacantán. The Chiapanec, to the west and south, disputed Zinacantán's monopoly of valuable natural resources. Competition between them, especially over salt deposits, periodically flared into open conflict.[30]

Early documents describe central highland peoples in considerable detail. The Quiché, the most powerful group, had their capital at Utatlán.[31] In the sixteenth century they were still expanding from their original homeland in the Quiché basin. Their territorial holdings, mainly of very recent acquisition, were imperfectly consolidated. Growth had evidently outstripped the evolution of systems of political control and administration. Quiché society had undergone enormous changes in the last centuries before the Spanish invasion, and it was still in a state of flux when the Spaniards arrived.

The Quiché aristocracy monopolized power, filling all important political, military, and religious offices. Quiché nobles based their claims to authority and legitimacy on two grounds: descent from Toltec lords and a special relationship with Toltec gods. Traditional histories even describe ceremonies in which Toltec lords invested Quiché rulers. So firm was the Quiché aristocracy's title to sovereignty that the Quiché ruler formally confirmed the succession of his Cakchiquel and Tzutuhil counterparts. The Quiché sovereign was the only highland Maya lord who wore the nose plug, the emblem of supreme authority among central Mexican peoples. Gold and jade jewelry, quetzal-feather ornaments, and a host of other status symbols reserved to the aristocracy set them visibly apart from common folk. Nobles dwelt in sumptuous palaces in the civic precincts of Quiché towns. Even after death, elaborate funerary rites confirmed the lords' exalted status. Posterity immortalized the greatest nobles, even deified them, preserving their remains as objects of veneration.

Quiché society, economy, and politics revolved around aristocratic kinship organization. At birth every noble child entered the lineage of his or her father. The most prominent lineages traced their ancestry back in the male line to Toltec lords. Marriage regulation was an ancient function of Quiché kin groups: no noble could wed a member of the same lineage. Political considerations created a preference for marriage outside of the community as well, and Quiché rulers often found noble wives among the Cakchiquel, the Tzutuhil, the Mam, and perhaps even among the Itzá of Yucatan. Obligations of mutual assistance linked all the members of a lineage, who were expected to act in concert, as a group. Making good on the bride price required to conclude a noble marriage was a lineage affair. Lineages were also corporate groups, with their own buildings and land. For some purposes, lineages were grouped into sets, although these "major lineages" and moieties seldom functioned as cohesive groups.

In the course of Quiché history, noble lineages played an ever-increasing role in affairs of state. Eventually they became subdivisions of the Quiché political system. Each lineage was linked to an important political office, from which it took its name. The lineage head automatically assumed that office. Lineages were ranked, those of greatest status providing the highest officials. The *ah pop*, or ruler, was the head of the Cawek lineage, while the *ah pop q'am haa* (assistant chief) came from a lower-ranking group in the same major lineage. Lineage members provided the head with a staff of subordinate officers to assist him with lineage affairs and with the duties of his political post. One set of minor officials included such titles as ambassador to foreign peoples, councilman, council debater, council announcer, council diviner, tribute collector, war leader, war dancer, guardian of the wall, guardian of orphans, chief carrier, messenger, blood sacrificer, tormenter, chief of the sweat bath, bracelet keeper, painter, flutist, rattler, banquet servant, saver of fowl, toaster, helper, and several others. The number of lineages grew steadily with Quiché expansion and the attendant internal political elaboration. By the sixteenth century there were sixty-four principal lineages, with hundreds of subdivisions. Relations between lineages and the composition of higher-order groupings changed with shifts in political and economic fortune.[32]

Utatlán, the Quiché capital, was a composite community occupying several plateaus separated by deep ravines. Three distinct civic centers, each occupied by different sets of lineages, formed the heart of the community. Q'umaric Ah,[33] home of the Cawek lineage, was preeminent in the sixteenth century. Within each civic precinct, discrete complexes of temples, palaces, and council chambers corresponded to each lineage.

Ordinary farmers, who made up the largest segment of Quiché society, lived in outlying residential suburbs. The fruits of their labor sustained the aristocracy, to whom they owed allegiance as well as service. Aristocratic status symbols were forbidden them, and they were excluded from rites pertaining to the Mexican tutelary gods of the nobles. Commoners had their own lineage groups, which functioned mainly to regulate marriage and family relations. Commoners, too, had to marry outside their lineages. Unlike nobles, they normally found spouses within the local community.

Several occupational groups ranked somewhere between lords and commoners. Military orders, merchants, and artisans evidently constituted something of an emergent middle class. Warriors were crucial to the political designs of the Quiché state. By the sixteenth century, military leaders had acquired titles indicating that they had now been elevated to a lower echelon of the nobility. These warrior nobles gained access to some restricted status symbols, moved into the civic precincts, and assumed greater roles in state affairs. Formal authority and the balance of political power remained in the hands of the old aristocracy. Merchants, too, had some attributes and privileges of high rank, including free association with nobles. Artisans also occupied intermediate social positions. Some were actually low-ranking members of noble lineages. In Utatlán, at least, other artisans may have been foreigners, residing in Mexican enclaves.

Below the commoners were landless "serfs" who worked the lands of nobles as sharecroppers. This group, consisting mainly of freed prisoners of war, grew as the Quiché state expanded by military conquest. Other prisoners went directly to the sacrificial altar. Others still became slaves, as did convicted criminals. The very poor could also be sold into slavery by their relatives or their lords. Most slaves were slated for eventual sacrifice on a variety of ceremonial occasions. Some died at once; others performed domestic service or agricultural labor for nobles before accompanying their lords to the afterlife.

The Cakchiquel, close relatives and perennial rivals of the Quiché, were their neighbors on the south and east.[34] From their capital at Iximché (Color Plate 8, Fig. 9-10) the Cakchiquel dominated much of the region around Lake Atitlán. In the years immediately preceding the conquest, the Cakchiquel had thrown off the yoke of the Quiché state. In the sixteenth century they were increasing their own territorial holdings and economic sphere of influence at the expense of the Pokom and other neighboring groups. In political, economic, and social organization, the Cakchiquel closely resembled the

Quiché, with whom they also shared much of their mythology and traditional history.

The Tzutuhil, at the time of the conquest, were under pressure from their expansionist near-relatives on the west, north, and east.[35] They resisted subjugation, but Quiché and Cakchiquel successes effectively blocked the Tzutuhil on almost every front. All indications are that the poorly documented Tzutuhil society was much like its better-known relatives. At the same time, their restricted horizons presented a more limited scope for political and economic complexity.

Farther east, the Pokom also had a recent history of territorial and economic expansion, particularly along the frontier facing the Central American peoples.[36] In most respects the Pokom were comparable to the Quichean peoples to the west. Naturally, influenced by the foreigners along their eastern flank, they present an eclectic cultural picture. To the south and east, solid Pokom distributions gave way to Pokom enclaves among Pipil, Xinca, Lenca, and other non-Maya peoples. Chalchuapa, in the southeastern highlands, was one such Pokom community, part of the eastern frontier of the Maya world and Mesoamerica.[37] Farther east, in Lenca territory, non-Mesoamerican cultural patterns were dominant.

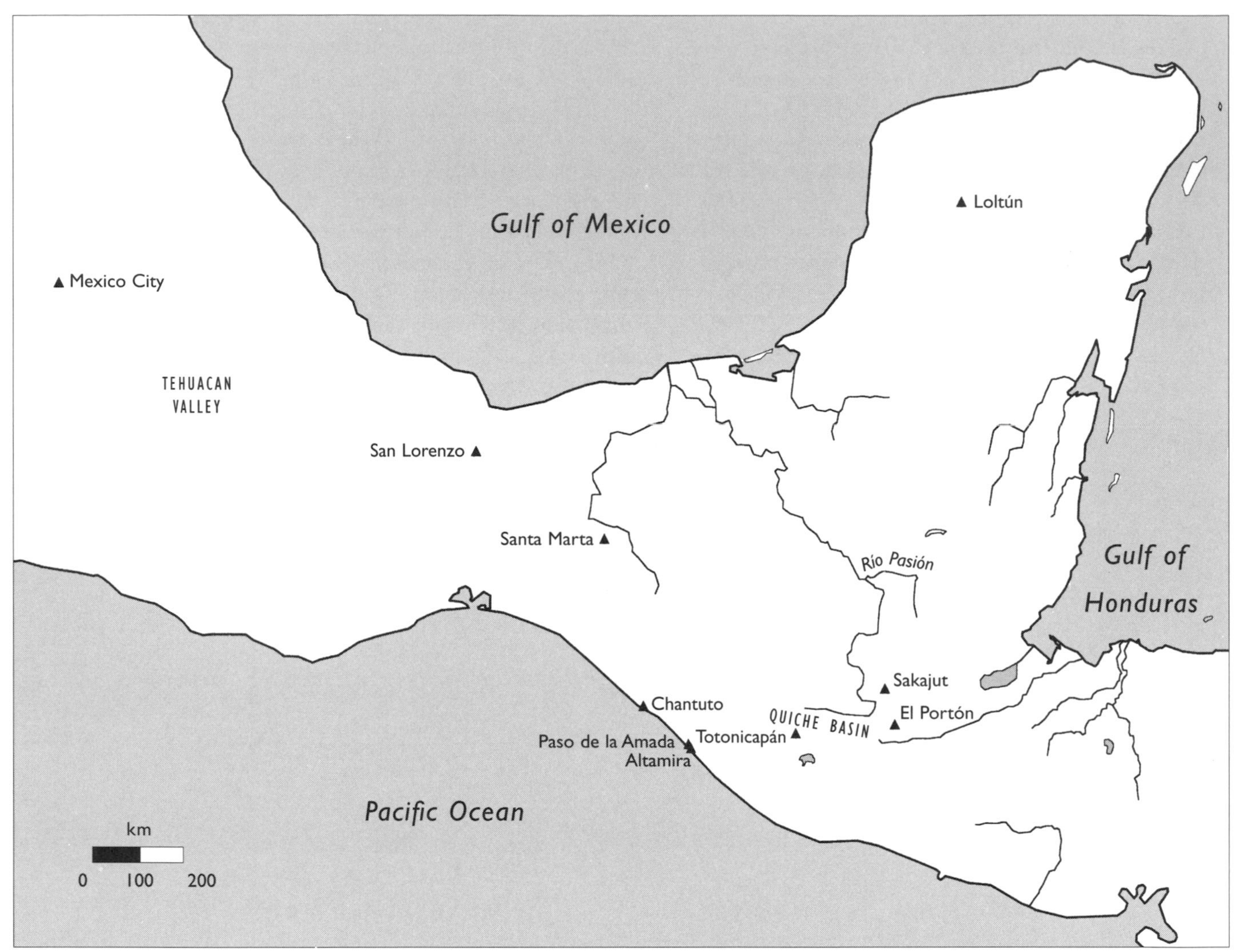

MAP 5. Early sites.

FOUR

Roots of Mesoamerican Civilization

The first inhabitants of the Maya world—small bands following seasonal migration cycles dictated by the availability of the wild plants and animals on which they depended for their food—are almost invisible archaeologically, especially in the heavily forested lowlands, but they were probably there soon after 10,000 B.C. Presumably, their descendants slowly began to cultivate plants and to follow more restricted seasonal rounds over the next several thousand years, as people in drier areas to the west (where archaeological data are far less scanty) certainly did. There is no reason to suppose that they were Maya in the sense of speaking one of the languages in the Mayan family,[1] and their remains certainly do not reflect the distinctively Maya patterns of later eras. By about 1500 B.C., settled farming life was established in most parts of Mesoamerica, including the Maya world. Shortly thereafter, before 1000 B.C., a new kind of society—with sharp contrasts in status and wealth, marked by differential access to such things as jade jewelry, and with centralized political power reflected in monumental architecture and sculpture—was emerging along the Gulf Coast. Most contemporary Maya societies seem not to have interacted very closely with Olmec centers, but the earliest manifestations of Maya civilization in the last centuries before the Christian era show a recognizable Olmec heritage.

Earliest Mesoamerica

The first Mesoamericans were people of Asian ancestry.[2] During the glacial epochs, millions of gallons of sea water were locked up in ice, and grassy tundra studded with shrubs and trees covered much of what is now northeastern Siberia, the Bering Sea, and Alaska. Great herds of game animals grazed these plains. Over the course of many millennia, small groups of people spread east and south from Asia into the Americas, not as part of a purposeful migration but simply as a slow natural expansion into new areas rich with resources untapped by human populations.

People reached South America well before 10,000 B.C.[3] Many thousands of years earlier, their ancestors had lived in Mexico and Central America. In the following millennia, small bands established themselves throughout Mesoamerica.

Before 7000 B.C. Paleo-Indian bands in Mesoamerica were small and very mobile. When food was plentiful, they temporarily formed larger groups, occasionally remaining together in a single camp for an entire season. More often, bands of a few related families moved about independently in a seasonal foraging cycle that required frequent changes of camp. Their lifestyle put a high premium on simple shelters and portable tools, and they left few lasting traces in their wake as they moved about the landscape. Archaeological remains of Paleo-Indian bands are quite limited: a few campsites with discarded stone tools and perhaps the bones of game taken in the hunt, an occasional kill site with stone spearheads or butchering tools associated with remains of the quarry. Paleo-Indian archaeological sites, never conspicuous, are most often found in relatively open highland environments. Where there are no dense forests, archaeologists can easily locate caves and rock shelters, obvious camping places for early bands. Lowland Mesoamerica, particularly the tropical rain forests of the Gulf Coast and Yucatan peninsula, offer limited prospects for locating early camps. Few have yet been found there. Some readily interpretable tools found in early camps, stone spear or dart points, are hunting implements. The most obvious functions of other common tools relate to the processing of carcasses: choppers and knives for skinning and butchering, scrapers for preparing hides. Plant remains rarely survive in very early sites. Animal bones normally provide the only direct evidence of subsistence, and even these do not survive unless soil and other conditions are favorable. When these factors are taken together, it is small wonder that Paleo-Indians, in Mesoamerica and elsewhere, are usually thought of as hunting peoples. Most known Mesoamerican Paleo-Indian bands were adapted to open, lightly forested environments, where group hunting techniques would be effective, particularly in the taking of large herd animals.

Kill sites, with remains of mammoth and other large Pleistocene mammals now extinct, are certainly the most impressive Paleo-Indian remains. Hunting was a major subsistence activity of early Mesoamerican bands, and several sites near modern Mexico City show that some occasionally succeeded in taking a great mammal (Map 5). These are not sufficient grounds, however, for supposing that they were basically big-game hunters, or even for describing them as hunters. Plants have been at least as important as meat in the diets of most later prehistoric and modern peoples. Most often, a great proportion of the animal food consumed by such peoples comes from activities that it would be better to label "collecting" or "foraging" than as "organized hunting": the gathering of insects, larvae, eggs, snails, shellfish, rodents, reptiles, and amphibians; fishing; scavenging and the opportunistic killing of small and slow game, particularly immature and injured animals. It is easy to recognize, in the abstract, that early bands were foragers, not hunters, but it is another matter to ascertain the relative importance of the variety of food-getting strategies they employed. Paleo-Indians relied on small animals and plants, but these foods have left few archaeological traces.

In the Maya area, as in the rest of Mesoamerica, Paleo-Indian remains have been found mainly in highland regions. The fullest evidence from the

Maya highlands comes from temporary campsites high in the Totonicapán mountains, northwest of Guatemala City.[4] A few stone points, knives, scrapers, engraving tools, and flakes of indeterminate use are all that remain to provide a partial glimpse of the way of life of one Paleo-Indian band. These camps, along with scattered finds of isolated tools, do at least indicate some occupation of the Maya highlands in early postglacial times. The lowland regions to the north are usually thought to have been unoccupied at this time, and for thousands of years afterward, because they do not offer environments in which open-country hunting would be suitable as a major subsistence strategy. It is true that there are few traces of very early occupations in the lowlands: stone tools found with the bones of Pleistocene animals at Loltún Cave in northern Yucatan, a few undated campsites with similar tools in the eastern lowlands, and an ancient sloth bone with butchering marks supposedly found with stone flakes in the Río Pasión drainage.[5] Given the nature of Paleo-Indian remains, though, negative evidence is hardly compelling. It would be foolish to conclude that Paleo-Indians were incapable of coping with lowland tropical-forest environments, even though no sites representing such an adaptation have been found. The odds against finding Paleo-Indian remains in such environments are overwhelming.

The Transition to Village Farming

The Paleo-Indian way of life—small, seminomadic bands that practiced a wide variety of foraging strategies, with a unique blend of food sources and patterns of seasonal movement in each region—is quite different from that of most later Mesoamerican peoples. Spaniards found Mesoamericans, almost without exception, living in substantial permanent settlements and relying on agriculture as the mainstay of subsistence. Communities ranged in size from tiny hamlets to huge cities. Some groups practiced basic milpa farming; others had intricate agricultural systems featuring *chinampas*,[6] canal irrigation, and other intensive techniques.

Discovering how and when ancient Mesoamericans made the transition from Paleo-Indian "hunting" to "village farming" has preoccupied Mesoamericanists for decades. In this quest, the natural tendency to create simplified categories has combined with an imperfect understanding of historic and modern Mesoamerican subsistence practices to cloud the picture. Thinking in terms of three ways of life—nomadic hunting, seminomadic hunting and gathering, and settled farming—archaeologists assumed at first that these are neatly separable lifestyles and that they represent stages of Mesoamerica's culture history. The history of subsistence in Mesoamerica is much more complex. In fact, "hunters" do many other kinds of foraging, depending heavily on plant foods, while "farmers" also hunt and collect wild plants.

Much of the problem stems from the supposed link between settled life and agriculture. Earlier generations of archaeologists believed that the relationship was clear-cut and absolute: sedentism is a "better" way of life and one that was naturally adopted everywhere when the development of agriculture increased productivity to such an extent that people could afford to give up nomadic ways. In an alternative formulation: agriculture is such an obviously superior mode of subsistence that, once it developed, people naturally chose the sedentary life it demanded. Recent archaeological and anthropological thought calls these links into question. Archaeological and ethnographic cases show clearly that nonagricultural peoples in resource-rich environments have led fully sedentary lives.[7] In some parts of Mesoamerica, varied environmental zones are closely spaced. A wealth of plants, small animals, fish, shellfish, and other wild foods provided the economic foundation for several early village communities. The notion that a settled agricultural life is superior and desirable reflects the values of farming societies. Nonfarmers have very different value systems revolving around mobile, foraging lifestyles.[8] They have often puzzled Westerners with their "irrational" refusal to convert to settled farming.

Certainly a connection exists between agriculture and settled life. Nearly all historically known farming peoples have been sedentary; conversely, few known foraging groups have been so. Well-documented foraging peoples have inhabited environmentally marginal areas; for the past few thousand years, farming societies have occupied nearly all of the world's richest environments. In earlier epochs, when foraging groups had access to areas rich in wild food resources, sedentism without agriculture must have been more common. All well-known farming peoples represent highly developed subsistence traditions; for the most part, they have had elaborate agricultural systems. Many prehistoric farming peoples were less closely tied to the land than their modern counterparts. Still, the agriculture–sedentism link persists in archaeological thought. Prehistorians are quick to interpret any permanent, settled community as agricultural unless there is obvious evidence to the contrary. There seldom is.

The relationship between settled life and agriculture is by no means a simple one. Nor was it always and everywhere the same. In some instances, agriculture and a settled way of life developed very gradually in tandem. The constraints of farming schedules created long-term pressures toward more permanent communities. As growing agricultural yields reduced the comparative advantages of a seminomadic food quest, increasing sedentism made greater investments of time and energy in plant cultivation more practical. In other circumstances, foraging groups adopted settled ways long before they began to incorporate agricultural activities into their subsistence systems. Simple cause-and-effect formulas (agriculture requires/permits sedentism; sedentism requires/permits agriculture) oversimplify and distort a wide range of very complex developmental processes.[9]

Agriculture is hard to define and harder still to recognize archaeologically. Mesoamerican peoples of the conquest period produced most of their food by means of a complex series of activities: preparing and clearing plots, planting crops, protecting them from other plants and animals, and often using more elaborate techniques as well. It is perfectly reasonable to call these practices "agriculture." Even today, though, native Mesoamericans do not rely solely on farming for their food: they hunt; they fish; they gather insects, mollusks, and other animals; they acquire plant foods in a variety of ways besides cultivating crops and collecting wild plants. People often protect fruit trees that they regard as their own, even though they have not planted them. They may plant trees but not tend them. They may clear unwanted plant competitors from berry patches or from around medicinal herbs. They may alter the distribution of any of these plants by dispersing their seeds—scattering berries near houses, for example—and the new locations may foster more intensive tending. In addition to obvious crops, most groups cultivate or otherwise encourage a wide range of other useful plants. These activities are not agricultural in the strict sense, but they can have similar functions. They provide important foods and medicines, and they have similar effects on plant populations. Modern ethnographers, like the Spanish colonists and conquistadores before them, have been distracted by those aspects of native subsistence which are most like modern farming. No outsider has produced a truly comprehensive description of native Mesoamerican plant use.

Archaeological remains never include the complete roster of useful plants, and there is seldom any way to judge what proportion they do represent. At best, when preservation is exceptionally good, fragments of some of the plants used by a prehistoric group survive along with some of the tools used in processing them. Such incomplete evidence does not always show whether plants were cultivated. Agriculture may produce physical changes in the crop plants themselves, such as increased seed size, but not in every instance. Simpler kinds of cultivation can also produce similar alterations. Affected plant parts do not always survive. Even if there were some way of determining the relative contribution of strictly agricultural activities to prehistoric diets, what proportion would define an "agricultural" way of life? The data will always be incomplete, and assigning early subsistence systems to such categories as "agriculture" and "hunting and gathering" will always be arbitrary and misleading.

The situation is not hopeless. Taken together with other remains, prehistoric plant material often provides considerable insight into subsistence activities. In most of highland Mesoamerica, maguey (agave, the century plant) ranked high among useful plants. The simplest (and probably the most common) method of consuming maguey is to chew the leaves after they have been slowly roasted, discarding the fibrous remains when the nourishment has been extracted. In late periods, at least, maguey was also the source of a fermented drink, now called *pulque*. Besides its food value, maguey was an important source of fiber from very early times. In the dry highlands of central Mexico, maguey was a dietary mainstay of early foraging bands, for it could be harvested year-round.[10] During the height of the dry season it was one of the few available plant foods. In the Tehuacán Valley, where ancient plant remains have survived unusually well, maguey quids found in early campsites represent the remnants of many prehistoric meals. Fragments of the shoots of maguey plants are common as well. Even in very early times, Tehuacanos harvested maguey at the most opportune moment in the plant's life cycle: after the shoot had appeared. By this time the plant had died, so that a natural fermentation process was already under way. Such timing of the harvest minimized the threat to the survival of the maguey population, for plants at this stage had already dispersed their pollen. Yet, since a plant may produce its shoot at any time of the year, this technique did not interfere with the continuous use of maguey. The archaeological remains do not show whether maguey plants were tended, nor do they indicate how aware early maguey users were of the ecological implications of their harvesting activities. In terms of its *effects*, though, this food-getting system is comparable to knowledgeable management of an important food resource. Other subsistence activities had equally subtle ramifications.

Attempting to pinpoint the beginnings of agriculture is a hopeless task. Reconstructing particular prehistoric food-getting systems in as much detail as possible is much more productive. Collectively, many scattered bits of evidence do indicate trends of change in subsistence patterns.

The Archaic Period (7000–2000 B.C.)

The Archaic period is not well represented in the Maya area.[11] Good archaeological evidence on the earlier part of the period has been found only in dry areas to the north and west, especially in the Tehuacán Valley, in the central Mexican highlands.[12] Data from these regions, of course, reflect specific adaptations to the environments and natural resources of semiarid highland zones. In the very different environments of lowland Mesoamerica, specific plant and animal foods, procurement activities, and scheduling practices would have been quite different. Reconstructions of early highland ways of life are not simply transferable to lowland settings, but they do provide very general insights into some of the processes involved in the evolution of Mesoamerican settlement patterns and subsistence systems.

In the most general terms, the early Archaic period was a time of slowly changing subsistence adaptations. The end of the Pleistocene epoch, with the withdrawal of massive ice sheets in northern latitudes, did bring noticeable environmental changes to Mesoamerica. Climates, previously a bit drier and cooler, shifted toward modern patterns. The combined effects of climatic changes and hunting drove some of the larger game animals, notably the mammoth and the horse, to extinction. Others, such as pronghorn antelopes and jackrabbits, moved into new territories. Plant distributions underwent comparable, even less dramatic adjustments. These environmental changes inevitably had an important impact on human adaptations, particularly on food procurement. New plant and animal foods came into use. Hunters now concentrated on small game almost exclusively, and plants were more prominent. There was no radical shift in the subsistence pattern, for Paleo-Indians always relied heavily on plants and small animals. In large part, new adaptations involved the gradual replacement of old food sources by comparable new ones, with corresponding shifts in procurement activities and scheduling. The same fundamental pattern of broad-spectrum foraging continued.

Within each region, food-procurement systems became a bit more standardized, with more regular scheduling of food-getting activities and more systematic seasonal rounds. Conflicting harvesttimes required choices among food resources, leading to greater reliance on some foods, especially certain plants. In this limited sense, subsistence adaptations became more specialized, with increased dependence on a narrower range of food resources, but overall subsistence strategies certainly continued to include a wide variety of food sources.

Many food plants important in the Archaic period were ancestral to the crop plants of later Mesoamerican agricultural systems. There is little doubt that cultivation was an increasingly important facet of human exploitation of many useful plants. An increasing number of plants represented in archaeological remains show morphological changes that resulted from human activities. In this sense, the Archaic period was a time of accelerating plant domestication.[13] This trend is a part of the historical background of later Mesoamerican agriculture, but it would be misleading to speak of a stage of incipient agriculture. Subsistence continued to be quite varied throughout the Archaic period, and hunting and collecting were still the chief food-getting activities. Analytically, it is useful to recognize a process of domestication at work in a set of changes in one aspect of subsistence: it is a convenient way of summarizing certain comparable trends in the few regions represented in the archaeological record. There is no reason to believe that Archaic period groups recognized domestication or cultivation as a separate component of their plant procurement, though, and it is very unlikely that they consciously chose to increase these activities to improve their diets.

When one looks at the regions of Mesoamerica individually, in terms of actual lifeways of specific human groups, the homogeneity disappears. In these more localized cases, there was no single process of domestication at all, just as there was no one subsistence adaptation common to all of Mesoamerica. Each region had its own specific food resources, scheduling patterns, and seasonal rounds. Different plants came under cultivation in each region, and at different times. The various domesticated plants played different roles in each local economy. There was interaction between regions, however, so that plants cultivated in one region were transferred to other areas, sometimes even beyond their normal ranges. The "process of domestication" in Archaic Mesoamerica dissolves into a mosaic of roughly comparable but quite varied local processes. Those highland regions where archaeological work has uncovered unusually complete remains of the early Archaic period cannot fully represent the history of domestication in Mesoamerica. Even for Tehuacán, the best-understood area, it is impossible to list all the plants that were cultivated in any given period. Most of the details of the domestication process are lost. In view of the fact that the Archaic period is a blank in most regions of Mesoamerica, especially the lowlands, it is likely that (1) nothing is known of most of the plants that were cultivated because they never became widespread agricultural crops; (2) many plants were domesticated independently in various areas at various times; and (3) none of the known cases of early cultivation actually represents the first or only domestication of the plants in question.

During the last thousand years of the Archaic period, plant cultivation was extensive in Tehuacán and in at least a few other regions of western Mesoamerica. Domesticated plants included, in one region or another, maize, beans, squashes, and chile peppers, the basic crops of later Mesoamerica. These plants were important contributions to the diets of human groups, but cultivation was not the dominant subsistence activity of any Archaic society. Nowhere is there direct evidence of the kind of elaborate cultivation techniques that characterized later agricultural systems.

Although the archaeological record of other zones is much sketchier than that of Tehuacán, there is some evidence of Archaic adaptations from a few environments of the Intermediate Zone along the western fringe of Maya country. Remains of early (ca. 7000–3500 B.C.) temporary camps in Santa Marta Cave, in the central depression of Chiapas, indicate that Archaic groups in this region were small bands of seminomadic foragers who followed extensive seasonal rounds.[14] The surviving material culture is limited almost entirely to stone tools, many of which could be used in processing animal and plant foods: grinding stones, nut-cracking stones, hammers, choppers, knives, scrapers, awls, gouges, and points. Collecting and trapping small animals (ocelots, armadillos, agoutis, tepescuintlis, squirrels, monkeys, birds, land crabs, snakes, snails) was evidently more important than hunting larger ones (deer, peccaries). Unidentifiable charred plant remains in the refuse and the low density of animal bones indicate the probable importance of plant foods in the diet. Some plants may even have been cultivated, although the absence of maize pollen suggests that the later Mesoamerican staple was not among them. Traces of larger and more permanent camps in the Quiché basin, to the east, suggest that the richer environments of the Maya highlands supported some larger bands with less extensive seasonal rounds.

More than a hundred poorly dated campsites along the eastern margin of the Maya lowlands probably reflect the activities of small mobile bands spanning the entire Archaic period, although they have not yet yielded detailed information on the lifestyles of early inhabitants of the lowlands. Changes in stone tools do appear to indicate increasing reliance on plant foods in the later millennia of the Archaic, and indications that at least some bands also remained in the same camps for longer periods may signal a corresponding trend toward a sedentary way of life.[15] Ancient pollen provides indications of environmental changes such as forest clearance that probably reflect the activities of small bands in this area and in several other parts of the Maya lowlands during the later centuries of the Archaic period.[16]

Late Archaic occupations (4000–2000 B.C.) on the Pacific Coast reflect the very different human adaptations in lowland Mesoamerica more fully.[17] A series of shell mounds represent many years' accumulation of refuse left by the shellfish-eating Chantuto people. Living in the mangrove forest and adjacent fresh-water swamps just inland from the beach, these early coastal people relied heavily on the rich animal-protein resources of the estuary-lagoon system. Marsh clams provided the bulk of their meat, supplemented by fish, turtles, iguanas, snakes, amphibians, birds, and occasionally mammals (deer, racoons). Although they left no archaeological trace, shrimp were probably an important part of the diet as well. There is no direct evidence of plant use, but *metates* and *manos* (grinding stones later widely used to grind maize and other plants) suggest the processing of plant foods. The Chantuto people followed a mobile seasonal round, but two oval clay floors with postholes indicate that, at least by the third millennium B.C., some people remained in the lagoon-estuary environment for enough of the year to justify the construction of substantial shelters. These structures may reflect a seasonal fluctuation in group size as the peak abundance of shrimp and other protein sources attracted more people from inland regions in the spring. The Chantuto people possessed a very simple material culture: mainly grinding stones and simple tools, useful for a variety of cutting, scraping, chopping, and pounding tasks. By 3000 B.C., these coastal groups were acquiring raw materials from distant regions, for now some of their cutting tools were made of obsidian, which occurs naturally only in the highlands. The obsidian trade is probably only one facet of flourishing exchange systems that brought inland products to coastal environments in exchange for shell, shellfish, and fish. This trade provides only the barest hint of the complex ties that must have linked late Archaic societies.

Occupation of the Chantuto region continued, evidently with little change, at least until 2000 B.C., and may have persisted for several centuries more. Pottery may already have come into use elsewhere in Mesoamerica, but it would make no appearance on the Chiapas coast until after 2000 B.C.

Linguistic reconstructions suggest that Proto-Mayan, the ancestral Maya tongue, constituted a separate, undifferentiated language stock during the late Archaic period (Fig. 2-4).[18] Most hypotheses about the history of the Maya family of languages call for an expansion from a "homeland" region in the west-central Maya highlands. Late Archaic populations in this area probably did speak Proto-Mayan, but the language was not necessarily restricted to a small highland core zone. Reconstructions of the Proto-Mayan vocabulary include words for lowland plants and animals as well as their highland counterparts. The ancestral Mayan language may have been quite widely spoken, but there is no way to plot its geographic distribution in detail, for the archaeological record of the Maya world is virtually blank before 1500 B.C.

Proto-Mayan began to diversify not long after the end of the Archaic period with the development of a distinct Proto-Huastecan language. Huastecan, isolated from the rest of the Maya world on the northern Gulf Coast, has no special relationship with any other Maya language. This early fission may have marked an actual separation of ancestral Huastecans from the main body of Mayan speakers and the beginning of a northward and westward movement to their historic homeland.

The Preclassic Period (2000 B.C.–A.D. 250)

Preclassic Maya societies,[19] like those of Mesoamerica at large, were never uniform. The first known Preclassic peoples in the Maya world evidently represent settled societies with mixed farming-and-foraging economies and a technology that included pottery making. Contemporary groups elsewhere in Mesoamerica had very different ways of life. In the Tehuacán Valley, the earliest Preclassic societies had mixed economies in which seminomadic seasonal rounds marked continued heavy reliance on animals and wild plant food in addition to domesticated plants.[20] Fully sedentary life developed only after 1000 B.C. At least one group along the Pacific coast of western Mesoamerica had settled in a permanent village by the beginning of the Preclassic period, but we have no evidence that its inhabitants cultivated plants.[21] Farther east, the late Archaic coastal-foraging adaptation persisted, with no indication of farming or pottery, until after 2000 B.C.

Most Preclassic communities do represent settled, pottery-making farming societies, but it does not follow that sedentism, agriculture, and ceramic technology are linked in a fixed process of cultural development. These patterns certainly did not appear everywhere in Mesoamerica at once. By the Late Preclassic period, though, a village farming way of life was established throughout the Maya world, setting the stage for the emergence of Maya civilization.

THE FIRST VILLAGE FARMERS (INITIAL EARLY PRECLASSIC PERIOD: 2000–1400 B.C.)

Not long after 2000 B.C., pottery making developed in southeastern Mesoamerica.[22] Mokaya pottery[23] appeared first at Altamira, Paso de la Amada, and other small villages, hamlets, and campsites in the lagoon-estuary zone of the Pacific Coast. Mokaya potters were in full control of basic ceramic technology, suggesting a long undocumented ancestry for Mesoamerican pottery making. The more ancient pottery tradition of lower Central America and northwestern South America is probably one ultimate source of the Mesoamerican craft. Early vessels from Mesoamerica do resemble southern pottery in general ways, and ceramic technology probably spread gradually north and west, through lower Central America into Mesoamerica. Especially in coastal zones, the overall way of life was much the same throughout this area: in each region, comparable village societies combined dependence on wild and cultivated plants with a strong orientation toward coastal and marine resources. No great differences in lifestyle presented barriers to communication. New ways of doing things probably spread freely and widely from community to community along both the Pacific and Caribbean littorals.

Within a few centuries the Mokaya pottery tradition had spread to communities throughout the Intermediate Zone and extended east as far as Sakajut and El Portón, well within the Maya highlands. The basic distribution of pottery in the Mokaya tradition corresponds to the probable homeland of the Proto-Zoquean language group, and these highland villages may represent an early eastern extension of its territory, although traditions of pottery manufacture can easily transcend language differences. Zoque and Maya peoples may have shared the Mokaya pottery tradition; there are no solid grounds for assigning Sakajut and El Portón to any specific linguistic group.

Although it represents a single basic tradition of manufacture, Mokaya pottery varies considerably from region to region. Nor were Mokaya communities uniform. Most were small villages with mixed farming-and-foraging economies, but local subsistence systems were quite variable. Maize was cultivated, but it does not seem to have been a staple crop. Beans and avocados were among the other domesticates. Clusters of obsidian chips, apparently the teeth of decayed grating boards, suggest that such root crops as manioc may also have been important contributors to the diet.[24] Coastal villages depended heavily on fish, shellfish, and other marine resources in addition to plant foods. Inland communities developed other blends of farming and foraging. Local groups in every region did not undergo simultaneous shifts in their lifeways. In the dry highlands of central Mexico, people still followed seasonal rounds to some extent until 1000 B.C. or later. Many

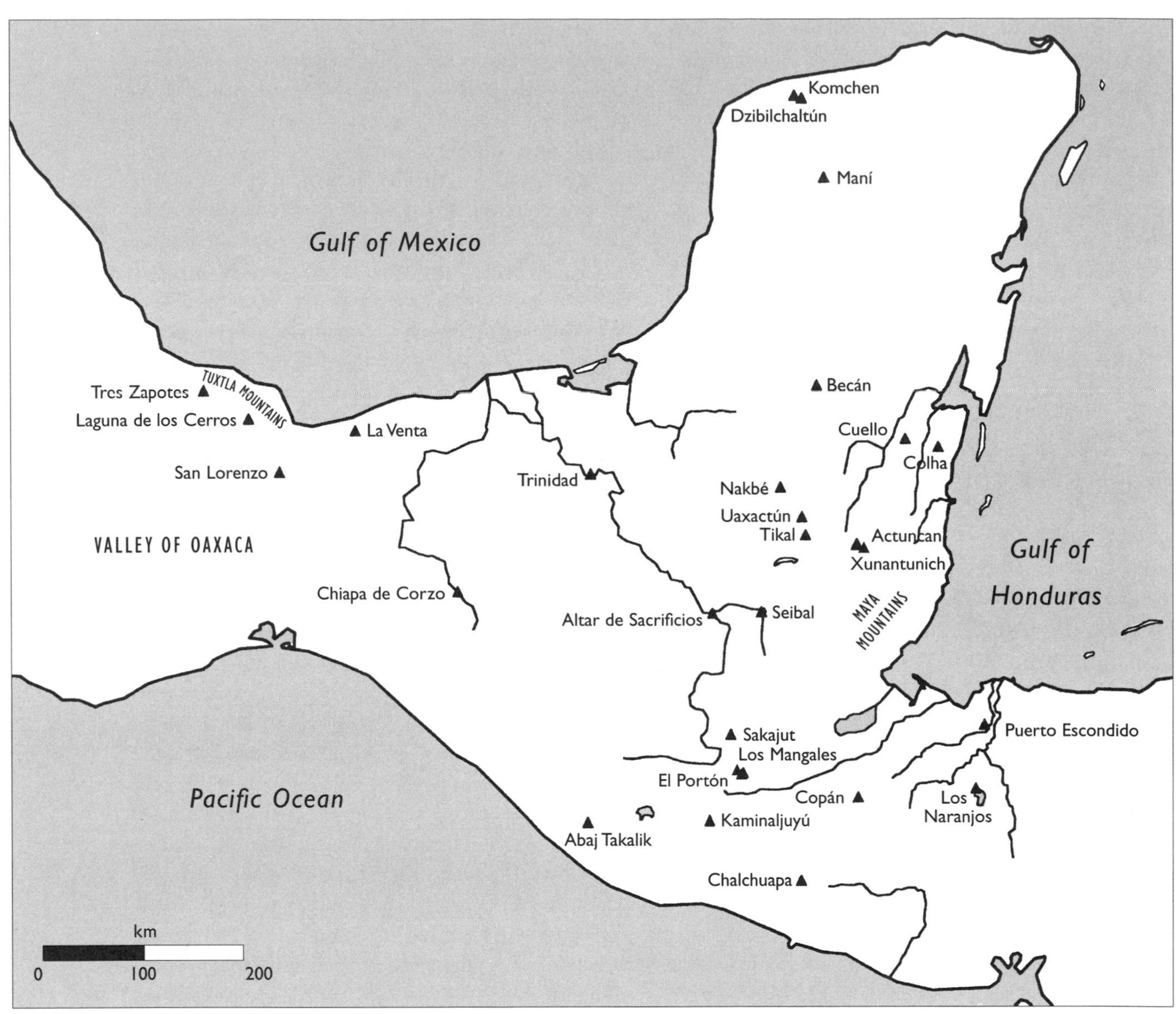

MAP 6. Early and Middle Preclassic communities.

of their lowland contemporaries presumably did the same.

Eventually some Mokaya communities grew into large villages, and a few even began to organize public construction projects. At Paso de la Amada, a large structure on a substantial platform, remodeled several times, was either a public building (such as a "men's house") or the residence of a chief. By 1400 B.C., a new kind of society—one that undertook public works projects, perhaps under the direction of a chief who could command the labor to construct a very special residence—was emerging in the Intermediate Zone.[25]

The people of San Lorenzo, in the Gulf Coast lowlands, undertook the greatest public works project of the age.[26] They moved great quantities of earth to modify and enlarge the natural plateau on which their settlement was located. Pottery and figurines already embodied a few features of the later Olmec art style, and by 1500 B.C. San Lorenzo villagers had also begun to produce basalt sculpture. Their descendants completed the development of the Olmec style and the transformation of the plateau into a building platform.

THE RISE OF CIVILIZATION IN THE INTERMEDIATE ZONE (EARLY AND MIDDLE PRECLASSIC PERIODS: 1400–400 B.C.)

By the latter part of the Early Preclassic period, precocious village societies in the Gulf Coast lowlands had developed into Mesoamerica's first complex culture: the Olmec civilization.[27] San Lorenzo (Map 6) had become an important center, producing large public constructions and monumental stone sculpture (Fig. 4-1).[28] Modification of the San Lorenzo plateau had been completed: many tons of earth fill formed an artificial construction platform supporting earth and clay mounds arranged around plazas. Larger structures were platforms for perishable public buildings, probably temples. Smaller mounds supported houses. Monumental basalt sculptures depicting political as well as ritual and mythical themes were arrayed among the buildings. Twenty or more artificial ponds, each lined with bentonite (consolidated volcanic ash) and connected to an elaborate stone drainage system, dot the plateau.

To judge by the two hundred or so residential platforms, fewer than a thousand souls lived on the plateau itself. A few hundred more probably lived in nearby residential communities, but San Lorenzo was never a great population center. It was nonetheless an important place, a center of religious, economic, and political power. Although San Lorenzo was not the capital of a huge centralized state, its leaders were beginning to exercise control over the human and natural resources of a large hinterland. La Venta, Laguna de los Cerros, and other contemporary Olmec centers in the Gulf Coast heartland could not match San Lorenzo in wealth, religious importance, or political power. San Lorenzo's public works projects testify to the power and managerial expertise of its leaders. They planned and directed construction projects that involved the quarrying and placement of tons of earth fill. They also organized the importation of raw materials on a large scale. The basalt used for the drainage system and for monumental sculpture—many tons of it—was brought from the Tuxtla Mountains, some 75 kilometers to the northwest. From distant areas, far beyond the Gulf Coast, came finished products as well as raw materials: obsidian for tools; iron ores, mica, shell, and other materials for jewelry and ritual paraphernalia. A variety of perishable goods, not preserved in the archaeological record, must have been imported as well.

The details of how these products came to the Gulf Coast are unknown. In some instances, Olmec merchants doubtless traded with foreign groups, but there are no indications of what products may have

FIG. 4-1. Colossal basalt head from San Lorenzo (Monument 2).

been exported from the Gulf Coast. In a few areas, where especially valuable commodities were available, Olmecs established outposts in order to secure access to them.[29] Olmec enclaves in the Valley of Oaxaca procured iron ores and products manufactured from them for Gulf Coast centers. Olmec culture had a strong impact on peoples beyond the Gulf Coast. Olmec-style pottery and figurines appeared throughout the Intermediate Zone and in many parts of central Mexico, most often in the houses and burials of wealthy, high-status people. The distribution of the Olmec style defines a sphere of economic and social interaction embracing much of Mesoamerica. Its most obvious economic function was to funnel valuable commodities to the Olmec centers on the Gulf Coast.

At about 900 B.C. San Lorenzo lost its preeminent position in the Gulf Coast, and La Venta emerged as the largest Olmec center.[30] La Venta was another vital civic center without a huge resident population. It, too, boasted a wealth of monumental basalt sculpture (Fig. 4-2), and its public architecture and massive construction projects surpassed those of San Lorenzo in size, in the formality of their layout, and in their organizational requirements. La Venta imported basalt from the Tuxtla Mountains on a truly massive scale. A new Olmec style of pottery and figurines defined a huge sphere interacting with La Venta and contemporary Olmec centers.[31] Olmec exploitation of valuable raw materials outside the Gulf Coast heartland intensified. Highland Mexican products included special pottery clays, obsidian, iron ores, mica, and other valuable minerals. Jade, the most precious substance of all, probably came from the Balsas Valley of Guerrero (Mexico) and the Motagua Valley in the Maya world. Southern and eastern areas provided serpentine, obsidian, and possibly another variety of jade. The Pacific slope and piedmont sector of the Intermediate Zone was a major cacao-producing region in later prehispanic times. Chocolate, eventually a medium of exchange as well as the source of a costly beverage, may already have become an important luxury item. Monumental relief carvings and other expressions of the Olmec art style, along with public architecture typical of the Gulf Coast, marked Olmec involvement in these and other areas where especially valuable commodities were to be had. In some of these regions, Gulf Coast centers may have maintained residential enclaves. La Venta continued to participate in a huge economic sphere until its collapse, around 500 B.C. In the following centuries, with no integrating force providing for continued interaction among its regions, no new Olmec centers emerged and the wider networks of interaction that had integrated the Gulf Coast and most of the rest of Mesoamerica dissolved.

MAYA COMMUNITIES AND THE OLMEC

Communities along the western edge of the Maya lowlands, bordering on the Gulf Coast, were more involved in the communication networks in which Olmec centers participated than most other villages in that region.[32] An Olmec relief carving at Xoc suggests that Gulf Coast communities maintained connections, perhaps outposts, to the south and east. Pottery at Trinidad, like that of most lower Usumacinta communities, reflects Olmec styles, but similarities with the pottery of the Pasión region also suggest interaction with upstream communities.[33] The pottery of Altar de Sacrificios and Seibal in the Pasión region reflects several Olmec norms of decoration, although neither community adopted the Olmec style fully. At Seibal, a jade bloodletter and a cache of jade celts laid out in a cross reflect Olmec ritual patterns.

Contemporary pottery from Sakajut and El Portón, near the headwaters of the Río Salinas in the northern highlands, also resembles that of the Pasión tradition.[34] Both villages, situated on natural routes

FIG. 4-2. Basalt "altar" (probably a throne) from La Venta.

connecting the highlands and southern lowlands, may have been part of the exchange system that provided early Pasión communities with highland raw materials. Pottery and public architecture indicate that Sakajut and El Portón interacted, at least indirectly, with Olmec centers, and the Pasión and Usumacinta would be the natural route of communication with the Gulf Coast.

Along the southern fringe of the Maya world, on the Pacific Coast, and in the piedmont and highland zones to the north, large platform constructions and monumental stone sculpture reflect the Olmec connections of several communities. Olmec-style relief carvings at Abaj Takalik probably reflect the interest of Gulf Coast centers in regional cacao production. To the east, Chalchuapa boasted monumental public architecture—a conical mound 22 meters tall is reminiscent of the main La Venta pyramid—as well as Olmec relief carving and Olmec-style pottery.[35] Elsewhere in the highlands there are few signs of intense interaction with the Gulf Coast.[36] Scattered Olmec-style pottery and figurines probably reflect Olmec interest in local resources, especially obsidian. Kaminaljuyú and its immediate neighbors were small villages with mixed farming-and-foraging economies. They show no signs of centralized economic and political organization, nor sharp distinctions between socioeconomic groups.

To the east, potters at Puerto Escondido in the lower Ulúa Valley shared elements of decoration with their counterparts in the Gulf Coast and along the southern fringe of the Maya world. Here, too, cacao, a major product of the region in later periods, was probably an important factor shaping the pattern of interaction.[37] By the end of the Late Preclassic period, other eastern communities had begun to participate in the Olmec world. Large-scale sculpture and jade celts in caches associated with public construction at Los Naranjos, on the shores of Lake Yojoa, reflect the adoption of Olmec symbols by emergent elites.[38] Jade mortuary offerings at Copán suggest a similar process at the village level.

VILLAGE SOCIETIES IN THE MAYA LOWLANDS (EARLY PRECLASSIC PERIOD: 1400–900 B.C.)

In most of the Maya world—in contrast with the fringe areas that participated fairly intensively in Olmec interaction spheres—the later Early Preclassic period was an era of slow growth. At first, typical communities were small but prosperous villages with mixed subsistence economies. Simple farming and gardening, combined with exploitation of tree crops and other wild plants, provided a variety of plant foods. Hunting and trapping contributed animal protein. Specific crop plants and wild food sources varied from region to region, as did supplementary food-getting activities. Along the rivers and coasts, fishing and shellfish collecting were extremely important. Trade linked communities into local and regional economic networks. Many villages were able to import such commodities as obsidian and chert for cutting and chopping tools, hard stone for grinding tools, and salt. Larger and wealthier communities could boast small-scale public works projects and a few small temples.

Communities of the later Early Preclassic period are the earliest known in most of the lowland Maya world.[39] Early Preclassic pottery-making traditions in several regions share very general features of form and decoration.[40] Red slips and low-sided dishes or bowls were widely popular, but each community and region manufactured pottery according to its own distinctive norms. Maya communities did not wholeheartedly adopt pottery styles that were widely distributed in the rest of Mesoamerica, and the internal spheres of communication that later led to widely shared ideas about pottery making evidently had not yet emerged.

Altar de Sacrificios, at the confluence of the Pasión and Salinas rivers, was the site of a small village by about 1000 B.C.[41] At least four buildings were clustered around a small plaza, and other houses were scattered nearby. These houses, small timber-frame dwellings with wattle-and-daub walls, [42] packed-earth floors, and thatched roofs, were built directly on the land surface. The economy was based on mixed farming and foraging and depended heavily on river resources. The surviving remains of jack beans, deer, and freshwater mussels represent only a small part of the diet. Most tools were fashioned from local stone, but igneous stone and obsidian were imported from the highlands. There is no indication that the community was other than homogeneous; the single known burial contained no funerary offerings at all. Apart from enigmatic objects, too often assumed to be ritual paraphernalia, and a little red-sandstone table that may have served as an altar, small, hand-modeled pottery figurines are the only possible evidence of ritual activity. The putative role of these female effigies in household fertility cults, however, is far from certain. Early pottery from Altar de Sacrificios reflects a distinctive regional manufacturing tradition that is also typical of Seibal, 50 kilometers upstream on the Río Pasión.[43] Seibal was presumably a similar village, but the actual archaeological evidence is limited to small concentrations of pottery and household refuse in two areas of high ground. The people of Seibal also had access to highland sources of obsidian and igneous stone.

The earliest known community at Tikal was evidently another small village,[44] but scanty data reveal no details of community organization. Like their contemporaries to the west, early Tikal villagers imported obsidian and hard stone from the highlands. Their pottery represents a local tradition of manufacture, sharing only the most general features with pottery from other regions. Nearby Uaxactún was probably a comparable small village during this early period, but it is represented only by small pottery collections similar to those of Tikal.

A settled community had emerged at Cuello, on the eastern edge of the southern lowlands, by 1200 B.C.[45] Its oldest structures were small timber-frame buildings with thatched roofs and set on low, plaster-surfaced platforms. These buildings, remodeled frequently, eventually formed a group neatly arranged around a small plaza. The early Cuello village had a mixed subsistence economy, combining cultivation and foraging. Manos and metates indicate the importance of plant processing. Maize was cultivated[46] and was probably the mainstay of the diet; beans and chile peppers, though long cultivated in western Mesoamerica, may have been among the wild plants exploited by Cuello villagers, as were avocados, nance, and other tree crops. Hunting, trapping, fishing, and collecting provided a variety of animal foods. Brockets and other deer, turtles, fish, and mollusks were the most important, followed by armadillos, rabbits, agoutis, and peccaries. Domesticated dogs were also a major dietary resource. Cuello villagers manufactured most goods from local raw materials: high-quality chert from Colha, not far to the east, was used for points, knives, scrapers, and other sharp tools; marine shell was fashioned into beads; hematite served as pigment. For heavy grinding tools, sandstone was imported, probably from the Maya Mountains, more than 100 kilometers to the south. Burials provide the only indication of ritual activity. Pottery vessels, plain or decorated, simple shell jewelry, and a variety of other items such as red hematite pigment were interred with the dead in simple graves. Funerary offerings are more or less comparable in all graves, suggesting a basically homogeneous community with no great differences in wealth or social status. The pottery made by the first Cuello villagers—jars, bowls, and low-sided dishes—was plain or very simply decorated. It represents another regional tradition of manufacture shared by communities in the eastern lowlands. Apart from their participation in patterns of interaction responsible for the shared norms of pottery making, little is known about most of these communities.

Villagers at nearby Colha exploited the extensive deposits of chert available in the local region—this was an excellent material for making cutting and chopping tools as well as points for spears, darts, or arrows—and they already had begun to export the raw material and/or the finished tools made from it. Such tools show no signs of standardization and seem to have been produced by many individual households; but in terms of form, function, and manufacturing process, they represent the beginning of a distinctive local tradition of toolmaking that would play an important role in the regional economy for many centuries.[47]

To the south, in the Belize Valley, the earliest known communities[48] reflect a way of life generally comparable to that of Cuello, but with its own regional flavor. Many vessels share very general features with contemporary pottery to the north, but there is no indication of particularly intense contacts. Groups of a few small wattle-and-daub dwellings on low platforms, roughly 50 meters apart, typically occupied riverbanks. These early houses may have had plaster floors laid on gravel foundations like their later counterparts, but none is sufficiently well preserved to provide details of construction or floor plan. Here, too, the economy was presumably based on mixed cultivation and foraging, but no direct evidence of farming has been found. Local raw materials—chert for cutting tools, marine shell for ornaments—were most important, but hard stone for grinding tools probably came from the Maya Mountains and some obsidian was imported from the highlands.

There is no good evidence of settlements in central and northern Yucatan during this early period, although the region was not necessarily unpopulated. Pottery found at Becán and Maní resembles that of early villages in the eastern lowlands, suggesting that the first northern communities remain to be found.[49]

Except on the margins, most early communities in the Maya world were small villages. Societies were homogeneous, with no sign of sharp differences in wealth or social status. These communities did not have centralized political leadership, and they did not undertake large public construction projects. They were essentially self-sufficient, relying on a combination of farming and foraging for subsistence and on local raw materials for most tools. Some villages did import such raw materials as obsidian, hard stone, and jade from distant regions, but there were no giant spheres of intensive economic interaction like those in which the Gulf Coast Olmec centers participated.

EMERGENCE OF THE MAYA WORLD (MIDDLE PRECLASSIC PERIOD: 900–400 B.C.)

After 900 B.C. the regionalism of the Maya area began to break down. Scattered regions formed larger and larger spheres of interaction. A "Maya world" emerged as a recognizable entity. This process is precisely the reverse of the one that was under way at the same time in the Intermediate Zone. The interaction networks connecting Gulf Coast centers to the rest of Mesoamerica had begun to dissolve even before the final collapse of La Venta. Perhaps increased communication and exchange within the Maya world disrupted these economic webs, contributing to the demise of La Venta and the networks in which it had participated. Such processes seldom have simple, one-way cause-and-effect relations, though. The decline of these economic spheres might easily have contributed to intensified trade with the Maya area by removing such obstacles as competing markets for key commodities.

The emergence of a recognizable Maya world is the first stage of a remarkable process of linked regional development. The regions of the Maya world never lost their own distinctive cultural traditions, but they were never again entirely independent. Ideas and institutions developed in one region could spread to many distant communities. This interaction was the key process in the emergence of Maya civilization.

The clearest sign of increasing communication throughout the Maya world is a definite trend toward greater homogeneity in pottery production among widely scattered communities. The first widespread Maya pottery style, called Mamom, reflects intensified interaction but not cultural uniformity.[50] Many kinds of interaction linked many diverse communities. Pottery making did not suddenly become uniform throughout the Maya world. The eastern lowland version of Mamom, for example, developed from local antecedents long before other communities began to produce similar vessels.

Even in pottery production, local differences were not entirely submerged. Regional diversity is still apparent beneath the new veneer of features common to the Mamom style. This pattern of regional variations on common themes continued to characterize the Maya world throughout its preconquest history. In the eastern lowlands, the Pasión zone, the Tikal zone, and the highlands, pottery embodies elements of earlier local traditions as well as features of the common Mamom style. The Mamom style does not reflect external influence; it developed in several regions from a series of localized but generally similar ancestors. These regional traditions came to share certain features and to follow convergent developmental paths as a result of increasing communication. Greater differences distinguish the northern and southern lowlands, although communities in both areas produced pottery in the Mamom style. Highland pottery represents a somewhat different tradition; ties between highlands and lowlands were weaker than those linking the lowland regions. Yet communication extended, at least indirectly, to the limits of the Maya world, for pottery made at Chalchuapa, in the eastern highlands, and at Chiapa de Corzo, in the Intermediate Zone, echoes the Mamom style.

The basic way of life of the peoples of the Maya world during the Middle Preclassic period was much like that of their ancestors. The typical community was still a small, homogeneous, self-sufficient village of farmers and foragers. Communities grew and multiplied as the population of the Maya world increased. Connections between regions, notably trade, intensified, though not uniformly.[51] Extensive exchange networks distributed raw materials more widely than ever, especially obsidian and igneous stone from the highlands to Altar de Sacrificios, Seibal, Cuello, and other villages in the central and southern lowlands. Even communities as small as Cuello began to import small quantities of Motagua Valley jade for luxury jewelry. Villages in the north relied mainly on local raw materials, but most communities did participate in expanded economic spheres.

As villages grew, internal differences in wealth and social status became wider. A few of the largest and most prosperous towns—each having perhaps a few thousand residents—had begun to show signs of emerging aristocratic groups and centralized political leadership, notably the appearance of buildings that reflect public construction projects. Such towns probably dominated their local areas, economically if not politically, but no Maya community matched the great Olmec centers. None undertook such massive public construction or controlled such extensive procurement networks. Maya societies were simpler politically and economically, if not socially. Maya elites were less distinct from ordinary folk. They had not concentrated power and wealth in their own hands to the same extent that Olmec leaders had. Temples testify to the public aspects of Maya religion, and it was probably inseparable from politics, but the Maya had not yet produced anything comparable to the dynastic monumental art of the Olmec.

At the Mirador group,[52] near Dzibilchaltún in northern Yucatan, a series of large platforms define a public plaza, and the construction of early versions of what would eventually become very large platforms at Komchen began before 400 B.C.[53] A formal plaza group at Altar de Sacrificios[54] was probably a ceremonial precinct. The platforms flanking the plaza, one of which was 5 meters tall, were faced with shell and plaster and had stonemasonry stairs. The timber-frame buildings atop the platforms have not survived, but their size and special construction features indicate that these were not ordinary dwellings. At Nakbé, terraced platforms some 15 meters tall atop a massive basal platform represent the largest complex of public buildings of that day. A stela was set in front of one of the smaller platforms either at this time or at the beginning of the following Late Preclassic period.[55] Cuello, Actuncan, Xunantunich and some of its neighbors in the upper Belize Valley, and probably other communities in the east, constructed modest stone-faced platforms coated with stucco. Modeled stucco masks adorned the façade of one platform at Actuncan.[56] Cuello's very modest structures—slightly larger versions of the traditional thatched timber-frame buildings atop oblong plaster-coated platforms—were more typical; but they do contain the seeds of the public, ritual functions of the later versions of the patio complex of which they are a part.[57] Several highland communities began to construct large earth platforms flanking plazas late in the Middle Preclassic period; these were not ordinary dwellings, but public (probably ceremonial) structures.[58] At El Portón and Kaminaljuyú, monumental stone sculpture was associated with these public precincts. At Los Mangales, fine residences and burials accompanied by offerings of jade and shell jewelry, trophy heads, and sacrificial victims testify to the emergence of a prosperous and powerful aristocracy.

Nakbé, El Portón, Kaminaljuyú, and a few other settlements had emerged as foci of centralized political and economic power. Monumental architecture and sculpture embody stylistic features that suggest an Olmec heritage, which would be reflected even more strongly in the elaborate architectural decoration and sculpture that embellished public precincts in the following Late Preclassic period. These towns probably dominated villages in their surrounding regions, but the overall patterns of social, economic, and political organization had not yet changed radically. Such changes would come in the Late Preclassic, as processes of population increase, community growth, and intensified interaction among regions throughout the Maya area continued. These trends, combined with the emergence of sharp social and economic differences within Maya societies, produced a new kind of social order.

THE OLMEC HERITAGE OF MAYA CIVILIZATION

The Maya world was largely outside the Olmec orbit. Some communities along the margins of the Maya area did participate in economic spheres that involved Gulf Coast centers. Some, especially in highland Guatemala and northern Honduras, were probably Olmec enclaves, perhaps Zoquean speakers in regions of Mayan speech. Others, particularly in the west, represent the fringes of the main Zoquean distribution, for in this early period Mayan-speaking peoples had not yet expanded to their eventual western limits. Zoquean and Maya peoples doubtless mingled in a variety of patterns along their common frontier. There are indications, mainly in pottery styles, of a fairly intense Olmec presence along the fringe of the Maya world: in the western lowlands, in the southern highlands and piedmont, and in the lower Ulúa Valley in the east. Local pottery-making traditions elsewhere in Maya country show only faint echoes of Olmec styles, and some communities imported a few Olmec pots and jade objects. Most of the peoples of the Maya world evidently were not directly involved in the Olmec economic sphere.

In another sense, Olmec civilization did have an enormous impact on Maya cultural development, for the foundations of Classic Maya civilization rest on an Olmec heritage.[59] Maya culture reached its developmental peak in lowland tropical forests with an ecology similar to that of the Olmec heartland. Basic organizational patterns of Maya civilization had been established centuries earlier by the Olmec. Classic Maya society revolved around impressive civic centers that were foci of public activity, social prestige, religious authority, and economic and political power. Here were temples, palaces, ball courts, and monumental art. Temples are the largest structures; they are also funerary monuments to important political figures whose deeds are recorded and celebrated in associated art and inscriptions. Few Maya centers had densely populated residential zones; most people lived dispersed in the surrounding territory. Procurement of jade and other luxury goods, as well as utilitarian items, was an important function of Classic Maya political and economic organization. Enclaves of Mayas living far beyond their home territories reflect a basic pattern of Maya territoriality, representing a strategy of ecological diversification. Such enclaves expanded access to valuable raw materials and to varied environments for crop cultivation. They also facilitated communication and interaction. All of these patterns are found, at least in embryonic form, in Olmec civilization.

Classic Maya civilization's Olmec ancestry is traceable through the Izapan culture, which spread throughout the Intermediate Zone and much of the Maya highlands in the Late Preclassic period. Olmec art foreshadows Izapan art in subject matter, in style, and even in specific iconographic elements and glyphlike symbols (Figs. 5-2, 5-4, 5-7, 5-8).[60] The continuities from Izapan art to Classic Maya art are even more striking. Olmec, Izapan, and Maya stelae all portray historical themes. The hieroglyphic inscriptions that accompany Izapan art resemble later Maya writing in the overall structure and layout of texts, in the forms of certain glyphs, and even in the use of the complex and distinctive Long Count system of recording dates. In a very real sense, Maya symbol systems began with Izapan culture, which in turn has an obvious Olmec ancestry. Olmec-Maya continuities extend to religious institutions and symbols as well: the ball game, the supreme importance of jade, the use of red pigments with jade, ceremonial bloodletting, and many items of ritual paraphernalia.

The importance of these continuities has led some Mesoamericanists to the conclusion that Olmec civilization was really the first flowering of Maya civilization; that is, that the creators of Olmec civilization were ethnically and linguistically Maya.[61] If the early people of the Gulf Coast spoke a Mayan language, there would have been a continuous zone of Mayan speech extending from the Huastec region to what is now the Maya lowlands. The corollary—that by the Classic period Mayan speakers had moved entirely out of the Gulf Coast and subsequently lived almost exclusively outside what had been the core of the Olmec world—is difficult to accept.

A more satisfactory hypothesis is that the early population of the Gulf Coast and the Isthmus of Tehuantepec, the creators of Olmec civilization, spoke Proto-Zoquean, the language ancestral to that of the Mixe and Zoque, who occupied much of the Intermediate Zone in late times.[62] The reconstructed vocabulary of Proto-Zoquean for the period around 1500 B.C. includes terms for many distinctively Mesoamerican items that were part of the Olmec cultural inventory: important plants, including basic crops; important domestic and wild animals; food-preparation terms; ritual and calendar terms; words relating to trade and commerce. Proto-Zoquean loan words are common in other Mesoamerican languages, some quite distant from the historic area of Mixe and Zoque speech. Proto-Zoquean must have been spoken by a group with wide-ranging connections. Probable Maya borrowings from Proto-Zoquean include words for cacao, gourd, tomato, papaya, tortilla, tamal, corn dough, incense, twenty years, dog, ax, sacrifice (?), turkey, lizard, bee, child, and elder brother. The cultural importance of these items implies that Proto-Zoquean speakers were once extremely prestigious and influential. The people of the Gulf Coast heartland and adjacent sectors of the Intermediate Zone were probably Proto-Zoquean speakers, as were many Olmecs residing outside this zone, in highland Mexico, eastern sectors of the Intermediate Zone, and parts of the Maya highlands; these Olmecs lived in enclaves among peoples who spoke different languages and who followed different cultural traditions. The wide adoption of Olmec pottery and figurine styles and of Proto-Zoquean words reflects the profound impact Olmec culture had on these local groups. In the lowlands, along the eastern edge of the Gulf Coast, in the Maya highlands, and in the piedmont zone to the south, Proto-Zoquean speakers mingled with their Mayan-speaking eastern neighbors. Many Maya communities in these regions adopted significant features of Olmec culture.[63]

Olmec civilization was a multiethnic, polyglot phenomenon, and the heritage of many Mesoamerican cultures can be traced to the Olmec. Interaction of Maya and Zoquean peoples continued as a historical process along a linguistic frontier that extended from the Gulf Coast through the highlands and piedmont to the Pacific Coast.[64] In the Late Preclassic period Olmec-influenced Maya groups were part of an "Izapan" world, an interaction sphere embracing diverse societies throughout the Intermediate Zone and parts of the Maya world. Many of the styles and institutions of the Izapan world represent basic patterns that became part of Classic Maya civilization.

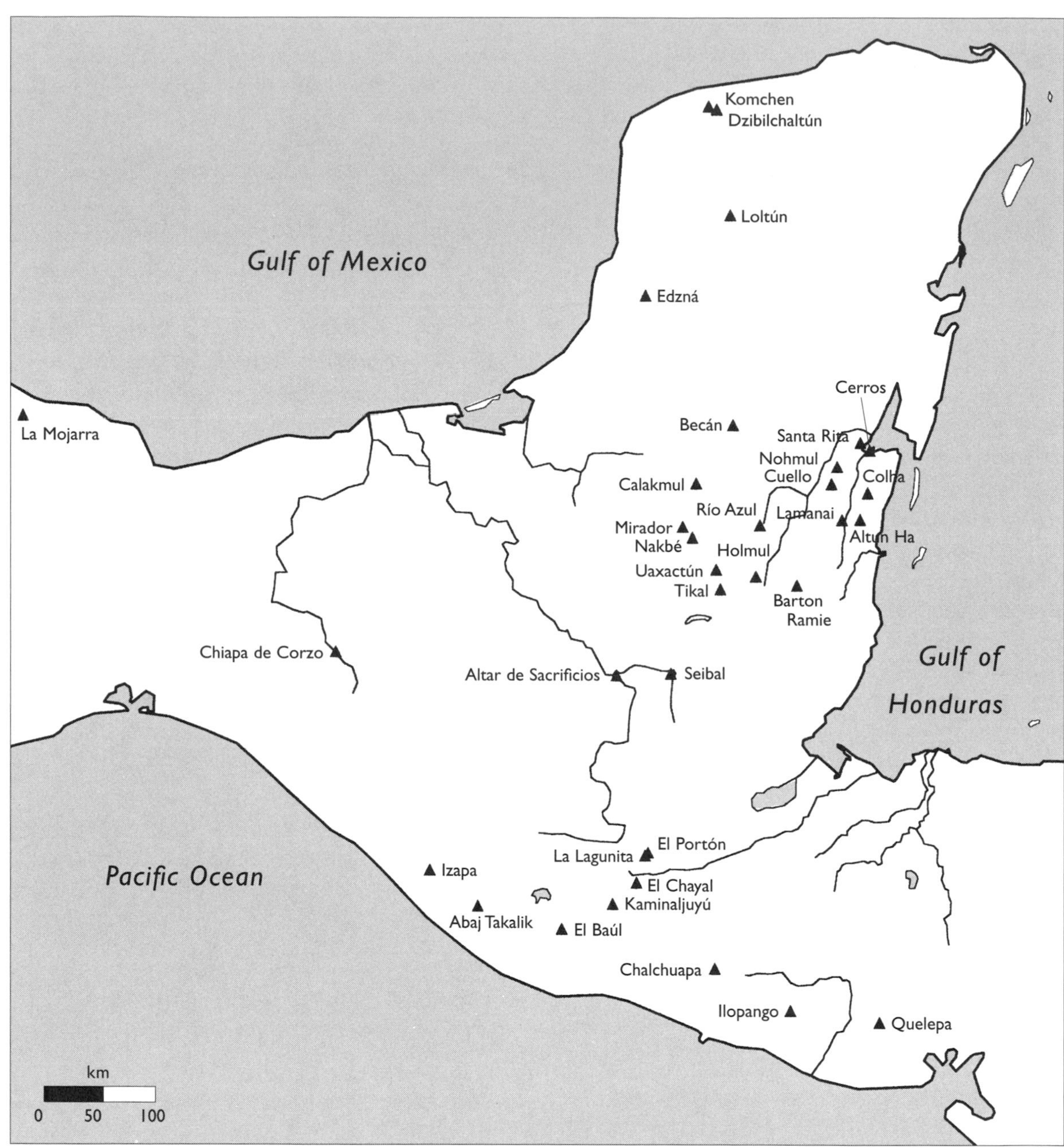

MAP 7. Late Preclassic communities.

FIVE

Foundations of Maya Civilization

Although some parts of the Maya world—mostly in the highlands—were firmly tied into the economic networks and related patterns of interaction of the Olmec world, centered to the west on the Gulf Coast, most early Maya communities, especially in the lowlands, were small, simple, egalitarian villages. By the end of the Middle Preclassic period, after 500 B.C., communities like Mirador were beginning to reflect a new developmental trajectory. Jewelry and other goods made from exotic raw materials indicate increasing prosperity, expanded economic ties to distant regions, and sharper differences in wealth and social status; large-scale, elaborately decorated public buildings reflect the emergence of powerful permanent leaders, chiefs or kings. These trends continued and intensified during the Late Preclassic period, setting the fundamental patterns of Classic-period Maya city-states.

The most distinctive features of political art and propaganda that would typify Maya states of the Classic period appeared first at Abaj Takalik and other towns in the highlands, the adjacent piedmont and coastal zones, and throughout the Intermediate Zone. Stelae with relief carving that depicted rulers in elaborate dress, studded with emblems of their office, also bore hieroglyphic texts recording their names, biographical details, and great deeds in the context of the Long Count calendar (Fig. 5-4). Standing before public buildings, often paired with altars, these monuments reinforced the power of the lords both by highlighting their genealogical and supernatural connections and by celebrating the fact of their offices. Some aspects of this dynastic political art can be found in towns scattered across the Maya lowlands, where it would reach its full elaboration, in the Late Preclassic period. But there is no evidence of the full pattern—notably, monuments with texts that include Long Count dates—until the Classic period.[1]

The Rise of Maya Aristocracies (Late Preclassic Period: 400 B.C.–A.D. 250)

The first sign of intensified interaction among the regions of the Maya area in the Late Preclassic period[2] was the appearance of a new shared style of pottery manufacture.[3] This Chicanel pottery tradition did not appear suddenly throughout the Maya world. It grew out of variants of the Mamom tradition in the several regions, with slightly different timing in each instance, much as Mamom had developed from antecedent regional styles. Within a century or two, though, virtually every community in the Maya lowlands (Map 7) manufactured pottery in the same basic Chicanel style.

Regional differences continued, reflecting the survival of distinctive local traditions. Northern and southern lowland communities remained distinct, but they shared many more patterns than before. Lowland peoples continued to import highland raw materials, and highland pottery reflects some features of the Chicanel style. Chalchuapa was now squarely within the highland Maya world, and many highland communities developed closer ties with those of the upper piedmont zone. To the west, the people of Chiapa de Corzo manufactured luxury pottery in the Chicanel style, and their public buildings—which by this time included complex palaces (Fig. 5-1)—also suggest ties with the Maya lowlands.[4] Villages in the far western Maya highlands shared a basic tradition of pottery making with Chiapa de Corzo, but they adopted fewer distinctively Chicanel features. Mayan-speaking peoples may have occupied both regions, but there is no reason that Zoquean groups could not have shared elements of architectural style and norms of pottery production with their Maya neighbors.

Part of the explanation for the intensified interaction among regions may lie in accelerating population growth. Communities grew and multiplied throughout the Maya world. Expanded populations, increasingly concentrated in and around larger towns, made increasing demands on subsistence systems. Many of the agricultural techniques that complemented the basic milpa farming in later periods were probably already in use in one or another region, as were water collection and storage facilities that would soon give rise to sophisticated water-management systems.[5] In the lowlands as well as the highlands, there are extensive remains of prehistoric terrace systems which converted otherwise useless slopes into a patchwork of level farm plots. In the central and southern lowlands, low-lying swampy areas too wet for ordinary rainy-season cultivation can be planted for an extra dry-season crop. In some lowland regions prehistoric land-reclamation projects transformed swamps into productive land. These wetland farming systems used ditches in swampy zones to lower the water level sufficiently to permit cultivation adjacent to the canals. Muck might also be piled along canal margins to further raise the planting platforms. In either case, canal-side fields, rich in rotting vegetation, formed giant soggy compost heaps that could be farmed almost continuously with enormous productivity. Canals within the wetland systems must have promoted fish cultivation, facilitated transport and communication, and provided a ready source of drinking water for the dry season. Even in the northern lowlands (where milpa farming is generally constrained by limited rainfall and thin soils), dry sinkholes, slight depressions, and even areas of loose rock provide pockets of soil and moisture that can support fruit trees as well as more productive milpa plots.

Exchange networks expanded as well, and more communities were importing more goods.[6] Obsidian from highland Guatemala was widely distrib-

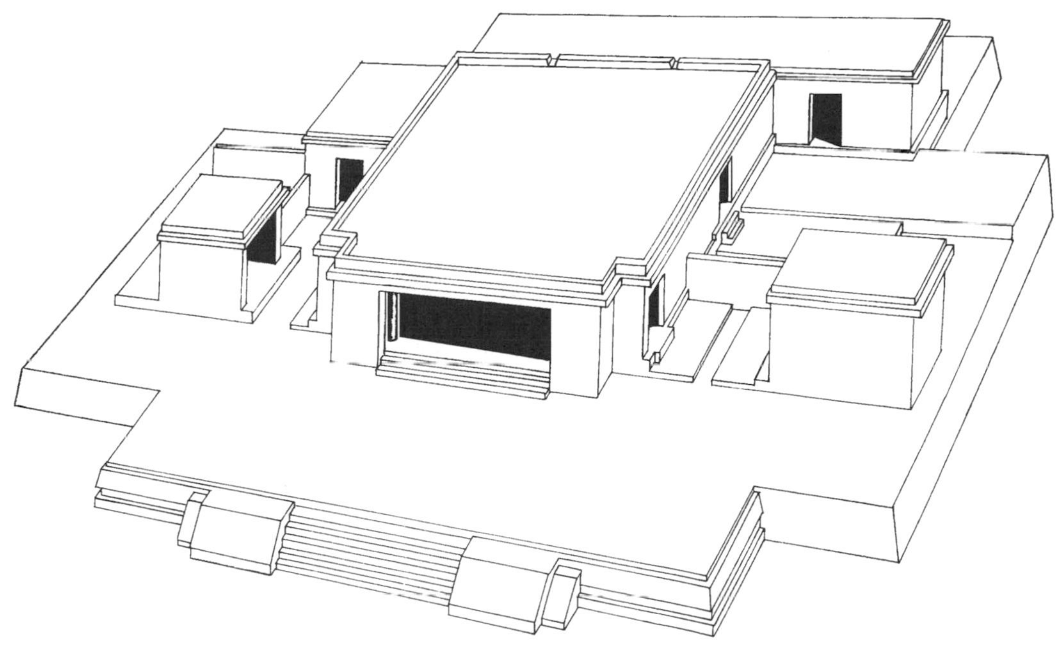

FIG. 5-1. Palace complex (Structure 5-H1), Chiapa de Corzo. Adapted from Lowe 1962:frontispiece.

uted. Jade traveled as far north as Dzibilchaltún. Tikal and its neighbors in interior sectors of the central lowlands began to import shell and stingray spines for jewelry and ritual paraphernalia.

This upsurge in luxury imports reflects another continuing process within Maya societies: the widening of social and economic gaps between emerging aristocratic groups and ordinary farmers. Massive public architecture—temples certainly, and possibly palaces and administrative buildings as well—reflects the new power and specialist roles of these leaders. Religion, in the process of transformation, moved more and more into the realm of public activity and began to require specialized priest-managers. Public buildings imply political leaders with the authority and power to command the human and economic resources of large areas. Richly stocked masonry tombs in civic building complexes contrast sharply with plain burials beneath the floors of ordinary houses, illustrating the social and economic differences that had developed within Maya societies.

While these generalizations hold for the Maya area as a whole, developments were by no means uniform. Specific patterns of growth and development differ markedly from region to region.

THE IZAPAN WORLD

The Maya highlands, though linked to the lowlands, were also an integral part of the "Izapan" world.[7] The heart of this diverse cultural sphere lay in the southern coast and piedmont zone. Izapa itself has the greatest concentration of relief carving, but it was not necessarily the place where any of the styles originated, and it was certainly not politically or economically dominant beyond its local region. Related styles of relief carving extend north and west through the Intermediate Zone to the Gulf Coast. This distribution recalls the old southeastern Olmec interaction sphere, although there is far more variability in these Late Preclassic styles and in most other features of the societies that produced them than there was among Middle Formative societies linked to the Gulf Coast Olmec. Even though there was no single Izapan cultural system comparable to Olmec civilization, these styles and iconographies do reflect a definite Olmec ancestry. Available archaeological data are insufficient for a thorough understanding of the patterns of similarity and diversity within the Izapan sphere. The variety probably reflects both regional cultural differences and developmental change within the several centuries spanned by Izapan art. The distribution of Izapan art reflects a multiethnic sphere of interaction, embracing Zoquean peoples in the Intermediate Zone as well as Maya societies to the east and north.

In style, one component of Late Preclassic sculpture provides a historical bridge between Olmec art and Early Classic Maya art (Figs. 5-4, 5-8).[8] Many elements of Classic Maya iconography and writing, intimately related to politics and religion, first appear on these monuments. Many Late Preclassic monuments take the form of stelae—vertical stone shafts, commonly carved with elaborate scenes in relief and often accompanied by low, cylindrical stone "altars." Many of these stelae depict richly dressed figures as well as cosmological themes. They foreshadow the Classic Maya stela complex, which glorified community leaders.

Hieroglyphic inscriptions occur on many, though by no means all, Late Preclassic monuments.[9] The earliest known, from El Portón in the Salama Valley in the northern Maya highlands, may have been carved as early as 400 B.C. The glyphs themselves vary, apparently representing (like the imagery) related but distinct evolving writing systems that record different languages. Several inscriptions from the Gulf Coast—notably, a very long text on an elaborately carved stela from La Mojarra—are written in Zoque. Several inscriptions from the eastern piedmont and Maya highlands are early Maya texts; other Late Preclassic texts represent quite distinct writing systems that may record yet other languages. A few Late Preclassic texts include calendar dates in a system ancestral to the Long Count, which typifies Classic-period Maya inscriptions (Figs. 5-2, 5-4).[10]

The Long Count is a calendar system that situates events in terms of the time elapsed since an arbitrary zero point in the distant past. Days are its elementary units, but its basic component is the *tun*, a period of 360 days (Fig. 5-3). A tun consists of 18 *uinals*, each of which contains 20 kins, or days. Twenty tuns constitute a *katun*. Twenty katuns in turn make up a *baktun*, the largest unit of the Long Count. The Long Count uses these units to record the number of days elapsed since the beginning of the current "Great Cycle."

Although there are earlier Great Cycles, each covers a span of thousands of years. On such a scale there is no ambiguity in placing historical events, although the Maya did not limit their calculations to what we would call the span of historical time. Maya concepts of time do not make a distinction between the historical and the mythical. Large numbers in some texts stretch back through millions of years to reach vastly remote epochs. The Long Count and the Calendar Round are complementary systems of time reckoning. A Long Count date specifies the position in the Calendar Round reached by the indicated number of elapsed days, and the portrait of the patron deity of the corresponding Solar Year month normally forms part of the sign that signals the beginning of a Long Count date.

Long Count dates typically stand at the beginning

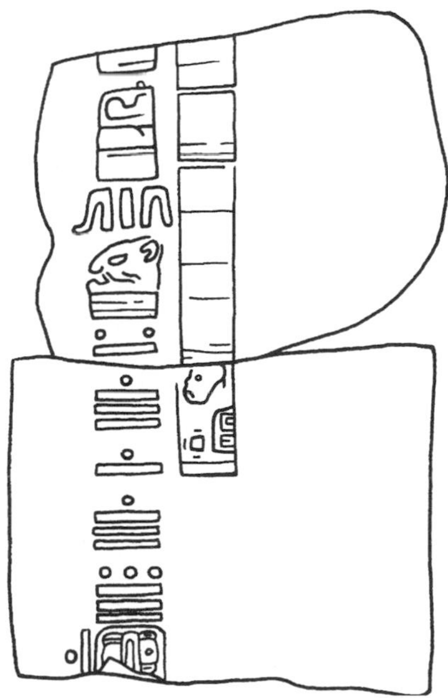

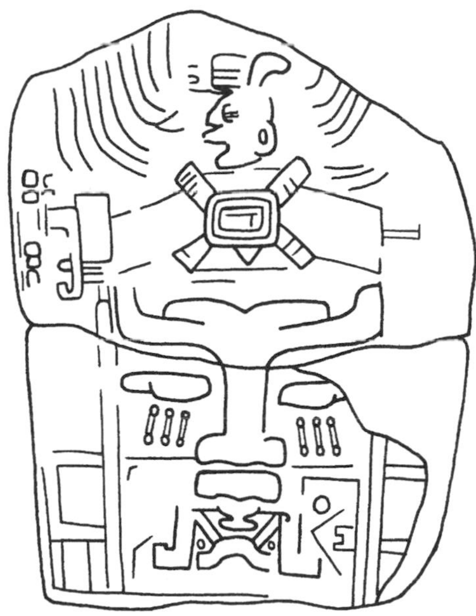

FIG. 5-2. Stela C, Tres Zapotes. *Left:* front, with text following the single-column format of early Maya calendrical inscriptions. The large glyph with a triple element surmounting a jaguar head marks the beginning of a Long Count date, conventionally transcribed 7.16.6.16.18. The five bar-and-dot numbers that follow constitute the date proper, tabulating the number of days elapsed since the beginning of the current "Great Cycle," far in the mythical past, in terms of a hierarchy of calendar periods:

7 baktuns	=	7 × 144,000	=	1,008,000 days
16 katuns	=	16 × 7,200	=	115,200 days
6 tuns	=	6 × 360	=	2,160 days
16 uinals	=	16 × 20	=	320 days
18 kins	=	18 × 1	=	18 days
Total			=	1,125,698 days

The Great Cycle began on a day 4 Ahau 8 Cumku in the Maya calendar, corresponding to a day in the year 3114 B.C.; the date on Stela C, 1,125,698 days later, falls in 31 B.C. The glyph at the bottom of the left column specifies that this day was 6 Etz'nab in the Ritual Almanac; the jaguar head in the Introducing Glyph represents the patron deity of the Solar Year calendar month in which the date falls, although the precise position in the Solar Year system is not specified (cf. Figs. 5-4, 6-4, 6-5). *Right:* reverse, with Izapan-style relief. Adapted from M. Coe 1976:fig. 4 and Marcus 1976b:fig. 7.

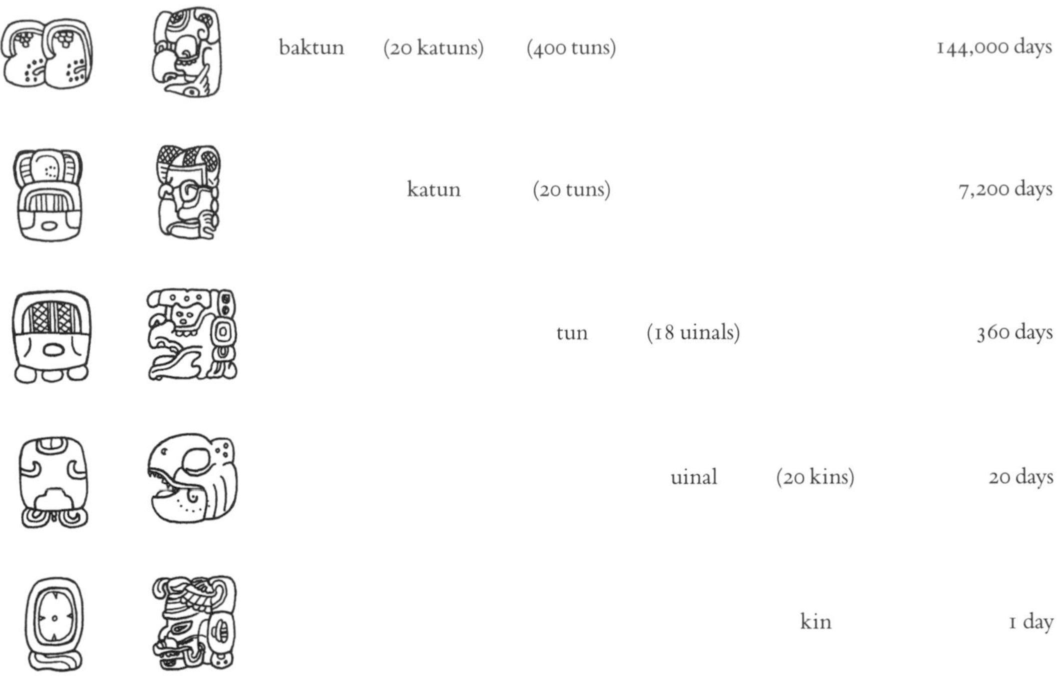

FIG. 5-3. Symbolic and portrait variants of the glyphs for the units of the Long Count in the style used in carved inscriptions.

of hieroglyphic texts, although they may be found in the bodies of texts as well, especially in early examples (cf. Figs. 5-2, 5-4, 6-4, 6-5). Opening with the oversized Initial Series Introducing Glyph, the date goes on to specify the number of elapsed days in terms of each of the constituent units of time. A Long Count date is, in effect, a five-digit number in a modified vigesimal (20-base) system. The earliest Long Count dates are relatively simple, with numbers making up the elapsed time tally followed by the Ritual Almanac position.[11]

Although the Long Count became a hallmark of lowland Classic Maya civilization, particularly in the south, early baktun 7 dates come from the highlands and from the Intermediate Zone. The earliest of these calendrical texts, from Chiapa de Corzo, corresponds to 36 B.C. The latest, in the early part of baktun 8, correspond to the first and second centuries of the Christian era.[12] The Long Count may have been in use in the Maya lowlands during baktun 7, but the earliest dates found there so far are some three centuries later. The development of the Long Count, like that of Classic Maya civilization itself, involved areas outside of what became the Maya world and included people who spoke non-Mayan languages.[13] On the La Mojarra stela and a few other monuments from the western Intermediate Zone, Long Count dates occur in texts that record the Zoque language. The dates from Abaj Takalik and other eastern centers are in texts written in an ancestral version of the Classic Maya script. An identical conceptual system—elapsed time tabulated from the same fixed starting point, divided into the same set of units, and recorded in the same way—was shared by culturally and linguistically distinct societies within the Izapan world.

Early Long Count dates from the eastern piedmont and adjacent Maya highlands are remarkably similar, in form and context, to those of the Classic-period lowlands—even in details of format and associated design elements—and they are carved on stelae, paired with altars and placed before public buildings. The stela complex, embodying the essence of Classic Maya art and iconography, developed in this highland-piedmont zone during the Late Preclassic period. As in later lowland cities, the early southern monuments reflect a complex and hierarchical social-political order. They must depict and celebrate the exploits of local leaders, who oversaw the construction of the elaborate public buildings and who were often buried within them.

Early Maya iconography was only one aspect of the art of the southern region in this period. Most of the important centers of the region boasted a considerable variety of monuments, suggesting a series of regionally distinct cultural traditions. At Izapa itself, dozens of carved monuments stood before stone-faced building platforms. Numbers and glyphs are quite rare, and the imagery appears to focus on mythical and cosmological themes. The lords of Abaj Takalik, in the piedmont zone to the east, placed a variety of carved monuments in association with terraces and platforms. Some of the stelae and altars are similar to those of Izapa; others, in an early Maya style, are more overtly political, with

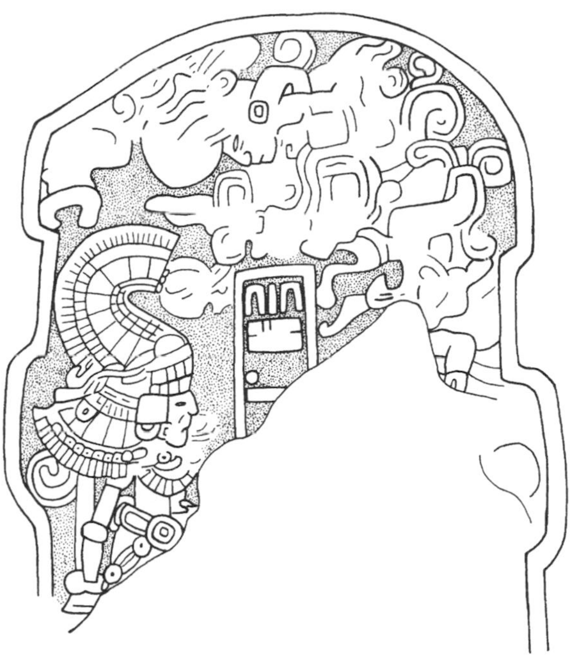

FIG. 5-4. Stela 2, Abaj Takalik. This monument, accompanied by a plain stone altar, was erected on a sloping stone pavement before a building platform. A richly dressed figure faces a vertical hieroglyphic text, and a face peers down from among swirling clouds above. The placement of the stela, as well as the format of its scene, the costume of the principal figure, and the hieroglyphic text with its Long Count date, typifies the early Maya stela complex. The text opens with an introductory glyph consisting of the typical three-part upper element and the earliest known use of the *tun* sign; the month patron is missing. The numbers are largely destroyed, but the first was certainly 7; if (as traces suggest) the second was 6, 11, or 16, the date would fall between 235 and 18 B.C. Charcoal found beneath the pavement on which Stela 2 was erected produced a date of 2100 B.P. ± 170 (373 B.C.–A.D. 80). Adapted from J. Graham et al. 1978:pl. 2 and M. Coe 1976:fig. 6.

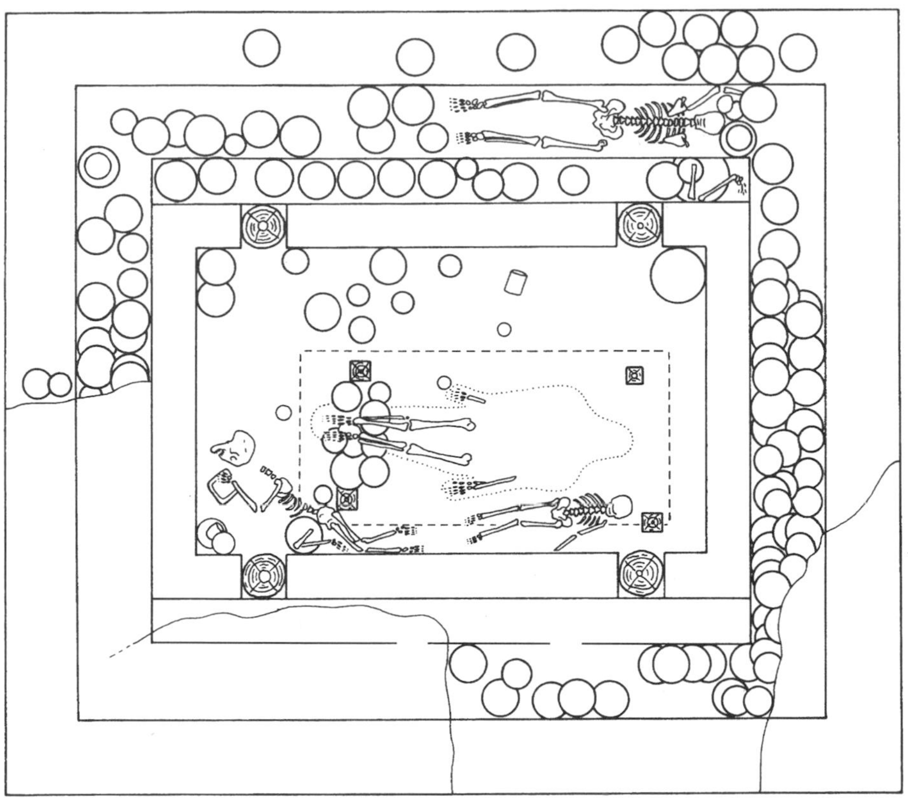

FIG. 5-5. Tomb II, Mound E-III-3, Kaminaljuyú: plan of the tomb of one of Kaminaljuyú's early leaders, dug into the floor of a temple platform. Five benches (uppermost not shown) step down into the burial chamber proper. The main occupant was laid out on a wooden litter (*dashed line*) covered with mats. The body (*dotted line*), painted bright red, was wrapped in a burial cloth with a mosaic mask of green stone over the face. The bodies of two children aged six to eight, probably sacrificed to accompany the lord, were laid along the west edge of the chamber. Offerings were arrayed around the corpse. In addition to the illustrated pottery vessels, some of which contained the residue of burned incense, these offerings include jade beads, stone ear ornaments, plaques encrusted with pyrite, gourds coated with stucco, obsidian and andesite blades, pebbles and chunks of minerals (iron oxide, hematite, mica, quartz), animal bones, fish teeth, stingray spines, several miscellaneous stone and bone objects, and probably a variety of perishable materials. The list of offerings, especially the jade, is surely incomplete, for the tomb was partially plundered in antiquity. The burial chamber was roofed with wooden beams supported by four large wooden posts, and a third sacrificial victim, a young adult, was laid face down along an upper bench amid additional offerings, including a hundred or more pottery vessels and a few stone beads. The entire tomb was filled with earth and capped by a new clay floor across the top of the platform, which continued to be used for ceremonial activities. The clay floor was renewed several times as the tomb fill slumped, and finally the old structure was entirely encased within a new clay-floored platform ascended by a broad stairway. The burial of an important person was often the occasion for such remodeling projects. An earlier (and even richer) tomb lay deep within Mound E-III-3. Adapted from Shook and Kidder 1952:fig. 15.

FIG. 5-6. Structure 4a, Mound B-II-1, Kaminaljuyú: reconstruction drawing of a dwelling in one of Kaminaljuyú's civic areas. A platform with three low terraces, rising not quite 3 meters above the adjacent plaza, supported the house itself, which had two rooms slightly sunken below the platform surface. Details of the timber frame and thatched roof are hypothetical. This building represents the sixth in a series of seven remodelings. Adapted from Austin and Lothson 1969:fig. 64.

portraits of richly dressed lords, hieroglyphic texts, and Long Count dates (Fig. 5-4). Other monuments include plain stelae and altars and potbellied boulder sculptures.[14]

Kaminaljuyú, in the highlands to the north and east, near the divide between the Pacific and Caribbean watersheds, was a substantial town consisting of several densely occupied neighborhoods.[15] Each had its own civic precinct, with earth and clay platforms supporting timber-frame thatched buildings coated with plaster. The largest public structure in each group was a tall, terraced temple platform, often containing a richly stocked tomb (Fig. 5-5). Smaller structures nearby include lower platforms that supported noble residences (Fig. 5-6). This community pattern, along with thrones and stelae (some with hieroglyphic texts), altars, potbellied sculptures, and a variety of other carved monuments, suggests a social order much like that of Classic Maya cities. Emergent aristocratic groups, combining many varied political, religious, and economic roles, dominated social life. Their prosperity may have stemmed from control of the extensive El Chayal obsidian quarries not far to the northeast. Carved monuments and public building platforms from La Lagunita, El Portón, and other Salama Valley communities indicate that the stela complex spread well to the north in the central highland zone.

To the east, Chalchuapa continued the pattern of public construction that had begun in the Middle Preclassic period. One carved stela includes a long hieroglyphic text in an early version of the Maya script. Local potters favored the Usulután technique of "negative" decoration, in which design motifs (typically, parallel wavy lines) were left plain while background areas were covered with a contrasting color. The production of Usulután pottery was highly complex and varied; the processes and their

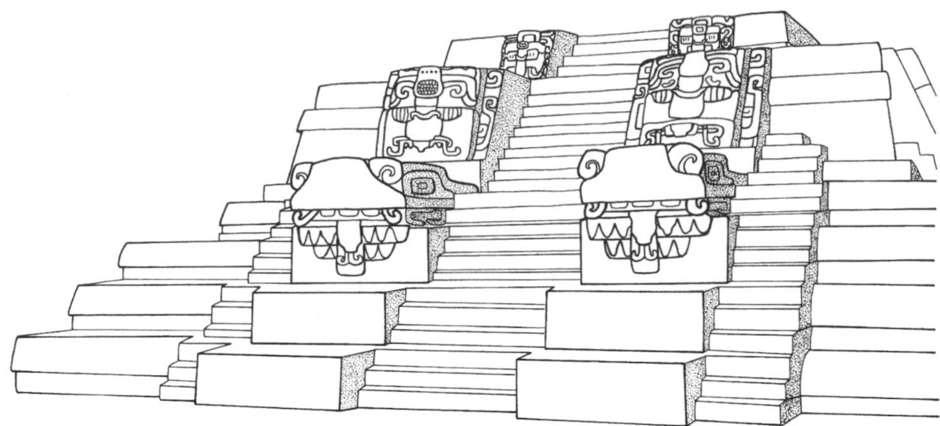

FIG. 5-7. Pyramid E-VII-sub, Uaxactún: reconstruction drawing of the front of a temple platform consisting of an earth-and-rubble core roughly faced with stone and plastered with an outer coating of stucco. The modeled stucco masks, which adorn all four sides of the pyramid, are done in the same early Maya art style that is expressed in stone relief carving in the southern highland–piedmont region. The platform surface, slightly more than 8 meters above the adjacent plaza, once supported a small timber-frame structure with a thatched roof. Adapted from Proskouriakoff 1963a:5 and Ricketson and Ricketson 1937:figs. 33, 39, 42, 43, 49, 50, pl. 30.

history are not fully understood, but it is clear that the Middle Preclassic potters of Chalchuapa and other communities in the eastern highlands were using techniques that were ancestral to the later Usulután vessels.

In the middle of the third century A.D., the eastern highland area was devastated by a massive eruption of the Ilopango Volcano. Chalchuapa and many nearby communities were buried by ashfall, and much of the surrounding region within 100 kilometers became uninhabitable for generations. Communities in many highland regions, even those well beyond the direct effects of the eruption, underwent a demographic and economic decline during this period (although this decline may have been part of a process already under way that was accelerated by the natural disaster). The attendant disruption of long-standing patterns of exchange and interaction probably contributed to intensified relationships between other southern regions and the lowlands to the north and set the stage for the Teotihuacán presence in the highlands during the Early Classic period. Decline was by no means universal in the highlands, though. In the Salama Valley, for example, La Lagunita enjoyed considerable growth and prosperity during the second and third centuries.

The complex relations among the several stylistic and cultural traditions represented in the Maya highlands and the adjacent piedmont zone cannot be analyzed properly without a better historical perspective on chronological change during the Late Preclassic period. It is certain, though, that one component of the cultural potpourri of the region during these centuries represents the foundation of Maya iconography, and of Classic Maya political-religious symbolism in particular.

THE MAYA LOWLANDS

As in the highlands, the appearance of large and elaborate public buildings reflect processes in which economic resources and political power were becoming concentrated in the hands of emergent aristocracies. Monumental public art, so typical of lowland Maya civilization in its florescent period, was less varied in the lowlands during this early developmental stage. Painting on tombs as well as painted and modeled stucco decoration on temple platforms (Fig. 5-7) and building façades echo the early Maya style of the southern highland–piedmont area.[16] Occasional fragments of stelae and other carved monuments indicate that lowland chiefs also commissioned relief sculpture. Hieroglyphic texts occur on a few portable objects and on a few fragmentary stelae, but no Long Count dates have yet been found in contexts that are definitely of the Late Preclassic period.

At Nakbé, in the central lowlands, large-scale construction activities continued during the last few centuries before the Christian era, as distinct eastern and western clusters of public buildings on broad platforms emerged and expanded to monumental proportions.[17] The tallest building reached a height of some 45 meters. Stela 1 (Fig. 5-8), erected in front of one of the smaller platforms, depicts two richly dressed figures facing each other. The overall style and composition, along with many particular motifs, especially costume details, strongly foreshadow Early Classic Maya lowland political art, while the mask between them (perhaps attached to the headdress of the right figure) clearly reflects the Olmec heritage of this style of monumental relief carving.

FIG. 5-8. Stela 1, Nakbé. The two figures and their costumes are carved in the style of the early highland–piedmont monuments. The profile head between the two figures reflects the strong Olmec heritage of early Maya political art. Adapted from Hansen 1991b:14.

FIG. 5-9. El Tigre group, Mirador. A triadic temple group atop its own terraced platform dominates this massive construction complex. Adapted from Hansen 1990:frontispiece.

The fragmentary remains of Stela 2 show eroded traces of an incised hieroglyphic text.

Nearby Mirador ranks as the largest lowland center.[18] Eastern and western building complexes, with "triadic groups" (composed of a large temple flanked by two smaller structures on a common platform) are comparable in form to those of Nakbé, but dwarf them in scale (Fig. 5-9). Elaborate painted stucco reliefs, often in the form of monstrous masks with reptilian features, adorn many of the platforms. Here, too, fragmentary stelae seem to bear traces of incised hieroglyphic texts.

Calakmul, some 40 kilometers to the north, could also boast monumental public architecture, including one platform with a height of 55 meters. An architectural group with a set of three buildings sharing a platform oriented north–south seems to mark the equinox and solstice positions of sunrise as viewed from a facing platform to the west.[19] A *sacbe* (causeway) that connects Calakmul to Mirador probably dates to this period and suggests an intimate political and/or economic relationship between the cities. Despite its precocious beginnings, Mirador suffered a process of decline, and was essentially abandoned by the early centuries of the Christian era. This turn of events may have provided the opportunity for Calakmul's florescence.[20]

The public building program at Río Azul, to the

FIG. 5-10. Structure N10-43, Lamanai. The terraced platform, which rises more than 30 meters above the adjacent plaza, supports a triadic temple complex.

east, was more modest in scale, with several temple platforms ranging up to 15 meters in height. Farther east, at Lamanai, a triadic temple atop an imposing platform more than 30 meters tall (Fig. 5-10) is more reminiscent of the buildings of Nakbé and Mirador. The form of the platform, which has a broad landing part way up, suggests that its design may already foreshadow the distinctive architectural style that would characterize the eastern edge of the lowlands in the Classic period. The foundations of the temple platform, begun a century or so before the Christian era, were laid over remnants of houses from a village that had grown at Lamanai by the fourth century B.C. At least one other monumental platform, decorated with a painted stucco mask, was built at about the same time.[21]

At Cerros, occupying a peninsula extending into Chetumal Bay on the Caribbean coast, a powerful elite that undertook monumental public construction projects emerged at about the same time.[22] Until a few decades before the beginning of the Christian era, Cerros was a simple village without monumental architecture or other indications of centralized political or economic organization. In the mid first century B.C., Cerros underwent a rapid transformation into a new kind of community, as new public buildings—first a temple atop a platform with elaborate painted stucco masks, like the temple at Lamanai

FIG. 5-11. Structure 5, Cerros. The construction of this small temple on the edge of Chetumal Bay marked the transformation of Cerros from a village to a town with public architecture. The terraces of the low platform were adorned with elaborately modeled and painted plaster masks (see Fig. 5-12) which are now covered by protective terrace facings.

(Figs. 5-11, 5-12), and shortly thereafter a series of triadic groups—covered the remains of the old village. Emblems in the form of the *kin* glyph for "sun" or "day" mark some of the masks as images of the sun god. Evidence of extensive burning and building demolition suggests that the transformation may have been sudden and self-conscious, perhaps under the influence of an inland center where the new patterns of centralized political organization had taken hold earlier. After a brief period of prosperity, marked by episodes of expansion and remodeling of its civic architectural core, Cerros was abandoned, before the beginning of the Classic period. Santa Rita Corozal, across the bay, grew during the same period, from a small village to a town of perhaps a thousand or two and continued to prosper during the subsequent Classic period.[23]

Cuello, to the south, followed much the same developmental trajectory, reaching its peak size, with as many as thirty-five hundred people, in the first centuries of the Christian era. Some buildings, with dressed stone masonry, now definitely had public ritual functions. To judge by two mass burials and the children's skulls that occasionally appear in caches along with pottery vessels, often paired bowls, and jade beads, human sacrifice accompanied the ritual activity that accompanied the dedication and/or deconsecration of these buildings. An uncarved stela may once have borne painted imagery.[24] Farther south, the small community of Altun Ha erected a

FIG. 5-12. Masks, Structure 5, Cerros. This photograph, taken shortly after excavation, shows two of the four painted-plaster masks flanking the stair of a low temple platform (see Fig. 5-11). Photograph courtesy David Freidel.

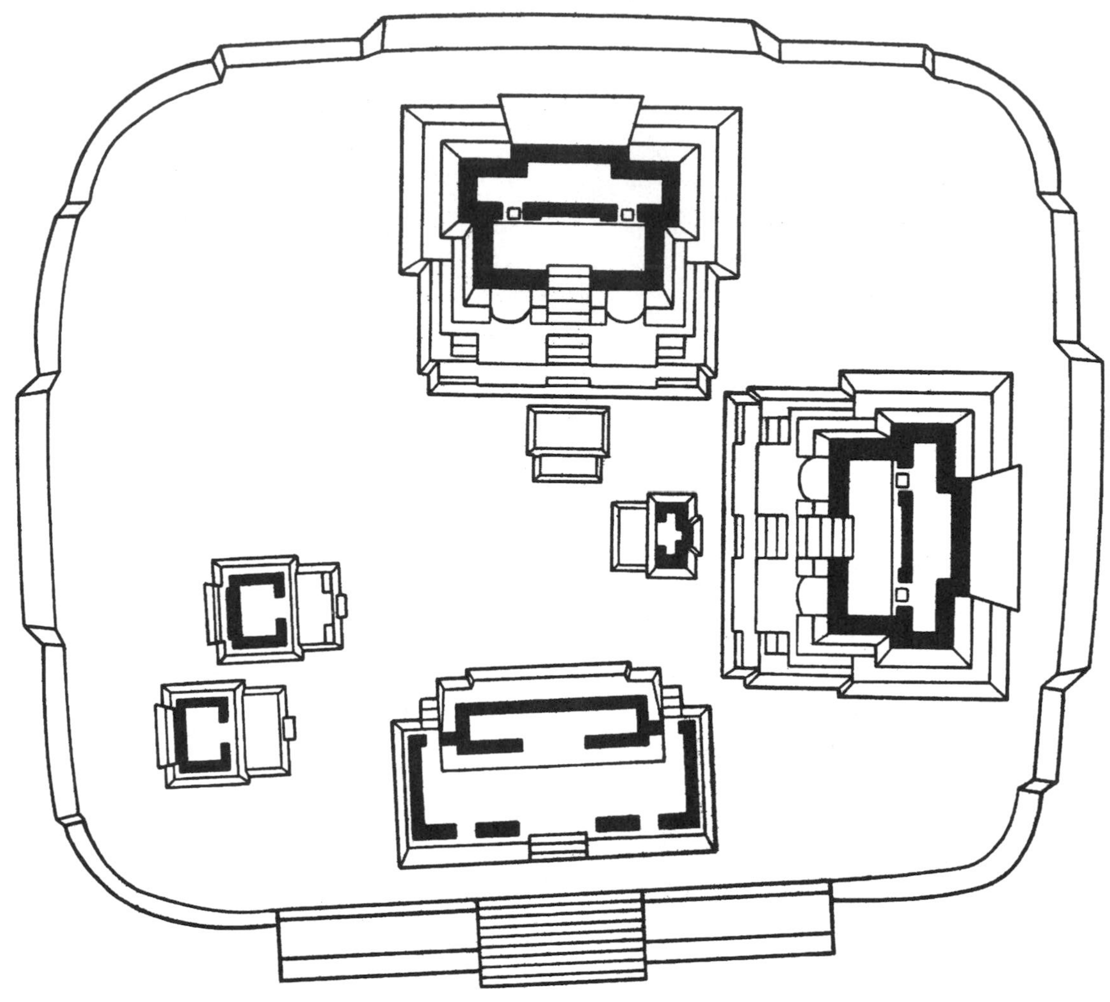

FIG. 5-13. Temple platforms, North Acropolis, Tikal: plan of a temple group built at about the beginning of the Christian era in Tikal's main ceremonial precinct. The northern (*top*) and eastern (*right*) platforms, rising about 4 meters above the acropolis floor, supported imposing temple buildings with modeled and painted stucco decoration. These two structures were nearly identical (see Fig. 5-14). A temple of different design, also with modeled-stucco ornamentation, stood on a lower platform at the head of the access stairs along the south edge of the acropolis. Two much smaller buildings occupied the southwest corner of the group. Tikal's early nobles, sometimes accompanied by their sacrificed retainers, were interred in vaulted tomb chambers within the acropolis itself. The tombs, painted inside with elaborate figures, were richly stocked with burial offerings. Adapted from W. Coe 1967:42.

modest temple adjacent to an artificial clay-lined reservoir.[25]

Colha, to the east, continued to exploit local chert resources and to export the products. By the first century B.C., the scale of chert tool-making had grown substantially, tool forms and manufacturing processes had become standardized, and it is likely that tool production was organized outside individual households, perhaps by guildlike groups, perhaps by central political authority within the community. Cerros, Cuello, and other communities in the region—as well as some distant ones—imported both raw material and finished tools. Tikal imported chert tools from Colha to complement those made from lower-quality local cherts.[26]

At Tikal, the construction of a small temple on a modest platform in the mid fourth century B.C. marks the beginning of a millennium of architectural history in an area that was to become the North Acropolis.[27] At about 200 B.C., this building was replaced by a much larger elevated platform for a larger temple and, shortly thereafter, the erection of a series of adjacent buildings marks the emergence of the North Acropolis as a focus of public architecture and civic affairs. In the first century A.D., central Tikal underwent another major architectural expansion, with a remodeling of the North Acropolis temples and the paving of the Great Plaza, forming a large forecourt to the south; shortly thereafter, the adjacent West and East Plazas were paved (Figs. 5-13, 5-14). Elaborately painted vaulted tombs under the North Acropolis temples were the final resting places of Tikal's early chiefs, along with their relatives and perhaps sacrificed retainers. The central temple contained the tomb of an individual whose missing head had been replaced by a jade mask; a variety of fine ceramic vessels accompanied the body. The small building in front of the eastern temple was built over the tomb of an adult, accompanied by another individual whose skeleton had been

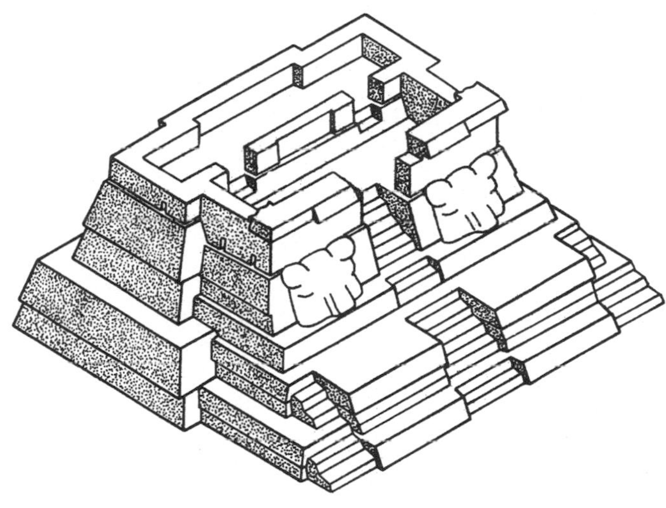

FIG. 5-14. Structure 5D-sub 1-1st, North Acropolis, Tikal: reconstruction drawing of a temple built in Tikal's center at about the beginning of the Christian era. The floor of the rear room stood about 4.5 meters above the acropolis surface. This building is the north (*top*) structure in the plan of the North Acropolis in Fig. 5-13; the eastern (*right*) building was nearly identical. The stucco masks flanking the stairway of the stucco-faced earth-and-rubble platform probably depicted jaguars. The projecting upper façade of the masonry building itself was ornamented with modeled stucco brightly painted in red, pink, black, and cream. The platform is very much like contemporary temple platforms at nearby Uaxactún, and the moldings along the sides and rear foreshadow the platform architecture of the Classic period (cf. Figs. 5-7 and 7-3). Adapted from W. Coe 1965:fig. 4.

FIG. 5-15. Group E, Uaxactún. This building complex, started near the beginning of the Christian era and subsequently elaborated, marks astronomical alignments. At the equinoxes, an observer atop the radial pyramid (E-VII-sub, see Fig. 5-7) looking east (the perspective of this photograph) would see the sun rise over the central temple on the facing platform. On the day of the summer solstice, the sun would rise directly behind the left (northern) temple; at the winter solstice it rose behind the southern temple (not visible here). Stela 20 (just visible in the foreground), in front of the radial platform, was added during the Early Classic period.

disarticulated before burial and the skeleton of an infant, as well as pottery vessels, painted gourds, and a green-stone figurine.

The Mundo Perdido complex to the southwest emerged as a focus of public architecture, at least as early as the North Acropolis, with the construction of a radial platform with stairs on all four sides facing an elongated platform across a plaza to the east. These structures represent an embryonic version of an astronomical complex that was designed to mark significant points in the seasonal cycle of sunrise positions and that would continue in use for at least a millennium. The platforms were remodeled and enlarged several times over the next few centuries, and the Mundo Perdido zone was connected to the North Acropolis by a formal causeway. By the first century A.D., the radial platform had become quite massive, with modeled stucco masks flanking the stairways. The architectural design of the astronomical complex was now fully evolved. Three temples atop the eastern platform marked, from the perspective of a viewer on the radial platform, the positions where the sun rose on the solstices and the equinoxes (Fig. 5-15).

At Uaxactún, a triadic building complex constructed in Group E, as early as the third or even the fourth century B.C., soon evolved into a compact cluster of public buildings. The adjacent Structure E-VII-sub (Fig. 5-7), embellished with elaborate stucco masks flanking its four stairways, is very similar to the radial platform of the Mundo Perdido astronomical complex. Here, too, an elongated platform facing it to the east eventually supported three temples that marked the key sunrise points (Fig. 5-15). By the beginning of the first century B.C., another public building complex in nearby Group H boasted elaborate decoration in modeled and painted stucco that included images of rulers and their emblems as well as portraits of the supernatural beings who bolstered their legitimacy. The buildings

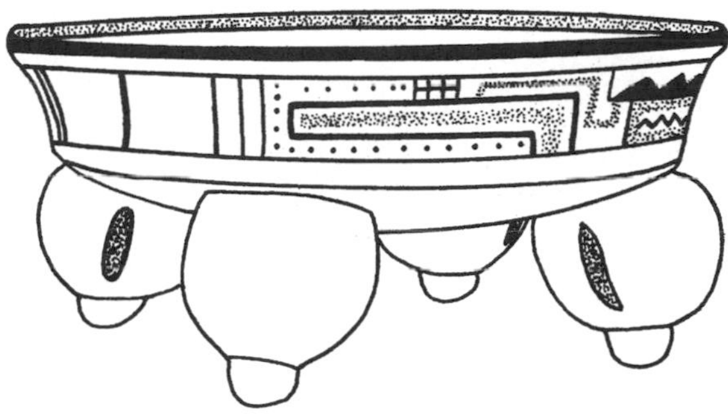

FIG. 5-16. Early polychrome bowl, Holmul. The four swollen legs are hollow and contain loose pottery pellets so that they serve as rattles. The geometric design is done in red and black paint over an orange ground. This bowl was one of several vessels interred with a noble in a burial chamber that was excavated into a platform mound just after the beginning of the Christian era. Adapted from Merwin and Vaillant 1932:pl. 18d.

must have presented a very grand setting for public political events.[28]

In the Río Pasión region, Altar de Sacrificios and Seibal experienced early population expansions and building booms. Altar enjoyed continued prosperity for several centuries, but Seibal soon entered a period of decline that culminated in near abandonment by A.D. 300. Here early monumental art consists mainly of the occasional modeled and painted stucco decoration on civic buildings. There are no hieroglyphic texts.[29]

Altar de Sacrificios, Barton Ramie, Nohmul, Holmul and other communities in an arc stretching across the eastern and southern flank of the lowlands added new features to the traditional Chicanel pottery style just before the beginning of the Christian era.[30] The Usulután technique of producing negative designs became widely popular. Vessels with swollen legs and true polychrome painting (red and black paint over an orange ground) (Fig. 5-16) are the most striking elements of the new style.[31] Many of these features have antecedents in earlier pottery-making traditions of the Maya highlands and adjacent piedmont regions.[32] This connection is especially obvious at Chalchuapa, in the east. The appearance of the new styles in southern lowland centers marks another, very intensive episode in the continuing relationship between highlands and lowlands. In few, if any, communities did new elements replace the Chicanel style entirely. New and old elements coexisted within each region, often marking a differentiation between ordinary and luxury pottery. Aristocrats in certain prosperous towns adopted polychrome pottery, using it for tomb offerings and in ritual activities. Ordinary people in these communities (and the residents of most smaller, less prominent villages) used pottery that added Usulután designs but that otherwise continued to reflect Chicanel norms. The great popularity of the new pottery styles in a few communities might indicate the arrival of people from the highland-piedmont zone.[33] If highlanders did live in these communities, they might have represented enclaves involved in the ongoing trade in obsidian, jade, and other raw materials, or they may have been permanent immigrants.

Other communities along this arc did not adopt the new luxury pottery tradition so wholeheartedly, nor did towns farther north and west.[34] Tikal, Uaxactún, and communities along the middle Río Usumacinta occasionally imported polychrome and Usulután vessels. Some features of the style were added to local pottery-making traditions, but there was no true shift away from the Chicanel style. Potters in some communities produced imitation Usulután designs in traditional ways, without using the actual negative production technique. Trade networks distributed vessels in these new styles as far west as Chiapa de Corzo. There, the imports contrast sharply with new local styles that marked a decided withdrawal from the Chicanel sphere.

Although they were regional phenomena, mainly restricted to the eastern and southern fringe of the lowlands, the new styles mark the advent of luxury polychrome pottery, which soon became an important feature of Classic Maya material culture. Like the early distribution of Maya sculpture and writing, the new pottery styles are another indication of intense highland-lowland contacts, suggesting that many of the foundations of Classic Maya civilization were laid in the Maya highlands. During the Late Preclassic period, many southern innovations spread gradually northward into the lowlands, where they were elaborated in later centuries.

Development was not uniform or continuous in the southern lowlands. In general, social changes, marked by large-scale public architecture and richly stocked tombs, proceeded quite rapidly until about the beginning of the Christian era. In many communities, the next few centuries represent a period of stabilization, with slackened population growth. Following its early population and building boom, Seibal experienced a period of decline that culminated in near abandonment by A.D. 300. Mirador, Nakbé, Cerros, and other communities were abandoned entirely. By contrast, Tikal, Lamanai and many other towns enjoyed steady growth and development through the beginning of the Classic period.

In central Yucatan, patterns of growth and development followed yet another course.[35] Becán began to produce Chicanel-style pottery at about the same time as centers farther south, but few other changes took place until the beginning of the Christian era. During the last centuries of the Late Preclassic period, Becán enjoyed a surge in population growth and its leaders began to organize public construction projects, including defensive structures. Architec-

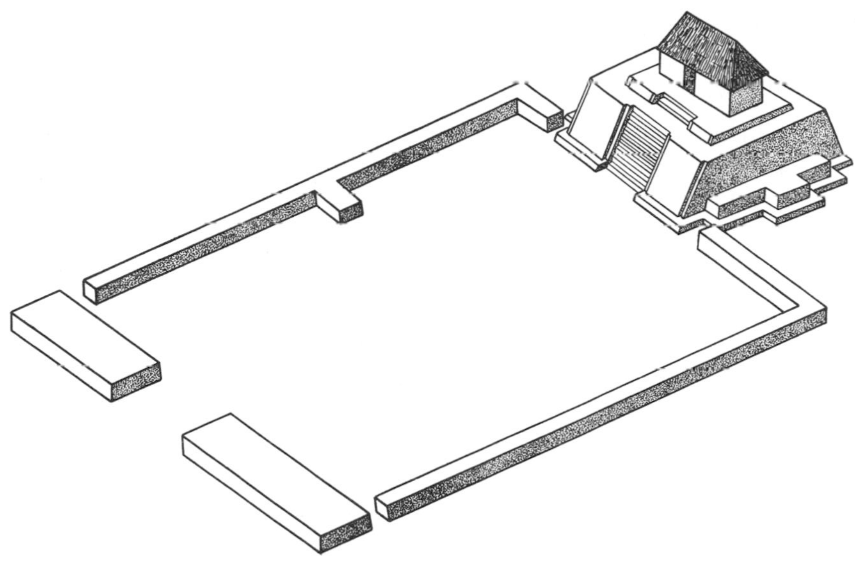

FIG. 5-17. Structure 450, Komchen: reconstruction drawing of a temple and its adjacent plaza. The main building platform has an earth-and-rubble core faced with stone. The building's walls are of heavy stone blocks faced with thick coats of undecorated stucco. Such details as the thatched roof are hypothetical. The masonry platforms at the end of the plaza probably supported timber buildings. A series of superimposed plaster floors indicates repeated remodeling of the complex. Adapted from Andrews IV 1965:fig. 1.

ture was modest in scale—with buildings on the tallest platforms reaching 15 meters in height—but a massive ditch and embankment, probably a fortification, represents a much larger public works project. The earthwork (16 meters wide and 5 meters deep, with a 5-meter interior embankment) is nearly 2 kilometers in circumference and encircles the entire center. There is no evidence here of early monumental art or polychrome ceramics. A large-scale hydraulic system at Edzná, to the west, featuring an elaborate network of canals and reservoirs, may also have had defensive functions.[36]

Farther north, population growth and centralization of political and economic power in the hands of elites also characterized the Late Preclassic period, although again developments were not uniform.[37] At Mirador, near Dzibilchaltún in the northwest, enlargement of the platforms flanking the central plaza continued, and one building appears to be a community sweat bath. Nearby Komchen quickly grew into the region's largest town, with several hundred buildings covering some 2 square kilometers, and a population probably numbering between 2000 and 3000. Five large platforms arranged around an open plaza form Komchen's civic core, with a causeway leading to another public building some 250 meters away (Fig. 5-17). Komchen probably exploited the rich salt beds of the nearby coast, but there is no indication that its leaders were involved in extensive systems of long-distance exchange. Nor is there evidence that material goods were used to mark wealth and status distinctions, although the appearance of more substantial burial offerings at nearby Dzibilchaltún indicates that the beginnings of this process were under way by the end of the Late Preclassic period. Komchen also evidently did not adopt the early tradition of monumental art. By the first century B.C. a process of decline had set in, and the community was abandoned by the third century A.D.[38]

A relief carving near the mouth of Loltún Cave and several portable pieces indicate that early Maya art and writing had already been adopted elsewhere in the north.[39] Northern lowland pottery represents a regional version of the Chicanel style, without a significant Usulután or polychrome component.

Regional Linkage and the Evolution of Maya Civilization

By A.D. 250 complex processes of growth and development had forever transformed homogeneous Maya societies. The old pattern of comparable villages had given way to elaborate settlement hierarchies. Towns provided social and economic focal points for surrounding villages, hamlets, and isolated farmsteads. In every part of the Maya world at least one town outstripped its fellows and rose to a position of regional dominance before the end of the Late Preclassic period. Smaller outlying communities may not have changed radically, but evidence of widening social and economic gaps abounds at larger civic centers. The contrast between simple burials beneath house floors and the elaborate vaulted masonry tombs stocked with luxury goods within public architectural complexes testifies to the emergence of aristocracies. Most of these public buildings were temples, and the practice of burying high-ranking individuals in sacred public places suggests the aristocratic ancestor cults typical of later Maya societies. Early stelae and altars also mark the inception of the Classic-period pattern of intertwined political, economic, and religious organization. Monuments to political leaders had strong sacred overtones in their iconography and in their association with temples.

Civic architecture and other massive public construction projects represent one obvious facet of the political and administrative roles that fell to the new leadership. They were able to command and mobilize human and economic resources on a regional scale, and they organized them to carry out well-planned public works projects. Aristocratic groups played key economic roles as well, for the imported luxury goods that adorn their tombs indicate far-flung procurement networks. Nobles must also have been involved in organizing the acquisition and distribution of obsidian, hard stones, and other widely used utilitarian goods. The emergent leadership may already have taken on managerial roles in subsistence economics, too, for the conversion of swamps and low river margins to new agricultural land had already begun, at least in the eastern lowlands.[40] The excavation and maintenance of canal systems and the concurrent creation of raised fields by landfill operations does not require administrative oversight, but specialists were certainly available and probably eager to expand their spheres of control.

Although all Maya societies experienced the same basic evolutionary transition between 400 B.C. and A.D. 250, the process was not uniform, and the Maya area did not become homogeneous. Developmental profiles vary from region to region, and even within regions. Styles of pottery and architectural decoration indicate the survival of vigorous local cultural traditions most clearly. Towns in the Maya highlands featured earth and clay public building platforms.

Associated monumental stone sculpture was quite varied, including a stela-altar complex memorializing leaders in relief carving and hieroglyphic text. Southern lowland public buildings often had stone construction and stucco decoration. Architectural decoration reflects the same emergent Maya monumental art style, but stone sculpture is rare and there is little evidence of writing. Some lowland centers also adopted a new highland style of luxury pottery. In the northern lowlands stone-and-stucco public buildings were large but quite plain. Pottery complexes there did not reflect southern innovations.

The stela complex of the highland-piedmont zone was ancestral to that of later Maya civilization. Early southern pottery also foreshadows many of the features of Classic Maya luxury pottery. The foundations of important aspects of Classic Maya civilization were laid in the south, but Maya civilization was not a highland invention transferred to the lowlands. Early public buildings in southern lowland towns, with stone facings and stucco decoration, set the pattern for monumental architecture of the Classic period. The development of Maya monumental art and luxury pottery was regional, while similar social changes occurred throughout the Maya world during these centuries. Individual features of Classic Maya civilization can be traced to developments in particular regions, but the emergence of Maya civilization itself was an areawide process.

The regions of the Maya area participated in parallel, linked evolutionary processes. Many factors were important in stimulating and fueling these developments.[41] There was no single cause. A huge fortification at Becán suggests that conflict and the need for defense may have contributed to the rise of powerful political leaders in central Yucatan, but defense was not an areawide preoccupation. The need to import exotic raw materials surely played a similar role elsewhere. Population growth occurred in every region, but demographic trends were far from uniform. Population pressure presumably contributed to the growth of new institutions in many regions, but it was not the single driving force. Connections among the regions of the Maya world created an environment in which a variety of localized causal factors contributed to the emergence of Classic Maya civilization. New political institutions that developed in one region under the pressure of conflict or population pressure might spread because they also facilitated commercial activities. Networks of communication stretched across the Maya world, bringing its several regions to the threshold of civilization at roughly the same time.

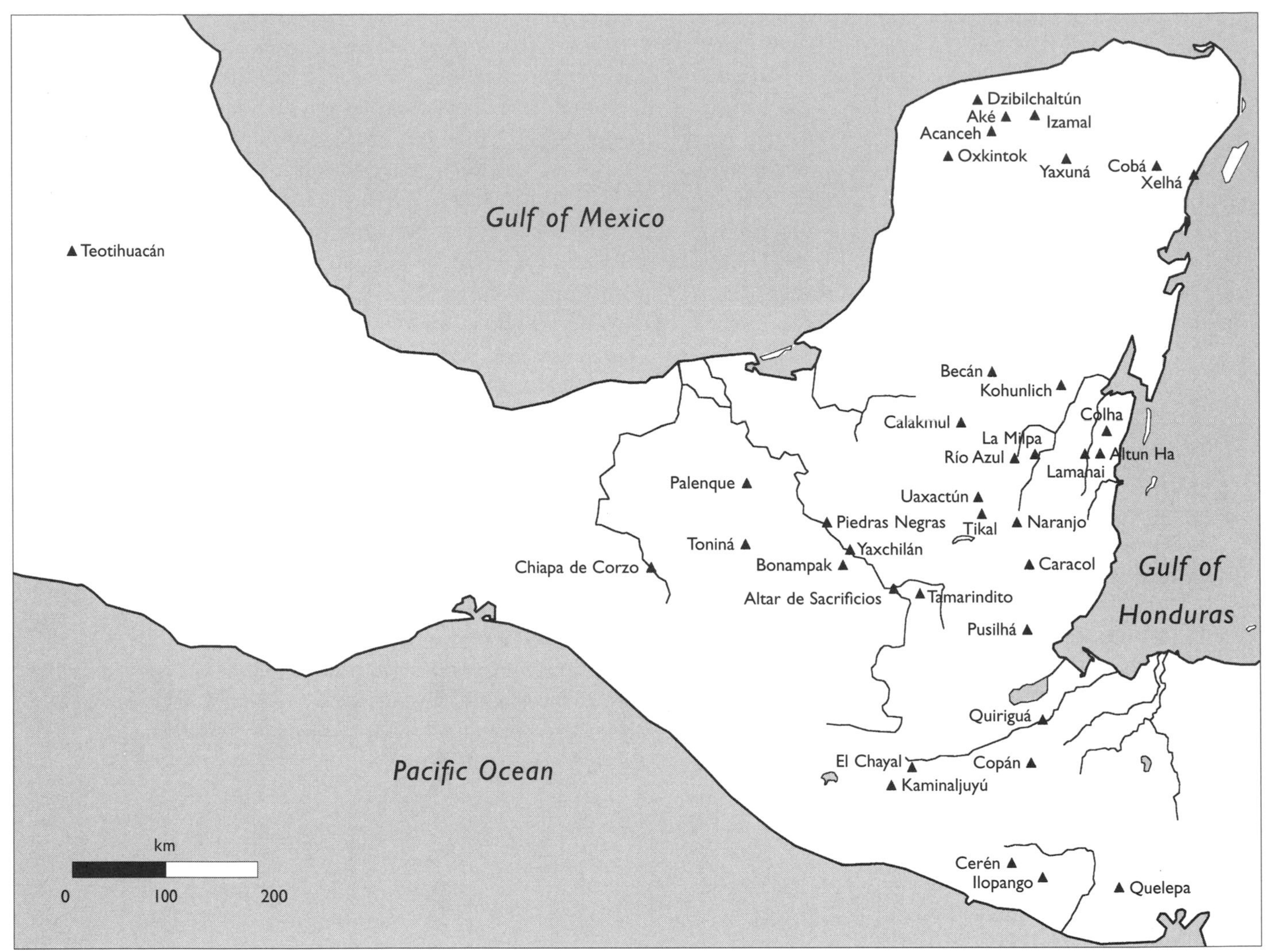

MAP 8. Early Classic cities.

SIX

The Crystallization of Maya Civilization

The Early Classic Period

Processes of growth and development that had begun in the Late Preclassic period—especially the concentration of political and economic power in the hands of elites and the associated elaboration of political and economic institutions and offices—continued during the Early Classic period as the new patterns of Maya civilization took hold throughout the lowlands.[1] Whether or not Late Preclassic Maya societies should be classed as states, there is no doubt that many Early Classic Maya polities were sufficiently large and complex to qualify. As in earlier centuries, of course, developmental trends were not uniform throughout the Maya world, nor were they smoothly continuous in any one region. Strikingly, highland societies did not continue along Late Preclassic trajectories: the practice of erecting stelae with Long Count dates and hieroglyphic texts celebrating local luminaries disappeared, at the very time it was being elaborated throughout the lowlands to the north.

The most striking development marking the onset of the Classic period is the florescence of the stela complex in the southern lowlands. A few Late Preclassic lowland towns had erected stelae with portraits of their richly dressed lords, and scattered finds indicate that writing was in limited use in the lowlands. But the Early Classic lords of some cities in the heart of the central lowlands adopted the regular practice of commissioning stelae on which dated hieroglyphic texts recording the main events of their lives complemented their portraits.

Several regions experienced intensified population growth. Well-developed hierarchies of communities—from tiny hamlets and villages with no indications of special political functions to large cities with all the trappings of centralized power—

FIG. 6-1. Stucco portrait, Pyramid of the Masks (Structure I-sub), Kohunlich. This mask, probably a representation of the sun god, echoes the style of lowland Late Preclassic architectural decoration (cf. Fig. 5-12).

FIG. 6-2. Corbeled vault, Copán. Higher courses project farther and farther toward the center until they can be spanned by a single block. Corbeled vaults require massive walls to counterbalance the outward thrust of the architectural burden they support; thus, interior spaces are much more restricted in size than those in buildings which are constructed with vaults that have true keystones.

appeared (Map 8). Many cities enjoyed a boom in building, especially in civic architecture. Some cities sought and acquired power beyond their immediate hinterlands, and regional states emerged. Marriage, alliance, and warfare variously characterized the relationships among autonomous states. Relationships with distant societies also intensified, as the great central Mexican city of Teotihuacán established a long-term presence in the Maya world, especially at Kaminaljuyú in the highlands.[2] Processes of increasing social stratification and occupational specialization intensified, and a variety of related changes characterized pottery and other craft styles.

Each of these developments has obvious roots in processes under way throughout the Maya area in the Late Preclassic period. The stela complex was directly descended from a much earlier tradition, developed in southern highland and piedmont centers, that had begun to appear in a few lowland centers during the Late Preclassic period. Late Preclassic public buildings at several southern lowland towns embodied the basic stylistic and construction features of Classic Maya civic architecture (Figs. 5-11, 6-1, 6-14). The new widely shared pottery style had evolved from Late Preclassic antecedents. In every way, Classic Maya civilization is an outgrowth of Late Preclassic Maya culture—an intensification and expansion of Late Preclassic cultural patterns.

Like earlier Maya societies, those of the Classic period were diverse. Regional differences, particularly in craft styles, became more pronounced. At the same time, expanding economic and political systems intensified communication among communities throughout the Maya world, so that the increasing regionalism is better interpreted as a reflection of closer ties among centers within regions, rather than diminished communication among regions. Many patterns were widely shared, but Classic Maya civilization was never homogeneous. It comprised several interacting cultures, each with its own regional flavor, its own variations on the same basic themes. Each regional culture represented a distinctive blend of its own unique local heritage with patterns developed in other parts of the Maya world. The Classic civilization of the southern lowlands, for example, was a synthesis of styles and institutions with diverse historical origins: public architecture had mainly local antecedents, while luxury pottery and political art owed much to earlier developments in the Maya highlands and the adjacent piedmont zone. Other regions achieved different syntheses of local developments and borrowed patterns. The sharpest contrasts developed between highland and lowland areas, although commerce continued. Styles and institutions were more widely shared within the lowlands, but differences between northern and southern sectors became more pronounced.

The Lowlands

The cultural synthesis that established the basic form of Classic Maya civilization took shape first in the central sector of the southern lowlands, in the Tikal-Uaxactún region.[3] There is no evidence of a substantial population increase at Tikal or Uaxactún at first, but the construction of public buildings did accelerate. As in the Late Preclassic period, most of these buildings are temples, although palaces and other elite residences become an increasingly prominent component of civic architecture. Architectural style, decoration, and construction techniques all follow patterns established in the preceding centuries. Corbeled vaulting (Fig. 6-2) was now certainly in use in above-ground buildings as well as in subterranean tombs. A new tradition of pottery making, featuring elaborate polychrome painting (Fig. 6-3), replaced Chicanel. This Tzakol style essentially represents the spread of an evolved version of the polychrome tradition (cf. Fig. 5-16) throughout the southern lowlands and beyond.

In the Great Plaza, already the architectural focus

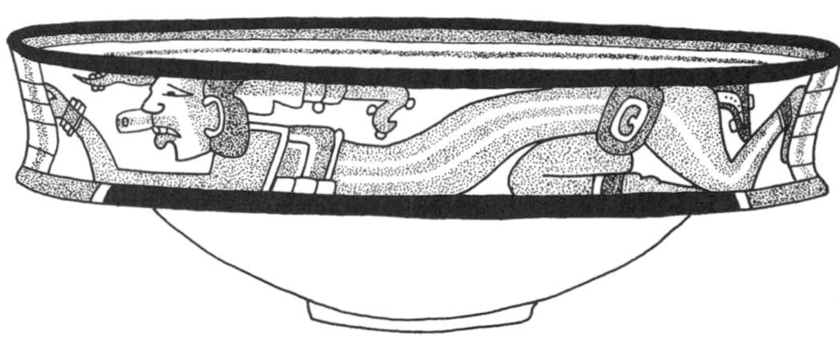

FIG. 6-3. Tzakol-style bowl, Uaxactún. The projecting flange is a typical Early Classic trait. The designs on this polychrome bowl, featuring human figures along with geometric elements, were executed in red and black paint over an orange ground. This bowl was one of nine vessels placed as funerary offerings in an Early Classic burial at Uaxactún. Adapted from R. E. Smith 1955:2, figs. 3e, 76b5.

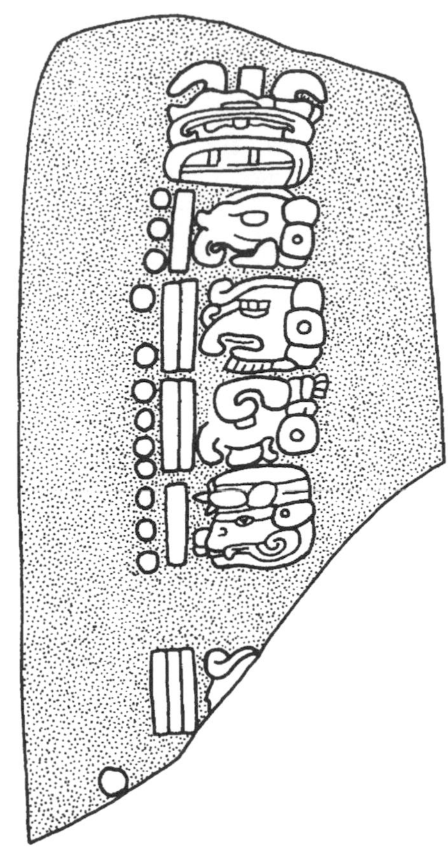

FIG. 6-4. Stela 29, Tikal. The Long Count position, 8.12.14.8.15 (A.D. 292), is the earliest known from the Maya lowlands. The date is arranged in a single column, like the earlier Cycle 7 inscriptions, but the numbers are now written vertically as coefficients of glyphs representing the periods of the Long Count, as in later dates (see Figs. 5-2, 5-3, 5-4, 6-5). The Introducing Glyph includes the patron of the Solar Year month (Zip). The dot just above the break is all that remains of the Ritual Almanac notation. The front of the monument (*left*) bears the portrait of a richly dressed noble with a scepter tucked under his right arm. As on many Izapan and early Maya monuments, the head of a deity or deified ancestor peers down from above. The headdress element on the head just in front of the noble's right hand is identical to the main sign in Tikal's "emblem glyph," the title of its kings (see Figs. 5-4, 6-12, 7-31, 7-32); here we see the first known use of this symbol. The monument, found broken in an ancient rubbish heap, must originally have been placed before an Early Classic public building, as were later Tikal stelae. Adapted from M. Coe 1976:fig. 15; W. Coe 1967:95; and Marcus 1976b:fig. 10.

of civic activity at Tikal for some five centuries, a major remodeling program was begun early in the third century: (1) the North Acropolis platform was enlarged; (2) new, larger temples were placed atop it, shifting its central axis; and (3) a monumental staircase was added, providing access from the Great Plaza. Substantial renovations continued as well in the Mundo Perdido complex, the other ancient focus of monumental construction activity, and that complex remained linked to the North Acropolis by a causeway.

A few broken monument fragments found in construction fills in the Great Plaza area at Tikal indicate that stelae or altars were being carved at least by the end of the second century A.D., but there is no direct evidence of hieroglyphic writing until the end of the third century. Stela 29 (Fig. 6-4), carved with the Long Count position 8.12.14.8.15, corresponding to A.D. 292, is the earliest dated monument to turn up so far in the Maya lowlands.[4] Like its highland ancestors, this monument celebrates the elaborately costumed lord who is portrayed on its face, bedecked with the emblems of his status, but the hieroglyphic text is limited to the date itself. His successors evidently did not universally revere his memory: the monument, missing its base, was found with a broken altar in a dump about midway between the North Acropolis and the Mundo Perdido building complexes.

A few decades later, in A.D. 328, nearby Uaxactún erected its first dated stela. For the next fifty years Tikal and Uaxactún were the only cities to do so. By the early fifth century, four or five smaller towns in the surrounding region were erecting monuments. During the second half of Cycle 8 of the Maya calendar (which ended in A.D. 434) the stela complex was restricted to a very small area in the heart of the southern lowlands around Tikal and Uaxactún, probably the centers from which the complex had spread. Uaxactún has by far the largest number of early dated monuments; together, Uaxactún and Tikal produced half of all Cycle 8 stelae. The practice of erecting stelae spread widely during the first katuns of Cycle 9, and by the end of the Early Classic period cities throughout the lowlands were erecting dated monuments. The widespread and reasonably standardized use of a fully elaborated version of the Long Count (Fig. 6-5) is the best evidence for the intensity of interaction throughout the Maya lowlands, cutting across a multitude of political boundaries. A few Long Count dates of the Classic period have been found beyond the Maya frontiers as well, although they may have been produced under Maya influence.

In style as well as content the earliest lowland stelae are squarely within the tradition of the Cycle 7–early Cycle 8 stela complex established in the highland-piedmont zone (Fig. 5-4). The disappearance of the stela complex from its original homeland in the Early Classic period evidently marks a change in highland sociopolitical systems, or at least in the mechanisms that reinforced the positions of highland aristocracies. There is no question that early lowland stelae (Figs. 6-4, 6-7, 6-13), like their highland ancestors, were memorials to powerful local political leaders and their families. These stelae reflect a social order in which aristocrats held the highest social ranks and dominated political, economic, and religious life. They filled specialized political roles that had economic and religious overtones. Ancestor motifs and other themes on the monuments appear to refer to noble family lines. Monuments are almost always associated with public buildings, and the practice of burying important people in well-built tombs within temple complexes continued. These patterns suggest aristocratic ancestor cults.

As the Classic period wore on, lowland lords increasingly relied on hieroglyphic texts to complement the imagery on their monuments with records of births, parentage, marriages, titles, accessions to

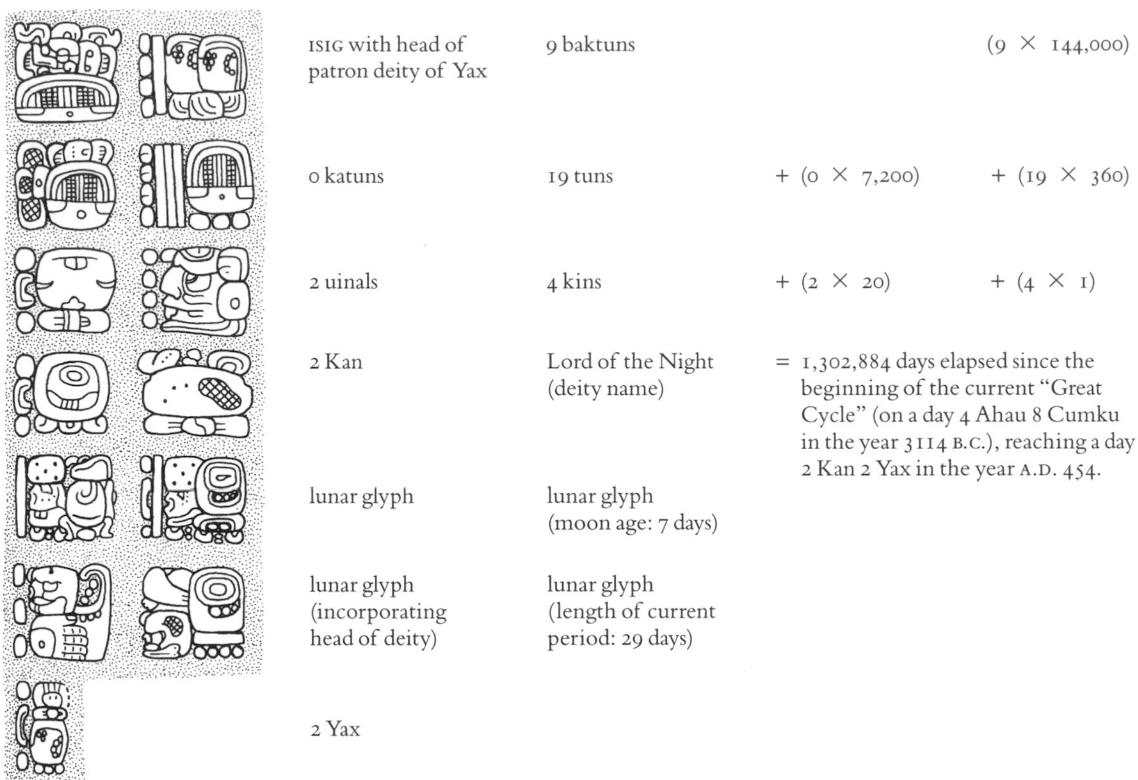

FIG. 6-5. Opening of the hieroglyphic text on Lintel 21, Yaxchilán. This text is typical of Classic-period inscription in that the Long Count date stands at the beginning of the text (therefore sometimes designated the Initial Series) and in the double-column format. The first seven glyphs and the final glyph are the date proper: 9.0.19.2.4 2 Kan 2 Yax. The intervening glyphs name the reigning Lord of the Night and record information about the moon, including its age (7 days) and the length of the current lunar period (29 days). The Initial Series Introducing Glyph (ISIG) contains the head of the patron deity of the month Yax. Adapted from I. Graham and Von Euw 1977:49.

office, alliances, and other selected aspects of their public lives. These biographical details, typically placed in the very precise chronological context of the Long Count, are the raw materials of history, but they cannot be blended in any simple way into an "objective" account of Maya history. Like all texts, those on Maya stelae reflect the perspectives and agendas of the lords who commissioned them; they are not necessarily straightforward factual statements.

Treated critically, however, texts do provide important insights into the politics of the Classic Maya world. During Cycle 8 of the Long Count, only the lords of Tikal used the emblem glyph (Figs. 6-4, 6-13)—a personal title meaning, roughly, "Tikal lord"—as part of their names. Whether or not these lords had actually been formally invested with that title as part of their accession to office (as opposed to claiming a status not yet actually achieved), the existence of such a title does at least imply that Tikal corresponded to a recognized political unit, although we know little of the nature of its institutions. The same emblem glyph appears at least once in the early inscriptions of Uaxactún, implying alliance or perhaps political domination.[5] The hieroglyphic texts of Tikal and Uaxactún also mention some of the same personal names and dates, doing so in ways that suggest close relationships between rulers of the two cities. The lord depicted as a warrior on Stela 5 at Uaxactún appears to be the same "Smoking Frog" personage named, with the "Tikal lord" title, in several texts at Tikal and elsewhere at Uaxactún. Textual evidence certainly suggests that Tikal and Uaxactún had something of a head start along the road to political power in the opening centuries of the Classic period.

By the fourth century, a major architectural expansion had begun to transform the Mundo Perdido complex. The radial platform of the astronomical complex was enlarged several times, eventually reaching a height of 31 meters, making it the tallest building in Early Classic Tikal. The eastern platform and its three temples were enlarged as well, and new structures sprang up around them. Several of these constructions, including another tall temple platform and a low platform without a superstructure on the astronomical axis west of the radial platform, were built in the architectural style of Teotihuacán, the great urban capital of highland central Mexico (Fig. 6-6, Color Plate 1), and an elaborately carved ball-court marker in the style of Teotihuacán was found a short distance from the Mundo Perdido zone. Rich caches and tombs in some of these buildings suggest that at least one branch of Tikal's aristocracy may have lived here. A fragmentary stela found in one of the rooms of the central astronomical temple carries a text with a Long Count date corresponding to A.D. 376 and the name of one "Jaguar Paw," a powerful fourth-century lord who may have ruled Tikal;[6] the final resting place of this stela was the result of a Late Classic relocation, but originally it was most likely erected nearby, perhaps on the centerline of the astronomical complex. It is possible that the Mundo Perdido area temporarily replaced or complemented the North Acropolis as a preferred location for royal burial and other construction activity.

The North Acropolis and Great Plaza were again the scene of major public construction programs by the late fourth century. The North Acropolis and its temples were remodeled, and the newly resurfaced Great Plaza acquired the layout that it would retain throughout the Classic period: buildings on the east and west sides, a small ball court, and a palace complex to the south (in the area that would become the Central Acropolis). The text on a ceramic vessel from a cache in this building complex names Jaguar Paw and places him as the ninth in a sequence of rulers. Whether or not Jaguar Paw was the heir to a dynastic line that had seen eight predecessors, the text

FIG. 6-6. Structure 5C-49, Mundo Perdido, Tikal. The terrace construction, with sloping lower sections topped by inset panels, represents the *talud-tablero* style of Teotihuacán. This temple platform, along with other examples of the Teotihuacán style in the Mundo Perdido zone and the Great Plaza area, reflect the foreign connections of Tikal's aristocracy.

reflects a claim to a royal title and a position in a (poorly understood) line of succession. Stela 4 (Fig. 6-7), set before Temple 34 at the southwest corner of the North Acropolis, is the earliest surviving lowland monument with a well-preserved hieroglyphic text that contains references to political affairs. The portrait and hieroglyphic text record the accession, in A.D. 379, of a lord known to Mayanists as "Curl Snout" (after the spiral nose of the animal head that is the main sign of his name glyph). A jade pendant in the shape of the same spiral-nosed animal was found among the mortuary offerings in a tomb beneath Temple 34, adding weight to the spatial argument that it was Curl Snout's final resting place.

Early fifth-century building activity in the North Acropolis area continued the same basic patterns: namely, the enlargement of existing temples and the construction of new ones, especially along the south edge of the North Acropolis facing the Great Plaza. Stela 31 (Fig. 6-13), which probably was originally set before the central Temple 33[7] seems to imply a corresponding political continuity. The monument, which bears a dedication date of A.D. 445, commemorates the accession of "Stormy Sky" one katun (i.e., a few months less than twenty years) earlier. The long text on the monument presents Stormy Sky as the son and successor of Curl Snout, mentions a variety of other names and events associated with his immediate predecessors, and refers to personages who would have lived long before the carving of the monument. Whatever the historical validity of Stormy Sky's claims—the alleged relationship with Curl Snout is perfectly plausible, but some of the other relationships referred to are obscure, and some of the events and personages mentioned are so ancient that they were surely mythical—Stela 31 provides an account of Tikal's history from Stormy Sky's perspective and potentially offers fascinating insights into how his particular view of the past served his own political ends. Temple 33 was

FIG. 6-7. Stela 4, Tikal. This monument is the first erected in honor of the early Tikal ruler nicknamed "Curl Snout," after the curlicue protruding from the face of the glyph that represents his name. The stela records the date of his accession to rule in A.D. 378 (8.17.2.16.7). Elements of Curl Snout's regalia and his frontal seated pose are typical of portraits of nobles at Teotihuacán, the great central Mexican city. Stela 4 was moved in the Postclassic period and re-erected upside down alongside an inverted altar. Its correct orientation has been restored, but its original location is unknown.

FIG. 6-8. Complex A-V, Vault Ih stage, Uaxactún: restoration drawing by Tatiana Proskouriakoff. This temple group, repeatedly remodeled during the fourth, fifth, and sixth centuries, was the location for the tombs of several of Uaxactún's nobles. The western (*left*) temple in the front row was erected over the burial with the most elaborate offerings (Burial A-22; Figs. 6-9, 6-10), perhaps that of the king depicted on Stela 22, which was erected in the back room and which bears a Long Count date equivalent to A.D. 504. Drawing by Tatiana Proskouriakoff. Photograph reproduced by permission of the Peabody Museum, Harvard University.

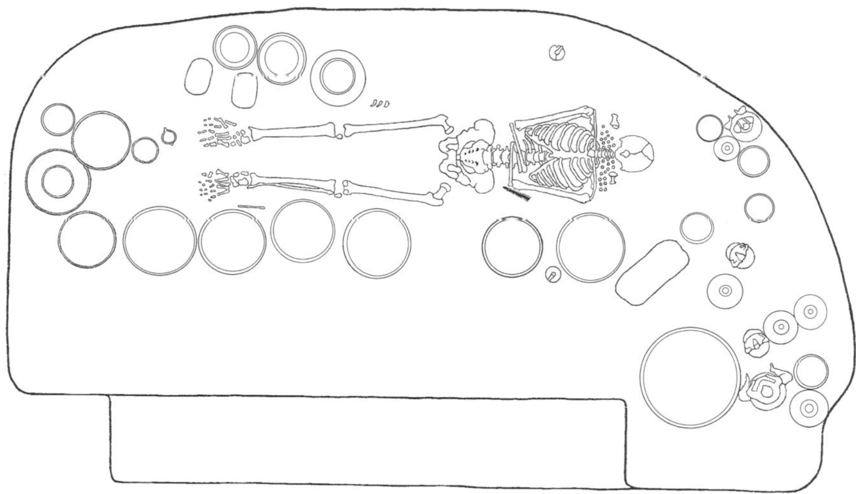

FIG. 6-9. Burial A-22, Complex A-V, Uaxactún. This lord, interred in the A-V temple complex (under the western temple in the front set), may be the ruler celebrated on Stela 22 erected in the back room of the temple (Fig. 6-8); if so, then he is also the king depicted on Stela 20 erected in Group E (Fig. 5-15). The mortuary offerings, the richest of any Uaxactún tomb, include thirty-five pottery vessels (Fig. 6-10), jade and shell necklaces and ear plugs, seashells, jaguar teeth, and copal incense; a stingray spine, painted red and placed near the pelvis, probably represents ritual bloodletting. The absence of this lord's teeth and facial bones, and the presence of red pigment covering the bones, suggest that the body may have been interred some time after death. Adapted from A. L. Smith 1950:fig. 121.

built over a richly furnished tomb—probably that of Stormy Sky himself, given the connection between this building and his elaborate memorial, Stela 31—and a Long Count date painted on the wall corresponds to A.D. 456, a plausible death date for Stormy Sky.

Uaxactún undertook a comparable program of renewal and aggrandizement of its public architecture in the fourth century. A new triadic complex in Group A (Fig. 6-8), located atop the most prominent of the hills on which the city is built, formed the core around which the grand new architectural focus for the public political activities organized by Uaxactún's rulers would develop over the following centuries. Five of Uaxactún's early lords chose the increasingly elaborate central building cluster of Complex A-V as the location for the tombs in which they were laid to rest, dressed in their jade jewelry and other finery and accompanied by pearls, elaborately painted pottery vessels, and other costly offerings (Fig. 6-9, 6-10). By the fifth century, a fine eighteen-room palace (Fig. 6-11), the largest at Uaxactún, occupied the adjacent plaza. In Group E, the astronomical commemorative complex was remodeled and Stela 20, which may depict one of the lords buried in the A-V group, was added (Fig. 5-14). A

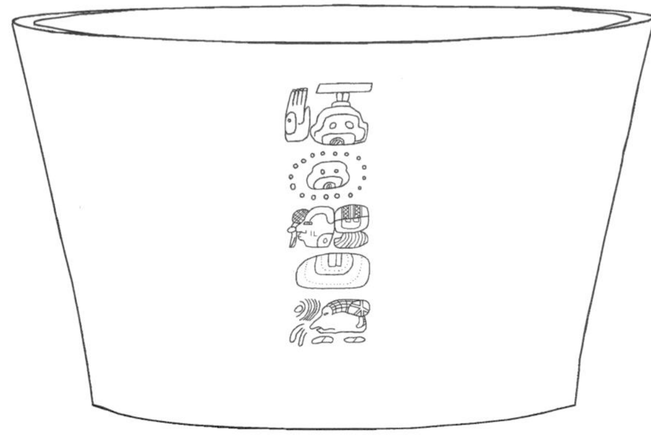

FIG. 6-10. Ceramic vessel and disk, Burial A-22, Complex A-V, Uaxactún. The hieroglyphic text incised on this orange bowl includes an ahau sign ringed with circles—possibly a version of the "emblem glyph" royal title, and possibly also referring to Curl Snout of Tikal (Valdés and Fahsen 1995:215). The disk, or lid, rested on copal incense that filled a smaller bowl inside the larger vessel. The painted design, repeated in incised form on the smaller bowl, represents a reptilian creature most commonly depicted on contemporary pottery from Kaminaljuyú. Several other vessels in the tomb also reflect stylistic connections with Teotihuacán or Kaminaljuyú. Adapted from R. E. Smith 1955:fig. 7a, c.

new triadic group was built over the adjacent building cluster, but it was not elaborated as the earlier complex had been, and it remained far smaller than the Group A buildings. The architectural complex in Group H was abandoned permanently.

This precocious political development at Tikal and Uaxactún may be related to the external connections of the two centers, for the aristocracies of Tikal and Uaxactún developed close ties with foreign nobles toward the end of Cycle 8.[8] Several monuments (Fig. 6-13) portray non-Maya costume elements and *atlatls* (spear throwers), Mexican weapons hitherto unknown in the Maya world.[9] A figure with an *atlatl* appears in a mural painting,[10] probably slightly later in date, in what may be a depiction of a confrontation between a foreigner and a local lord. Curl Snout's inaugural monument (Fig. 6-7) depicts him less than two years later in a pose and costume typical of the nobles of Teotihuacán. His tomb contained, in addition to the usual ritual paraphernalia, imported vessels with Mexican-style painted stucco decoration (Fig. 6-12) and other objects indicating a Teotihuacán connection. The mortuary offerings closely parallel those in contemporary tombs at Kaminaljuyú, a Teotihuacán outpost in the Maya highlands.[11] At about this time, three other burials at Tikal involved Mexican-style cremation rites. Uaxactún's lords were also buried with objects indicating a Teotihuacán-Kaminaljuyú connection (Fig. 6-10).

The relationship continued, though perhaps less intensely, during the reign of Stormy Sky, who succeeded Curl Snout in about A.D. 425. Stela 31, erected to celebrate the first katun of the new leader's reign, depicts Stormy Sky in typical Maya regalia, but with Mexican emblems among his accoutrements (Fig. 6-13). Two subordinate figures in highland Mexican dress flank Stormy Sky; they carry atlatls and shields adorned with the goggle-eyed face of a central Mexican god connected with warfare.[12]

FIG. 6-11. Structure A-XVIII, Uaxactún. This large and elegant palace was probably the residence of the lords buried in Complex A-V, to the west. A bench on the second floor, just above the central door, may have served as a throne for audiences on public occasions.

FIG. 6-12. Design painted on a stuccoed bowl, Burial 10, Tikal. The figure, painted in red, green, and white over a thin stucco coating on the outside of the vessel, is done in the style of Teotihuacán and Kaminaljuyú. The bowl itself is not of local manufacture and shows strong similarities with Thin Orange pottery from western Mesoamerica. Adapted from Culbert 1993:fig. 15.

Stela 31 emphasizes Stormy Sky's genealogical links with his Mexican-influenced predecessor, for Curl Snout is the "ancestor figure" gazing down on him. The text mentions the accession of both rulers. By the time of Stormy Sky's death in the mid fifth century, Tikal's Mexican connection was definitely on the wane. His tomb, beneath Temple 33 in the North Acropolis (Fig. 7-6, Color Plate 2), was, like his monuments, more traditional than Curl Snout's, with fewer Mexican imports. The monuments of his successors (Fig. 7-10) reflect a sharp change in style, with the virtual absence of foreign design elements.

For a very brief period, then, Mexican cultural elements became popular among the rulers of Tikal and Uaxactún. It is even possible, though far from certain, that Curl Snout himself was of foreign descent. He certainly established a ruling line with a strong Mexican affiliation at Tikal. Stormy Sky's monuments emphasize his ties to Curl Snout, but they incorporate Mexican symbols only as minor elements. The quick decline of Mexican emblems does not square with the notion that foreign rulers took over Tikal. It suggests instead an episode of especially intense alliance, perhaps including marriage ties, between local Maya rulers and foreign aristocrats. Buildings with Teotihuacán architectural features in the Mundo Perdido zone suggest either that aristocratic Tikal families adopted Teotihuacán styles in both the domestic and the public sphere, or that central Tikal housed a resident enclave of foreigners. These foreign connections may have

FIG. 6–13. Stela 31, Tikal. This monument was erected at about A.D. 445 to mark the end of the first katun of Stormy Sky's rule. His costume is essentially Maya, but such elements as the skull in his headdress are Teotihuacán-inspired. The figures on the sides of the stela are dressed as Teotihuacán warriors. They carry atlatls, and the shield at the right is decorated with the face of a central Mexican deity who resembles later Aztec depictions of the rain god, Tlaloc; however, the meanings associated with this fifth-century supernatural would have been different and would have included a connection with warfare. The head gazing down from above is that of Stormy Sky's predecessor, Curl Snout. The Tikal emblem glyph appears in the headdress of the head in the crook of Stormy Sky's arm. Stormy Sky's name glyph appears as part of his headdress. The deity head emerging from this glyph, along with elements of the headdresses on the heads at his belt, may be other lineage emblems. The hieroglyphic text mentions Curl Snout's accession as well as that of Stormy Sky, emphasizing the genealogical link between them. Stela 31 originally stood before one of the Early Classic temples of the North Acropolis (Fig. 7-6, Color Plate 2). In the eighth century it was moved up into the rear room of the temple itself. Here it was burned and incense burners were broken around it; then the upper part of the temple was destroyed, and the whole building was encased in a new construction. Two nobles were buried in the heart of the structure before the remodeling, and the ceremonial "sacrifice" of the ancient monument may have marked some momentous event in the affairs of Stormy Sky's descendants, who had returned to power at Tikal late in the seventh century, after a long lapse. Adapted from Robertson et al. 1972:pls. 133–35.

influenced the course of political development at Tikal and Uaxactún, but they do not represent the implantation of a foreign civilization in the Maya lowlands. Lowland Maya societies had already developed the essential features of civilization. The stela complex, reflecting the basic patterns of Classic Maya political organization, had been present in the heart of the southern lowlands for at least a century by the time Curl Snout came to power.

Although Maya tomb offerings include green obsidian from central Mexico, and although Maya pottery has been found at Teotihuacán, the ties between lowland Maya centers and Teotihuacán were probably not direct. Teotihuacán maintained an active presence in the Maya highlands, most notably at Kaminaljuyú (Map 8).[13] Stylistic nuances of Mexican material found there point to an enclave of Mexicans, albeit more likely from some part of Teotihuacán's southeastern dominion than from the Central Mexican metropolis itself. Teotihuacán's sphere of influence embraced most of the Intermediate Zone, from the Gulf coast to the Pacific coast and piedmont. Curl Snout's burial at Tikal is very much like the Mexican tombs at Kaminaljuyú. The Mexicans who came to Tikal, and who may have maintained a resident enclave there, were almost certainly "colonial" Teotihuacanos from Kaminaljuyú. Commerce was surely an important component of this interaction, as lowland aristocracies added central Mexican obsidian and Teotihuacán-style pottery to the traditional imports from the Maya highlands. After Curl Snout's reign, Mexican imports fell off rapidly, although economic ties with the highlands continued. Local potters still manufactured a few Teotihuacán-inspired vessels, and Mexican emblems did not disappear entirely from monumental art, but these are plainly minor elements in overwhelmingly Maya contexts. Teotihuacán architectural features continued to be used at least occasionally in remodelings (in the Mundo Perdido zone) and new construction (in the East Plaza, Fig. 7-9) as late as the earlier part of the Late Classic period.

The heart of the southern lowlands experienced renewed growth during the late fifth and early sixth centuries.[14] Tikal enjoyed a burst of monumental construction activity and a population surge. Inscriptions at centers as distant as Yaxchilán mention Tikal, already emerging as a powerful political center with influence extending far beyond its local area. Tikal had begun to take on the features of a regional capital, a status it certainly achieved in the Late Classic period.

This growth was interrupted in the sixth century. Between 9.5.0.0.0 and 9.8.0.0.0 (A.D. 534–593), Tikal, Uaxactún, and many dependent towns ceased to erect new stelae and sharply cut back their public building activity.[15] In part, this slackened growth may be related to political and economic reorientations following the withdrawal of Teotihuacán's presence. Shifting political alliances and conflict with emergent powers elsewhere in the lowlands may also have played a role. Hieroglyphic texts do indicate that interactions among the cities of the region had begun to intensify and may have included warfare, but they do not provide clear evidence of the nature of the political landscape.[16]

Elsewhere in the southern lowlands, development of the regional patterns of Classic Maya civilization was even more gradual. Mexican ties were much less intense.[17] Tomb offerings and special caches sometimes include imported central Mexican obsidian and Teotihuacán-style pottery (Fig. 6-16). Local potters adopted some features of the Teotihuacán style, and Mexican symbols sometimes appear in monumental art, but there is nothing comparable to the Mexican interlude at Tikal.

Tikal's political influence, though not necessarily its sphere of actual control, may have stretched well to the north in the Early Classic. References to Tikal and its rulers in the texts and images at Río Azul, a city with a substantial civic architectural core of several hundred buildings, seem to imply a very close political relationship, if not formal domination, by the power to the south.[18]

The lords of Calakmul and nearby cities began to commission stelae in the fifth and sixth centuries. Calakmul, which carved the northernmost text with a date in Cycle 8 of the Long Count, was already a substantial city, and the developmental trajectory that would make it a major regional political force in the Late Classic period was under way. One early lord had himself entombed beneath a palace on a bed of ceramic dishes; he was heavily adorned with jade and shell jewelry, and was accompanied by stingray spines and other ritual paraphernalia. By the mid sixth century, Calakmul's political connections stretched at least as far as Yaxchilán and Naranjo, and in the early seventh century extended beyond to Caracol. Hieroglyphic texts suggest that these alliances often had a military dimension, usually directed against Tikal, and indications that the accession of at least one king of Naranjo took place under the aegis of the lord of Calakmul suggest that the alliances sometimes involved a hegemonic relationship.[19]

In the east, where early polychrome pottery was so popular, the new ceramic style was in widespread use from the beginning of the Classic period.[20] Otherwise, the basic way of life was much the same as it had been in the closing centuries of the Late Preclassic period. Population growth continued. Some older centers faded into obscurity, but new, larger ones replaced them. Monumental public architecture and richly stocked burials testify to the expanding political and economic power of local aristocracies at Caracol and other eastern cities. Eastern lords began to commemorate themselves on stelae as early as the mid fifth century, and the practice burgeoned in the sixth century as public construction activity fell into temporary eclipse to the west. A mid-sixth-century king of Caracol evidently assumed the throne under the authority of the king of Tikal.[21] The rapid rise of Caracol is sometimes interpreted as the result of successful military action against Tikal. A ball-court marker at Caracol refers to Tikal in connection with glyphs that refer to conflict. Subsequently, Caracol continued to prosper and grow, while Tikal experienced a rentrenchment in terms of carved monuments and monumental architecture.[22] Lamanai, on the New River Lagoon, maintained the modest regional power that it had enjoyed since the Late Preclassic period. Public construction activity took place throughout the central zone of the community, which occupied several square kilometers. Some buildings reflect a marked conservatism, as at least one of the earlier buildings was remodeled with relief masks that strongly echo older sculptural styles (Fig. 6-14). One of these masks includes a headdress with crocodilian features that seem to foreshadow later imagery and may indicate that the city was already known as "the place of the submerged crocodile," the name that Spanish invaders corrupted to "Lamanai."[23] Altun Ha, a much smaller community to the east, had a population of only a few thousand within the central square kilometer that included its main public buildings. This community's civic core shifted away from its Late Preclassic location during the Early Classic period, to focus on a pair of plazas flanked by temples and palaces. Altun Ha was probably within Lamanai's economic and political shadow, if not under its direct political control, but its aristocrats were nonetheless quite prosperous. One noble was laid to rest in a tomb in one of the temple platforms accompanied by pottery vessels, stingray spines, chert "eccentrics,"[24] shell jewelry, several hundred jade beads and pendants, and the remains of a codex. Here and at Lamanai, general similarities in architectural, sculptural, and craft styles testify to a continuing interaction with the cities of the lowland core to the west. But a distinctive eastern architectural style

FIG. 6-14. Structure N9-56, Lamanai. The masks flanking the stairways of this temple platform echo Preclassic architectural decoration and, more distantly, reflect the Olmec heritage of Classic Maya monumental art.

—featuring a multiroomed building constructed across the platform stairway and often having no superstructure on the summit—emerged in the Early Classic period (Fig. 6-15).[25] Colha not far to the north, continued to be the primary source of chert and manufactured chert tools for the region, as well as for a substantial number of more distant communities.[26] To the west, La Milpa was emerging as a regional power.[27]

The same general pattern holds for the southeastern region, where Copán was erecting monuments in association with temples and palaces very early in Cycle 9.[28] Copán's early pottery reflects widely shared lowland styles, but represents a distinctive regional sphere of interaction. Dedication of stelae continued through the sixth century, although the lords of Copán commissioned many fewer monuments during the interval from 9.5.0.0.0 to 9.8.0.0.0. Quiriguá, 50 kilometers to the north on the Río Motagua, erected two stelae in the fifth century that are very much like the monuments of Petén cities to the northwest. The early lords of Quiriguá may have maintained a special connection with Tikal, but references to individuals who are also named in Copán texts suggest that relationships with their southern neighbor were more salient. To judge by architectural scale, Copán is likely to have been the more prosperous and influential city during the Early Classic period.

To the west, along the Río Pasión, the first two centuries of the Early Classic period saw no appreciable change in the traditional way of life.[29] Seibal was still in decline. At Altar de Sacrificios the Late Preclassic building boom continued in the Early Classic period, but new pottery styles and the stela complex did not appear until the mid fifth century. Public building activity declined during the late fifth and early sixth centuries, but Altar continued to erect sculptured monuments. Altar de Sacrificios was one of the first cities in the west to take on

FIG. 6-15. Structure B-4, Altun Ha. This platform, with a row of rooms built across the stairway, represents a distinctive eastern architectural style. Instead of a temple, the platform summit supports an altar which bears traces of burned offerings; like the platform, the altar was resurfaced and enlarged several times. The masonry block protruding from the upper section of the stair housed a richly stocked tomb.

the full Classic pattern of Maya civilization. By the sixth century, local aristocracies were beginning to emerge in the Petexbatún region to the south; hieroglyphic texts suggest that the lords of Tamarindito were dominant there initially. At about the same time, the rise of Yaxchilán and Piedras Negras, downstream on the Río Usumacinta, signaled the end of Altar's prominence in the west. Yaxchilán's texts mention early lords of Bonampak, not far to the southwest, and that town was probably already formally subordinate to its larger neighbor. The texts also indicate a close relationship between the rulers of Yaxchilán and the lords of Piedras Negras which would persist for several centuries, although references to Piedras Negras in the texts of Yaxchilán suggest that Yaxchilán's kings may not yet have achieved the wider sphere of dominance that they evidently enjoyed in the Late Classic period. In style, the early monuments of western cities closely resemble those of Tikal and Uaxactún, and the westward and northward spread of the stela complex may reflect an expanding sphere of political influence. Yaxchilán texts refer to Tikal from the beginning of the sixth century. During that century, a marked interruption in stela dedication reflects an unsettled period of reduced growth comparable to that in some of the regions to the east.

Farther north, middle Usumacinta communities had not yet adopted the full pattern of Classic Maya civilization.[30] No important Early Classic civic center has been identified in this region. Local pottery complexes are quite varied, with only occasional echoes of the styles popular to the south and east. Regionalization also affected the Palenque area, away from the river. Typical Chicanel complexes gave way to an essentially localized pottery tradition at the beginning of the Early Classic period. Not until the fifth and sixth centuries do imported southern polychromes and local versions of the Tzakol style indicate a significant renewal of ties with the rest of the southern lowlands. Monumental public construction also began at this time, but on a modest scale. Palenque did not become a major center with large-scale public architecture and monuments until the Late Classic period.

At Becán, too, few real changes marked the beginning of the Early Classic period.[31] Pottery making reflects a regional variant of the Tzakol style as well as strong influence from northern traditions. Public works activity continued. The ditch-and-bank fortification was kept in repair and some new civic architectural complexes appeared, but the basic form of the older community was hardly altered, and a population decline set in before the end of the Early Classic period. Many Late Preclassic buildings evidently remained in use until they were replaced in the Late Classic period. Fifth- and sixth-century pottery indicates intensified contacts with cities to the south and a corresponding weakening of northern ties. At the same time, Becán's potters adopted a few elements of the Teotihuacán style, and imports include small quantities of central Mexican obsidian. A cache of Teotihuacán-style figurines in a structure that had Teotihuacán architectural features (Fig. 6-16) might even indicate a foreign enclave. If so, it must have involved Mexicanized Mayas from the south rather than central Mexicans or colonial Teotihuacanos. Tikal's intense Teotihuacán ties were already waning by this time, and Becán's Mexican connection must have been even more indirect.

Early Classic developments in northern Yucatan were varied.[32] Acanceh, Aké, Izamal, Yaxuná, and a few other towns undertook public works projects during the first centuries of the period, but Dzibilchaltún, already in decline in the Late Preclassic period, was abandoned. Renewed public construction at Dzibilchaltún in the fifth century heralds a general period of revival and renewed external ties in the north. After 9.2.0.0.0 (A.D. 475) Oxkintok and other northern cities were erecting stelae and carving

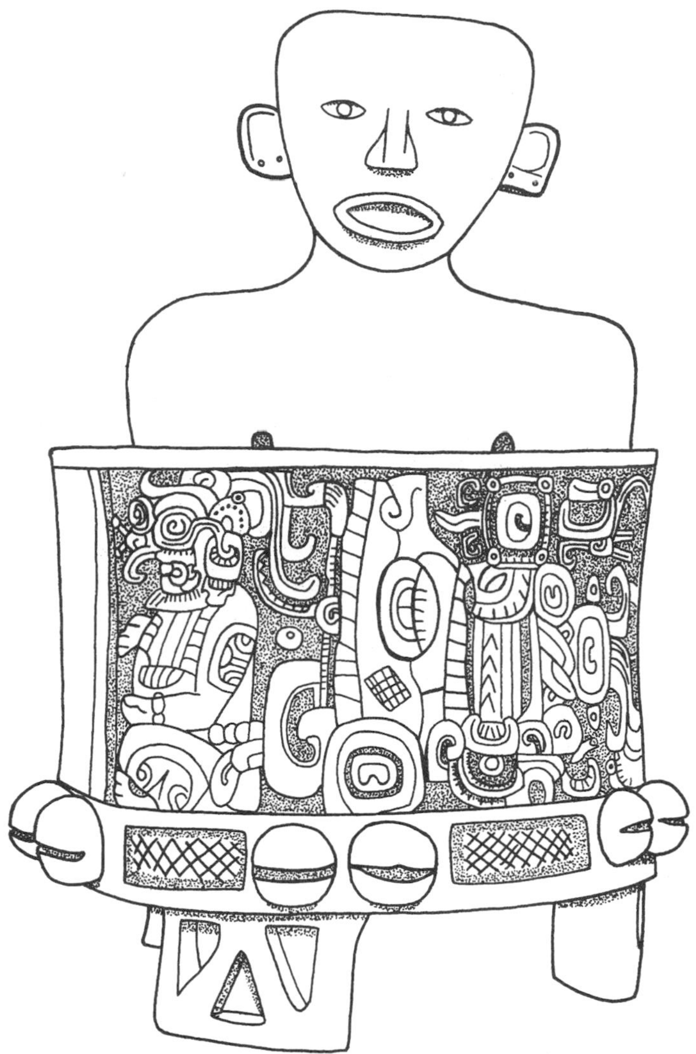

FIG. 6-16. Tripod vase and figurine, Becán. These objects were part of a cache placed in the rubble of an Early Classic building on the occasion of a major remodeling operation. The vase is Maya. Its carved design, filled in with red pigment, represents Chac, the Maya rain god, seated before the open mouth of a monstrous reptilian creature. The ceramic statuette, found seated within the vase, is in the Teotihuacán style. It is hollow, and the front and back are separate pieces. Within it were ten smaller, solid-pottery figurines, including a Central Mexican "Tlaloc" figure, three Teotihuacán warriors, and what seem to be emblems of Mexican military orders, along with four non-Teotihuacán warrior figures. The new structure erected over the ruins containing the cache seems to have been built in the distinctive *talud-tablero* style, typical of Teotihuacán platforms (see Fig. 6-17). Adapted from Ball 1974b:cover ill.

hieroglyphic inscriptions, and the spread of the stela complex continued during the rest of the Early Classic period, with no indication of an episode of slackened growth. Pottery-making traditions were even more diverse than their Preclassic ancestors; some complexes echo southern stylistic features, and some centers imported luxury pottery from the southern lowlands. Salt, extracted along the coast, was probably the principal export. Scattered Mexican pottery shapes and design features indicate that sporadic and very indirect interaction with the Teotihuacán world was the norm, although a Teotihuacán-style mural at Xelhá suggests a closer relationship, perhaps via a maritime connection with one of Teotihuacán's outposts on the Gulf Coast. Cobá and other towns in the northeast dedicated their first monuments during the sixth century.[33]

The Highlands

A disastrous eruption of the volcano Ilopango about A.D. 250 produced widespread ruin in the highlands and piedmont.[34] Settlement patterns and trade networks underwent radical shifts, particularly in the east (although Quelepa, far to the east, was apparently beyond the zone of direct impact). Chalchuapa and many smaller centers were abandoned, and many surviving communities suffered drastic population declines. Kaminaljuyú, still the major highland Maya town, survived with reduced influence. Civic constructions were much more modest than those of the Late Preclassic period, and Kaminaljuyú produced no new monumental art. Pottery represents a development of the local Late Preclassic stylistic tradition. Some features shared with the lowland Tzakol style reflect continuing trade relations.

Beginning in the fifth century, Kaminaljuyú enjoyed a period of renewed growth as it became closely involved with the Teotihuacán world. At the same time, lowland-style polychromes mark intensified contacts with the rest of the Maya world to the north. The southern fringe of the Maya world contracted in this period as the piedmont and coastal zone became part of the Teotihuacán interaction sphere, stretching from Veracruz south and east through the Intermediate Zone. Cacao was a major product along much of the Pacific coast and piedmont in later periods, and access to prime cacao production areas may have provided much of the attraction for the highland city. Disruption in the aftermath of the Ilopango disaster probably paved the way for this Teotihuacán expansion.

Eastern communities, nearer the volcano, rebounded more slowly. Traditional ties with other highland regions to the west were broken, and new trade networks linked the eastern highlands with the southeastern fringe of the Maya lowlands. A village that emerged at Cerén, in the Zapotitlán Valley, not long before A.D. 600 may have been one of the earliest communities to reappear in the area east of Ilopango.[35] Another, much more localized, volcanic eruption entombed Cerén beneath a deep ash deposit after only a century or so. The remarkable preservation of houses and outbuildings with all their domestic paraphernalia, along with garden plots and outlying fields, provides unparalleled insights into village life. Maize, maguey, cacao, and a variety of other plants were cultivated; mature cobs were found on doubled-over stalks awaiting harvest, indicating that the eruption occurred late in the growing season, probably in August. Households consisted of special-purpose structures: living/sleeping buildings, kitchens, and storerooms. Even the least elaborate of these households was prosperous, having more than seventy-five pottery vessels. Imports included obsidian, jade, and hard stone for axes (from the north) as well as seashells and salt (from the Pacific Coast). Special facilities that probably served multiple households, perhaps the entire community, include a steam bath, what may have been a shaman's house, and a building large enough to accommodate dozens of villagers for community events.

Kaminaljuyú's connection with Teotihuacán began as an exchange relationship, probably indirect, marked by the appearance of central Mexican obsidian and a few other Mexican imports in aristocratic burials. Late in the fifth century, Teotihuacán-style tomb offerings became more popular, and public buildings began to incorporate elements of Teotihuacán's distinctive architectural style. Teotihuacán's influence on Kaminaljuyú peaked early in the sixth century, as a series of new public building complexes in a thoroughly Teotihuacán style transformed the center. Even the construction techniques and materials followed Teotihuacán norms, foreign to the local architectural tradition (Fig. 6-17). Tombs in these buildings were richly stocked with Teotihuacán-style pottery and central Mexican imports (Fig. 6-18). The Teotihuacán presence was quite localized in these building complexes at Kaminaljuyú. They must have housed enclaves of foreigners, probably noble merchants from one of Teotihuacán's eastern provinces. Other parts of the town reflect the local Maya tradition. Outside Kaminaljuyú, Teotihuacán architectural elements are quite rare. As the economic center of the Maya highlands, Kaminaljuyú was an ideal staging point for foreigners seeking obsidian (especially from nearby El Chayal), jade (from the Motagua Valley), and other highland products. Here they could also establish contact with Kaminaljuyú's lowland trading partners. The lords of Teotihuacán reinforced the relationship by fostering a small Maya enclave within their own city.

By the late sixth century, the Teotihuacán presence at Kaminaljuyú was on the wane. Teotihuacán architectural and pottery styles had a lasting impact on the tastes of the Maya aristocracy and on local craft production, but Teotihuacán elements would play a progressively reduced role within the overall

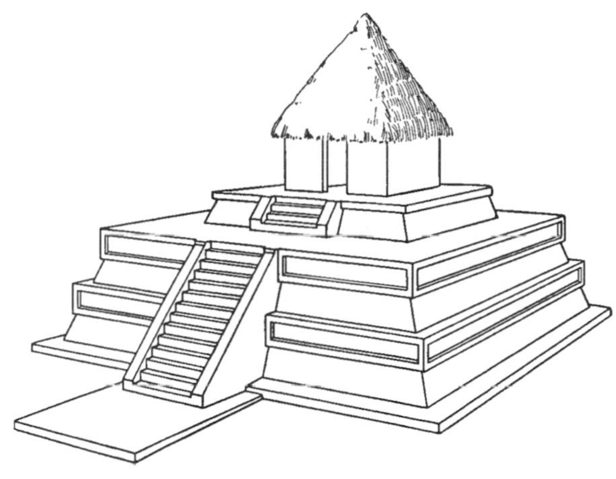

FIG. 6-17. Structure A-7, Kaminaljuyú. The construction of this temple platform represents a massive enlargement of the structure that preceded it. A tomb chamber in front of the stair (A-V), containing the body of an Early Classic noble interred with his jade and shell finery, may have provided the occasion for the remodeling. Each terrace of the platform consists of a sloping lower section (*talud*) surmounted by a vertical, inset panel framed by a projecting molding (*tablero*). This platform design is typical of the architecture of Teotihuacán. The reconstruction of the temple building atop the platform is conjectural; only the holes of the cornerposts survive. Adapted from Kidder et al. 1946:fig. 108.

FIG. 6-18. Tripod vase, Kaminaljuyú. This vessel was one of a pair included among the funerary offerings placed with the body of the noble in a tomb chamber (B-I) beneath the stairway of a Teotihuacán-style temple platform (B-4; similar to Structure A-7, Fig. 6-17). The design, representing a Teotihuacán warrior, is executed in red, green, and black paint on a thin stucco coating over the black fabric of the pottery. This vase may be an import from central Mexico rather than a local copy in the Teotihuacán style. Adapted from Kidder et al. 1946:fig. 174d.

highland Maya tradition. Local styles were universal again by the mid seventh century.

The fluid Maya-Zoque frontier in the western highlands stabilized during the Early Classic period, as the distribution of Maya peoples took on the basic contours that would persist until the conquest.[36] Chiapa de Corzo and other far western towns in the central depression of Chiapas drifted away from the Maya world before the end of the Late Preclassic period. In the western highlands, Early Classic pottery reflects fully Maya styles for the first time, although the Tzakol style did not penetrate this far west. Local traditions of pottery production and decoration represent another regional style that evolved independently from a variant of the Chicanel tradition. Populations grew and new hilltop settlements replaced valley communities. Sharp changes in craft styles may mark an influx of new peoples; if so, the Tzeltal and Tzotzil, inhabitants of the region at the time of the conquest, would be the leading candidates. The Tzeltalan branch of the Mayan language family separated from the proto-Cholan stock not long after the beginning of the Christian era. A westward expansion of Tzeltalan peoples from the southern lowlands or from an adjacent foothill region of the northern highland slopes could account for the advent of Maya pottery styles in the west. The stela complex appeared at Toniná and a few nearby centers in the sixth century.

By the sixth century, then, the basic patterns of Classic Maya civilization were firmly established. Cities with elaborate public architecture reflected powerful aristocracies with well-defined leadership roles. Stelae provided public confirmation of their power and prestige. A few lowland cities, concentrating authority and power to an unusual degree, moved toward positions of regional dominance. In the lowlands, only the west lagged behind in adopting the full pattern of Classic Maya civilization. Regional differences, sharper than before, marked distinct northern and southern lowland areas. Even sharper contrasts set the Maya highlands apart. After their early lead in the development of Maya monumental art and writing, central and eastern highland centers ceased to memorialize their leaders with stelae and hieroglyphic texts. Like Teotihuacán's expansion, this retreat may have to do with massive ruin caused by the eruption of Ilopango. Highland Maya communities did not revert to homogeneous village societies. Towns and aristocracies survived, but they no longer relied on the stela complex to celebrate the lives and works of their leaders.

MAP 9. Late Classic cities.

SEVEN

Late Classic Maya Civilization

Growth processes that began during the Preclassic period culminated in Maya civilization of the seventh and eighth centuries: one of the most splendid achievements of native America. Populations continued to expand. Cities grew larger and more powerful. The gap between aristocrats and common people widened. Nobles acquired greater political and religious authority, and wielded more power. Specialists multiplied in every field. Architecture, arts, and crafts all reached new aesthetic peaks. In writing and the intellectual sphere generally, Classic Maya sophistication was unrivaled in the Americas. The Classic period was a time of cultural florescence throughout the Maya world (Map 9).

Remarkable, almost uniform, growth and development took place throughout the Maya lowlands during the Late Classic period. Settlement systems were transformed into complex hierarchies as more communities grew into cities, smaller cities became larger, and the largest cities amassed greater power. Cities were hubs of social, religious, economic, and political activity for extensive surrounding regions. A few of the most powerful were able to translate prestige and influence into broad political power, fashioning states of regional scope. Northern cities, building on smaller, simpler Early Classic foundations, progressively came to rival their southern lowland counterparts. Ubiquitous stelae and hieroglyphic texts testify to comparable social and political institutions throughout the lowlands. Aristocrats took on new managerial roles. Occupations became increasingly specialized, particularly in the realm of craft production and the building trades. Subsistence, more varied than ever, involved intensive agricultural techniques. Trade networks expanded, embracing wider areas and handling a greater volume and diversity of materials. Populations grew, becoming particularly dense in the immediate environs of powerful civic centers.

Processes leading to intensified regional differences and to increased homogeneity were at work simultaneously in the Late Classic Maya world. Shared patterns went beyond the very basic similarity in the overall way of life that had always existed within the Maya world. Settlement systems, cities, and the social order they imply had always been generally comparable. Now monumental art, the stela complex, and writing had spread throughout the lowlands. A common basic belief system sustained social and political institutions everywhere. The symbol systems used to express these concepts were so similar from region to region that they almost imply a single Maya religion.

Specific shared elements were largely confined to the aristocratic segments of lowland Maya societies. They were mainly products of interaction among the ruling groups of the several regions of the Maya world. Monumental art and hieroglyphic texts document some of the social and political ties that linked the aristocracies of various cities. Similar interchanges took place in the intellectual sphere among priests devoted to astronomical, astrological, and other esoteric investigations. Between A.D. 687 and 756, for example, inscriptions reflect the adoption of a new and uniform system of tabulating lunar periods.[1] Long-distance exchange, increasingly centralized in the hands of noble merchants and administrators, also promoted communication. The emergence of regional states with expanding spheres of influence was a powerful stimulus intensifying these connections.

On closer inspection, though, the apparent homogeneity of the Maya world dissolves into a kaleidoscopic picture of regional variations on the same set of basic themes. Late Classic Maya monumental art has stylistic coherence and stands apart from the art of other Mesoamerican peoples. At the same time, regional styles of sculpture and painting are readily apparent. No one could mistake the modeled stucco decoration from Palenque for the work of a Copán artist, nor confuse the stelae of Quiriguá and Tikal. Styles of public architecture and architectural decoration show the same pattern of diversity within a single basic tradition. Regional differences in crafts are still more pronounced. Pottery manufacture involved a tremendous array of regional styles, although symbolic scenes and designs on luxury vessels were comparable everywhere.

Demography and Settlement

Maya populations reached their greatest size and widest distribution during the seventh and eighth centuries.[2] The distribution of swampy land, variable farming conditions and communication facilities, the clustering of people around major cities, and other factors produced considerable variation in population density. All of the best areas for settlement had been occupied for hundreds of years.

The basic unit of settlement everywhere was the domestic plaza complex with three or four or more small thatched wattle-and-daub buildings (Fig. 2-3) grouped around open courtyards.[3] These one-room dwellings, each on its own low platform, correspond to the single-family dwellings of today's Maya. Each housed a couple with their unmarried children. Plaza complexes grew as sons married and established new households in adjacent buildings around the courtyard. Clusters of several domestic plazas form hamlets in rural areas and neighborhoods within larger centers. Kinship and marriage ties must have been especially strong within these communities of a hundred or a few hundred souls, and they must sometimes have corresponded roughly to lineages and other formal kin groups, although there is no solid ground for assuming that they always did so. Houses and domestic plazas larger and more elegant than the norm must be the dwellings of family and lineage heads with local political, economic,

1. Temples 5C-49 and IV at Tikal (Classic period) in the heart of the southern lowland tropical forest. Temple IV, in the background, rises 65 meters above the adjacent plaza; its terraced platform is unrestored.

2. Main mortuary temple complex (North Acropolis), Tikal (Classic period).

3. Ball court, Copán (Late Classic period). The Great Plaza with stelae celebrating Copán's kings is visible in the background.

4. Temple of the Sun, Palenque (Late Classic period).

5. Temple of the Magician, Uxmal (Terminal Classic period).

6. Temple of the Warriors, Chichén Itzá (Terminal Classic period).

7. Small temple at Tulum, on the east coast of Yucatan (Late Postclassic period).

8. Temple, Iximché (Late Postclassic period).

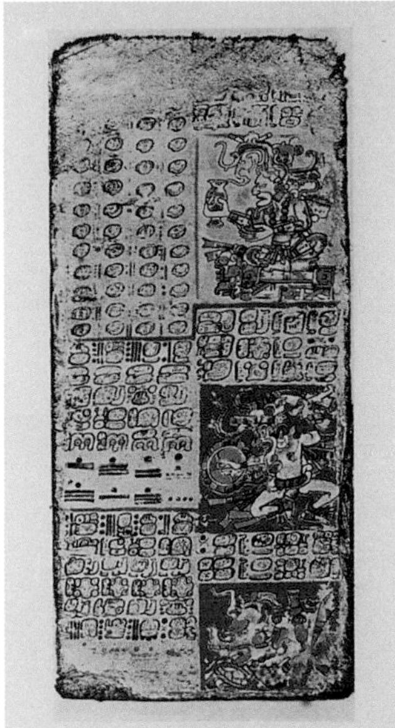
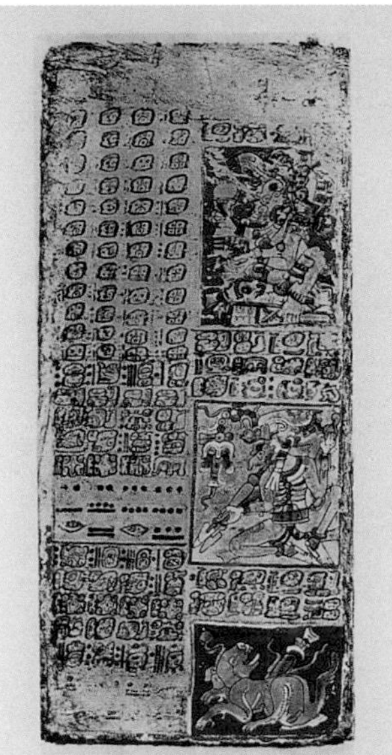
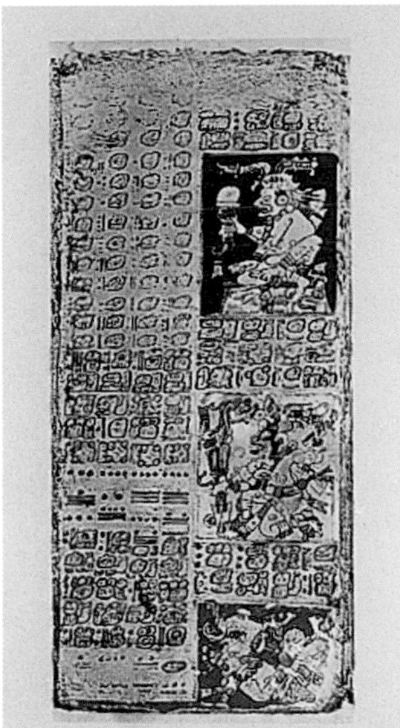
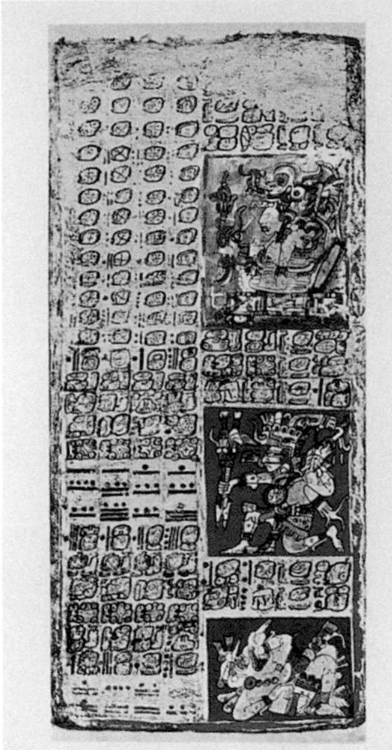
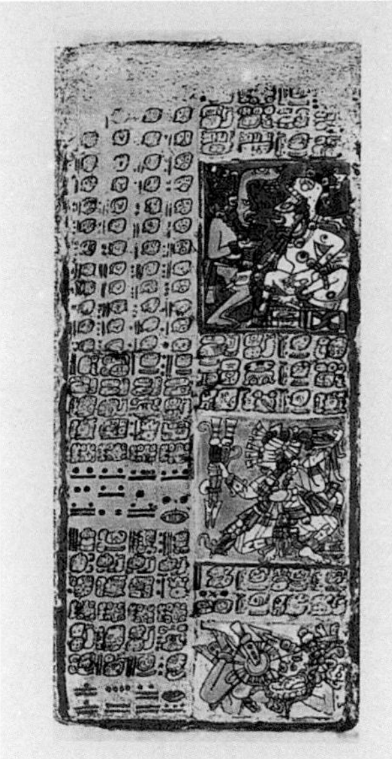

9. Astronomical table, Dresden Codex. These pages tabulate the appearances and disappearances of the planet Venus as morning and evening star and set out the associated supernatural influences on human activity. The codex was painted in Yucatan, probably in the thirteenth century.

10. Cakchiquel market at Sololá, near Lake Atitlán, Guatemala, in the Maya highlands.

11. Ancient sculpture with modern offerings of candles, flowers, and *aguardiente* (cane liquor), El Baúl, Guatemala. The head (Monument 3), carved in the Cotzumalhuapa style of the Late Classic period, is known as "Dios Mundo" to the Maya who propitiate him as a supernatural being in control of everything that happens here on earth. Participants in the cult of Dios Mundo come from the highlands to work on the surrounding cane plantation; they are not the direct descendants of this sculpture's creators, whose understanding of its significance is unknown.

and religious leadership roles. Minor civic structures—small temples and aristocratic residences—were focal points for smaller communities. They reflect the more formal minor offices of administrative systems. Even in outlying areas, these minor civic complexes were usually subordinate to larger ones. At the apexes of these hierarchies were such great regional capitals as Tikal.

Calculating actual population sizes and densities is a very inexact project at best. Even gross estimates, though, help us to understand Maya society and economy. Estimating ancient Maya populations requires (1) an accurate count of houses in the area under study, (2) precise dating to determine how many were occupied simultaneously during the period of interest, and (3) a reliable indication of the number of people who lived in each house. The third factor is the most difficult, for even the most intense archaeological investigations seldom produce evidence for such a precise reconstruction. The usual solution is to resort to census information gathered in Maya communities early in the colonial period. Estimating the first two factors accurately presupposes very extensive archaeological investigation. Domestic buildings are the least conspicuous Maya structures, and only an intensive search will produce a reliable count. Only excavation can distinguish with certainty between residences and small structures having other functions. Determining contemporaneity is even more difficult, requiring a very fine-scale chronological framework and good samples of datable objects (usually pottery) from each house. Only specially designed investigations will provide these data. In the Maya world, where impressive public buildings have consumed so much attention, a great deal of work remains to be done on dwellings.

In the southern lowlands, the best data for population estimates come from Tikal, one of the largest and most thoroughly investigated Maya cities.[4] Yet even here only a sample of the many thousands of structures could be excavated. Unlike that in most lowland cities, where settlement thins out gradually away from the civic nucleus, house density at Tikal drops off sharply beyond the bank-and-ditch constructions that define the basic residential community on the north and south. Excavation of more than two hundred small buildings showed that 80 percent were houses dating to the eighth and early ninth centuries, the period of Tikal's greatest florescence. Because most houses had been remodeled, they appear to have been occupied continuously during most of this time span. Some were surely occupied for shorter periods, but inconspicuous and destroyed houses missed by the survey should compensate in part for this error. When these figures are extrapolated to the center as a whole and multiplied by a factor of five (a rough average of the number of people per family during the early colonial period), one comes up with about 10,000 people in central Tikal alone. This figure makes no allowance for the occupants of palaces and other large buildings. Estimates of the population of the community within the bank and ditch run as high as 50,000. "Greater Tikal," including the surrounding region under the center's direct influence, must have embraced many thousands more who came often to the civic center for markets, social events, and ceremonies. However imprecise these estimates may be, they decisively eliminate the possibility that Tikal was a sparsely populated "ceremonial" center.

Tikal, if not the largest of all Maya cities, was certainly among the most populous. Even at its peak it remained relatively open, without the extreme density of structures and people usually associated with such urban centers as Teotihuacán. Still, at Tikal and the other great Maya cities, daily life and social relations must have had something of an urban flavor. Certainly Maya centers performed all the civic functions of central places.

Copán is near the other end of the size range for major Maya cities. The civic core of the city housed the royal family, their retainers, and a modest number of lower-status aristocrats. Other aristocratic extended families and their retainers occupied nearby suburban complexes, especially in the Sepulturas zone. The bulk of the population (ordinary farmers) lived in homesteads on the surrounding slopes and scattered throughout the valley. The overall population of the Copán valley probably reached its peak—roughly 25,000—in the eighth century.[5]

Subsistence

The concentration of even 10,000 people in a single city indicates that subsistence was diverse and involved intensive agriculture.[6] Basic milpa farming was the cornerstone of Classic Maya subsistence, and maize was a mainstay of the diet, but this could not have been the only farming system. Estimates of the productivity of prehistoric maize farming are far less reliable even than population estimates. Changes in climate, soils, and the plants themselves mean that estimates of prehistoric yields of maize per hectare are sheer guesswork. It is also difficult to determine the amount of land each community used for maize farming. Today Maya farmers often cultivate milpas many kilometers from their homes. It is impossible to know how far Classic Maya farmers were willing to travel to reach their fields, although ethnographic studies suggest that most farmers would probably have cultivated fields within 5 kilometers of their dwellings.[7]

Scanty direct evidence in the form of occasionally preserved plant remains, along with indirect indications provided by historical documents and ethnographic studies, do suggest some of the subsistence strategies that complemented milpa farming. In the first place, maize was never the sole crop. Milpas typically include beans, squashes, chiles, and other plants. Garden plots and wild plants added a tremendous variety of fruits, vegetables, and spices, not to mention medicinal herbs. Most of these plant products are not potential staples, but a few are. Manioc, sweet potatoes, and other root crops known to later Maya peoples produce higher yields than maize, although they are low in protein. Animal food was a relatively minor component of the Maya diet, but along the rivers and coasts fish and shellfish were heavily exploited. In some areas, the Maya may even have dug special canals to serve as fisheries. Where marine foods provided a ready source of protein, root crops could have been important foods. Manioc is mainly a lowland crop, but it can be grown as high as 2,000 meters. In the eastern lowlands manioc was certainly eaten, and probably cultivated, beginning early in the Preclassic period.

The *ramón* or breadnut tree, growing wild today in many parts of the lowlands, is another potential prehistoric staple. Recent Maya peoples have used ramón trees as a source of emergency food in times of famine. Ramón nuts, high in vegetable protein and fat, can be processed, like maize, into a nutritious flour. Ramón nuts also store quite well. Experiments conducted in prehistoric *chultunes*, the bell-shaped underground chambers found in many Maya sites, show that ramón nuts stored in them will last up to eighteen months, while maize rots within a few weeks. Ramón trees can produce much more food than maize (more than 1,100 kilograms per hectare), and with much less human effort. The trees require little or no cultivation. They are more reliable than maize, and will produce some nuts even in very dry years. Ramón trees continue to produce for decades, so that an orchard might provide a continuous source of food for a century or more without a single fallow period. Ramón trees need not even have been planted. Allowed to proliferate in fields, around houses, or in open areas within urban centers, they could provide a significant dietary supplement. Ramón trees—along with a variety of fruit- and fiber-producing trees, *balché* trees (whose bark is the source of a fermented ceremonial beverage), and *pom* trees (whose resin is used for incense)—represented a significant component of Maya economies. Even in very dry northern environments, localized pockets of soil and moisture can support economically important trees. Aristocrats probably owned, or at least controlled, most trees of economic value and almost all of those with ceremonial importance.

Strategies for intensified food production varied with environmental circumstances. Seasonal cultivation of sinkholes (mainly in the north) and swampy areas (mainly in the south) was the simplest available technique and probably the most widespread response. In areas with substantial sloping land—in the highlands and in such lowland regions as the Maya Mountains and the Pasión—terracing offered a somewhat more expensive strategy. Terracing was not a major strategy everywhere, however, even when the topography was suitable; farmers in the hilly Puuc region constructed only occasional terraces to collect soils at the bases of slopes. Wetland cultivation systems, much more expensive in terms of capital investment and maintenance, nonetheless probably expanded substantially in those parts of the lowlands where environmental conditions were suitable, particularly in the river systems and swamps along the northern edge of the southern lowlands. In many seasonally inundated areas—the Pasión region, for example—the water table fluctuates too much to permit effective wetland farming.[8]

Within cities, sophisticated water management systems involved carefully planned architectural drainage, channel construction, and modification of land surfaces to ensure that rainy season runoff found its way into reservoirs for storage and use during dry periods. Some of these systems may have served to channel water to cultivated plots, both within and beyond urban areas.[9]

Large cities may have imported food from less densely populated regions. The coastal towns probably exported their nearly inexhaustible supply of fish and shellfish. The widespread exchange networks that crisscrossed the Maya world might have distributed food as routinely as they did imperishable commodities. Certainly they must have functioned sporadically to transfer local surpluses to areas where crop failure or population growth had produced food shortages.

It is very unlikely that the population of the Maya world at large ever approached the limits of these societies' productive capacities, but it is possible that subsistence systems were near their limits in the most densely populated zones. Along with accelerating land clearance for farming, large-scale timber cutting to provide wood for construction and fuel—for burning limestone to produce the huge quantities of lime plaster required by the building programs as well as for everyday cooking and heating—must have led to deforestation and erosion in many areas. Faced with an endemic strain on normal subsistence strategies and with increasingly frequent food shortages, some aristocracies may have chosen counterproductive responses. Shortened fallow cycles would provide immediate relief at the expense of long-term environmental degradation, as soil nutrients were exhausted and erosion intensified. Increased labor input could have raised productivity, but only at the cost of greater strain between peasant and ruler. Even if they avoided these traps, the Late Classic leaders of some lowland cities must have presided over societies with very fragile subsistence economies. The largest cities were quite vulnerable to the vagaries of weather and to a host of other disruptive elements. Food shortages probably contributed to the decline that affected so many Maya states at the end of the Late Classic period.

Economy, Society, Politics

The economies of the great cities and of the regions they dominated must have been as intricate as their subsistence systems.[10] The quality and standardization of craft products, especially pottery, suggest that economic specialization was well developed (Fig. 7-1). Although the evidence is less conclusive, larger cities could probably also boast specialists in stone flaking and grinding, lapidaries, jewelers, weavers, tailors, tanners, feather workers, woodcarvers, painters, sculptors in stone and plaster, carpenters, masons, and other building-trade specialists. Some neighborhoods or outlying satellite communities probably housed concentrations of specialists in the same activity, resulting in a form of community specialization. Most people in every region were full-time farmers, and many craft specialists must have maintained some involvement in farming. Most households also produced at least some of their own stone tools, mainly simple ones made from local raw materials. Other basic tools were centrally produced and widely distributed, as in the case of chert tools from Colha. More specialized obsidian and chert tools—such as those used by craft specialists like woodcarvers and shell-jewelry makers—were made locally from imported raw materials.[11] Makers of luxury goods and other craftsmen most closely involved in the activities of the aristocracy sometimes maintained large dwellings in or near the public sectors of the great cities, suggesting an elevated socioeconomic status.

If craft specialization typified an emergent "middle class," other specialist roles were the province of the upper levels of Maya society.[12] Aristocrats monopolized positions of authority and power and those requiring extensive mastery of esoteric knowledge. Political, religious, and economic organization were inextricably intertwined, with aristocracies providing the key personnel. The highest-ranking members of the most noble families filled the top positions in the rulership and priesthood. Cadet lines and lesser aristocratic families produced lower-ranking priests and religious functionaries, scribes, long-distance merchants, architect-engineers, minor military officers, and a variety of political and economic administrators. The lower echelons of the aristocracy probably included many part-time farmers and craftsmen.

It is unlikely that these social groups were rigidly bounded classes. Relative status and power within the aristocracy fluctuated as old noble families lost influence and new ruling dynasties emerged. Mechanisms of social mobility probably permitted advancement from group to group as well. Although social gaps widened throughout the Classic period, with great differences between ordinary farmers and high-ranking nobles, there is no reason to suppose that the system was ever closed or inflexible.

Institutions like the modern *cargo* system could have been important in social integration.[13] Cargo systems consist of sets of ranked religious and civil offices (cargos) held by adult males. Because the national governments of today dominate the political life of most Maya communities, the religious cargos are more prominent. In Zinacantán, a Tzotzil community in the western highlands, the cargo system is a central feature of social and religious life. A cargo holder must leave his home in the countryside to live in the ceremonial center of the community for his period of service. He must pay for his own subsistence, for hospitality, and for ceremonial materials. Full participation in the system—a year at each of the four levels of the hierarchy—is very expensive indeed in lost income and direct expenses. Not every Zinacanteco can afford (or wishes) to conform to the ideal. For those who do, though, the rewards in personal fulfillment and social prestige are great. A cargo holder enjoys great prestige and much attention during his term of office, and a man who completes all four cargos becomes an honored community elder. In Zinacantán the cargo system provides a successful organizational framework for the religious life of a community of more than 8,000 Maya dispersed throughout an area of more than 100 square kilometers. The cargo system of neighboring Chamula successfully serves more than 40,000 people. These systems are not simply remnants of ancient institutions. They are also responses to contemporary social conditions. Zinacantán's cargo system is much more elaborate today than it was a century ago, and modern Zinacantecos are much more eager to participate than were their great-grandfathers. Although today's cargo systems owe something to Spanish religious institutions, they also have roots in precolumbian Mesoamerica.

Comparable prehispanic institutions might have functioned to distribute minor offices far down the social scale and to allow people who normally lived in outlying areas to participate directly in the political and religious affairs of civic centers. Families whose members performed these offices exceptionally well, or who used these periodic sojourns in the centers of status and power to forge lasting alliances, might over the course of a few generations rise to the lower echelons of the aristocracy.

Success in commerce and exceptional military achievement were other potential routes to permanently elevated status, and both mechanisms operated among the Quiché at the time of the conquest. The Aztecs had institutionalized such mechanisms of social advancement: several important political offices were reserved for commoners elevated to noble rank because of notable performance on the field of battle.

At the apex of the social order, all public activities merged in the person of the ruler. Stelae and other monuments in the great cities depict rulers in religious, political, and military roles. There is no question of their economic ascendancy. The distribution of minor palaces and temples defines administrative subdivisions within cities, reflecting an internal hierarchy of political and religious offices. To judge by the settlement patterns of surrounding territories, regional bureaucracies were equally complex. Several levels of subordinate centers with public buildings served as hubs of civic affairs for outlying villages, hamlets, and farmsteads. Whatever the extent of nonaristocratic participation at lower levels, the direction of political and religious activity was firmly in the hands of the aristocracy. Long-distance commerce, largely concerned with procuring luxury goods, was another essential aspect of public activity. Nobles organized and controlled this trade.

Ultimately the aristocracy dominated the entire economy. Merchants may have delivered imported food and utilitarian goods, along with luxury imports, to the ruler, who then saw to their distribution. Much craft production was directly geared to consumption by the aristocracy, and many other specialists were concerned with public activity. Nobles and craft specialists alike depended on farmers, and rulers must have collected and distributed food surpluses. On occasion, political leaders must have extended their influence into the sphere of agricultural and craft production, particularly during the Late Classic period. With increased specialization, administrative intervention was probably necessary sometimes to avoid the collapse of fragile economic systems in the face of crop failure or problems with the supply of raw materials. There is no reason to suppose that economic transactions among social groups were like those in a monetary economy. It is quite conceivable that officials routinely collected the bulk of all production—food, utilitarian craft goods, and luxury items alike—for redistribution. Undoubtedly farmers and craftsmen exchanged some of their surplus products directly at local and regional markets, but here too the aristocracy would have had a supervisory role, at least in maintaining order. Perhaps, as in Aztec markets, there were also officials to regulate weights and measures and to standardize exchange rates. Classic Maya economies involved a balance of market and redistributive features, and political officials and other aristocrats surely exercised considerable influence, but there is little evidence of strong centralized control. Evidence on the production and distribution of pottery and stone tools suggests a considerable degree of decentralization.[14]

Religion, too, was intimately bound up with politics. Rulers were political officials, but they were also religious figures. Monumental art and architecture, above all the stela complex, presented public statements of the divine sanction that was the basis of political sovereignty.[15] Elite ancestor cults were part of the same belief system: along with high priestly roles, rulers had godlike personal qualities stemming from divine ancestry (Figs. 6-4, 6-13, 7-12, 7-18–7-20, 7-24, 7-26, 7-39).

Religion influenced political activity in other ways as well. Maya belief systems universally feature a unitary conception of time and the universe in which supernatural elements have direct roles in current events. Because time determines these influences, they are cyclical and predictable. Astrology was the chief science, embracing religion, astronomy, history, and prophecy. The calendar system lent meaning and order to every facet of life.

Archaeological investigations, which are focused on a few of the largest cities, do not provide a comprehensive picture of the Maya world. Even without archaeological documentation of the full range of cities, towns, villages, and hamlets that made up each region, however, basic patterns of economic organization and interaction can be reconstructed. Hieroglyphic texts can provide clues—admittedly difficult to interpret—about social and political relationships among the communities that formed the regional hierarchies and about relations between regional systems. At the local level, Maya societies were highly integrated, and the key personnel of the political, religious, and economic systems were recruited from the upper echelons of the social hierarchy. Connections among aristocracies also produced the most important links among communities and regions. Tikal and a few other very powerful cities held sway over political systems of regional scope, but there was never a single state that embraced all of the Maya world. Economic networks that distributed luxury goods and exotic raw materials are only the most obvious mechanisms that connected the regions of the Maya world into a larger sphere. The single system of calendar notation and hieroglyphic writing in use at all cities indicates continuing communication throughout the lowlands during the Classic period.

Farmers and craftsmen must occasionally have undertaken to procure special foods or raw materials from distant regions on an ad hoc basis. In general, though, most ties between communities, especially over long distances, involved nobles. Communication among aristocracies, essential to the continued functioning of many aspects of Maya civilization, was in many ways institutionalized. Enclaves of Mayas living away from their home communities in other parts of the Maya world, and even beyond, must have been as common in the Classic period as they were in later times. Some were probably established quite purposefully by ruling groups; others were not. These enclaves—whether of nobles forging alliances, merchants procuring exotic goods, craftsmen tapping distant markets, or farmers taking advantage of different environmental conditions—contributed to communication at every level, from local to interregional. Kinship ties and political alliances between noble families of different cities played key roles in the emergence of regional political systems, and they often linked the cities of distant regions. These ties were especially intense within the southern lowlands, where monuments and burial offerings frequently record intermarriage, formal or ceremonial visits, and other sorts of interchange among aristocracies.[16]

A polychrome vessel found in the richly stocked eighth-century tomb of a noblewoman at Altar de

Sacrificios (Fig. 7-1) provides vivid documentation. The painted scene records important aspects of the beliefs and ceremonies that surrounded the death of an aristocrat, and it may depict the lady's actual funeral rites. The hieroglyphic text, which refers to Tikal, Yaxchilán, and at least one other city, seems to identify participants—whether they are meant to represent noble emissaries taking part in a historical event or deities in the underworld—with these places. Other offerings in the tomb included pottery imported from the Yaxchilán–Piedras Negras zone, from the Tikal area, and from the Chamá region of the highlands.

The cultural decline that swept across the Maya world in the ninth and tenth centuries also reflects the close connections among Maya centers and the extent to which aristocracies depended on them.[17] In the southern lowlands, foreign interference in communication networks touched off a process of decline that eventually brought about the collapse of every major city. To the north and south, societies were better able to deal with these pressures, and the processes of decline were less drastic.

Regionalism

Comparable cities, widespread styles of monumental art and craft production, the stela complex, hieroglyphic writing, and the Long Count calendar give Classic Maya civilization an air of overall uniformity. Beneath this veneer is a wealth of regional diversity. Subdivisions of the Maya world—southern lowlands, northern lowlands, and highlands—reflect real spheres of interaction. Similarities are certainly paramount within each of these areas, but none is uniform, and many lines of communication crossed area "boundaries" to link distant cities.

THE SOUTHERN LOWLANDS

Early investigations in the heart of the lowlands laid the foundations of Maya archaeology. Indeed, the styles, institutions, and organizational features of Tikal and Uaxactún have often been treated as the basic cultural patterns of the southern lowlands, and even of "true" Classic Maya civilization in general.

Late Classic pottery (Fig. 7-1) represents a widespread regional style shared throughout the southern lowlands and beyond.[18] In part, its spread may reflect Tikal's enormous social, political, and economic influence. Tepeu pottery is by no means uniform, though; there is no "standard" Late Classic Maya pottery style.

Tikal (Map 9, Fig. 7-2), one of the largest cities in the southern lowlands in the seventh and eighth centuries, was among the most powerful as well.[19] Civic activity at Tikal in the Late Classic period, and for a millennium before that, revolved around the Great Plaza, flanked by the city's mightiest temples and most elegant palaces (Figs. 7-3–7-8, 7-10, Color Plate 2). The architectural grandeur of the Great Plaza and the symbolic messages communicated by its buildings, sculpture, and texts were largely the result of a building program begun early in the eighth century during the reign of Ah Cacao.[20]

To the east, Temple I (also called the Temple of the Giant Jaguar) soars to a height of more than 45 meters (Fig. 7-3). Nine superimposed terraces form the steep pyramid that supports the temple, reached by a single majestic stair. The intricate insets and moldings of the terraces form a field for the play of light and shadow. The temple building has three high, narrow, vaulted rooms with carved wooden lintels spanning the inner doorways. The innermost lintel depicts a huge jaguar, perhaps a divine protector of Ah Cacao and the royal family, towering over the enthroned ruler; the associated hieroglyphic text records Ah Cacao's parentage and his accession to rule in A.D. 682, and may refer to the defeat of the great city of Calakmul to the north.[21] The hollow "roof comb" atop the temple had an ornamental function, leading the eye upward from the line of the stair and

FIG. 7-1. Design on a polychrome vase, Altar de Sacrificios. This scene, painted in black and several shades of red over a creamy brown slip, records some of the beliefs and ritual associated with the death of a middle-aged noblewoman. The cylindrical vase was found with the body of a younger woman, evidently a relative, who was buried with her. One interpretation treats the scene as a depiction of the funeral ceremonies themselves and identifies the figure at the lower left—shown in the act of committing suicide with a large flint knife—with the younger tomb occupant, who was in fact buried with such an implement. The glyphs seem to identify some of the figures with particular cities, including nearby Dos Pilas and Yaxchilán. The fifteen imported vessels found in the tomb— from the middle Usumacinta, the central lowlands, and the Chamá region— would have been brought or sent by foreign lords from those regions, showing the importance of the kinship networks that linked aristocrats from widely separated centers. Many Late Classic polychrome vessels were made expressly as mortuary offerings, and they often depict funerary rites and underworld deities without representing any identifiable historical individuals. An alternative interpretation of the Altar vase, identifying all of the figures as supernaturals, is equally plausible. Adapted from R. E. W. Adams 1971:frontispiece; R. E. W. Adams 1977a:figs. 1–3; and G. Stuart 1975:774–76.

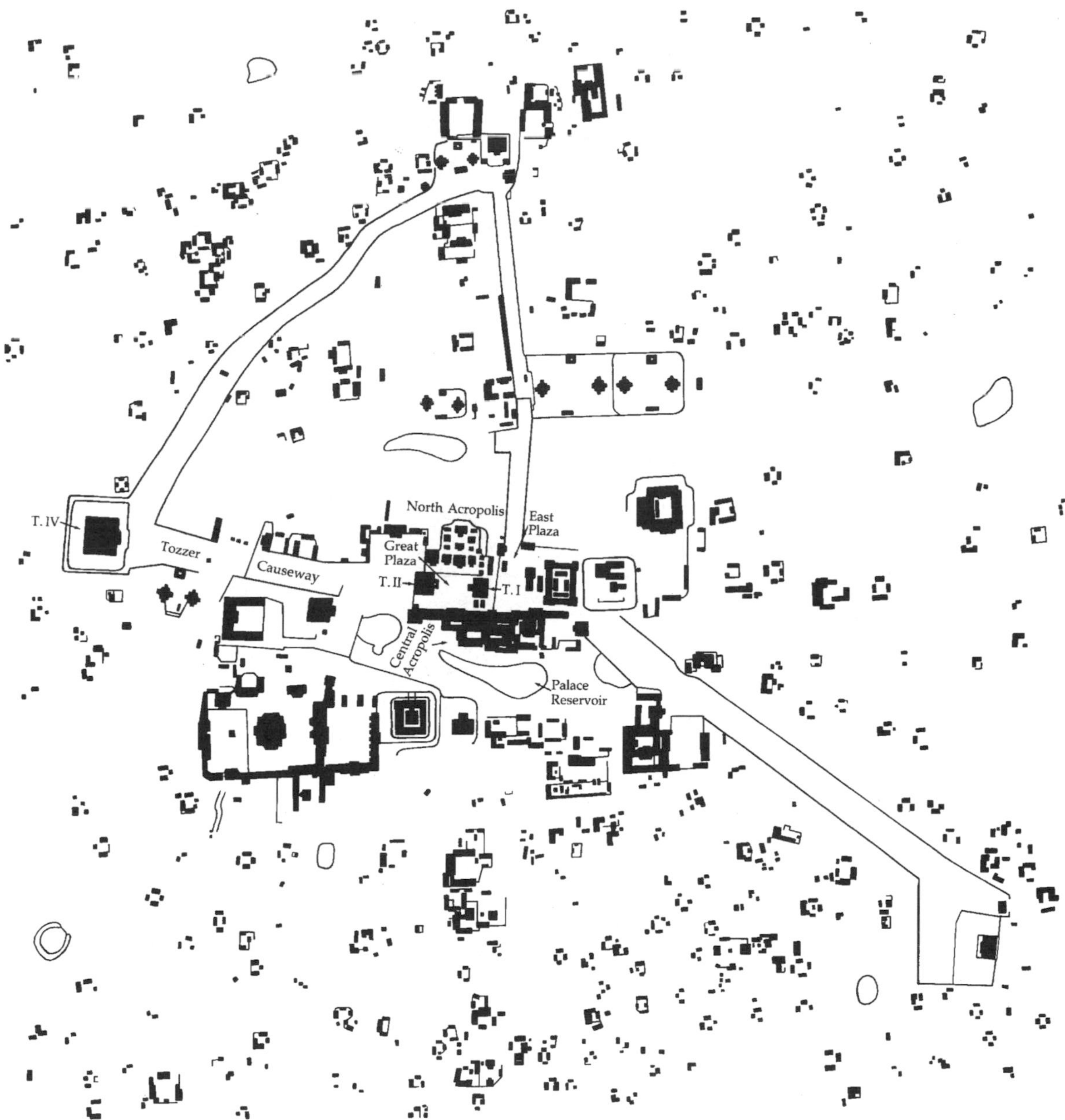

FIG. 7-2. Plan of central Tikal. The area shown is slightly more than 2 kilometers on a side. Adapted from Carr and Hazard 1961.

FIG. 7-3. Temple I, Tikal.

FIG. 7-4. Ball court, Great Plaza, Tikal. The foot of Temple I appears in the background, just beyond the open end of the ball court.

providing an additional field for decoration. The face of the roof comb, now badly eroded, once portrayed a huge seated lord, probably Ah Cacao himself, flanked by scrolls, brightly painted in cream, red, and perhaps blue and green. The temple itself, like others at Tikal, may also have been painted red. A tomb chamber dug into the bedrock beneath the pyramid contained the mortal remains of Ah Cacao, laid to rest clothed in royal finery, adorned with jade jewelry, and accompanied by an array of elaborately painted pottery, seashells, pearls, carved bones, mosaic-jade portrait vases, and other finely crafted offerings. A small open-ended ball court, without markers, stands at the foot of the temple (Fig. 7-4).

Temple II (the Temple of the Masks), lower but equally well proportioned, faces the Temple of the Giant Jaguar across the Great Plaza (Fig. 7-5). Elaborate masks, now mostly destroyed, once flanked the central stairway. The temple building, like its opposite number, has three vaulted rooms, and the wooden lintel over the middle door is carved with the portrait of a noblewoman, presumably a relative of Ah Cacao. Temple II's decorative roof comb depicts a huge face. On special occasions priests or lords must have come out of the temple onto the great stone platform jutting from the stairway to review activities in the plaza below, to address the populace, or to perform ceremonies in full view of the crowd assembled there.

FIG. 7-5. Temple II, Tikal. Temples III and IV are visible in the background.

The North Acropolis, a huge complex of temple buildings, closes off the north side of the Great Plaza (Color Plate 2, Fig. 7-6). Stelae and altars set before the temples and along the north edge of the plaza record the exploits of Tikal's great rulers (Fig. 7-10). Many of Ah Cacao's predecessors were entombed within the temple platforms. One of the most ambitious building projects of Ah Cacao's reign was the remodeling of the central temple (Fig. 7-6), the mortuary temple dedicated to Stormy Sky;[22] already enhanced once during the Early Classic period, Temple 33 was now massively enlarged with a design very much like that of Temple I. Stela 31 (Fig. 6-13), celebrating Stormy Sky's accession in A.D. 426, was moved from its original location, probably in front of Temple 33, to the rear room of the temple, above Stormy Sky's tomb. There the monument, its base broken away, was reset; after elaborate ceremonies which left the stela burned at the base and surrounded by broken incense burners, the room was carefully packed with fill and the new building was built over it. Stormy Sky's accession had taken place precisely thirteen katuns before Ah Cacao's, presumably by the latter's design; evidently, Ah Cacao wished to assert his connection to the earlier lord in unmistakable public fashion with an immense architectural marker. Fragments of many earlier monuments dating to the late sixth and seventh centuries were incorporated into the fill of the new Temple 33. This apparent episode of destruction—some of the monuments were deliberately broken—probably relates to other facets of Ah Cacao's use of the past.

The Central Acropolis (Fig. 7-7), an immense building group south of the Great Plaza, is Tikal's greatest palace complex. At its peak it consisted of a series of long, multiroomed buildings up to three stories high, grouped around six courts connected by stairways and passages (Fig. 7-8). The buildings had elaborate carved decoration, and room interiors

FIG. 7-6. Structure 5D-33, North Acropolis, Tikal. This temple, at the center of the North Acropolis cluster facing onto the Great Plaza, was remodeled several times. Built as a mortuary temple for Stormy Sky, it was enlarged in the seventh century by Ah Cacao, who evidently wished to connect himself with his Early Classic predecessor. The stairway at the right represents Ah Cacao's construction, which was mostly dismantled during excavation in order to reveal parts of the Early Classic building, including the stairs to the left and plaster masks beneath the thatched canopies.

FIG. 7-7. Central Acropolis, Tikal.

FIG. 7-8. Interior court, Central Acropolis, Tikal.

FIG. 7-9. Mexican-style building, East Plaza, Tikal. The *talud-tablero* design of the platform recalls the architecture of Teotihuacán, but the foreign involvement of the central Mexican city was already on the wane by the time it was built, suggesting that Tikal's ties with central Mexico did not end with the decline of Teotihuacán.

were fitted out with domestic features: dowels from which to hang curtains across doorways, benches, niches, and even thronelike seats with stone armrests. Tikal's aristocrats certainly used these buildings, though probably not for domestic purposes alone. The palaces were also suitable for a variety of administrative activities: royal audiences, meetings of nobles, and many everyday bureaucratic functions. In fact, they have no obvious kitchen areas, so food was probably prepared elsewhere and brought in. A small, thatched kitchen building stands just outside the palace complex.

More temples, another ball court, and several other public buildings occupy the adjacent East Plaza. A large quadrangle defined by a series of long, low buildings may have been Tikal's marketplace, for here the rooms have none of the benches or other domestic fixtures found in palaces. A platform along the south edge of the East Plaza, in a Mexican architectural style (Fig. 7-9), might be a reflection of foreign involvement in Tikal's market, although buildings in the Mundo Perdido area were also remodeled in this style early in the Late Classic period. By this time, a process of retrenchment with respect to foreign involvements was well under way at Teotihuacán, soon to be followed by economic and political collapse, so Tikal's Mexican connection would most likely have been with an outlying part of the Teotihuacán sphere. These late Mexican architectural elements recall buildings in Gulf Coast cities and at Xochicalco (Fig. 8-30), where architectural styles of Teotihuacán inspiration continued to flourish after the decline of the central Mexican capital itself.

Nearby is a small building fitted inside with a water channel and a fire pit. Here Maya nobles reclined on wide benches as they enjoyed the steam baths prescribed in connection with curing and other ritual activity. Additional public building complexes cluster around the Great Plaza area on every side. Nearby are four of Tikal's ten reservoirs, natural ravines or quarries sealed and converted to water storage in order to ensure a steady supply of water through the dry season.

The Great Plaza, the hub of public life, embodied Tikal's greatness. The aristocrats who lived and worked in the palaces were at the center of political, economic, religious, and social life. Ceremonies in the nearby temples confirmed their fitness to reign. Reliefs and hieroglyphic texts on stelae, altars, lintels, and elsewhere recorded their great achievements and those of their ancestors (Fig. 7-10).

Past rulers died, but they did not depart. Entombed within the temple complexes, they remained to protect and guide their descendants. The Late Classic buildings were but the latest in a long series of superimposed remodelings. Most of the temples were not just scenes of ceremonies: they were funerary memorials to the illustrious dead. The Great Plaza complex as a whole was a monument to Tikal's aristocracy and its ancestor cult.

Public activity was not entirely centered on the Great Plaza. Broad raised causeways, paved with plaster and flanked by parapets, connected this civic core with other complexes of public buildings: temples, palaces, ball courts. To the west, the Tozzer causeway leads to Temple IV (Color Plate 1, Fig. 7-5), probably dedicated to Ah Cacao's son and successor. With its roof comb reaching a height of 65 meters, Temple IV is among the tallest standing precolumbian structures in the Americas. More than 190,000 cubic meters of building material went into its construction.

Farther away from the Great Plaza, public buildings become smaller and less elaborate and stelae and altars less frequent, although here, too, Ah Cacao and his successors erected monuments celebrating their reigns. At the end of each katun from the mid seventh through the end of the eighth century, the current ruler built a "twin-pyramid complex" (Fig. 7-11) whose focal point was a stela bearing his por-

FIG. 7-10. Stela 9, Tikal. This monument, carved in A.D. 475 to honor "Kan Boar," who probably succeeded Stormy Sky on the throne, still stood along the north edge of the Great Plaza during the Late Classic period.

trait within an unroofed enclosure (Fig. 7-12). Eastern and western pyramids (without superstructures) recalled the daily course of the sun; a nine-roomed southern building, suggesting the underworld realm, completed the grouping, symbolically locating the royal portrait in the celestial realm. Uncarved stelae erected before the eastern pyramid may have provided for flexible propagandizing, with painted texts and images tailored to specific occasions. Other outlying building clusters probably represent lower levels of the administrative hierarchy: subordinate civic units that served the immediate needs of the people who lived in the dwellings clustered around them. Ordinary farmers occupied most of the houses, but some residential groups contained workshops of potters, stone knappers, woodworkers, masons, sculptors, and other craft specialists. One compound evidently housed dental workers, cosmeticians patronized by nobles who wished to improve their front teeth with inlays of jade, pyrite, and other precious stones.

As one moves farther from central Tikal, the density of public and domestic buildings alike thins out gradually. Beyond the ditch-and-bank constructions that define the primary settlement to the north and south, building density drops off sharply. The basic Tikal community covers an area of about 125 square kilometers. At its Late Classic peak, Tikal housed a population in the tens of thousands.

Tikal's political and economic control embraced a large territory, and its interaction network was vast.[23] Hieroglyphic texts at Yaxchilán suggest that Tikal nobles played important roles in local political affairs on at least one occasion, probably on the strength of marriage alliances with the local aristocracy. Tikal's connections extended northwest to Palenque and southeast to Copán. These regional capitals all mentioned one another in hieroglyphic texts. Uaxactún (Figs. 6-8–6-11), a smaller city less than 20 kilometers to the north, is well within what would

FIG. 7-11. Schematic representation of a twin-pyramid complex. For about a century and a half during the latter part of the Late Classic period at Tikal and a few nearby cities, the ruler on the throne at the end of each katun commissioned a twin-pyramid complex. The architectural layout is designed to reflect fundamental symbolic aspects of rulership. A building with nine doorways stands at the south edge, evoking the underworld; the eastern and western platforms, without superstructures, represent the path of the sun. Thus, the stela and altar in the northern enclosure, celebrating the current ruler, symbolically occupy the celestial realm. Restoration drawing courtesy Tikal project, University of Pennsylvania Museum, negative 66-5-49.

FIG. 7-12. Stela 16 and Altar 5, Twin-Pyramid Complex N, Tikal. Stela 16 bears the portrait of Ah Cacao, who built this complex to mark the katun ending at 9.14.0.0.0 (A.D. 711). Texts on both monuments celebrate his ancestry and the events of his reign. The entry of the roofless enclosure in which the monuments stood is just visible in the foreground.

otherwise be reconstructed as Tikal's immediate sustaining area.[24] The two cities may have been peers in the Late Preclassic period, but Tikal gradually gained the upper hand. Uaxactún's nobles began to mention Tikal in their monumental texts early in the Classic period. In the Late Classic period, Uaxactún occupied a distinctly subordinate status, one of many dependent towns dominated by Tikal. Evidently Tikal chose to control part of its immediate sustaining area as it did outlying areas, through a separate but subsidiary administrative center. To the southeast, the civic architecture of Yaxhá, on the shores of one of the lakes that stretch across the lowlands, closely resembles that of Tikal: an astronomical building complex marks sunrise positions, and here we find the only other known twin-pyramid complex. These patterns probably reflect a subordinate status within Tikal's political sphere. The main element of Yaxhá's emblem glyph—the distinctive component, which refers to the particular polity (not the place per se)—can be read as *yax ha*, "green (or first) water." This is one of the few cases in which a Classic-period name survives to the present.[25]

Styles of architecture, sculpture, and pottery indicate long-term interaction with some communities to the north, but Tikal's political dominance may not have stretched far in that direction during much of the Late Classic period. Calakmul, once a city of modest size, could now boast a thousand buildings in its central civic precinct, along with more than a hundred stelae. A series of paired male and female portraits may depict rulers and their wives. Some six thousand structures occupy the area around the city center, delimited by a 6-meter-high wall, and the population of the city and its environs may have reached 50,000. By the seventh century, Calakmul was one of the largest and most powerful Maya cities. Its political and economic sphere embraced a substantial region, and hieroglyphic texts at Naranjo, Caracol, Dos Pilas, Yaxchilán, and elsewhere suggest that its lords were intimately involved in even wider webs of alliance. Palenque and especially Tikal, on the other hand, were evidently serious rivals, and hieroglyphic texts suggest periodic armed conflict between them. The complexity and dynamism of the Late Classic political landscape in the southern lowlands may relate in large part to continuing competition between the great cities of Calakmul and Tikal for dominance over large spheres of influence. By the end of the seventh century, Tikal had evidently emerged victorious, for a text carved on one of the lintels of Ah Cacao's mortuary temple seems to refer to the defeat of Calakmul.[26]

East of Yaxhá was Naranjo, which dominated a sizable region, stretching at least as far as the upper valley of the Belize River. Xunantunich and Buenavista del Cayo, both with substantial clusters of

FIG. 7-13. Courtyard D, Cahal Pech. The outer wall of the corridor of this elite residential compound has fallen, revealing the back wall and entrances to its rooms. The arch over the central door is unusually wide.

temples and palaces, may have vied for control in the local region, but surely were politically subordinate to Naranjo. Cahal Pech (Fig. 7-13) and Pacbitún are smaller communities still further down the political hierarchy. Hieroglyphic texts at Naranjo indicate that the local ruler married the daughter of the lord of Dos Pilas in the late seventh century. Such marriage alliances often marked relationships between dominant and subordinate cities, which served to enhance the status of local ruling lines and to cement the positions of minor centers within the orbits of regional powers, so Dos Pilas may have sought to exert influence in the east through its connection with Naranjo. Both cities evidently acknowledged the king of Calakmul as overlord.[27]

Caracol, farther east and south, emerged as a rival to Tikal in the Late Classic period.[28] In the seventh century, Caracol grew to great size (Fig. 7-14), with a civic architectural core of temples, palaces, ball courts, and other public buildings connected to outlying building complexes by a series of causeways that extended out from the center as far as 8 kilome-

FIG. 7-14. Caana temple complex, Caracol. A "triadic" group of three temples on their own occupies the summit of the terraced platform. The multiroomed construction across the stairway at the top of the lower terrace reflects the eastern architectural style.

ters. The residential area surrounding the city center covers dozens of square kilometers, and the overall population of the city may have exceeded 50,000. A ball-court marker commemorating a seventh-century Caracol king seems to allege that an earlier king of Caracol had achieved some sort of military victory over Tikal at the middle of the previous century. Whether or not such an event actually transpired, the monument clearly does indicate the rivalry of these two great cities. Other texts indicate hostilities with Naranjo, closer to home, and alliances with the lords of Calakmul.

The eastern fringe of the lowland core was probably beyond the direct political or economic control of any of these cities. Lamanai enjoyed continued prosperity, based in part on its strategic location on the shores of New River Lagoon, which provided a variety of foods as well as easy access by water to the coast and its exchange networks. A port facility on the edge of the lagoon was surely in use by this time, as was a substantial zone of wetland cultivation. The community had grown to occupy at least 4.5 square kilometers, and its lords undertook new public building projects, remodeled earlier structures in the distinctive eastern architectural style (Figs. 6-15, 7-14), and dedicated monuments to themselves.[29] Altun Ha, farther east, was still a much smaller community, although its lords continued to remodel the temples and palaces flanking the central plazas and to furnish their crypts with rich offerings of jade, shell, and pearl jewelry. The lord buried in a stone crypt within the masonry block that projects from the stairway of one large platform (Fig. 6-15) was accompanied by a jade head weighing more than 4 kilograms. Politically and economically, Altun Ha probably remained in the shadow of its larger neighbor.[30] Colha, just to the north, continued to be a major producer and exporter of chert and chert tools. The community had a small cluster of public structures and dozens of workshops scattered over an area of more than 6 square kilometers. Colha products were exported in substantial quantities at least as far west as Yaxhá, Tikal, and nearby communities in the heart of the central lowlands.[31] Nohmul and La Milpa, to the west and north, were independent towns that controlled modest surrounding territories. A series of prosperous coastal communities served as ports in the active maritime-exchange network that stretched north to Yucatan and south to the lower Ulúa Valley and beyond.[32]

FIG. 7-15. Altar, Great Plaza, Copán. This grotesque two-headed beast, standing before Stela D at the north end of the public precinct, may have functioned as a throne.

The Southeastern Frontier. The southeastern region of the Maya lowlands had its own very distinctive styles of architecture, sculpture, and polychrome pottery painting. Copán, on the banks of a small river flowing through hilly forested uplands on the fringe of the Maya highlands, was the greatest city in the southeast.[33]

Copán was not isolated from the great cities to the north and west. The Sky family, which held great power in southeastern cities, may have shared one component of its ancestry with a leading family at Tikal. The Copán emblem glyph appears occasionally in Tikal texts, and one Copán stela (Fig. 7-19) mentions Tikal[34] along with Calakmul and Palenque. Other texts indicate that Yax Pac, who ruled Copán during the late eighth and early ninth centuries, was the son of a woman from Palenque.[35] These alliances notwithstanding, Copán was not subordinate to Tikal or to any other center.

Public activity at Copán revolved around a compact central zone of temples and palaces, thick with monuments to local leaders (Color Plate 3, Figs. 7-16–7-20). Copán's civic core is less extensive than Tikal's and individual buildings are smaller, but the two precincts were functionally equivalent, each the heart of a powerful regional capital. Copán's buildings are relatively simple in design, but most are elaborately decorated with reliefs in stone and stucco (Figs. 7-21–7-23, 7-25, 7-27). As at Tikal, sculpture and hieroglyphic texts associated with public buildings record the achievements of great rulers; but at Copán their style is quite distinctive. Architectural decoration and free-standing monuments alike feature very deep relief (Figs. 7-15, 7-18–7-20, 7-22). Some stelae almost have the character of sculpture in the round rather than relief. Costumes and other pictorial details are very elaborate, as are the hieroglyphs. The overall effect is almost florid. The main ball court (Color Plate 3), unlike those at Tikal, is elaborately decorated: sculptures of macaws adorn the upper façades of the temples that top the flanking platforms; macaw-head markers line both sides of the playing area; and relief plaques are set flush into the floor along the centerline.

Much of the architectural grandeur and sculptural magnificence of Late Classic Copán was the result of energetic building programs undertaken by its powerful eighth-century kings. The Acropolis, the focus of temple and palace construction since the fifth century, grew even higher with yet another episode of reconstruction. These buildings (Figs. 7-21, 7-25, 7-27), along with those of the lower Cementcrio zone to the south, are best interpreted as the royal household. The Cementerio complex includes a series of modest plazas flanked by relatively small structures with built-in benches and other domestic features. These building groups are good candidates for the actual residences of the relatives and retainers of Copán's rulers. The more elaborate Cementerio buildings—with vaulted roofs and sculptural decoration on the façades—may have housed the royal family itself.[36] The East and West courts of the Acropolis itself are more spacious, and the flanking buildings are far more imposing, with elaborate sculptural ornamentation on their façades. Since access to these courts is sharply limited by the structures that enclose them, the buildings are best interpreted as "semiprivate" temples and palaces to which privileged persons—high-ranking officials, priests, visiting dignitaries—were admitted in order to participate in affairs of state.

In sharp contrast, a series of spacious plazas to the north took form as the public focus of Copán's civic precinct early in the eighth century (Color Plate 3). Here were stelae (Figs. 7-18–7-20), altars (Fig. 7-15), a radial platform ascended by four stairs (Fig. 7-16, visible in Color Plate 3 before reconstruction), and a great ball court. Along one edge of the Great Plaza was a multiroomed building that probably functioned as a residence for young men receiving religious and military training.[37] The Great Plaza, flanked on three sides by long, low terraced platforms, provided a showcase for sculpture celebrating Copán's kings. Most of the stelae in the main plaza are monuments to "18 Rabbit," who ruled, according to the hieroglyphic texts, as thirteenth in a succession, from A.D. 695 to 738. Collectively, the portraits of 18 Rabbit and the accompanying hieroglyphic texts represent the multifaceted public image of a king, projected in Copán's principal civic space.[38] Monuments erected by his predecessors were relegated to the edges of the plaza or, as in the case of a stela that once stood on the radial pyramid,[39] were removed and defaced.

At the east edge of the public precinct, Stela J commemorates 18 Rabbit's accession to the throne of Copán in an elaborate hieroglyphic text carved on the stone as though it had been painted on the strips of a woven mat, itself a key symbol of royal power. Standing at the end of a causeway leading to a series of substantial residences, Stela J would have greeted visitors arriving from this elite suburb. The rest of 18 Rabbit's monuments were set in the Great Plaza. Each stela bears a high-relief portrait of the king with emblems of royal authority. He wears a distinctive belt with pendant plaques and anthropomorphic heads (perhaps trophy heads of sacrificed enemies, perhaps supernatural beings) and he holds an elongated "ceremonial bar" with a reptilian head at each end. Mat designs are ubiquitous, as are celestial symbols; representations of bloodletting implements used in sacrificial ritual adorn all but one of the portraits. Other headdress and costume details, supernatural symbols, and the associated hieroglyphic texts vary. The stelae appear to have been carefully placed within the Great Plaza in order to present the full array of royal qualities in relation to important symbolic dimensions: east/north/west/

FIG. 7-16. Structure 10L-4, Copán. This radial platform, between the main plaza (*to the left*) and the ball-court complex (*right background*), once supported a stela honoring one of Copán's early kings. It was removed and buried during a remodeling operation, probably the redesign of the main plaza complex as a setting for 18 Rabbit's stelae, one of which (Stela A) stands adjacent to the platform.

south, right/left, old/young, male/female, celestial/terrestrial/underworld.

Stela D (top center in Color Plate 3) was placed in the north so that 18 Rabbit's gaze takes in all the other monuments and the royal household in the Acropolis. The text, done in florid full-figure glyphs (Fig. 7-17), records the latest Long Count date of the group, corresponding to A.D. 736. Stela C (Fig. 7-18) presents a double portrait, with a youthful 18 Rabbit adorned with a phallus facing east and an older, bearded king on the opposite side facing to the west. Stelae A and H (Figs. 7-19, 7-20), designed as a pair, face one another across the south end of the Great Plaza. Stela H portrays 18 Rabbit in an unusual costume that combines the jaguar-skin kilt often worn by kings with a long beaded skirt usually found on images of women; it is the only portrait without sacrificial implements associated with the drawing of blood from male genitalia. The symbolic message appears to be that Maya kingship entailed roles such as nurturing that might otherwise be associated only with women. The text on Stela H may be a continuation of that on Stela A, which couples Copán's emblem glyph with those of Palenque, Calakmul, and Tikal.[40]

Caches placed beneath the monuments contained offerings that provide additional indications of the scope of 18 Rabbit's external relations. In addition to local pottery vessels and stone implements, the offerings included jade beads, seashells, pottery in-

FIG. 7-17. Opening of the hieroglyphic text on Stela D at Copán, transcribed 9.15.5.0.0 10 Ahau 8 Ch'en. Glyphs for numbers and Long Count units are full-portrait figures (compare the heads with portrait variants in Figs. 1-1, 5-3). The Initial Series Introducing Glyph features a portrait of the moon goddess, patron of the month Ch'en. The sun god, carrying a jaguar-skin bundle, is the Lord of the Night, appearing between the Ritual Almanac day (10 Ahau) and the Solar Year day (8 Ch'en). Adapted from C. Thomas 1904:pls. 76, 77.

cense burners (some with lids modeled to represent imports such as cacao), elaborately painted pottery imported from the Ulúa region to the east and south, and two legs from a figurine cast in *tumbaga* (a gold-copper alloy), imported from lower Central America.[41]

If, as is usually assumed, these stelae were erected on the dates corresponding to the Long Count positions that appear to be the dedicatory dates in the texts, then they would have been commissioned by 18 Rabbit himself, as part of the early eighth-century building program that included (1) the low platforms and men's house flanking the Great Plaza, (2) the latest reconstruction of the radial platform, (3) the penultimate in a long series of enlargements of the ancient Structure 26, and (4) the final remodeling of the ball court. In this orthodox interpretation, these monuments would reflect 18 Rabbit's own program of legitimizing his position and glorifying himself. Apart from the Long Count dates in the texts, the items deposited in the caches beneath the stelae provide the only direct indication of the dates of their placement, and these offerings are consistent with the possibility that the stelae were erected later in the eighth century in honor of a former ruler.[42] Even if the monuments *were* erected by 18 Rabbit himself, it is important to recognize that his successors left them in place, adding their own stelae only along the south edge of the public precinct and not effacing his imagery in the ball court, so that the image of royal qualities and power that they reflect must also be understood as integral to the legitimation strategies of subsequent kings. Presumably, glorification of a great predecessor was central to these symbolic agendas.

The grand public arena of the Great Plaza is best interpreted as an extension of the royal household to the south. Here, in the more private space of the East Court of the Acropolis, the elegant Structure 10L-22 (Figs. 7-21–7-23) provided a setting for ritual and

FIG. 7-18. Stela C, Great Plaza, Copán. This image of the mature, bearded 18 Rabbit contrasts with a younger king portrayed with symbols emphasizing masculinity on the opposite face of the stela.

FIG. 7-19. Stela A, Great Plaza, Copán. The small stone chamber below the monument was the repository for pottery and other offerings associated with its dedication in A.D. 731. The hieroglyphic text links Copán to Tikal, Calakmul, and Palenque.

FIG. 7-20. Stela H, Great Plaza, Copán. This portrait of 18 Rabbit was designed to highlight female aspects of his royal persona, depicting him in a costume that combines the jaguar-skin kilt with a long skirt typical of representations of women.

FIG. 7-21. Structure 10L-22, East Court, Copán. This building, which was probably the venue both for administrative and ritual activities, is part of the royal household complex of the Acropolis zone.

FIG. 7-22. Entry, Structure 10L-22, East Court, Copán. The doorway was designed to represent the gaping mouth of a huge reptilian creature, so that entering the building took the visitor into the maw of the beast. The fangs and front teeth of the lower jaw are visible on the top step.

administrative activities aimed at a much more restricted set of privileged participants. Here, too, the imagery links 18 Rabbit to royal emblems and to aspects of the supernatural.

Very few monuments bear Long Count dates corresponding to the decades following 18 Rabbit's last stela, and the mid eighth century seems to have seen a sharp decline of construction in the city center as well.[43] The next lord of Copán to be the protagonist of a substantial number of monuments and texts is Yax Pac, who was probably responsible for the last major architectural expansion of Copán. According to the texts, Yax Pac came to power in A.D. 763 and ruled at least through the first decade of the ninth century. A few monuments refer to "Smoke Monkey" and "Smoke Shell" as having ruled between 18 Rabbit and Yax Pac, but some of them are certainly retrospective, and the few that may be contemporaneous are ambiguous.

The orthodox interpretation of Copán's political history during these intervening years[44] focuses on a text at Quiriguá that celebrates the local lord,

FIG. 7-23. Corner of Structure 10L-22, East Court, Copán. Heads of long-nosed creatures adorn the corners of the building, which itself was conceptualized as a gigantic living creature. These heads are similar to those on northern lowland buildings (cf. Figs. 8-12, 8-14, 8-15) which are often called "Chacs." Ah Bolon Dzacab, associated with aristocratic lineages, was also commonly depicted with a long nose or upper lip and would be a more logical subject for this sort of architectural imagery than the rain god. The *cauac* ("stone") symbols above the eyes of the Copán heads refer to stone and, by extension, to the earth or to mountains.

"Cauac Sky" (Fig. 7-24), and couples 18 Rabbit's name with a glyph in the form of an axe. One interpretation identifies the axe glyph as a reference to beheading or some other form of execution, so the text may allege that Cauac Sky beheaded or otherwise did away with 18 Rabbit on the associated Long Count date, which corresponds to A.D. 738. This date—shortly after the dedication date on 18 Rabbit's last stela and less than a year after the last date that seems to be a contemporaneous reference to him—is in fact the beginning of a sharp decline in building and monument dedication at Copán and therefore perfectly consistent with the interpretation of a military defeat at the hands of its onetime subordinate, Quiriguá. A building adjacent to Structure 10L-22 in the East Court of the Acropolis (Fig. 7-25) has been interpreted as a council house in which lords from powerful families met to conduct state business in the supposed power vacuum of Smoke Monkey's troubled reign.[45] The very long text and royal portraits on the Hieroglyphic Stair of Structure 10L-26, the temple adjacent to the great ball court, has been interpreted in the same vein as a celebration of the achievements and warrior qualities of Copán's past kings, commissioned by Smoke Shell (Smoke Monkey's successor) to refurbish the tarnished image of his predecessors.[46]

In fact, there is no evidence at Copán of siege, destruction, military occupation, or even the installation of a foreign overlord or puppet ruler.[47] The council house may very well have been the venue for conclaves of powerful nobles, perhaps in the context of feasting, which is clearly reflected in associated archaeological remains,[48] but such a function need not have been a response to diminished royal authority, and not necessarily to a loss of power in the aftermath of 18 Rabbit's execution by Cauac Sky. Texts associated with the building refer to Yax Pac as well as to Smoke Monkey, so it presumably remained in use under a lord whose authority has not been called into question.

The only clear references to royal succession in the period between 18 Rabbit and Yax Pac are on the monuments of Yax Pac. His famous Altar Q (Fig. 7-26), which represents him as the sixteenth in a succession of lords beginning with Yax Kuk Mo, lists Smoke Shell, Smoke Monkey, and 18 Rabbit as his immediate predecessors. The orthodox interpretation of the Hieroglyphic Stairway and of other monuments ostensibly from this period is consistent with Yax Pac's version of Copán's royal succession, but these monuments do not unequivocally confirm it. Unfortunately, the collapse of the Hieroglyphic Stairway has made the order of the glyph blocks and therefore the reading of the text very problematic. Smoke Shell is the last ruler definitely referred to, but it is by no means certain that he was the author of the text. One of the two stelae that seem to portray Smoke Shell appears to refer to Yax Pac[49] (and to 18 Rabbit) as well as to Smoke Shell and Smoke Monkey. If Smoke Monkey erected stelae, none has been found. It is even possible that Yax Pac was the author of all of the monuments referring to Smoke Monkey and Smoke Shell.

The dearth of monuments dedicated in the years following 18 Rabbit's reign might indicate a period in which the power of Copán's kings was in eclipse. If so, the diminished royal profile might or might not have been the result of a defeat at the hands of Quiriguá. Cauac Sky's text might have been an attempt to gain political advantage at home by taking credit for the death of 18 Rabbit even if it had resulted from some other cause entirely. Alternatively, the absence of monuments dedicated between 18 Rabbit and the accession of Yax Pac might reflect a very different kind of political process, such as the aftermath of a problematic succession. In such cases, the successful contender may rewrite history in order to create a fictitious line of succession and connect himself to the last king generally recognized as legitimate. Such a scenario is certainly consistent with Yax Pac's interest in glorifying 18 Rabbit and with the possibility

FIG. 7-24. Monument 5 (Stela E), Quiriguá. This monument, dedicated in A.D. 771, is the tallest (10 meters) of all Maya stelae. It bears the portrait of Quiriguá's great early ruler Cauac Sky, whose life is the subject of the hieroglyphic text on the sides. The text mentions 18 Rabbit in a context that seems to be a retrospective claim that Cauac Sky defeated or executed the lord of Copán.

FIG. 7-25. Structure 10L-22A, East Court, Copán. This building is often interpreted as a "council house" in which heads of lineages met to fill the power vacuum created by 18 Rabbit's demise. The mat designs could symbolize such an institution, but they are also a symbol of royalty.

that Yax Pac produced at least one of the monuments ostensibly erected by Smoke Shell. In any event, the Great Plaza remained a memorial to 18 Rabbit in the tenth century, when the lords of Copán had commissioned the last sculptured monument and ceased to sponsor public building programs.

In the same way, Yax Pac's version of Copán's earlier history may be more a fictive claim than a straightforward account of what actually happened. Yax Pac's account of Copán's history is not therefore less interesting: the importance of Altar Q is in the access it provides to the version of history promulgated by its author and in what this tells us about the Maya concept of history and the role that historical accounts played in such high political affairs as succession to the throne and maintaining royal authority. Consistencies between some earlier texts and Yax Pac's monuments do not necessarily constitute confirmation of all his allegations. The fact that the texts of 18 Rabbit and a few earlier kings place them in the same positions in a succession from Yax Kuk Mo as does Altar Q may reflect no more than Yax Pac's attempt to connect himself to a line of succession that some of his predecessors also claimed. Relationships between personages mentioned in Copán's early texts and the founder figure, Yax Kuk Mo, and his immediate successors are tenuous.[50] The discovery that Copán maintained connections with

FIG. 7-26. Altar Q, West Court, Copán. On this monument Yax Pac, the last great king of Copán, had himself portrayed with the fifteen figures he claimed as royal ancestors. The central pair of figures carved on this side represent Yax Pac (*on the right*) receiving a scepter, symbolic of the legitimacy of his power, from the founder figure, Yax Kuk Mo.

Teotihuacán or its eastern outposts in the Early Classic period—when Yax Kuk Mo, who Yax Pac portrays with Mexican costume elements, would have lived—does not confirm the historical veracity of Yax Pac's references to him. Other texts—some of them found in construction fills and rubbish heaps and therefore presumptively suppressed by later rulers—suggest that alternative versions of the history of Copán's kings had currency in some periods. These texts refer to rulers not named in Yax Pac's monuments as well as to some of the same kings, but in connection with other succession sequences and other founder figures.[51]

Altar Q (Fig. 7-26), with its celebration of Yax Pac as successor to a line of past kings, was placed in the West Court of the Acropolis, before Temple 16, an ancient temple which Yax Pac extensively remodeled with imagery focusing on warfare and death (perhaps in the context of royal ancestors). The dedication of the monument involved the burial of more than a dozen jaguars just behind it.[52] Structure 10L-11 (Fig. 7-27), at the north edge of the Acropolis, facing out into the public precinct as well as south into the more private space of the West Court, functioned in private administrative and ritual activities as well as on occasions of public spectacle. The much smaller temple of Structure 10L-18, in the East Court, portrays Yax Pac as a warrior.

FIG. 7-27. Structure 10L-11, West Court, Copán. Administrative as well as ceremonial activities probably took place in this building; the stairways provided access from the relatively private royal household area of the Acropolis. The opposite face of the palace overlooks the ball court and Great Plaza.

Residential complexes are found throughout the Copán Valley. Several imposing building complexes not far from central Copán appear to combine residential and civic functions. Smaller residences are the norm in outlying areas. A causeway connects the main civic precinct with a densely populated area just upstream that had been a residential zone for many centuries. Plazas surrounded by platforms supporting masonry buildings cluster into larger groupings, each of which probably housed one of Copán's prominent families and its retainers. One of the largest residential complexes, Group 9N-8 (Fig. 7-28),[53] with a dozen plazas,[54] probably housed several hundred people, including servants and retainers in the time of Yax Pac. The largest platform, facing the main plaza, supported a masonry building with vaulted rooms which were fitted with plastered stone benches. A hieroglyphic text on the bench in the central room invokes Yax Pac and records the parentage of the head of the extended household. The text, along with sculptural imagery found on and around the building, indicates that the head of

FIG. 7-28. Plaza A, Sepulturas, Copán. The building in the background (Structure 9N-82) dominates the largest plaza in this residential complex on the Río Copán, about 1 kilometer upstream from the city core. The façade, once much higher and topped by a vaulted roof, was elaborately ornamented with sculpted images, featuring busts of scribes who flanked the central doorway. A hieroglyphic text on the elaborate bench inside the main room links the lord of the compound to the king, Yax Pac.

FIG. 7-29. Part of the design on an Ulúa polychrome vase, lower Ulúa Valley. The figure, holding a "fan," is seated inside a building shown in cutaway view. The overall composition, the style of the figure and the building, and the glyphlike signs behind them reflect Maya artistic canons (cf. Fig. 3-1).

household was a scribe, and material found in the two flanking buildings suggest that weaving and the ball game were also important concerns of those who lived in the complex. The principal family may have resided in these buildings, although the main plaza surely had communal functions as well; the platform opposite the main building was a shrine without a superstructure. High-ranking family members also lived in the large residences that surrounded smaller but spacious plazas immediately to the north. The lineage's noble dead were buried with their luxury pottery and jade jewelry in tombs beneath the platforms or under the plaza floor. Subsidiary building groups, surrounding smaller plazas in the complex, housed lower-ranking family members and retainers and were the scene of shell-jewelry making and probably a variety of other craft production activities as well. Fancy painted pottery and figurines imported from the Ulúa sphere to the east and south (Figs. 7-29, 7-30) are common, as they are in other residential areas, including those occupied by much less prosperous families.[55]

Below the city, the Río Copán flows west and north into the Río Motagua. Quiriguá, 50 kilometers away on the banks of the Motagua, was ideally situated to control the distribution of obsidian and jade from the west.[56] Domination of Quiriguá and its subsidiary sphere thus extended Copán's effective control over a large zone to the north. Sculpture and architecture reflect close ties between the two cities from a very early period. The Acropolis, a group of administrative and residential buildings, flanked on the north by a ball court and a great open plaza with sculptured monuments, replicates the basic structure of Copán's core. Quiriguá enjoyed a political and economic florescence during the sixty-year reign of Cauac Sky (Fig. 7-24), who came to power in A.D. 724. Shortly after the alleged defeat of 18 Rabbit of Copán in A.D. 738, Cauac Sky undertook a major remodeling of Quiriguá's public buildings;

among the monuments he dedicated to himself is the tallest stela ever carved in the Maya world. Whether or not Cauac Sky actually conquered Copán, he certainly presided over a period in which Quiriguá emerged from Copán's political shadow; his monuments reflect the first use of Quiriguá's own emblem glyph. The rupture of A.D. 738 may have taken Quiriguá out of Copán's economic sphere as well, for Late Classic pottery shows few links with the luxury styles of Copán. Even distinctive Copador vessels, with their glittering-red hematite paint, so widely distributed south of Copán, are quite rare at Quiriguá.

Styles of architecture and sculpture at Pusilhá, Lubaantún, and Nimli Punit suggest an interaction sphere extending well to the north along the Caribbean coast.[57] These cities were probably part of an economic network in which Copán and Quiriguá were the dominant participants, but there is no evidence that the southern cities extended their political control so far afield.

Smaller towns subordinate to the regional capital dot the area immediately east of the Copán Valley. Copán's connections stretched farther to the east and especially to the south, where luxury pottery styles indicate close ties with Chalchuapa and neighboring communities in the southeastern Maya highlands. The distinctive Copador pottery, manufactured in Copán, and related local styles are particularly common in the south, but elaborately carved stelae with hieroglyphic texts are absent.[58]

Copán's sphere of direct influence probably did not extend very far beyond El Puente, Los Higos, and other small towns in the upper Chamelecón drainage. At La Sierra, farther down the Chamelecón, and at Gualjoquito, on the middle Ulúa, pottery and architecture reflect some typical lowland features, but community layouts are different and there are no stelae or hieroglyphic texts.[59]

The lower Ulúa Valley, the Lake Yojoa basin, and

FIG. 7-30. Ceramic figurine, Pineda, lower Ulúa Valley. This elaborately coiffed lady, adorned with necklace and ear ornaments, carries a bowl on her head.

the Comayagua Valley of central Honduras to the south were part of the Ulúa sphere, best defined by a series of closely related styles of painted pottery.[60] These elaborate Ulúa polychromes (Fig. 7-29) share fundamental color palettes, design structures, and motifs with the rest of the Maya world; but designs and forms are more varied, and they are better made than most Maya polychromes. Ulúa iconography is distinctive and quite complex, although it does not include formal hieroglyphic texts.

In the lower Ulúa Valley, the heartland of the Ulúa sphere, craftsmen produced some of the finest Ulúa polychrome vases and excelled in the manufacture of ceramic figurines (Fig. 7-30), elaborate figural incense-burners, and stone vessels with carved relief designs.[61] Travesía and other prosperous communities boasted ball courts and imposing public buildings with dressed stone, plaster facings, and sculptural ornamentation in the Maya architectural tradition. Stelae graced these towns as well, although they were entirely plain or featured simple carved designs or painted-stucco coatings rather than the elaborate royal relief portraits of Copán and other Maya cities to the west.

The Ulúa sphere was part of a frontier zone in which Maya and Central American peoples mingled to produce an intricate mosaic of contrasting cultural patterns. Communities were cosmopolitan and multicultural, with enclaves of foreign Mayas, non-Mayas, and probably people of hybrid cultural identity as well.

Río Pasión–Petexbatún. Late Classic styles of architecture, monumental art, and luxury pottery indicate a continuation of close relationships between Pasión centers and the Tikal region.[62] Tamarindito and Altar de Sacrificios were still the most prominent centers in the region in the initial decades of the Late Classic period. In the mid seventh century, Dos Pilas emerged as the dominant center in the Petexbatún zone, under lords who used an emblem glyph identical to Tikal's. There is no evidence of a Tikal takeover, but Ruler I, the apparent founder of the new dynasty, had the same "sky" glyph in his name as did Tikal kings, and he may well have come from the Tikal ruling family. A central plaza flanked by temples and palaces is at the core of the civic center at Dos Pilas. Hieroglyphic texts on monuments erected here record the consolidation of local political control in the Petexbatún region and beyond as far as Seibal. Alliances with more distant cities included the marriage of a daughter of Ruler I into the ruling family of Naranjo as well as continuing political connections with the lords of Calakmul. In the eighth century, the center of power in the Petexbatún zone shifted from Dos Pilas to Aguateca, evidently without a break in dynastic succession. By the late eighth century, the dominance of the ruling dynasty had come under challenge, and the overall political situation in the region had become highly unsettled. At Dos Pilas, stones from abandoned palace buildings were used to enclose surviving civic buildings within a defensive rubble wall topped by a palisade. At Punta de Chimino, on a promontory in Lago Petexbatún, a defensive ditch-and-wall system protected public buildings and a canoe port. Even the lords of Aguateca, atop a high bluff, had to throw up palisades to defend themselves against attack. By the end of the century, Dos Pilas was abandoned; Aguateca apparently survived a bit longer, but its regional dominance had come to an end. Early in the ninth century, Seibal—now with strong new foreign connections—emerged as the most powerful city in the Pasión region.

In the west, Altar de Sacrificios remained independent, maintaining alliances with Yaxchilán, down the Usumacinta, as well as with other Pasión centers and with Tikal. One of the lords of Yaxchilán, perhaps the great eighth-century king "Bird Jaguar," may have participated in the funeral rites of a

FIG. 7-31. Record of Bird Jaguar's birth and accession to rule at Yaxchilán: excerpts from a hieroglyphic text spanning Lintels 29, 30, and 31, all from Structure 10. (a) The text opens with the date 9.13.17.12.10 8 Oc (A.D. 709); (b) 13 Yax (end of Initial Series); "upended frog" glyph, marking this as the birth date of Bird Jaguar, whose name glyphs follow, along with the dual Yaxchilán emblem glyph; (c) a distance number (omitted) leads to the Calendar Round day 11 Ahau 8 Zec (corresponding to 9.16.1.10.0, or A.D. 752); the "toothache" glyph marks this as the date on which Bird Jaguar came to power. Bird Jaguar's name glyphs, a notation of his age (he was in the third katun of his life), and the Yaxchilán emblem glyphs follow. Adapted from I. Graham and Von Euw 1979:67–71.

noble Altar lady along with nobles from several other regions (Fig. 7-1).

Río Usumacinta. Another set of variations on the themes of Classic Maya civilization characterizes the Usumacinta region.[63] Late Classic pottery at Yaxchilán, Piedras Negras, and nearby cities embodies a distinctive regional variant of the Tepeu style. Architectural features point to downstream connections.

Yaxchilán, a very large city built on a series of terraces cut into the low hills along the middle course of the Río Usumacinta, was the capital of the region's most powerful state during the Late Classic period. Despite its importance, no extensive excavations have been undertaken at Yaxchilán, so almost all available data come from studies of its hieroglyphic inscriptions (Figs. 7-31, 7-32). To judge by the texts, Yaxchilán reached its peak of political power in the late seventh and eighth centuries during the successive reigns of kings who ruled under names glossed as "Shield Jaguar" and "Bird Jaguar" (the second and third kings of Yaxchilán, respectively, to adopt these traditional names).[64] Both

FIG. 7-32. Capture scene at Yaxchilán. Lintel 8 shows Bird Jaguar, ruler of Yaxchilán (*on the right*), and a noble companion taking prisoners, whose names and titles appear on their thighs. The main text opens at the upper left with the Calendar Round date 7 Imix 14 Cazeu, corresponding to 9.16.4.1.1, or A.D. 755 (Cazeu is the Chol equivalent of Yucatec Zec), followed by *chucah*, or "captured" (cf. Fig. 1-3e), and "Jeweled Skull," the name of Bird Jaguar's captive. It continues in the upper right with a title, Bird Jaguar's name, and the Yaxchilán emblem glyph. A loose translation would be: On the day 7 Imix 14 Cazeu (in the year A.D. 755) Bird Jaguar, lord of Yaxchilán, captured Jeweled Skull. The secondary text, above the captives, designates Bird Jaguar's companion as captor of the second prisoner. Adapted from I. Graham and Von Euw 1977:27 and Proskouriakoff 1963b:fig. 1.

FIG. 7-33. Judgment of captives, Bonampak. This small section, from a narrative mural sequence recording a raid on another center, shows a nude prisoner pleading his case before the victorious lords. Other captives, whose hands are bleeding, sit on the lower terrace alongside a sprawling corpse whose foot rests against the severed head of a sacrificed prisoner.

rulers were evidently energetic builders, and they transformed the city with buildings that incorporate images and texts glorifying themselves. Bird Jaguar's monuments, which strikingly replicate the themes of those commissioned by his father, seem to be designed to emphasize his legitimacy. The prominent depiction of his wife and of subordinate lords may also indicate that the foundations of Bird Jaguar's authority depended heavily on factors other than his parentage, a hypothesis that would be consistent with indications in the texts that his mother was not Shield Jaguar's principal wife.[65] The lords of Yaxchilán dominated a very large zone of the middle Usumacinta during these centuries, and their broader sphere of political activity stretched well beyond the limits of the state itself—at least to Piedras Negras downstream and perhaps as far upriver as Altar de Sacrificios.

Bonampak, on a tributary stream 25 kilometers to the southwest, is the most famous of Yaxchilán's dependencies. Bonampak's architecture and low-relief sculpture reflect the impact of Yaxchilán styles. Hieroglyphic texts confirm the relationship, again suggesting marriage alliances between local lords and aristocratic women from the regional capital. One of these noblewomen appears with the late eighth-century ruler Chan Muan on stelae and in the famous murals recording a successful raid on a nearby center (Fig. 7-33). She was probably the mother of the heir to the throne who is depicted in one of the murals; the designation of this child as heir apparent may have been the occasion for the military action and associated ritual. A tentative reading of the eroded texts in the murals suggests that the noblewoman may have been the sister of the king of Yaxchilán.

Piedras Negras, down the Usumacinta, was a large city, although many of its temples and palaces were roofed with beams and thatch rather than stone vaults. Eight steam baths suggest an unusual regional emphasis on this ceremonial activity.[66] It was the patterns of names and dates on this city's monuments (which the lords of Piedras Negras regularly dedicated to themselves at five-tun intervals) that led Tatiana Proskouriakoff to her initial recognition that Classic Maya texts actually recorded dynastic history. In the earlier part of the Classic period, Piedras Negras may have rivaled Yaxchilán in importance, but Yaxchilán emerged as the dominant center during the Late Classic period. References to Yaxchilán in the texts of Piedras Negras include an account of Bird Jaguar's participation in what appears to be a rite designating the heir to the throne.

In the eighth century, Yaxchilán asserted its dominance in the Usumacinta region. Bird Jaguar (Figs. 7-31, 7-32) or a close kinsman assumed a major role in the succession at Piedras Negras. Through Piedras Negras, Yaxchilán could control El Cayo and other subsidiary towns. Yaxchilán's external links stretched southeast to Altar de Sacrificios, where Bird Jaguar or his representative might have participated in local affairs (Fig. 7-1). Northwestern connections were even stronger. The mansard roofs, roof combs, and façades of Yaxchilán's buildings strongly recall those of Palenque, where texts occasionally refer to Yaxchilán. A variant method of recording dates at Yaxchilán, like the Mexican elements in its art, points to northern connections, in this instance with western Yucatan.

The Western Frontier. The western regional variant of Classic Maya civilization, most fully represented at Palenque, is as distinctive as that of Copán's sphere in the southeast.[67] Beyond Palenque to the north lies the frontier zone in which Maya groups mingled with Mexican peoples of the Gulf Coast. Signs of contact with the culturally diverse peoples of the frontier are prominent at Palenque and other cities in its region.

Pottery in the west reflects this frontier status.

FIG. 7-34. Palace, Palenque.

FIG. 7-35. Relief panel, Palace, Palenque. Pacal, on the right, seated on a bench or throne carved to represent a double-headed jaguar, receives a headdress or crown from Zac Kuk, his mother.

FIG. 7-36. Portraits of captives at Palenque. The first four figures make gestures of submission with their arms across their breasts; the fifth has his arms bound behind his back.

FIG. 7-37. Palace tower, Palenque.

Some luxury vessels reflect styles dominant in the south, but most western pottery represents a distinctive regional tradition. From the very beginning of the Late Classic period, a "fine paste" pottery tradition, typical of the frontier and the Gulf Coast, is prominent. This pottery often has a strongly Mexican flavor in style and iconography. Over time, fine paste wares grew in importance as Tepeu-style polychromes declined, reflecting the increasing influence of frontier people and a progressive northward reorientation of lines of communication. These trends were intimately connected to the processes of decline that brought sweeping changes to the Maya world at the end of the Late Classic period.

Palenque, not particularly prominent in earlier centuries, dominated an extensive political sphere in the Late Classic period. By the end of the eighth century, though, processes of decline had set in, and Palenque was among the first southern centers to lose its power. Palenque's temples and palaces are striking architecturally, but few are immense. Mansard roofs, roof combs, and trefoil arches are all quite distinctive. Stelae are rare. Most of Palenque's monumental art consists of architectural ornamentation: delicate, painted relief panels of stucco and stone (Figs. 7-35, 7-36). The ball court, by contrast, is small and plain. Palenque's elevated situation, in the foothills overlooking the coastal plain, provided local planners with considerable scope to blend architecture with topography. The layout of the central civic precinct reflects exceptional care in the placement of buildings in relation to one another and to the uneven terrain.

The Palace (Fig. 7-34), a maze of interior courts and subterranean rooms and passages, is Palenque's most unusual building. Relief carvings and texts (Figs. 7-35, 7-36) suggest that it was the administrative heart of the city as well as an aristocratic residence complex. A unique four-level square tower (Fig. 7-37) dominating the Palace provides a stunning view of the surrounding countryside stretching north to the sea. Behind the Palace, the small stream flowing through the center was channeled into a vaulted aqueduct.

The Temples of the Sun, Cross, and Foliated Cross form a compact group behind the Palace (Figs. 7-38, 7-39, Color Plate 4). They and the nearby Temple of the Inscriptions (Fig. 7-40), Palenque's most imposing structure, are monuments to the dynasty of Palenque's greatest ruler. Pacal ("Shield") came to power in 9.9.4.2.8 (A.D. 615) and presided over Palenque's swift rise to regional dominance until his death in 9.12.11.5.18 (A.D. 683). His son and successor, Chan Bahlum ("Serpent Jaguar"), began his reign in 9.12.11.12.10 (A.D. 684). The Temple of the Inscriptions was built above Pacal's crypt, which is reached by a vaulted stair that descends from the floor of the temple building through the heart of the pyramid to a level below ground. Pacal's body lies in an immense sculptured-stone sarcophagus along with his jade mask, ear spools, necklaces, rings, and a treasure trove of other jade and mother-of-pearl ornaments.[68] Nine stucco reliefs representing the chief gods of the underworld adorned the walls of the crypt. Pottery vessels and beautifully sculptured stucco portrait heads littered its floor, sprinkled with red cinnabar pigment. The corpses of five or six sacrificial victims, slain in connection with Pacal's funeral rites, were interred in a stone box outside the crypt to guard the sepulcher and its antechamber. After the funeral ceremonies the crypt was closed with a huge stone block, the antechamber and stair were filled with rubble, and the temple floor was sealed with large flush slabs. Only a slender pottery tube leading upward from the crypt to near the temple floor provided for communication between Pacal and his descendants in the upper world.

Reliefs on Pacal's sarcophagus identify him in death with the sun god, as does a jade effigy of the sun god buried with him. Reliefs in the Temple of

FIG. 7–38. Temple of the Cross, Palenque. The front wall has fallen, revealing the doorway to the inner chamber and the shrine celebrating Chan Bahlum's succession to the throne after the death of his father, Pacal (see Fig. 7–39).

FIG. 7-39. Inner shrine, Temple of the Cross, Palenque: restoration drawing by Tatiana Proskouriakoff. The scene on the shrine's back wall shows the transfer of royal emblems from Pacal (*left*, in his mortuary shroud) to his son, Chan Bahlum (*right*). The panels on the doorjambs show Chan Bahlum, arrayed in the symbols of kingship, facing an underworld deity who smokes a cigar. The sequence of images and associated hieroglyphic texts celebrate the installation of a legitimate successor. Drawing by Tatiana Proskouriakoff. Photograph by C.I.W., reproduced by permission of the Peabody Museum, Harvard University.

the Cross (Fig. 7-39), one of the buildings celebrating the succession of Chan Bahlum, reaffirm this association. The whole symbolic arrangement represents the transfer of royal authority and power from Pacal to Chan Bahlum, under the special auspices of the sun god. The accompanying hieroglyphic texts and the imagery and texts of the other temples in the Cross group record the same events and symbolic associations. The rituals that designated Chan Bahlum as heir to the throne were scheduled at summer solstice, and the texts seem to say that in the process he "became" the sun.

Palenque's architects designed these buildings with such sophistication that the sun itself appeared to confirm the symbolic associations. As the sun sets on the day of the winter solstice, when it is lowest and weakest, its last light shines through a notch in the ridge behind the Temple of the Inscriptions, spotlighting the succession scenes in the Temple of the Cross. At every other time of year they are in shadow. Observers in the Palace saw the sun, sinking below the ridge behind the Temple of the Inscriptions, follow an oblique path along the line of the stair to Pacal's tomb. Symbolically, the dying sun confirmed the succession of Chan Bahlum, then entered the underworld through Pacal's tomb. No more dramatic statement of the supernatural foundations of the authority of Palenque's ruling line is imaginable. The design of Palenque's civic precinct blends architecture, natural topography, monumental art, and belief systems into a structured environment that symbolically confirms the social and political order.

The imagery and texts of the Temple of the Inscriptions and the Cross group go beyond this symbolic identification with the sun in asserting the divine qualities of Pacal and Chan Bahlum. The Temple of the Inscriptions refers to Pacal's mother with glyphs otherwise used to name a goddess who ruled at the beginning of time.[69] The façade of the

FIG. 7-40. Temple of the Inscriptions, Palenque. This building is a monument to the dynasty of Pacal, Palenque's great seventh-century ruler. Pacal's crypt, almost directly beneath the small altar at the base of the stairway, is reached by a vaulted stair that descends into the pyramid from the upper temple building.

FIG. 7-41. Temple, Toniná. The openwork roof comb of this temple, standing high on the hillside terraces that support Toniná's public architecture, recalls the architectural style of the city's rival, Palenque (cf. Fig. 7-38, Color Plate 4).

temple depicts Chan Bahlum as an infant, perhaps on the occasion of his designation as heir, with the features of God K, the patron of kings and royal lineage. The texts of the Cross group recount the history of the births and accessions of gods in mythic time just before and after the beginning of the current Great Cycle. The dates are patterned so that the birth of Pacal falls on a date that is, in calendrical terms, the historical equivalent of the birth date of the ancient goddess.[70]

Through a hierarchy of lesser towns, Palenque controlled a substantial region. Texts at Tortuguero mention noble Palenque women as well as men, suggesting that here, too, marriage alliances counted among the ties that bound subsidiary centers to the regional capital. Pomoná, the most prominent of Palenque's dependencies, probably lay near the frontier with the Piedras Negras–Yaxchilán political sphere. Palenque's texts occasionally refer to the latter city. References to Tikal in Palenque texts, and to Palenque on carved bones in the tomb of a noble buried beneath Tikal's Temple of the Giant Jaguar, suggest that close alliances linked the two capitals, at least occasionally. Hieroglyphic texts indicate other ties stretching as far south and east as Copán. Texts also link Palenque with Toniná (Fig. 7-41), lying to the south at the edge of the western highlands.[71] There are some stylistic links as well, although Toniná's small stelae, carved as full round figures, are quite distinctive. Many of Toniná's monuments seem to record hostilities with other cities, and an eighth-century king of Toniná claimed the capture of Kan Xul, a younger son of Pacal who succeeded Chan Bahlum on the throne of Palenque.

Tortuguero and Jonuta lay near the western and northern limits of Palenque's sphere, on the fringe of the frontier zone. Comalcalco, a major town near the coast, was well within the frontier zone. Its architecture and stucco reliefs include features of Palenque style, but other elements indicate ties with

FIG. 7-42. Palace complex, Comalcalco. The brickwork, here with a narrow vertical window, is unique to this frontier city.

Mexican groups and with western Yucatan. Its architectural techniques, featuring brick construction (Fig. 7-42), are unique in the Maya world. Comalcalco was beyond the limits of the typical polychrome style and the stela complex. Like lower Ulúa Valley centers, Comalcalco was part of a culturally complex frontier zone, where peoples of Maya, non-Maya, and hybrid cultural identity mingled. Comalcalco's blend of styles reflects this diversity of cultural traditions.

THE NORTHERN LOWLANDS

Late Classic Maya societies in the northern lowlands were only loosely linked with their southern contemporaries. Northern styles of architecture and monumental art are quite distinctive, but they are clearly part of the lowland Maya tradition. The stela complex, the calendar, and the writing system also reflect basic Maya patterns, although even hieroglyphic writing shows considerable regional distinctiveness. Few northern texts are so well understood as those of southern cities, and details of the political histories and foreign alliances of northern centers are correspondingly sparse. Southern styles of polychrome luxury pottery faded rapidly from northern pottery-making traditions during the Late Classic period, especially in western Yucatecan towns. Such imported goods as obsidian and jade reflect some

FIG. 7-43. Temple of the Seven Dolls, Dzibilchaltún. The windows and towerlike roof are unique. The building is named after a group of clay figurines buried inside during the Postclassic period, when the ruined temple was reused for ceremonies.

continuing connections with the south, probably increasingly indirect. During the eighth and ninth centuries, many northern regions interacted with southern centers only through the geographically and culturally intermediate communities of central Yucatan.

The Northern Plains. Dzibilchaltún grew into a large city in the Late Classic period.[72] Clusters of houses and small public buildings surround the core of temples, palaces, and stelae. Raised causeways connect the major public building complexes. Nearly 8,400 structures on platforms occupy central Dzibilchaltún, and many more perishable buildings without platforms once stood among them. The Temple of the Seven Dolls (Fig. 7-43), one of the earliest vaulted buildings in the city, was also among the most unusual in its architectural design. The temple itself stands on a radial platform, and four stairs lead up to the four doorways which give access to a vaulted corridor running entirely around the building; windows in the eastern and western walls make the corridor unusually bright and airy. The central room has a vaulted ceiling that projects above the

FIG. 7-44. Palace, Edzná. The terraces of the platform that supports the templelike structure with the roof comb consist of linear arrangements of rooms of the sort usually found in residential-administrative complexes. The rooms are progressively set back so that each set stands on solid fill.

roof of the surrounding corridor to form a low tower.

Outlying building groups extend well beyond the central zone of 20 square kilometers. Dzibilchaltún was a very large community with a population on the order of 20,000–25,000 in the late eighth century. It was surely a regional capital with an extensive political and economic sphere, although Tiho, only 15 kilometers to the south, may have emerged as a political and economic rival during the Late Classic period. Dzibilchaltún is located in the driest part of the northern lowlands—the cenote adjacent to the main plaza provided a significant proportion of the city's water—and intensive farming was not the foundation of the city's economy. Dzibilchaltún's prosperity was probably based in large part on control of extensive salt-evaporation facilities on the nearby coast.

Western Yucatan. Early Classic traditions persisted in the cities of western Yucatan during the first century or two of the Late Classic period.[73] Local styles of architecture, sculpture, and pottery reflect continuing ties with the south, especially at Edzná, which

FIG. 7-45. Restored version of Structure 2, Hochob, in the Museo Nacional de Antropología, Mexico City. The elaborate façade, in which the doorway represents the open mouth of a reptilian monster, typifies central Yucatecan architecture, particularly in the Chenes region. The roof comb features rows of standing human figures.

erected monuments with Long Count dates spanning most of the seventh and eighth centuries. In addition to architectural construction programs, the lords of Edzná undertook large-scale hydraulic works,[74] including an elaborate canal system that probably functioned to control drainage and to manage the water supply; a moatlike central canal hints at defensive functions as well. Buildings at Edzná (Fig. 7-44), Oxkintok, Xcalumkin, and other towns in the region reflect the development of a distinctive architectural style that would reach its fullest elaboration at Uxmal and adjacent cities in the Puuc hills during the ninth and tenth centuries (cf. Fig. 8-13). The island of Jaina, just off the west coast, appears to have been especially sacred ground, for aristocrats from several western mainland towns chose it for their final resting place. The small island accommodated many hundreds of tombs stocked with rich offerings, including the famous polychrome figurines.

Central Yucatan. Communities in Central Yucatan maintained ties with northern and southern cities alike.[75] Central Yucatecan buildings have many features in common with those of the western Yucatecan Puuc tradition, which reached its peak later, in the Terminal Classic. Stone mosaics ornamented elaborate façades. Unlike Puuc structures, though, these are usually faced with plaster; masks of long-nosed creatures are especially common on building corners. Doorways often resemble the mouths of grotesque monsters,[76] particularly in the Chenes region, in the northwest (Fig. 7-45; cf. Figs. 7-22, 8-2). Farther south and east, in the Río Bec region, the architecture echoes southern styles more strongly. Towers attached to low buildings imitate the form, but not the function, of tall southern temple pyramids (Fig. 7-46). Stairs are too steep to climb, and the "temples" atop the towers are solid

FIG. 7-46. Structure I, Xpuhil. The tower, part of a temple complex, resembles temples on tall platforms in southern cities (cf. Fig. 7-5), but the stair is too steep to climb and the upper structure is a solid construction with a false door and no interior rooms.

constructions with false doorways. Pottery styles follow a similar pattern: the potters of Santa Rosa Xtampak and Dzibilnocac maintained stronger northern connections, while their counterparts at Becán and nearby communities used more southern features. There is, in effect, a gradient from the Río Bec region through the Chenes zone to the Puuc area, marked by decreasing evidence of contacts with the southern lowlands and a progressively later timing of peak development. In the eighth century, Becán's increasingly regionalized pottery suggests that external relations, particularly with southern centers, were weakening.

Eastern Yucatan. Cobá was the largest and most powerful center in eastern Yucatan.[77] The city has many complexes of palaces and temples (Fig. 7-47) connected by a network of internal causeways and surrounded by extensive residential zones. Architecture and ceramics indicate close connection with southern cities. An unusually large number of stelae memorialize women, and some of the portraits incorporate motifs usually reserved for male rulers: ceremonial bars symbolic of authority and prisoners beneath the noble's feet. Similar stelae at Tancah, Ichpaatún, and other cities suggest that royal women played exceptionally important roles in parts of the north, where they evidently often assumed high political offices in addition to their roles as royal spouses. A causeway more than 100 kilometers long connects Cobá with Yaxuná, just south of Chichén Itzá, pointing to close ties with areas to the west. Cobá probably controlled Yaxuná (and perhaps a significant part of the surrounding region) during the Late Classic period, before Chichén Itzá emerged as a major power, although Izamal and Ek Balam were also large and prosperous cities that probably wielded substantial political influence in the region.

THE HIGHLANDS

Communities in the Comitán Valley, in the western highlands south of Toniná, erected dated stelae in a distinctive regional style. The stela complex and monumental art evidently did not extend farther west into the highlands, although some communities imported pottery from the southern lowlands. Settlement systems indicate political regionalization, with no really dominant towns. Most communities were quite small, located in defensible positions on ridges and hilltops.

Central and eastern highland regions were less closely linked with the rest of the Maya world during the Late Classic period.[78] The stela complex, Long Count calendar system, and hieroglyphic writing, first developed in highland and piedmont communities, went out of use at the beginning of the Classic period. Such architectural features as corbeled arches, universal to the north, did not extend to highland towns. The mechanisms of communication that spread these traits throughout the rest of the Maya world evidently did not embrace most of the highlands. After the decline of Teotihuacán's influence, the central highlands underwent a process of regionalization, marked by the resurgence of local traditions. In some areas, particularly along the northern fringe of the central highlands, traditions of pottery making continued to reflect lowland styles. Lowland towns still imported jade, obsidian, and other highland commodities, but few if any central highland communities maintained close ties with lowland cities. In the east, lowland connections were stronger, especially between Chalchuapa and Copán's sphere.

No highland community could compare with the great lowland cities in size, architectural grandeur, or political and economic influence. None controlled a political and economic zone comparable to the areas dominated by lowland regional capitals. Cotio, a small town in the Valley of Guatemala, is typical of many Late Classic highland communities. A compact cluster of low platform mounds, faced with adobe plaster, supported small thatched buildings. These structures, along with a single small ball court, comprised the entire civic precinct.

By most measures, lowland cities of the Late Classic period represent the apogee of Maya civilization. The florescence of the Puuc region and of Chichén Itzá was still in the future, but most southern lowland cities had reached their peak in terms of population size, scale of public architecture, and internal diversity. Communities within regional settlement systems were more diverse in size and function than ever before. Political, economic, and social systems reached their maximum complexity; aristocracies and bureaucracies expanded, and political art—especially as expressed in monumental stone sculpture—burgeoned. Minor arts and crafts flourished, and economic specialization in general proliferated. Several cities (notably Tikal) concentrated authority and power to an unusual degree and dominated extensive regional states. Economic spheres also contributed to a general sharpening of regional contrasts, reflected in distinctive styles of architecture, pottery, and various crafts. Sharper contrasts set apart the smaller highland towns, whose aristocracies still eschewed the stela complex. By the end of the eighth century, many regions, at least in the southern lowlands, were testing the limits of their natural resources to sustain growth. Beginning in the ninth century, in region after region, new stresses set off processes of change that would eventually transform the Maya world.

FIG. 7-47. Nohoch Mul temple, Cobá.

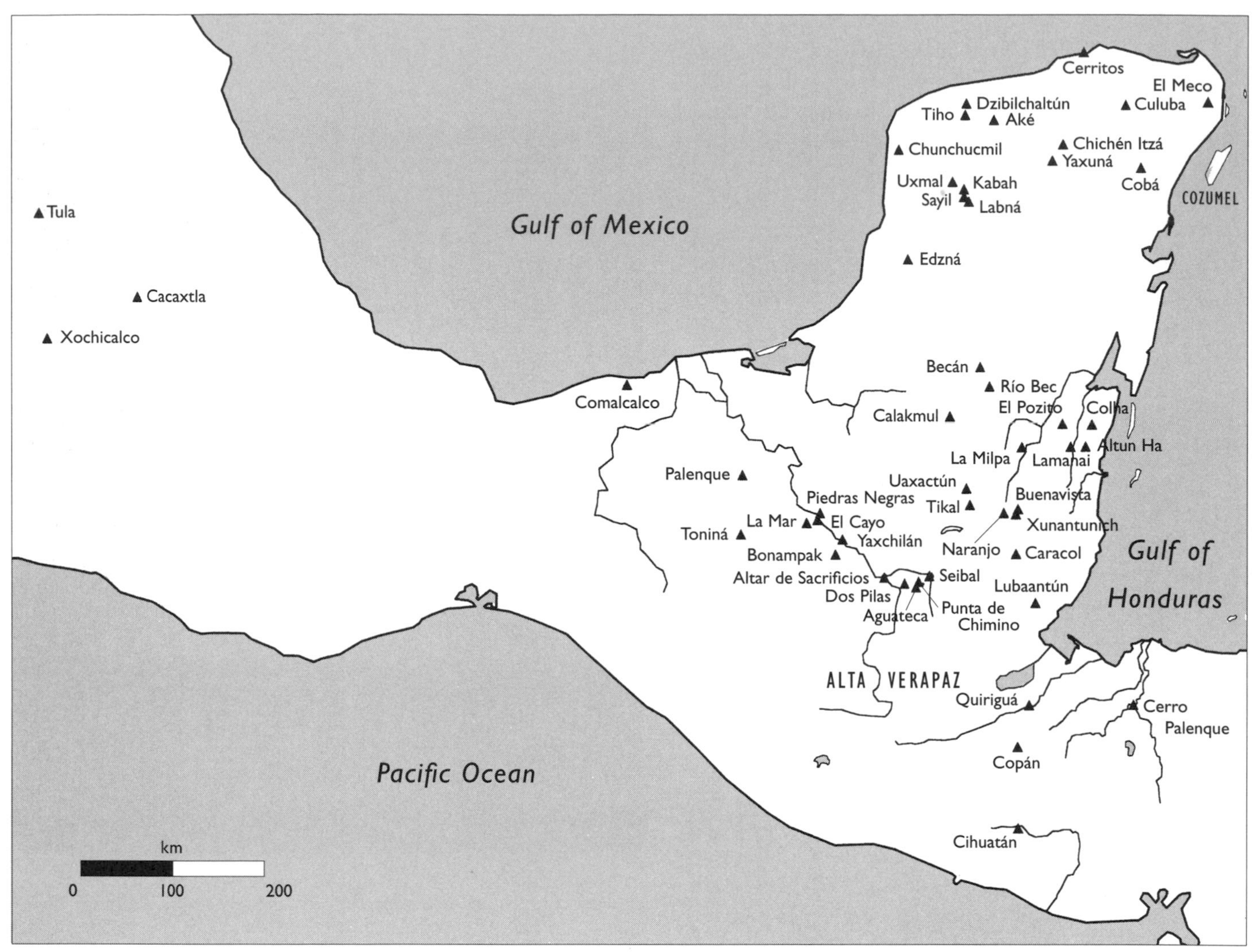

MAP 10. Terminal Classic cities.

EIGHT

Transformations

The Terminal Classic Period

The Classic period embraces both the great florescence of Maya civilization and a period of radical sociopolitical transformation.[1] In the ninth century, new processes—involving internal strains as well as external pressures—disrupted long-standing trajectories of growth and expansion, and eventually transformed the entire Maya world. This episode, which was once conceptualized as a sudden and universal collapse of all facets of Maya civilization at the end of the Classic period, now appears to have been a series of interlocking processes that operated over several centuries with different timings and outcomes in the various parts of the Maya world. Most of these processes, and the trajectories of growth and decline that they produced, were always in operation; in a sense, the Terminal Classic transformation was unusual only in that most regions went through a deep decline stage of the developmental cycle at about the same time. Some regions (notably northern Yucatan) enjoyed continued, sometimes intensified growth while others were in the process of transformation.[2] The earliest and most devastating effects were felt in the southern lowlands, where nearly every great city—and the states whose centers they were—presently ceased to function. Even at its most intense, the process was chiefly a decline of state institutions, with consequent transformations of aristocracies and aristocratic economies; in most regions, village and household life went on, albeit in the context of much-simplified political and economic systems. Even political decline was not universal: Lamanai in the east (Map 10) continued to flourish, seemingly little affected. Related processes were at work in the north, but with different timings and results. The great cities of the Puuc region in the west reached their peaks in the Terminal Classic, as

FIG. 8-1. Temple of the Magician, Uxmal. This view shows the rear of the building.

did Chichén Itzá in the central part of the peninsula.[3] Highland Maya societies participated less directly in these processes, but they too felt the effect of pressures from Mexican Mesoamerica. These pressures, along with a disruption of communication and exchange networks resulting from the decline of lowland cities, produced radically reoriented economic and social systems in the highlands as well.

The Northern Lowlands

As the Terminal Classic period wore on, the long-standing involvement of Mexican and Mexican-influenced frontier peoples in the affairs of northern Yucatan intensified. The fragments of Maya history recorded in the colonial period provide only distant echoes of Terminal Classic conditions, and they are couched in the language of metaphor, but they do nonetheless hint at some of the central historical processes.[4] European and Maya histories refer again and again to the complex comings and goings of the Itzá, a Maya group foreign to northern Yucatan, to Mexicans who often accompanied them, and to Kukulcán.[5] Diego de Landa, third bishop of Yucatan, in his account of preconquest history, explained: "It is believed among the Indians that with the Itzas who occupied Chichen Itza, there reigned a great lord, named Kukulcan. . . . They say that he arrived from the west; but they differ among themselves as to whether he arrived before or after the Itzas or with them."[6]

All histories link the Itzá to Mexicans and to Chichén Itzá. The Itzá were Maya, but foreign to northern Yucatan. According to the books of Chilam Balam, compendiums of Yucatec history and prophecy written during the colonial period, the Itzá were "the fatherless ones, the motherless ones," who "speak our language brokenly."[7] The Chontal of the western frontier spoke a related but distinct Mayan language, and would have had to develop local kinship ties by marrying into Yucatec families. The Chontal fit descriptions of the Itzá quite well.[8] Disparaging comments about Itzá sinfulness and lewdness in Yucatec histories may refer to phallic cults introduced into Yucatan as part of the Terminal Classic interaction with Mexican and frontier-Maya peoples, but they might also imply no more than unfamiliar, and therefore "heathen," religious practices. The "foreign presence" in northern Yucatan during the Terminal Classic period is best understood as a reflection of a continuing process of intense interaction with Maya, Mexican, and culturally hybrid peoples of the Gulf Coast region. Gulf Coast peoples were also intimately linked to central Mexican societies: the region was an important part of the Teotihuacán world, and the Nonoalcas (Mexican neighbors of the Itzá along the western Maya frontier) were closely tied to the Toltec state. The Gulf Coast region was always an intermediary between central Mexico and the Maya world, and the Terminal Classic intensification of Gulf Coast and Mexican involvement in the Maya world reflects in part the long-term effects of the massive social, political, and economic disruptions of Mexican societies that began with the collapse of Teotihuacán in the Late Classic period.

The chronology of the arrivals of the various groups of foreigners who were said to have come to northern Yucatan is very confusing.[9] Yucatecan histories refer to a series of penetrations of Mexicans and Mexican-influenced Mayas from the west, not to a single group of Itzá led by a lord named Kukulcán. Archaeological evidence reinforces this historical picture, indicating a continuing Mexican and frontier-Maya presence in western Yucatan during the Terminal Classic period.[10]

WESTERN YUCATAN

By the ninth century, southern features had faded as highly distinctive new regional styles emerged. The

FIG. 8-2. Doorway, Temple of the Magician, Uxmal. This Chenes-style doorway, framed by the jaws of a grotesque monster, is part of a construction stage that was superseded by the final, Puuc-style temple.

advent of the western Yucatecan style is roughly coeval with the beginning of the decline within the Usumacinta lowlands. New Mexican elements accompanied both developments. Disruption of communication networks in the west may have severed a principal link between northern and southern lowlands at the same time that newly intensified contacts with Mexican and Mexican-influenced peoples of the frontier zone affected both areas.

Uxmal, in the Puuc hills of western Yucatan, a small community during the Late Classic period, grew to become one of the largest and most powerful of the northern cities, with a sphere of influence that put it in the same class as the southern capitals.[11] The Puuc zone is particularly distinctive in its architectural tradition, which had roots in both the central Yucatecan styles and (especially) in the Late Classic architecture of Edzná and other cities in the southwestern part of the peninsula. Notable in the dry Puuc region is an emphasis on systems of water storage, necessary to ensure a year-round supply of drinking water and to permit a truly effective exploitation of the region's fertile soils.

Early versions of Uxmal's Temple of the Magician and Governor's Palace were built in the Chenes style (Fig. 8-2, Color Plate 5), as was at least one building at Chichén Itzá. Public buildings—temples, palaces, ball courts—correspond functionally to those of southern cities, but architectural style and construction techniques differ sharply. Rubble-cored walls faced with thin, carefully fitted stone veneers, freestanding and engaged columns, and plain lower-building façades topped by intricate stone mosaics combine to produce a sharp contrast with southern civic buildings.

Uxmal's civic core embodies the fullest expression of the Puuc architectural style. Wide plazas and other open areas lend Uxmal a feeling of spaciousness unknown in the more crowded southern cities. The Temple of the Magician (Figs. 8-1 and 8-2,

FIG. 8-3. Nunnery Quadrangle, Uxmal. The arched entry is at the top of the stairs that ascend the platform at the left.

Color Plate 5) is Uxmal's most massive structure. This unusual smoothly faced elliptical pyramid, surmounted by an elaborately ornamented temple building, was rebuilt at least four times. The adjacent Nunnery Quadrangle, four multiroomed buildings with mosaic façades arranged around a central court (Figs. 8-3–8-5), was probably both a palace and an administrative complex. A stela stands before the main building, opposite the arched entranceway. A small ball court at the edge of the Nunnery Quadrangle building platform has decorated stone rings mounted in the side walls, representing the most spectacular way to score in the ball game. Abbreviated dates on the rings, and in two of the Nunnery Quadrangle buildings, suggest that these complexes were dedicated at the beginning of the tenth century, probably during the reign of "Lord Chaac," who is mentioned several times in these texts. Another broad platform supports two of the most pleasingly proportioned of all Maya buildings: the Governor's Palace and the House of the Turtles (Figs. 8-6–8-8). The Governor's Palace has a very linear

FIG. 8-4. Nunnery Quadrangle, Uxmal. A stela stands before the main two-story palace, which is decorated with elaborate stone-mosaic scenes and masks.

FIG. 8-5. Mosaic decoration, Nunnery Quadrangle, Uxmal. Feathered serpents writhe across a geometric background.

FIG. 8-6. Uxmal. The Governor's Palace (*left*) and the House of the Turtles (*right*) occupy a massive substructure. The Great Pyramid (*center background*) is a free-standing construction. The corner of the ball court is just visible at the lower right.

FIG. 8-7. Governor's Palace, Uxmal.

FIG. 8-8. House of the Turtles, Uxmal: detail showing turtle effigies along the upper façade.

FIG. 8-9. Tzompantli, Uxmal. The crossed bones and skull reliefs on this low platform reflect its function, displaying the remains of sacrificial victims.

FIG. 8-10. Arch, Kabah. This monument marks Kabah's end of a paved causeway connecting the center with Uxmal.

design, with two dozen rooms stretching 100 meters along the platform. Elaborate mosaic decoration on the façade, featuring mat designs, confirms the connection with royal authority and is consistent with administrative functions that might include council meetings. Construction of the Governor's Palace probably also took place early in the tenth century under Lord Chaac, who is mentioned in a text found nearby. The Great Pyramid, a large temple ornamented with mosaic masks of a grotesque supernatural being, stands on an adjacent platform. Surrounding building complexes reflect the same simplicity of design combined with ornately decorated façades. Mexican elements are common in Uxmal's monumental art, and its pottery incorporates fine paste styles of the western frontier. Uxmal even had a tzompantli, or skull-rack platform (Fig. 8-9), identical to those on which central Mexican peoples displayed the heads of sacrificial victims. Perhaps the city housed an enclave of Mexicans.

The distribution of Puuc-style buildings in the surrounding region probably reflects a sphere in

FIG. 8-11. Codz Pop, Kabah. Some 250 mosaic masks of long-nosed beings decorate the façade.

FIG. 8-12. Codz Pop, Kabah: detail of mosaic masks on the lower façade. The two square, pierced objects at right center are the ear ornaments of adjacent heads. The lighter-shade projecting stone is the grotesque nose of the head on the left. These long-nosed masks are often interpreted as images of the rain god, Chac, but they are just as likely to represent Ah Bolon Dzacab, another long-nosed supernatural associated with royal lineages.

which Uxmal was able to exercise direct political and economic control. A paved causeway runs 16 kilometers southeast from Uxmal, ending at a formal archway which stands at the edge of the civic precinct of Kabah, a smaller dependency (Fig. 8-10). A text inscribed on an altar standing before the main palace building, which is elaborately ornamented with long-nosed masks (Figs. 8-11, 8-12), refers to Lord Chaac of Uxmal, presumably the city's overlord.

Sayil was even more extensive, with temples, palaces (Fig. 8-13), craft production areas, and residential complexes spread out over nearly 4.5 square kilometers.[12] Some 10,000 people lived in the houses interspersed among the civic buildings and in the immediately surrounding area, with another 5,000 to 10,000 slightly farther out. Even in the city center, however, gardens were attached to each domestic complex; so the city must have been relatively cool and green. These domestic gardens could be intensively cultivated and fertilized with no need to transport materials or labor and—along with the fruit trees that would have been planted around each house—they must have produced a significant

FIG. 8-13. Palace, Sayil. The upper stories are set back so that they stand on solid construction fill.

FIG. 8-14. Puuc-style building, Chichén Itzá.

proportion of the community's food. Labná, just to the east, was a third prominent town within Uxmal's political and economic shadow.

The Puuc architectural style spread quite widely, extending at least as far east Chichén Itzá and Culuba (Figs. 8-14, 8-15), but there is no reason to suppose that it reflects an expansion of Uxmal's hegemony beyond the Puuc hills. At least by the later Terminal Classic, if not before, the potters of Uxmal and Chichén also shared ceramic styles.[13] Texts at Chichén refer to Lord Chaac, so there may be political links as well as economic ties between the two cities, although there is no evidence to indicate that they did not remain politically autonomous. By the eleventh century, a process of decline was under way in the Puuc cities, and most were abandoned before the end of the century.

THE NORTHERN PLAINS

At Dzibilchaltún, in the northwest, the prosperity of the eighth century continued during the ninth and tenth centuries, and the population may have grown a bit beyond the 20,000–25,000 estimated for the Late Classic period.[14] Construction of public buildings continued in the civic core of the city, and some of the new buildings reflect the Puuc style, although Dzibilchaltún was surely not a dependency of Uxmal. Here, too, potters adopted fine paste

FIG. 8-15. Iglesia ("church"), Chichén Itzá. This building reflects the architectural styles of central Yucatan as well as that of the Puuc area.

styles, and unusual inscriptions and a tzompantli indicate strong Mexican connections. Like Uxmal, Dzibilchaltún may have housed an enclave of Mexicans or Mexicanized Mayas from the western frontier region. By the end of the tenth century, Dzibilchaltún was in decline, with a reduced population, and no new major construction projects were undertaken. This shift in Dzibilchaltún's fortunes probably relates to the growth of Tiho, only 15 kilometers to the south. Tiho may have been larger than Dzibilchaltún by the end of the Terminal Classic period and was certainly a formidable political and economic rival.[15]

Chichén Itzá had emerged as a substantial town by the beginning of the Terminal Classic period, and it soon became the dominant political and economic power in the northern peninsula.[16] The city core came to cover some 5 square kilometers, surrounded by a much larger zone of perhaps 25 square kilometers which is dense with residential remains. Several related but distinctive styles of architecture and sculpture reflect the cosmopolitan character of the city. Some elements indicate connections with the Puuc and Chenes spheres (Figs 8-14, 8-15); some point to a strong foreign component, including both frontier Maya (Itzá) and Mexican elements; and others probably reflect a local heritage. The most imposing buildings (with most of the Mexican elements) are part of the main civic precinct, while most of the Puuc-style buildings are located to the south of this core zone. These differences in spatial distribution probably reflect differential functions of the buildings in different zones of the city, differential use of some stylistic elements in political art, as well as differences in cultural identity among segments of the city's population.[17] Murals and reliefs that depict nobles in Mexican garb, accompanied by Mexican-style name glyphs,[18] provide strong evidence that at least one segment of Chichén's aristocracy claimed a non-Maya cultural identity. Pictorial representations also suggest that the influx of foreigners was not entirely peaceful (Fig. 8-16). Scenes of combat depict figures with Mexican characteristics—presumably the Itzá and their allies—as victors; Maya warriors generally appear slain, fleeing, as prisoners, or consigned to the sacrificial altar. At the same time, Mexican emblems do not always mark dominance, for some images show bound figures in Mexican dress.

Building designs and decorative schemes in the center of Chichén—the public face of the state and the focus of state activities—reflect foreign tastes as well as elements of Yucatecan tradition, suggesting that the Itzá were key participants, if not the dominant element, in Chichén's political order. This foreign dimension of the Chichén state may in part account for the fact that hieroglyphic texts do not celebrate individual kings and their dynasties with the same emphasis as the texts of earlier Maya cities. Later historical sources speak of a more complex political system in which council-like institutions exercised much of the power held by earlier kings.[19]

Chichén's prosperity and regional dominance lasted through the tenth century and may have continued well into the Early Postclassic period.[20] As time passed, processes of acculturation were at work on Itzá aristocrats and their Mexican affiliates as they formed alliances with Yucatec families and developed a taste for local ways of doing things. Architecture, arts, and crafts all reflect the growth of a hybrid Yucatec-Itzá-Mexican culture at Chichén Itzá. In the end, the local Maya tradition proved most durable and influential, and foreigners were largely assimilated into Yucatec societies. The Yucatan invaded by the Spaniards retained surprisingly few signs of the previous foreign impact.

The civic heart of Chichén Itzá, set apart by a formal boundary wall, was an immense platform on which three great building complexes define a spacious plaza area. The ball court to the west

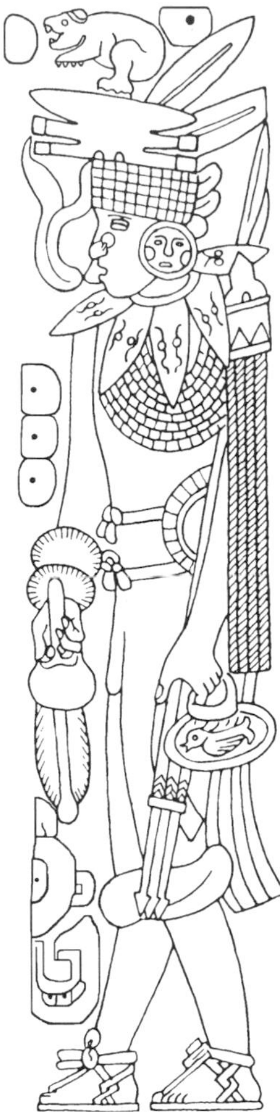

FIG. 8-16. Inner doorjamb, Upper Temple of the Jaguars, Chichén Itzá. The warrior figure, done in a style that reflects many foreign elements, carries spears and an atlatl usd to throw them. The hieroglyphic sign above his head, "2 Rabbit," is a day in a Mexican-style calendar and probably records his name. Adapted from Coggins and Shane 1984:fig. 19.

(Fig. 8-17) is the largest in all Mesoamerica, has an I-shaped playing area 150 meters long, and features a small temple at either end. Tall platforms flank the main playing alley, and rings are set high in the side walls (Fig. 8-18). Reliefs along the lower walls depict ball-game ritual, including the sacrifice of losers by the victors. A temple looks down into the ball court from atop the east platform, with a lower chamber opening outside into the main plaza.

The Castillo (Fig. 8-19), Chichén's most important temple and one of the few to follow the ancient high-terraced pyramid design, stands at the south edge of the Great Plaza. Landa, who visited Chichén Itzá in the sixteenth century, says that this building was called Kukulcán. It probably was dedicated to the great god-hero, for feathered serpents are prominent in the decoration of the pyramid and the temple building. The feathered serpents that flank the balustrades of the Castillo's northern stair are among the most remarkable of all Maya architectural ornaments. They are carved so that twice a year, at the spring and autumn equinoxes, the late-afternoon sun brings them to life. As the afternoon advances, a shifting pattern of light and shadow transforms the balustrades into images of slowly writhing diamondback rattlesnakes.

The final remodeling of the Castillo encased and preserved an earlier version of the Kukulcán temple. A red-painted stone jaguar throne, with jade insets for eyes and spots and chert fangs, still remained in the temple chamber along with a chacmool sculpture. The throne is identical to those of the lords portrayed in the murals of the Temple of the Chacmool, another early building later covered by the Temple of the Warriors.

The Temple of the Warriors (Color Plate 6) is the most imposing building of the complex that borders the main plaza on the east. Behind a colonnade of square pillars, each adorned with relief carvings of warriors in Mexican dress, rises a low platform

FIG. 8-17. Great Ball Court, Chichén Itzá.

which supports the temple. Standard-bearers guard the top of the stair, and a chacmool (Fig. 8-20) reclines before the main entrance. The serpent columns flanking the doorway once supported the lintel. The inner sanctum is complete with an altar borne by tiny Mexican-style warriors (Fig. 8-21). Long colonnaded halls furnished with benches border the large adjacent court—a hub of civic activity combining palace, administrative, and market functions. Several low platforms within the Great Plaza itself never supported buildings (Fig. 8-22). One is a tzompantli, where the heads of sacrificial victims were displayed. Two others, according to Bishop Landa, were "stages . . . where they say that farces were represented, and comedies for the pleasure of the public."[21]

No doubt the plaza was the scene of many rites and festivals similar to the Chic Kaban ceremony, performed in later times at Maní in honor of Kukulcán:

> On the 16th of Xul, all the priests and lords assembled in Mani, and with them a large multitude from the towns, who came already prepared by their fasts and abstinences. On the evening of that day they went forth with a great procession of people, and with a large number of their comedians from the house of the lord, where they were assembled, and they went very quietly to the temple of Kukulcan, which they had previously properly adorned, and having arrived there, and making their prayers, they placed the banners on top of the temple, and they all spread out their idols below in the courtyard, . . . and having kindled new fire, they began to burn their incense in many places and to make offerings of food cooked without salt or pepper and of drinks made of their beans and the seeds of squashes. The lords and those who had fasted remained there without returning to their houses for five days and five nights in prayer, always burning copal [incense] and engaged in their offerings, and executing several sacred dances until the first day of Yaxkin [the following month].

FIG. 8-18. Great Ball Court, Chichén Itzá: view of the playing area, with rings set high in the side walls. Temples stand atop the side platform and beyond the end court.

FIG. 8-19. Castillo ("castle"), Chichén Itzá. This building is Chichén's main temple, dedicated to Kukulcán. The balustrades of the main stair, like the columns that support the lintel over the doorway to which it leads, represent feathered serpents. At sunset on the equinoxes, the edges of the platform terraces cast shadows which form a diamond pattern along the balustrade. Photograph courtesy Anthony Aveni.

FIG. 8-20. Chacmool and serpent columns, Temple of the Warriors, Chichén Itzá.

The comedians went during these five days among the principal houses, playing their pieces and collected the gifts which were given to them, and they carried the whole of them to the temple where, when the five days were ended and past, they divided the gifts among the lords, priests and dancers, and they got together the banners and idols and returned to the house of the lord, and from there each one to his own house. They said and considered it as certain that Kukulcan came down from heaven on the last day of these (five days), and received their services, their vigils and offerings.[22]

The Mercado, a large colonnaded building with a spacious interior court—perhaps a council hall—occupies an extension of the great building platform to the east. Nearby are three more ball courts, one associated with a ritual steam bath.

North of the main plaza lies the sacred cenote (Fig. 8-23) from which Chichén Itzá ("mouth of the well of the Itzá") took its name. "From the court in front of these stages," reports Bishop Landa, "a wide and handsome causeway runs, as far as a well which is about two stones' throw off [300 meters]. Into this well they have had, and then had, the custom of throwing men alive as a sacrifice to the gods, in times of drought, and they believed that they did not die though they never saw them again. They also threw into it a great many other things, like precious stones and things which they prized. And so if this country had possessed gold, it would be this well that would have the greater part of it, so great was the devotion which the Indians showed for it."[23]

Although the Maya did little metalwork, copper, gold, and tumbaga ornaments, bells, rings, masks, cups, figurines, and beautifully embossed plaques were among the offerings dredged from the cenote.[24] Most of these metal objects were imported from Mexico, Honduras, and eastern Central America. Jade jewelry and plaques, along with many other luxury items were also imported or made from im-

FIG. 8-21. Altar, Temple of the Warriors, Chichén Itzá. The Atlantean supports represent miniature, foreign-style warrior figures.

ported materials. Most of the pottery and such perishable materials as carved wood, textiles, and incense were more local.

Human bones confirm the cenote's role in sacrifice. These rites were both divinatory and propitiatory: they were meant to determine the disposition of the rain god and to placate him. According to the sixteenth-century *Relación* of Valladolid:

In this cenote the lords and important men of all these provinces . . . were accustomed, having fasted for sixty days without raising their eyes in this time even to look upon their wives nor upon those who brought them food, and this they did as a preliminary to, upon reaching the mouth of that cenote, throwing into it at break of dawn some Indian women belonging to each of those lords, whom they had told to ask for a good year and all those things which seemed best to them (the lords). And thus, these Indian women having been thrown in without being bound, but flung down as from a cliff, they fell into the water striking it with great force. And at exactly midday the one who was to come out shouted for them to throw her a rope to take her out, and when she came above half dead they made great fires around her, censing her with copal. And when she came to, she said that there were many of their race below, men as well as women, who received her, and that when she raised her head to look at some one of

FIG. 8-22. Venus platform, Chichén Itzá. This small platform, decorated with symbols of Kukulcán and the planet Venus, never supported a superstructure. It was probably a stage for public ritual performances. The causeway from the Great Plaza to the sacred cenote leads away from the Venus platform into the background.

them, they gave her severe blows on the neck so that she would keep her head bowed down, all of which occurred within the water in which they say there were many hollows and holes. And they replied to her whether they would have a good or bad year according to the questions which the Indian woman put. And if the demon was angry with one of the lords of those who threw in the Indian women, [no one asked] to be taken out on the point of noon.[25]

So sacred was this cenote that its cult still flourished hundreds of years after the decline of Chichén. Certainly ritual activity continued there when Bishop Landa visited the site in the sixteenth century. He wrote: "On the top close to the edge is a small building in which I found idols made in honor of all the principal buildings of the country, almost like the Pantheon at Rome, . . . And they held Cozumel and the well of Chichén Itzá in the same veneration as we have for pilgrimages to Jerusalem and Rome, and so they used to go (to visit these places) and to offer presents there."[26] The popular belief that only beautiful maidens were hurled into the cenote, after being deflowered by depraved priests, is pure Victorian embroidery. The most reliable early sources mention men, women, and children alike, and human bones taken from the cenote are indeed those of children and adults of both sexes. As one analyst who studied the bones remarked, "All of the individuals involved (or rather immersed) may have been virgins, but the osteological evidence does not permit a determination of this nice point."[27]

FIG. 8-23. Sacred cenote, Chichén Itzá. This natural sinkhole was still the scene of sacrificial ceremonies long after Chichén itself went into eclipse.

Except for the sacred cenote, the layout of Chichén's main plaza recalls that of the civic heart of Tula, the Toltec capital. The Temple of the Warriors complex is strikingly like Tula's Pyramid B (Fig. 8-24; cf. Color Plate 6), a Quetzalcoatl temple with adjacent colonnaded halls. Chichén's ties with Tula, however indirect they may have been, were strong enough to

FIG. 8-24. Pyramid B, Tula. The similarities with Chichén's Temple of the Warriors (Color Plate 6), though real, are exaggerated in this reconstruction.

produce very similar civic architecture at the core of each center.[28] The relationship was certainly not one of slavish copying of a metropolitan capital by a colonial outpost. The chief difference between the two centers is that Chichén has by far the better architecture, and the buildings at Tula which most resemble those of Chichén were erected relatively late in its history. The relationship between the two great capitals was complex and involved the eastern Gulf Coast in an intermediary role. Each center reflects a complex amalgam of several cultural traditions; the culture of Chichén, although it owed much to Mexican influence, had its own impact on the Toltecs.

Smaller complexes of public buildings, including several more ball courts, surround the main group at Chichén Itzá, and many of them are linked to the civic core by causeways. One causeway leads south to a funerary temple called the High Priest's Grave (Fig. 8-25), a smaller version of the Castillo containing the tomb of a great noble. Nearby is the Caracol (Fig. 8-26), a round building that probably functioned as an observatory.[29] Windows opening off the spiral stair inside its dome define lines of sight that mark the positions of such interesting astronomical events as sunset and moonset at the equinoxes. By analogy with round buildings elsewhere in Mesoamerica, the Caracol would also have been sacred to Kukulcán. Beyond, civic architecture stretches far to the south.

Chichén Itzá rose to a position of political and economic supremacy in the central part of the Yucatan peninsula and, after the demise of Cobá, in the east as well. The core of Chichén's sphere may have corresponded to the earlier domain of Izamal, to the northwest.[30] Izamal, and perhaps other towns like Ek Balam to the northeast, was probably autonomous early in the Terminal Classic period, taking on the status of a subordinate outpost as Chichén's power grew. Chichén's actual control may also have stretched well to the south, deep into the heart of Yucatan. Here, few if any powerful political and economic centers survived beyond the early decades of the Terminal Classic, and most communities were village societies with limited external contacts. The near absence of large communities with civic architecture in the central peninsula may be a measure of the thoroughness of Chichén's control. It may also reflect Chichén's growth process, which seems to have involved a transfer of people from the surrounding region into the city.[31]

FIG. 8-25. High Priest's Grave. The serpent balustrades flanking the stairway of this temple, just south of the central sector of Chichén, recall those of the Castillo.

Cotton, a major crop in the north during the sixteenth century, was surely an important product, but coastal resources were increasingly central to Chichén's economy, and salt from the extensive north-coast beds was probably the principal export. Cerritos, on an island and adjacent mainland on the north coast, had a port facility that may have been a special attraction for Itzá merchants. It soon became Chichén's chief port, providing maritime links that stretched southeast and southwest to the limits of the Maya world and beyond.[32] These economic networks brought Fine Orange pottery from the Gulf Coast, jade from the upper Motagua Valley, Plumbate vessels from the Pacific coast and piedmont, turquoise from northern Mexico, and metal

FIG. 8-26. Caracol, Chichén Itzá. Windows opening out of the dome from the interior spiral stair were used for astronomical sightings.

ornaments from lower Central America. Maya highland sources continued to provide obsidian, but the bulk now came from central Mexico. Maya histories recorded after the European invasion emphasize Chichén's connections with Honduras, famous for cacao, feathers, as well as gold and other metals. Honduran markets could also provide products that originated farther south and east, beyond the limits of Mesoamerica, such as the Panamanian gold objects that have been found among the offerings cast into the sacred cenote.[33]

EASTERN YUCATAN

Cobá remained a political and economic force in the eastern part of northern Yucatan during the ninth and tenth centuries, albeit with new patterns of external relationships. With southern cities in decline, polychrome vessels disappeared and pottery began to reflect northern norms. The long sacbe connecting the city to the small center of Yaxuná, just south of Chichén Itzá, indicates a special relationship between Cobá and at least the Yaxuná region. Terminal Classic construction activity at Yaxuná included some new structures (mainly in the ball-court complex) along with the remodeling of many existing civic buildings. Many of these structures are oriented to the sacbe, and thus to Cobá, but local lords also built some buildings in the Puuc style. It may be that Cobá attempted to bring the central part of the peninsula within its orbit. If so, the emergence of nearby Chichén Itzá as a focus of regional power brought to an end Cobá's pretensions to political and economic hegemony in the west; at the same time Yaxuná's prominence waned, and many of its buildings and sculptures were thrown down. Chichén evidently established a presence first at towns like El Meco on the northeast coast and on Cozumel, effectively encircling Cobá.[34]

In general, northern cities continued to flourish during the tenth century, although a process of decline may have begun in a few places as external pressures intensified. Large numbers of Mexicans and Mexican-influenced Mayas moving into Yucatan from the west may have accelerated a process of decline that had already set in. The appearance of fortifications at Aké, Chunchucmil, Uxmal and several other towns suggests that this process may not have been entirely peaceful.[35] In any case, Uxmal, Dzibilchaltún, Cobá, and most other cities declined rapidly. Most were effectively abandoned, even though regional populations were not decimated. Chichén Itzá maintained its power and prosperity longer, probably well into the eleventh century and perhaps even into the twelfth.

The Southern Lowlands

Beginning about A.D. 800 in the west, center after center across the southern lowlands stopped erecting stelae. Public building activity slackened or ceased altogether, populations declined, and most centers quickly lost power and central administrative functions. Social, economic, and political systems were devastated, reduced to faint shadows of their climax forms.[36]

Changes were not instantaneous. Some communities continued to function as civic centers for a brief period. Public construction continued at some cities, on a reduced scale, for a few decades after the last stelae and hieroglyphic texts were carved. Seibal even experienced a ninth-century boom in public building and a peak of monument dedication while other cities in the region were in decline; before the end of the century, though, it too was eclipsed. By 10.4.0.0.0 (A.D. 909), the last Long Count date had been carved and almost all southern lowland cities had lost their power. Lamanai, in the east, continued to function as a city, but by the middle of the tenth century the civic core of virtually every southern city was an abandoned ruin. Surrounding areas retained at least remnants of their former populations,

FIG. 8-27. Graffito, Temple II, Tikal. The scene depicts an episode of human sacrifice. Adapted from Maler 1911:fig. 10.

and squatters in the ruins of a few cities made pitiful attempts to recapture lost grandeur.

At Tikal, survivors tried to maintain corrupt versions of the old institutions.[37] They reerected broken stelae, sometimes with the hieroglyphic inscriptions upside down. Ashes and fragments of crude incense-burners in temples testify to a continuing but simplified ceremonial regime. The old sacred buildings, still holy places, were now refurbished only with graffiti scratched on the walls (Fig. 8-27).[38] The aristocratic component of Maya civilization had been swept away—along with, in some regions, a good portion of the peasant population that had sustained it.

Conflict with Toniná seems to have resulted in the capture and execution of Palenque's king—Kan Hok Xul, Pacal's younger son—early in the eighth century. Hostilities between the two cities continued, at least sporadically, for the rest of the century and may well have played a significant role in the decline of Palenque and perhaps of some of its neighbors. In any case, public construction waned at Palenque in the mid eighth century.[39] The latest Long Count date (9.18.9.0.0), on a carved pottery vessel, corresponds to A.D. 799. Shortly thereafter, aristocratic activity ceased altogether. The lords of Toniná, on the other hand, continued to commission sculptures emphasizing militaristic themes throughout the ninth century, and one monument bears the latest of all Maya Long Count dates, 10.4.0.0.0 (A.D. 909).[40]

By the end of the opening decade of the ninth century, Piedras Negras, La Mar, El Cayo, Bonampak, and all of the smaller towns in the Usumacinta region had erected their last dated monuments. Yaxchilán alone may have held out for another decade or two, until just after the beginning of the tenth cycle (10.0.10.0.0, or A.D. 840). As at Palenque, the last monumental public architecture and the end of the aristocracy soon followed.

At all these cities the decline is related to contacts with the north and west: the Gulf Coast frontier, where Maya and Mexican peoples intermingled. The distinctive "fine paste" pottery tradition, the most widespread indicator of this interaction, developed first on the Gulf Coast among Mexican or Mexican-influenced Maya peoples who were marginal to the Classic Maya world. Its appearance in Maya communities, often accompanied by Mexican elements in architecture and sculpture, reflects a process of foreign influence on Maya societies by Mexicans, or by frontier peoples with hybrid cultures, or by both.

On the western fringe of the lowlands, fine paste pottery appeared as early as the seventh century, along with southern-style polychrome pottery. At Comalcalco, part of this frontier zone, pottery within the fine paste tradition appears early and in quantity. Fine paste wares became progressively more dominant at western Maya centers during the eighth century as southern features waned. For Palenque this was also a time of declining public construction. By the end of the eighth century, as aristocratic activity ceased at Palenque, a new fine paste style with strongly Mexican decoration had appeared.

Farther south, similar developments are associated with the slightly later decline of the centers of the Usumacinta region. Mexican elements appeared on the stelae of Piedras Negras and Yaxchilán as early as the eighth century. The people who occupied Piedras Negras in the early ninth century, after the decline of the aristocracy, manufactured fine paste pottery, and the later fine paste style made an appearance toward the end of the century.

Altar de Sacrificios, farther upstream at the confluence of the Usumacinta and Pasión rivers, continued to dedicate monuments late in the eighth century, as public construction declined and fine paste pottery appeared alongside remnants of the old polychrome tradition.[41] Toward the middle of the ninth century the late fine paste style appeared at Altar, at first as an import, but with growing popularity. By the beginning of the tenth century, major construction activity had ended, and the remaining population which occupied Altar until midcentury manufactured pottery exclusively in the late style.

In the Petexbatún region, the disruption of economic and political systems, intimately related to intensified warfare, was well under way before the appearance of fine paste pottery.[42] At Dos Pilas, a palisade on a wall built with stone taken from abandoned palace buildings indicates serious military pressure well before the end of the eighth century, and the city was apparently almost abandoned by the beginning of the ninth century. Similar hastily built defensive works appeared at other cities at about the same time. Punta de Chimino was also abandoned near the beginning of the ninth century, while Aguateca, the dominant political center in the region, survived longer and local potters did begin to manufacture fine paste ware.

Events associated with the decline of Seibal, perched atop a high bluff overlooking the Pasión, illustrate the complexity of the external pressures involved in the transformation process.[43] Until the late eighth century, Seibal was subordinate to the powerful Petexbatún state, and its architecture and sculpture reflected styles typical of the region. With the collapse of Aguateca at the beginning of the ninth century, Seibal emerged as the dominant political center in the region and embarked on a major construction program incorporating stylistic elements with a decidedly foreign, northern flavor (Figs. 8-28, 8-29). At first, new stelae depict leaders in typical southern-lowland aristocratic dress with unusual facial features. Later monuments portray figures whose countenances and garb point north, to western Yucatan. Seibal's round platform is one of several architectural reflections of a northern connection. Throughout the ninth century, the late fine paste pottery style progressively displaced the polychrome

FIG. 8-28. Structure A-3, Seibal. This temple, with stelae at the bases of the stairs and another inside, was built in the mid ninth century when Seibal reemerged as the dominant regional center.

tradition. Seibal continued to dedicate stelae until 10.3.0.0.0 (A.D. 889), but after that date the center quickly lost importance and was abandoned early in the tenth century. Seibal evidently came under the domination of a foreign group during the ninth century, and the alien features are extensive enough to suggest the possibility of an actual influx of new people. Burials provide the best evidence for the presence of a new element in the population. Apart from the appearance of fine paste vessels, with or without northern or "Mexican" designs, as offerings in some graves, mortuary practices changed sharply with respect to grave locations and how bodies were laid out. Skeletal remains show new fashions of cosmetic body-alteration (head deformation and tooth filing) as well as increased stature.[44] Stylistic evidence points both to the Gulf Coast region and to western Yucatan, which was itself influenced by Mexicanized peoples of the frontier zone.

There is no reason to associate the foreign elements everywhere with a single people. Mexicanized Maya peoples of the eastern Gulf Coast, including the groups referred to as Itzá in colonial-period sources, maintained connections westward into Yucatan and southward up the Usumacinta,[45] as did their descendants, the Mexican-influenced Putún, who later occupied the Acalán region. Peoples of hybrid Maya-Mexican culture, and even non-Maya Mexicans, were probably involved as well. Each Maya city faced a unique concatenation of foreign influences. The common thread is an increasing impingement of people with cultural patterns foreign to southern Classic Maya civilization, emanating ultimately from the western frontier of the Maya world.

This interaction also carried elements of Maya culture from the Gulf Coast to the north and west in the ninth and tenth centuries.[46] Maya-style relief carvings and hieroglyphs on buildings at Xochicalco (Fig. 8-30), in the central Mexican highlands, may

FIG. 8-29. Stela 3, Seibal. The format of this late ninth-century stela, namely the three registers, and many of its stylistic elements suggest a strong northern influence. The seated figures in the upper register are particularly foreign-looking with their goggle-eyed "Tlaloc" masks; the glyphs above them in the square cartouches, probably their names, are also foreign calendar names.

FIG. 8-30. Terrace face, Temple of the Feathered Serpent, Xochicalco. The figure seated within the coils of the serpent is executed in a thoroughly Maya style.

reflect an exchange of esoteric information among priests or aristocrats. Mural paintings in a palace at Cacaxtla depict battle scenes and nobles in a thoroughly Maya style (Fig. 8-31), although Mexican glyphic texts accompany them. Even if these local lords were not themselves actually Maya, the fact that they chose to have their portraits painted in the Maya manner suggests close economic and/or diplomatic relations, perhaps involving marriage ties, with distant Maya centers in the Gulf Coast frontier region or along the Usumacinta. Fine paste and Plumbate pottery[47] found in several communities in the Cacaxtla region also point to a pattern of interaction with the western fringe of the Maya world. Mural paintings at Chichén Itzá[48] depicting confrontations between Mexicanized Maya or Itzá groups and local people in both tropical forest and drier highland settings may be references to Itzá incursions into the upper Usumacinta and Mexican highland areas.

Pressures from the frontier were less intense east of the Usumacinta. At Tikal and Uaxactún, building activity and the dedication of stelae slackened early in the ninth century.[49] The latest Long Count date at these cities is 10.3.0.0.0 (A.D. 889), but there was no major construction after 10.0.0.0.0 (A.D. 830). At Tikal, population apparently dropped substantially from its eighth-century peak, but there was no sudden demographic disaster. Over the course of several generations, a reduced birthrate and increased mortality among key groups, especially women of childbearing age, could easily account for the overall loss. Fine paste pottery appeared alongside remnants of the polychrome tradition, though after the decline had set in. To the north, the last stela commissioned by the lords of Calakmul (in A.D. 810) appears to mark the onset of a comparable decline. Here, too, fine paste pottery suggests a continuing occupation, and subordinate towns continued to erect dated monuments for another two decades at least.[50]

Farther north, cities in the Río Bec zone of central Yucatan were in eclipse by the early decades of the ninth century.[51] Outlying populations were declining but not decimated. Becán initiated no major construction after about A.D. 830, and squatter occupations soon appeared in the old public buildings. Pottery of the late ninth and early tenth centuries reflects fine paste norms as well as ties with northern lowland styles.

Lubaantún and some other cities in the eastern lowlands ceased to function during the course of the ninth century. Caracol may have maintained some of its regional sway during the early ninth century but was soon in decline, its monuments thrown down. At Xunantunich (Fig. 8-32), some Late Classic building groups fell into disrepair during the ninth century, but the central cluster of temples and palaces continued in use as a more compact architectural setting for political affairs, perhaps a reflection of newfound independence now that Naranjo and Buenavista were probably in decline. A colonnaded structure built on the edge of the largest temple platform, suggests a new pattern of interaction with the north, probably with cities in the Puuc region. In contrast to the west, fine paste pottery is quite rare.[52] If peoples of the western frontier had an impact in the east, it was quite indirect. Farther north, Colha maintained the prosperity based on local chert until

FIG. 8-31. Portrait of a noble, Cacaxtla. The figure and his costume are thoroughly Maya in style, but the hieroglyphs represent a Mexican writing system. The sign above and behind the figure is probably his calendar name: "3 Deer." Adapted from Foncerrada de Molina 1979:fig. 7 and López and Molina 1976:5.

FIG. 8-32. Structure A-6, Xunantunich. This massive temple platform, remodeled several times, was the focus of the Xunantunich's civic architecture.

late in the century, but then the community was abandoned. To judge by the evidence of destroyed buildings, probably elite residences, and an associated cache containing the skulls of thirty decapitated individuals, Colha's decline was rapid and involved intense conflict. By the late tenth or eleventh century, Colha was again a center of chert tool manufacture, albeit as part of a very different technological tradition and organized quite differently.[53]

Elsewhere in the east, developmental trajectories were quite different. In the Belize Valley, the decline of local aristocracies was not immediately disastrous for the population as a whole. Here, as in most regions, away from the major civic centers domestic life went on as it always had and vigorous village communities survived well into the tenth century, at least. At Altun Ha, for example, temple and palace construction declined in size and quality beginning late in the eighth century, and ceased altogether by the end of the ninth. Desecration of aristocratic tombs suggests that the collapse of centralized political control involved considerable hostility on the part of former subjects. People continued to reside in the area, however, and some of them rebuilt abandoned temples to serve as residences.[54]

Centralized power, aristocratic privilege, and city life did not come to an end everywhere in the east: Lamanai, for example, enjoyed continued prosperity. Reduction in the overall scale of public construction and shifts in its location suggest changes in organization, but the lords of Lamanai continued to undertake substantial public building projects long after most cities and their aristocracies in the southern lowlands had fallen into decline (Fig. 8-33). Residences were built in areas formerly devoted to civic buildings, and most new construction was located south of the old civic core. A ball court built at this time featured a large stone-floor marker, covering an offering that included a vessel which contained liquid mercury. Features such as colonnaded porticoes on several buildings reflect architectural affinities with northern Yucatan, and ceramics suggest a new emphasis on interaction with Chichén Itzá and other northern communities as well. El Pozito, not far to the north, shared pottery styles with northern Yucatan to a far greater degree; several buildings at Nohmul, a bit farther north, are very reminiscent of structures at Chichén Itzá. A Yucatecan-style dwelling was built at La Milpa as well, but in the former main plaza, where many stelae were now being rearranged and sometimes recarved.[55]

In the southeast, the Quiriguá kings lost control of state functions in the later ninth century.[56] The community itself survived for another century after the demise of the aristocracy, but it undertook only minor remodeling of existing public buildings and was no longer a regional power. Pottery styles suggest intensified interaction with communities to the north, along the east coast of Yucatan, and there are indications that groups from some of these towns may have resided at Quiriguá. The community was evidently abandoned by the middle of the tenth century.

At Copán, problems in royal succession and general signs of weakened state institutions became apparent not long after A.D. 800, and centralized authority was lost before midcentury. Population, which had increased in the Copán Valley throughout the Classic period, peaked at 25,000 or more in the Terminal Classic. This demographic pressure—a comparable population in the valley today strains agricultural systems—along with evidence of heavy deforestation and erosion of soils from the valley slopes suggests that an imbalance between population and available resources contributed to the demise of the Copán state. Some of the palaces in the city center were intentionally burned at the time they were abandoned, and some aristocratic tombs may have been looted, suggesting an element of

FIG. 8-33. Structure N10-9, Lamanai. This temple remained in use and continued to be remodeled through the period when monumental construction and public functions had ceased in most lowland states.

rebellion as part of the decline process. A new ball court and a few other modest civic structures were built near the old city center at about this time, and fine paste pottery suggests that the Putún were somehow implicated in this small-scale public activity, which lingered for a few decades at least. Some aristocratic families, in outlying residential complexes, were able to maintain a semblance of their former power and prosperity even longer, but all traces of centralized power and aristocracy had disappeared by the end of the tenth century. For farmers, who continued to live and work in the valley until the twelfth century, life probably continued much as usual except that they were relieved of the demands of the state and the aristocrats who controlled it.[57]

In the lower Ulúa Valley and adjacent regions, the old social order was transformed, as fine paste pottery replaced Ulúa polychrome styles, public construction projects came to an end, and many communities were abandoned. Scattered villages were all that remained of the eighth-century settlement hierarchies. At the same time, Cerro Palenque grew from a small town into a large and prosperous city with no regional rivals.

The Highlands

In the western highlands small communities, already located along ridges and on hilltops, show few signs of disruption in the Terminal Classic period, although the influence of the western frontier did reached the region, and several communities imported fine paste luxury vessels for funerary offerings.[58] The appearance of new settlement layouts and architectural styles and fine paste pottery in communities along the northern fringes of the central highlands reflect the impact of Gulf Coast peoples here as well. These traits may reflect a continuation—via the Chixoy and other upper tributaries of the Usumacinta—of the thrust that brought Itzá settlers to the Pasión and Petexbatún region. Elsewhere most highland societies underwent radical alterations late in the tenth century, as civic centers ceased to function and many communities were abandoned. New towns that emerged in the eleventh century were almost uniformly situated on hilltops and in other defensible locations. Some were actually fortified. The newly pressing need for defense may reflect increasing foreign penetrations, for the highland region was subject to external pressures from more than one quarter. Influences emanating ultimately from central Mexico continued to reach the Maya highlands by way of the southern coast and piedmont throughout the Terminal Classic period.

Connections between central Mexico and southeastern Mesoamerica did not end, and may even have intensified, with the collapse of Teotihuacán and the breakup of its sphere.[59] Widespread cultural instability and population shifts attended the collapse of the great central Mexican city, and the chain reactions eventually extended far to the east. Linguistic and ethnographic evidence suggests that the ancestors of the Pipil groups scattered along the coast and piedmont at the time of the Spanish invasion had split from their central Mexican parent populations during the Late Classic period. The increasing popularity of fine paste pottery in highland Maya communities during the Terminal Classic also indicates closer contacts with the Gulf Coast frontier region. At first these links may have been quite indirect, reflecting the close ties that already existed between the northern highlands and the southern lowlands, but northern influences persisted long after the failure of southern lowland communication-and-exchange networks. After A.D. 1000, highland aristocracies maintained close relations with the Maya-Mexican rulers of northern Yucatan. A cache of heirloom Gulf Coast pottery in a council building at Utatlán reflects the importance that Late Postclassic Quiché lords attached to their Gulf Coast heritage.[60]

The strong Mexican flavor of the Cotzumalhuapa style of monumental sculpture, which was fashionable in the southern piedmont and coastal region, may reflect interaction with central Mexico and with the Gulf Coast. Distinctive Plumbate pottery manufactured in communities not far to the west probably circulated through Itzá exchange networks, appearing at Chichén Itzá as well as in western Mesoamerica at Cacaxtla (along with fine paste vessels) and as far north and west as Tula.

Communities in the Paraíso basin to the east were radically reorganized about A.D. 900; there, new styles of pottery and other craft products represent a clear break with the past.[61] Cihuatán, with its walled civic and elite-residential zone, emerged as the dominant regional center. Fine paste pottery and a variety of ceramic deity effigies are the most obvious markers of the strong impact of Mexican cultural patterns, perhaps by way of Itzá and Gulf Coast linkages. Plumbate pottery from the west and Nicoya-style polychromes from regions to the east and south testify to other dimensions of Cihuatán's foreign interaction.

Accounting for the Transformation

While peoples of the western frontier played key roles in the decline of cities in the Usumacinta and Pasión regions, and perhaps in parts of the southeast, they were certainly not directly responsible for the collapse of cities everywhere in the south. Even in the west the collapse cannot simply be blamed on a foreign invasion, for there is little evidence of widespread population intrusions; moreover, indications of conflict predate the appearance of foreign elements. Rather, the decline involved complex processes in which external pressures exacerbated stresses inherent in the structure of Maya societies.[62] Different combinations of factors resulted in slightly different processes and timings in each region.

One serious internal stress resulted from the population expansion of the preceding millennium. By the eighth century, populations throughout the lowlands had reached new peaks of size and density.[63] Aristocratic segments of society, well fed and cared for, were probably expanding most rapidly. Subsistence systems were able to feed these larger numbers of people, though at considerable cost. An increased degree of management and greater labor requirements would have increased production, but created new stresses. The temptation to intensify food production at the expense of environmental stability by shortening fallow cycles must have been nearly irresistible. At the same time, growing demands for household firewood, timber for construction, and fuel for producing the plaster that covered virtually every public building and plaza floor, would have intensified the deforestation of the landscape.[64] The inevitable result—best documented at Copán—was environmental degradation. At the same time, there is evidence of environmental shifts involving reduced rainfall in at least some parts of the Maya world during the ninth and tenth centuries. Although they were not felt uniformly across the Maya world and were probably not extreme enough to bring about major sociopolitical transformations by themselves, climatic changes certainly would have exacerbated the effects of such internal stresses as population growth and of other external pressures as well.[65] In any event, newly intensified farming systems became increasingly fragile. With subsistence systems stretched to their limits, even slightly reduced production resulting from minor environmental fluctuations could assume emergency proportions. In this situation, any further increase in population, agricultural intensification, or environmental damage could only increase the frequency and severity of food shortages. Intensification of farming systems, pressure on resources, and environmental degradation were highly variable regionally across the Maya world. The Petexbatún region, for example, shows no signs of excessive forest clearance or soil erosion.[66] The intense warfare and other radical societal changes that were part of the transformation process here have to do with other factors. Part of the explanation may be that cities in regions which did experience environmental degradation might have tried to compensate by importing food. This strategy would have had the effect of distributing the strains to other communities, with the probable side effect of increased competition and friction among cities and regions. Serious food shortages, even very fleeting ones, could only widen social and economic gaps, already a source of tension between wealthy aristocrats and peasants eking out a bare existence. Increased pressure on all segments of society was inevitable as aristocrats faced greater and greater administrative burdens and as their demands for increased labor from the peasant sector escalated.

The continued success of Maya civilization demanded the maintenance of an intricate web of articulation among many complex systems. Pressure at any key point could disrupt the fragile balance, setting off self-reinforcing cycles that magnified difficulties and spread them throughout the Maya world. The penetration of the western lowlands by foreigners carrying Mexican cultural patterns was one such trigger. Armed incursions were not necessary, although they probably occurred sporadically and on a small scale.

Any substantial intrusion of foreign elements into communication networks would result in serious disruption of the lifelines between Maya centers, causing chaos throughout the southern lowlands. In the first place, any disruption of exchange-and-distribution networks would make cities extremely vulnerable to local crop failures. Second, the aristocratic segment of Maya civilization depended on easy interaction among cities. Local aristocracies were cosmopolitan, with wide-ranging social, political, and economic ties. Efficient communication networks were as essential to the maintenance of local political and religious systems as was the uninterrupted flow of luxury goods. Anything that interfered with such practices as the ceremonial confirmation of local rulers' legitimacy at regional capitals, or that increased the difficulty of nobles' participation in special events (marriage rites, inaugural celebrations, funerals, and the like) at distant centers struck at the very foundations of southern lowland Maya society. International facets of aristocratic life were the first to go—hence the disappearance of the stela complex, monumental art, the Long Count calendar, and the writing system and the dissolution of luxury pottery styles. Presently, as the malaise deepened in each region, aristocracies lost control, centers ceased monumental construction activity, and all other signs of public activity faded.

Foreign elements spread, filling partial vacuums. External influences and the spread of Mexican cultural patterns are implicated in the decline of southern cities as both cause and effect. In the west they were a trigger mechanism, setting off a chain reaction that eventually weakened all of the interconnected southern cities, even on the eastern fringes of the lowlands. At Tikal, foreign elements appeared only after the decline was under way. Farther east they are barely represented at all, and cities like Lamanai continued to function, perhaps in part because they continued to participate in reoriented exchange networks which now bypassed their western neighbors. Coastal port towns had become more prosperous than ever as their involvement in maritime exchange intensified during the eighth and ninth centuries. By the late tenth century, coastal settlements were experiencing a radical transformation in tandem with changes in the exchange networks.[67]

The processes of decline that brought Maya civilization to an end throughout the southern lowlands affected northern cities differently.[68] Here, too, aristocracies had close connections with peoples of the western frontier in the Late Classic period, perhaps even closer than their southern counterparts. Ninth- and tenth-century pottery at Uxmal, Sayil, Kabah, Dzibilchaltún, Chichén Itzá, and many other centers reflects fine paste styles as well as Yucatecan traditions. Other indications of Mexican influence are common, particularly at Chichén Itzá but also at cities such as Uxmal and Dzibilchaltún, where non-Maya sculptural motifs and tzompantlis suggest the presence of enclaves of foreign, Itzá, and/or Mexican aristocrats.

These signs of foreign influence coexisted for a considerable time with the peak of cultural development at northern centers. If foreign intervention triggered the decline of southern cities, it evidently had a different, or at least a delayed, effect in the north. Part of the reason lies in the long-standing differences between northern and southern cities. Although trade continued, northern centers were marginally involved in the communication networks that linked the cities of the southern lowlands in the Late Classic period. Northern monumental art and architecture became very distinctive, and southern styles of luxury pottery were hardly represented at all in the north. Social and political ties between northern and southern aristocracies grew weak in relation to the intensity of contacts within each region. The northern area was also more regionalized internally, with more localized patterns of interaction that in the southern area. In the north, new alliances with Mexican or Mexican-influenced peoples of the western frontier may have partly replaced ties with southern cities. Northern aristocracies, less dependent on external communication and more receptive to foreign alliances, were less vulnerable to intensified pressures emanating from the western frontier.

The drier climate of the northern lowlands should have made northern communities more vulnerable to the effects of the reduced rainfall that evidently characterized at least some lowland regions during the ninth and tenth centuries; in fact, though, this is the period of florescence in the north. The timing of the drying process may have been later in the north, or perhaps northern farmers, already adapted to thinner soils and lower rainfall, were better able to cope with climatic change. A slower population increase in the north, partly a function of sharper environmental constraints on farming that limited the possibilities for agricultural intensification, may also have helped retard decline.[69]

Like the northern lowlands, the highlands did not constitute a single sphere of interaction. Highland aristocracies were even less dependent than their northern lowland counterparts on communication with distant cities. They were less vulnerable to foreign intervention. Still, faced with increasing external pressures and influxes of foreigners, even they succumbed.

By the end of the eleventh century, if not before, virtually every part of the Maya world had been transformed. Nearly every powerful Classic-period state dissolved. The aristocracies that had created and controlled the great states vanished, and with them went the architecture, art, and material wealth that had reflected their prestige and sustained their power. Most of the big cities fell into ruin, although rural peasantries continued to farm the countryside. Relieved of the burdens of state demands and with the best farmland, however degraded, no longer monopolized by aristocrats, the quality of life may even have improved for many Maya families. Factors responsible for the transformation were many and varied; the process, its timing, and the precise congeries of causes differed from region to region. In most areas, though, two processes stand out: (1) a severe strain on natural resources owing to dense populations and heavy state demands, perhaps exacerbated by drought; and (2) a disruption of communication-and-exchange networks and of local political systems by incursions of foreigners from the Gulf Coast.

A few cities survived and retained their economic and political power, presumably because of exceptional local circumstances. Lamanai, for one, continued to build and refurbish public buildings and maintained its prosperity, perhaps because of its location on the New River Lagoon, which represented both an unusually rich source of aquatic foods and a means of easy access to exchange partners, now far more widely spaced with the disappearance of so many Classic-period cities. Lamanai and such newly prominent cities as Mayapán reflect a clear Classic-period heritage, but the organization of Postclassic states was quite different: aristocracies and the central institutions of the state, kingship in particular, were transformed.

MAP 11. Postclassic cities.

NINE

New Orientations

The Postclassic Maya

The sharp contrast formerly drawn between Postclassic and earlier societies does contain a kernel of truth, but the differences have been seriously exaggerated.[1] Postclassic societies, and the new cultural orientations they reflect, have definite roots in the Classic period;[2] continuities have been underemphasized. Widespread decline and cultural reorientation did mark the Terminal Classic period, but there was no areawide collapse. Postclassic communities are not well represented in the archaeological record, partly because in many regions there were so few of them. Many Postclassic settlements (Map 11) are architecturally much less conspicuous than their Classic-period predecessors, and they have been both more difficult to locate and less rewarding—in terms of monumental art and architecture—to excavate.[3] Even in the southern lowlands the decline was a process in which foreign intrusion, not necessarily sweeping military conquest, was one of many factors. In the northern lowlands and in the highlands, continuities from Classic to Postclassic are quite prominent.

Late Maya societies, on the threshold of history,[4] seem more different from their predecessors than they really were. Warfare and sacrifice are prominent in the Postclassic period, but they are also well represented in earlier Maya art and inscriptions (Figs. 7-32, 7-33, 7-36, 8-9, 8-27).[5] Reliance on coastal resources and long-distance exchange increased, and agriculture was correspondingly less central to economic systems, but this trend was a logical outgrowth from patterns already well established in the Classic period. Political systems shifted away from a near-exclusive focus on the person of the ruler, to new, more flexible forms of organization that involved a much broader distribution of power. Political art and public architecture changed correspondingly. The public roles of religion, especially in providing supernatural sanction for kingly authority, were reduced, but ritual maintained a central place in domestic life. Usually conceptualized in terms of a supposed "cultural decadence," the reduced scale of Postclassic architecture and the lower quality of the masonry and architectural decoration also point to changed architectural functions, new mechanisms for legitimizing political authority, and reduced economic drains on the people. The same considerations apply to decorated pottery and to the aesthetic quality of many other Postclassic craft items, and in this respect the norms of Classic-period city-states are of limited use in defining a frame of reference for Postclassic societies. Postclassic Maya societies were not identical to their Classic-period ancestors—some aspects of political and economic organization, and with them some values, *had* changed—but neither were they so radically different as older views suggest.

The Lowlands

Mayapán emerged as an important political center in the north in the Postclassic period, perhaps as early as the eleventh century, when Chichén Itzá was still a prosperous and powerful city. When Chichén fell into decline as a political and economic center—in the twelfth century, if not before—Mayapán replaced it as the dominant political force in the northern peninsula.[6] Chichén retained its importance in historical tradition and as a focus of pilgrimage, though, for offerings cast into the sacred cenote include many Postclassic objects, particularly ceramic incense-burners.[7]

Yucatec histories recorded after the Spanish invasion provide very detailed circumstantial accounts of the circumstances of Mayapán's displacement of Chichén as the dominant northern city. Most versions attribute the end of Chichén Itzá's hegemony in northern Yucatan to a political upheaval engineered by the lords of Mayapán, who were allied with the Itzá and other Mexicanized frontier elements. On the eve of Chichén's overthrow, the ruler was Hunac Ceel, famous as a man of supernatural influence, having survived the plunge into Chichén's cenote to emerge with a prophecy favorable to himself. At the wedding festivities of the lord of Izamal, Hunac Ceel used a love charm concocted from the plumeria flower to inflame Chac Xib Chac, the ruler of Chichén Itzá, with a passion for the bride. Chac Xib Chac carried her off, adding insufferable insult to Izamal's long-standing grievance over the sacrifice of its youths to Chichén's serpent god. Hunac Ceel, with new allies reinforcing his Mexican mercenaries, orchestrated the sack of Chichén.[8]

The Cocoms maintained their alliances with Mexican and Mexicanized frontier peoples to the west, but foreign elements would never be so prominent again. The last centuries before the European invasion saw a renaissance of native Yucatecan noble lines and traditions. The Book of Chilam Balam of Chumayel, an eighteenth-century compendium of Maya history, describes an "interrogation" administered in ritual language by a great chief. Those who respond correctly to the obscure questions and demands are confirmed as lords; those who lack the appropriate esoteric knowledge are to be tortured and put to death. The passage evidently consists of riddles designed to verify the cultural knowledge—and thus appropriate ethnic identity—of the lords:

> This is the convocation and review,
>   The examination and correct review
> Of the lineages
>   Of the governors
> In the land
>   Here.

. . .
Thus then will be the seating of lands
And houses
Of the lineages
Of the Mayan people
Here
In the region of Yucatan.[9]

Although Mayapán's heyday is several centuries closer in time to the historical sources in question than Chichén's, these accounts, like those which ostensibly describe the rise and fall of Chichén, must be treated as metaphorical allegations designed to further the political agendas of their authors. Landa's account of the Cocoms' accession by acclamation, for example—"the nobles agreed, in order that the government should endure, that the house of the Cocoms should have the chief power; because it was the most ancient or the richest family, or because at this time he who was at the head of it was a man of the greatest worth"[10]—must be suspect, since one of his principal informants, Juan Nachi Cocom, was a descendant of those estimable nobles. On the other hand, references to the Cocoms in hieroglyphic texts at Chichén establish them as important players on the political stage of Postclassic Yucatan. Colonial-period histories may not contain straightforward narratives of events, but they do refer to real groups and processes.

Whatever the actual circumstances, sometime after A.D. 1000, Mayapán replaced Chichén as the dominant city in the north.[11] All indications are that Mayapán did not exercise the same degree of centralized political control as had Chichén, nor did its influence reach as far. Mayapán's sphere had something of the character of a confederacy involving some of the former provinces of Chichén Itzá; Mayapán may have maintained fairly direct control of the old provinces in the northwestern part of the peninsula, but to the south and east its influence was probably hegemonic at best.

In any case, the city's new status and power demanded new architectural settings, and an extensive building program provided the needed temples, palaces, and administrative buildings. The Maya-Mexican heritage of Chichén Itzá is still evident in the new order established at Mayapán. The main temple, sacred to Kukulcán, echoed Chichén's Castillo in every major feature; the Caracol and other buildings have their counterparts as well. Mayapán was planned as a new Chichén, but the execution did not measure up to the quality of the model. Mayapán's architecture is unimpressive, even slipshod, in comparison with Chichén's. Plaster replaced delicately carved stone, and corbeled vaults gave way to wooden roofs. Specifically Mexican elements are relatively few, and some older Maya patterns reappear. Mayapán had no tzompantli, but at least twenty-five stelae were erected. Oddly, there is no ball court. Dense residential construction testifies to an expanded population. Elite residences surround the concentration of civic buildings at the core of the settlement; farther out were closely spaced ordinary houses with rough masonry walls defining individual residential compounds. Some four thousand buildings, mostly dwellings, were packed within the 4 square kilometers enclosed by the low stone wall surrounding the city, and more than 10,000 people lived and worked there. In its day, Mayapán must have seemed a confusing warren of buildings and alleyways, with none of the spaciousness of such earlier cities as Chichén and Uxmal.

Colonial-period histories are a bit more helpful in suggesting aspects of Mayapán's social and political organization than they are in reconstructing its political history. Organizational patterns are more likely to find expression in architectural and other material remains, so it is easier to test organizational models derived from documents against archaeological data. Certainly the thirteen major colonnaded halls in Mayapán's core are plausible candidates for the palaces and administrative offices of the governors of Mayapán's dependent provinces who, according to Landa, resided at Mayapán:

They built houses for the lords only, dividing all the land among them, giving towns to each one, according to the antiquity of his lineage and his personal value. . . . [T]hey ordered that other houses should be constructed . . . where each one of them could keep some servants, and to which the people from their towns could repair, when they came to the city on business. Each one then established in these houses his mayordomo, who bore for his badge of office a short and thick stick, and they called him *caluac*. He kept account with the towns and with those who ruled them; and to them was sent notice of what was needed in the house of their lord, such as birds, maize, honey, salt, fish, game, cloth and other things, and the *caluac* always went to the house of his lord, in order to see what was wanted and provided it immediately, since his house was, as it were, the office of his lord . . . The lords appointed the governors, and if they were acceptable confirmed their sons in the offices. . . . All the lords were careful to respect, visit and to entertain Cocom, accompanying him, making feasts in his honor and repairing to him with important business.[12]

In effect, the Cocom ruler held his subsidiary lords hostage for the good behavior of their provinces.

The appearance of smaller political centers in the north during the Postclassic period is also consistent with the histories' suggestion that the Cocoms did not maintain the same degree of centralized control as had the lords of Chichén Itzá.[13] Even Dzibilchaltún, quite far down the settlement hierarchy, again constructed small-scale public buildings. The Temple of the Seven Dolls, long in ruins, was rededicated with the construction of a new altar and the placement of an offering of seven ceramic figurines—after which the building is named—before it. Still, however indirect it may have been, Mayapán's political and economic hegemony embraced most of northern Yucatan.

Economic ties with the western frontier, reflected by imported pottery, remained strong, as did social and political alliances. Landa reports that the Cocoms brought in Mexican mercenaries from the trade center of Xicalango, on the Laguna de Términos.[14] Exchange networks also linked Mayapán with areas far to the south and east. Salt from the north coast beds was the main export. Jade from the Motagua Valley and obsidian from the Maya highlands were high-volume imports, and occasional objects of hard volcanic or igneous stone came from there or from the Maya Mountains. Landa mentions that the only Cocom to escape slaughter in the overthrow of Mayapán happened to be abroad at the time on a trading venture in the Ulúa region of Honduras.[15] Honduras, linked to the north through exchange networks that stretched along the east coast, certainly provided Mayapán with tools and jewelry of gold, copper, and tumbaga (an alloy of the two metals). Honduran markets could also boast other Central American products alongside the cacao, feathers, and other perishable goods for which it became famous.[16]

Mayapán maintained its sway over northern Yucatan through much of the Postclassic period, but its hegemony dissolved at least a century before the arrival of the Spaniards.[17] Bishop Landa provides one account of the fall of Mayapán and the events that led up to it:

Among the successors of the house of Cocom was a very haughty man, an imitator of Cocom, and he made another league with the men of Tabasco, and he introduced more Mexicans into the city, and he began to play the tyrant and to make slaves of the poorer people. On this account the nobles joined with the party of Tutul Xiu, who was a just statesman like his ancestors, and they conspired to put Cocom to death. And this they did, killing at the same time all his sons, except one who was absent. They sacked his house and took away the lands which he had in cacao and in other fruits, saying that they paid themselves for what he had taken from them.[18]

Again, Landa's version is not without bias, for Gaspar Antonio Chi, another principal informant, was the grandson of a Xiu ruler,[19] but the contention that Cocom rule had grown increasingly onerous is perfectly plausible. In any case, Mayapán was sacked, its buildings destroyed, its wall leveled.

Mayapán's sphere disintegrated into its constituent provinces (Map 4),[20] and never again did a single city hold political or economic sway over all of northern Yucatan. In the years between Mayapán's fall and the Spanish invasion, these independent states engaged in a bewildering series of conflicts and shifting alliances as they competed for local political and economic advantage. Western provinces maintained their traditionally close ties with the frontier region and with Mexican peoples. In Ah Canul, at least, the old political hierarchy dissolved entirely. The main centers, controlled mostly by men of the Canul family, generally acted in concert, but there was no paramount ruler.

The same situation obtained in east-central Yucatan, where the Cupul family controlled most of the towns. Chakán and Chikinchel were even less unified; little more than casual alliances linked the main towns. By contrast, Maní, the home province of the Tutul Xiu, retained the old political system. A halach uinic at least theoretically ruled the entire sphere through subordinate batabs who were in charge of the several minor centers. Neighboring Sotuta, the home of remnant Cocom groups, was ruled by a halach uinic who derived sovereignty from the old Mayapán dynasty. Landa followed their history:

The son of Cocom who escaped death through absence on account of his trading in the land of Ulua, . . . when he heard of the death of his father and of the destruction of the city, returned very quickly and joined with his relations and vassals, and settled in a place which he called Tibolon. . . . And they built in those wooded places many more towns. From these Cocoms proceeded numerous families, and the province where this lord reigns is called Sotuta.[21]

The east coast province of Ecab was probably never under Mayapán's direct control, and no local town managed to establish dominance after the decline of Cobá. Eastern communities were oriented toward the flourishing maritime-exchange networks that stretched along the coast, linking Yucatan with Honduras and Central America beyond. The island of Cozumel, just off the coast, was an important commercial and transshipment center with ties to Acalán in the west and to the Chetumal and Gulf of Honduras trading centers to the south.[22] The internal organization of Cozumel was physically decentralized, without a single dominant town. The island was also sacred to worshipers of Ix Chel, the moon goddess and patroness of weaving, divination, medicine, and childbirth. Pilgrims came to Cozumel from all parts of Yucatan and beyond to consult the famous oracle in her shrine.

The stretch of coast opposite was one of the most densely occupied regions of the Maya world during the last centuries of the precolumbian era.[23] Tulum, which so impressed the men of the Grijalva expedition when they sighted it from the sea in 1518, was a major mainland port on the northeast coast.[24] Tulum stands on a bluff directly overlooking the sea (Color

FIG. 9-1. Town wall, Tulum.

Plate 7). A structure just north of the town center where a channel offers safe passage through the offshore reef may have served as a landmark for arriving vessels. A wall, pierced by arched gateways and topped by a parapet and walkway, enclosed the community on the landward sides (Fig. 9-1). Within the city wall, the layout of public buildings and private houses suggests some attempt at community planning: several buildings stand along what looks like a main avenue, and a low inner wall sets off the core of civic structures. Tulum's public buildings echo the architecture of Chichén Itzá in their serpent columns and other features, but the seemingly shoddy quality of the construction is much more reminiscent of Mayapán (Figs. 9-2, 9-3). Buildings are small, with thick plaster masking the irregular masonry. One building contained a stela (with a Long Count date corresponding to A.D. 761) which was probably brought from nearby Tancah long after it was carved.

Modeled and painted plaster was the standard mode of architectural decoration. The most popular architectural ornament was an inverted relief figure, often set in a niche over the main doorway (Fig. 9-4). These "diving gods," many of whom are fitted out with insect stingers on their posteriors, may be images of Venus, known as Xux Ek, or "Wasp Star." They probably are also meant to evoke the Ah Muzencabs, bee gods who were particularly prominent in Ecab, where honey and wax were especially important in the regional economy.[25] Murals painted on plaster wall-facings (Fig. 9-5) were also quite popular at Tulum and at other contemporary towns along the east coast.[26] Some of these wall paintings closely resemble scenes in the surviving Yucatecan painted manuscripts, particularly the Paris Codex. The content of the paintings and associated hieroglyphic texts is uniformly Maya, but the execution of some reflects the strong influence of the Mixteca-Puebla style of central Mexico, reversing the pattern of the Cacaxtla murals. The adoption of this style at Tulum, Chetumal,[27] and other east coast cities indicates very strong, though not necessarily direct, ties with central Mexico. The maritime exchange networks that stretched around the coast of Yucatan could have brought Mexicans and Mexican ideas to the east from Xicalango and other Gulf Coast trade centers. One mural at Tulum, depicting Chac, the rain god, seated on a four-legged creature, may have been inspired by Spaniards on horseback, the noise and flash of their firearms suggesting a connection with Chac, who brings thunder and lightning along with the rain.[28]

Smaller communities and isolated watchtowers are located all along the east coast. Xelhá, Tancah, and other minor centers near Tulum were secondary ports within its orbit, and many of them shared Tulum's penchant for mural painting. Inland, Cobá—apparently abandoned during the first centuries of the second millennium—was reoccupied. Its new lords built several public structures in styles very reminiscent of Tulum, including a temple featuring "diving god" figures atop the old Nohoch Mul pyramid.

To the south lay the major commercial center of Chetumal,[29] in Yucatan's main cacao-producing zone. A key port in the maritime-exchange networks that linked Yucatan with the Gulf of Honduras, Chetumal was also at the eastern end of an overland trade route from western Yucatan. Cacao, gold, copper, and feathers were among the southern products imported for reshipment to the north. Salt, textiles, and other north Yucatecan exports moved through Chetumal in the opposite direction. Mexicans, or at least Mexican ideas (most clearly reflected in murals that depict Maya deities in a thoroughly Mexican style), also reached the Chetumal region by means of these networks.

Farther south, many older ports were abandoned and, in many coastal regions at least, new communities emerged as the focus of commercial activities, probably in response to the reorientation of maritime exchange.[30] Colha emerged again as a center of chert tool manufacture, and presumably export, in the late tenth or eleventh century, but the tools represent a different technological tradition, and production was organized differently. Pottery styles suggest connections with communities to the to the south and west, at Lamanai and beyond in the core of the southern lowlands. Indications of connections with communities to the north in Yucatan are even stronger and might indicate an influx of new people.

A small, dispersed population continued to reside in the vicinity of Altun Ha, to the south, during the earlier centuries of the Postclassic period; an offering of Lamanai-style incense burners suggests that they maintained at least occasional contact with their more prosperous western neighbors. In the fifteenth century, the old town center was reoccupied by people whose pottery—like that of their contemporaries at Colha and Lamanai—reflects strong ties to northern Yucatan.[31]

At Lamanai, community patterns continued very much as they had been in the Terminal Classic period.[32] Remodeling of public buildings continued, and styles of architecture and pottery reflect ongoing interactions with northern Yucatan. Incense burners, for example, look like locally manufactured versions of the censers of Mayapán, and later pottery includes a local variant of northern redwares.[33]

FIG. 9-2. Castillo and adjacent structures, Tulum. Tulum's buildings echo the architecture of earlier, larger cities, especially Mayapán.

FIG. 9-3. Temple of the Frescoes, Tulum. Polychrome murals (Fig. 9-5) adorn the interior walls.

FIG. 9-4. Descending figure, Temple of the Diving God, Tulum. This inverted figure, with its head facing directly forward, may symbolize Venus (known as "Wasp Star") as well as a bee god.

FIG. 9-5. Mural, Temple of the Frescoes, Tulum. The figure is the Maya goddess Ix Chel, but the style is heavily influenced by the Mixteca-Puebla school of western Mesoamerica.

Obsidian imports had diminished by the twelfth century, but in general Lamanai maintained and even enhanced the scope of its external economic connections during the remainder of the precolumbian era. The city, on the New River lagoon, was itself an active maritime commercial center and also maintained close relationships with Marco Gonzalez on Ambergris Caye and other coastal port towns. Imported copper bells and jewelry and thin gold sheet that sheathed such perishable materials as wooden staffs accompanied prosperous individuals in their tombs. The copper—like the style of mural paintings in coastal towns to the north—may indicate connections with Oaxaca in Mexican Mesoamerica, to the west, while the gold probably reflects southern ties. A gold bell found at El Pozito, not far to the north, is made in the Veraguas style of Panama.

The entire zone to the south of Chetumal was known as Dzuluinicob in the sixteenth century. Tipú, in the region's extreme southwest, was its economic and political focus, although it may not have exercised centralized political authority. Christian churches built at Tipú and Lamanai in the sixteenth century reflect Spanish interest in the substantial communities that existed there at the time of the invasion and that survived until late in the seventeenth century.[34]

Active trade routes linked several independent peoples along an arc through the interior of the peninsula. Acalán, in the west, was the heartland of the Chontal-speaking Putún.[35] Acalán maintained close relations with Mexican peoples of the nearby frontier. Several Nahua-speaking communities existed as enclaves within Chontal country, and a few of Acalán's rulers even had Mexican names. Itzamkanac, Acalán's capital, was a town with large temples and administrative buildings and many stone-walled houses. Putún nobles were great traders and played a leading role in the maritime commerce of coastal Yucatan. Chontal may even have become something of a lingua franca in port towns. At the same time, Putún economic connections stretched west to central Mexico, south and east through the Itzá region around Lake Petén Itzá, and beyond to Nito, on the Gulf of Honduras.

By the mid thirteenth century, a process of resurgence was under way in the interior of the southern lowlands, and a few communities had grown intó substantial towns.[36] Topoxté, occupying a cluster of islands in Lake Yaxhá, controlled the surrounding region. Pottery basically continued local traditions, but the new popularity of effigy incense-burners may have had its inspiration in the north. Topoxté's temples and low palace/administration buildings had beam-and-mortar roofs in place of vaults. They recall Mayapán and Tulum rather than the local architectural tradition of the Classic period, and pottery styles reflect the same pattern of northern connections. Northern groups certainly did not displace local populations entirely, but some may have established themselves in the region as early as the Terminal Classic, and in some places they gave rise to aristocracies claiming foreign ancestries. The Itzá label, indiscriminately applied to all the invasion-period peoples of the central Petén lake district, was certainly appropriate for some dynasties in the region who claimed descent from the lords of Chichén Itzá, but it also obscures considerable political and ethnic variability as well as continuities from the earlier local tradition.[37]

By the sixteenth century, with Topoxté perhaps already in decline, Itzá lords dominated the region around Lake Petén Itzá from Tayasal (Tah Itzá), another island capital.[38] Descriptions left by Cortés and other early Spanish visitors indicate that Tayasal was a town comparable to Topoxté, with temples, palaces, administrative buildings, and some two hundred houses. At the end of the seventeenth century, still independent, Tayasal controlled a population of more than 20,000. Tayasal was an important link in transpeninsula trade, maintaining connections with the Putún to the northwest, with Tipú and the province of Dzuluinicob to the east, and with southeastern trade centers along the Gulf of Honduras. Canek, the sixteenth-century ruler of Tayasal, even maintained an enclave on the east coast to grow cacao for him.

Nito, in Chol country on the Gulf of Honduras, was another major port in the commercial network linking Honduras and Yucatan. Nito attracted merchants from as far away as Acalán, and the brother of the ruler of Itzamkanac headed a large Putún enclave there. Nito's economic ties stretched northwest into the interior, north by sea to Chetumal and beyond, and south to Naco and the great commercial centers of the lower Ulúa Valley in northwestern Honduras.[39]

A small community existed at Naco as early as Late Preclassic times. Naco grew slowly, but in the Late Postclassic period it became the most prominent commercial center in northwestern Honduras. Naco dominated the middle Chamelecón region, and extended its political and economic sphere well into the frontier region of the lower Ulúa Valley. Naco's central precinct contains temples, including a strange round structure capped by a plaster "emblem" (Fig. 9-6), aristocratic residences, and a ball court with stone rings. Humbler dwellings cluster around these buildings, extending for a considerable distance along both banks of the Río Naco. Early Spanish visitors estimated 2,000 houses and 10,000 people in Naco itself, without counting dependent villages.

FIG. 9-6. Platform summit, Structure 4F-1, Naco. This unique plaster "cogwheel" emblem capped the summit of a round platform in Naco's civic center. Round structures elsewhere in Mesoamerica are associated with Kukulcán or Quetzalcoatl.

Naco's commercial ties extended in every direction: north through the lower Ulúa Valley to the Gulf of Honduras and Yucatan; west to the Maya highlands; south to the Lake Yojoa region; and beyond to the Pacific Coast and Central America. Naco distributed regional products as well as long-distance imports. The Sula plain was one of Mesoamerica's premier cacao-producing zones. Several neighboring regions produced gold and copper tools and ornaments, and feathers were a famous Honduran export. Products of lower Central American metalworkers probably flowed through Naco, as did obsidian from highland Guatemala and salt, textiles, and other goods exported from Yucatan.

Naco, on the fringe of the cultural potpourri of the eastern Maya frontier, was a cosmopolitan place. Its primary population was presumably Maya, and the bulk of its Late Postclassic pottery indicates an affiliation with Maya groups of the eastern highlands. Vessels used by the people who lived in Naco's central zone, however, represent a slightly different style suggesting ties with lowland regions to the north and west. Naco's nobles, like the Mexicanized aristocrats among the Quiché and their neighbors, may have claimed a cultural identity and heritage different from those of the populace at large. Early documents also hint at the possibility of a Nahua-speaking enclave, affiliated with Pipil groups to the south. There were certainly Nahua enclaves in central Honduras and along the north coast. Chetumal maintained commercial outposts in the Ulúa Valley, and other northern centers may have done so as well. The valley was a mosaic of enclaves of peoples of many cultural identities—Chol, Chortí, Yucatec, Jicaque, Lenca, Paya, and probably others—and Naco may have been similarly polyglot.

The Highlands

Chichén Itzá's connections reached as far as the Maya highlands, at least indirectly.[40] Ties with the Gulf Coast, already in evidence at the end of the Classic period, continued after A.D. 1000, as did influence from central Mexico via the Intermediate Zone. The southward and eastward diaspora of Nahua-speaking Pipil groups was another ongoing process. Central Mexican styles of arts and crafts became increasingly prominent in the Maya highlands and southern piedmont. Toltecs had an economic interest in the region, both as a source of cacao and as a commercial link with areas farther east. Plumbate pottery, a finely glazed luxury ware manufactured in the Tajumulco region, was a popular import in Tula. Occasional Nicoya polychrome vessels from Costa Rica probably reached Tula via the Maya highlands. By the time of the Spanish invasion, highland Maya peoples showed many signs of Mexican impact, particularly in aristocratic status symbols and in the trappings of rulership of the Quiché and Cakchiquel states in the central highlands.

As in Yucatan, highland Maya histories often reflect, dimly, events and conditions of the eleventh and twelfth centuries. Several highland aristocracies explicitly claimed Toltec ancestry. References to leaders called Kukulcán or Gucumatz (Q'uq' Cumatz, "quetzal bird–snake" in Quiché and Cakchiquel) abound. Many of these claims may be fictional, reflecting local Maya rulers' attempts to bolster their claims to legitimacy, but highland Maya aristocracies were certainly Mexicanized. Some highland peoples probably even had culturally hybrid Maya-Mexican ruling groups comparable to those in such northern cities as Chichén Itzá.

Much of this Mexican influence came to the highlands from the north, from the Gulf Coast and Yucatan, not from Tula. Nahua loan words in Quiché and other highland languages reflect the influence of Gulf Coast dialects, not of Nahuatl as it was spoken in central Mexico. The Quiché lords of Utatlán included pieces of heirloom Gulf Coast pottery vessels in a cache placed in a bench in one of the capital's council buildings.[41] Chichén Itzá itself may have been the primary center from which Mexican influence radiated to southern regions of the Maya world. Chichén might also have been an intermediate provider of fine paste pottery to highland communities. Certainly there were economic links, for Chichén imported Plumbate pottery. Highland histories refer explicitly to Tula or Tollan, but this name had taken on a wider symbolic significance, connoting a semimythical place of past cultural grandeur, the font of Toltec sovereignty. It could easily designate Chichén Itzá, a new or surrogate Tula. The appellation Tulán Zuiva, Vucub Pec, Vucub Zivan (Tollan Zuiva, Seven Caves, Seven Ravines) in the Popol Vuh and other Quiché documents denotes the place of origin of the Quiché people or their gods. It is usually interpreted as a double reference to Tula and to another mythical birthplace homologous to the Chicomoztoc (Seven Caves) of central Mexican origin myths. Zuiva also appears as a place of origin in the traditional histories of northern Yucatan. Actually, the references may be to Chichén Itzá, for Uucil Abnal (Seven Hollows or Seven Bushy Places) was an ancient name for Chichén.

In the far west, communities of the Late Classic period were already located on ridges and in other elevated, defensible situations. After A.D. 1000, this settlement pattern changed. Early Postclassic villages were oriented around new towns in broad valleys. In other respects, continuities between Late Classic and Early Postclassic societies are very strong. Western highland societies were relatively isolated and may have escaped many of the external pressures felt by their eastern neighbors. They did not continue to import fine paste luxury vessels, and rarely even acquired Plumbate pottery. Political and economic spheres remained quite local in scope, as the area underwent a process of regionalization.

The Tzeltal, Tzotzil, and their neighbors occupied independent communities linked by a variety of social, political, and economic ties.[42] No great cities emerged to create large states or spheres of economic hegemony. Zinacantán, controlling a modest region in Tzotzil country, was among the most prominent western towns. With access to abundant supplies of amber, quetzal feathers, animal pelts, and salt, Zinacantán was a prosperous commercial center. It was subject to constant pressure from the Chiapanecs to the west and south. Even the Aztecs made persistent attempts to control the area; they were largely unsuccessful, although they did finally establish a foothold at Zinacantán. Cultural patterns at the time of the conquest do suggest that Toltecs or Mexicanized Mayas eventually had some impact on western highland peoples, but it must have been mild and indirect.

Zaculeu, among the largest Early Postclassic highland towns, is situated on a plateau surrounded by deep ravines in the west-central highlands.[43] Like many of its contemporaries, Zaculeu evidently had to cope with considerable local conflict, and perhaps with external military pressure as well. By the Late Postclassic period, Zaculeu had become the capital of a powerful Mam state. Nearly fifty buildings—temples, palaces, administrative buildings, "dance" platforms, and a small ball court—make up the compact public core (Figs. 9-7–9-9). Humble residences are scattered throughout the surrounding countryside. Though quite plain, Zaculeu's temples and colonnaded halls recall those of Mayapán and other late Yucatec centers. A few of the latest buildings may represent a garrison established by the Quiché, the conquest-minded eastern neighbors of the Mam.

The many local groups comprising the Quiché and their close relatives were probably much alike early in the Postclassic period, for linguistic reconstructions suggest that Quiché, Cakchiquel, and Tzutuhil did not develop into distinct languages until about A.D. 1000.[44] Beginning as early as the Terminal Classic, local central-highland aristocracies absorbed foreign ideas and symbols, and some highland societies probably assimilated Mexican and

FIG. 9-7. Structure 1, Zaculeu. This temple is the largest in the town.

FIG. 9-8. Stage, Zaculeu. This small platform, standing before Structure 1, never supported a building; it was probably the scene of ritual performances.

FIG. 9-9. Ball court, Zaculeu. The I-shaped playing area, like the one at Iximché (cf. Fig. 9-10), is completely enclosed.

northern Maya nobles as well. Many elements of architecture, pottery, and arts and crafts reflect Mexican styles. The result of this process of acculturation was a series of thoroughly Mexicanized aristocracies that asserted "Toltec" ancestry, although they came to speak highland Mayan languages. Many ruling lines based their claims to legitimacy on real or fictive connections with Tula or its surrogate, Chichén Itzá.

Quiché and Cakchiquel histories describe ceremonies in which the lord Nacxit invested highland Maya rulers with authority and sovereignty in his palace at Tollan. The Annals of the Cakchiquels explains:

> They came before Mevac and Nacxit, who was truly a great king. Then they entertained them, and the Ahauh Ahpop and Ahpop Qamahay [ah pop q'am haa] were chosen. Afterwards, they dressed them, they pierced their noses, and they gave them their offices. . . . And turning to all of them, the Lord Nacxit said: "Climb up to these columns of stone, enter into my house. I will

give you sovereignty. . . ." And thereupon they climbed up to the columns of stone. In this manner ended the granting of sovereignty to them in the presence of Nacxit, and they began to give shouts of joy.[45]

The Popul Vuh, the great book of Quiché tradition, has a fuller description:

And then they said as they left,
"We are going there to the sunrise,
Whence our fathers came,"
. . .
Actually they crossed over the sea,
And then they arrived there at the sunrise.
They went to receive the lordship.
. . .
And when they arrived
Before the lord,
Nacxit was the name of the great lord,
The sole judge
Of a huge jurisdiction.
And it was he who gave out the signs of authority,
All the insignia.
Then came the sign of the [ah pop, the ruler]
And [ah pop q'am haa, the "Assistant Chief"]
And then came the sign of the power
And authority
Of [ah pop]
And [ah pop q'am ha]
In the end Nacxit gave out
The insignia of lordship.
These are the names of them: Canopy,
And Throne,
Nose Bone
And Earring,
Jade Labret,
And Gold Beads,
Panther Claws
And Jaguar Claws,
Owl Skull
And Deer,
Armband of Precious Stones
And Snail Shell Bracelet,
Bowing
And Bending,
Filled Teeth
And Inlay,
Parrot Feather Crest,
And Royal Crane Panache.
And so they took them all and came away;
Then they brought back across the sea
The Tula scripture,
The Scripture.[46]

Yucatecan chronicles link Nacxit with Chichén Itzá and with Kukulcán, both as a name for the god and culture hero and as a royal title.[47] More than one early leader bore the name or title Q'uq' Cumatz, the Quiché equivalent of Kukulcán. Another document reports that Guatemalan lords sent tokens of peace and friendship to the ruler of Chichén Itzá. These gifts may have been meant to signal acknowledgment of Chichén as the source of their sovereignty. Whether or not highland Maya rulers derived legitimacy from ties to Chichén, or even journeyed there for symbolic investiture, they were surely independent in day-to-day activity.

Early Quiché towns are unimposing and occupy easily defended localities atop steep ridges and hills along the north edge of the Quiché basin. Public buildings embody elements of Gulf Coast architectural styles, suggesting the likely source of Mexican features for later Quiché society. These northern connections may have been maintained via the Motagua and maritime networks as well as along overland routes coming through the upper drainage of the Usumacinta.[48] Although Quiché histories portray ancestral rulers as great kings, this is largely a matter of descendants aggrandizing themselves by glorifying their forebears. None of the early Quiché nobles controlled anything greater than a very localized sphere of influence.

Local political and economic spheres grew and multiplied during the thirteenth and fourteenth centuries.[49] Shifting alliances and changing power relations were the order of the day. The Quiché state eventually emerged as the most powerful in the Maya highlands.[50] Utatlán, the Quiché capital at the time of the conquest, occupies a series of plateaus separated by deep ravines in the broad Quiché basin. Three distinct civic centers, each corresponding to one set of Quiché kinship groups, formed the heart of the composite community. Q'umaric Ah, eventually the preeminent civic precinct and home of the most powerful lineage, was founded about A.D. 1400. Presently it would boast an impressive array of temples, palaces, administrative buildings, and ball courts. Discrete architectural complexes, each with its own temples, palaces, and "council chambers," corresponded to the several noble lineages that lived there. Ordinary farmers, artisans, and landless "serfs" occupied outlying residential areas. During the fifteenth century, Quiché society underwent radical changes as Utatlán's political and economic sphere expanded beyond the Quiché basin on all fronts. Control of lower, warmer valleys to the north and east secured access to precious stones, metals, feathers, and a variety of other lowland products. Thrusts to the southwest, into the broad, fertile highland basins and the cacao-producing piedmont and the coast beyond, provided a major economic boost to the Quiché state. Garrisons, often with scaled-down copies of Utatlán's civic buildings, marked Quiché penetration of neighboring territories.

Eventually Quiché territorial expansion outstripped the evolution of administrative systems. Late in the fifteenth century the Cakchiquel broke away from the Quiché sphere and established an independent capital at Iximché, some 60 kilometers southwest of Utatlán.[51] The new town, with its temples, palaces, "council chambers," and ball courts, was very much in the Utatlán tradition, though more compact (Fig. 9-10, Color Plate 8). As at Utatlán, Mixteca-Puebla stylistic elements reflect the Mexican heritage claimed by the aristocracy as well as continuing ties with central Mexico. These connections could be quite direct at times: in 1510, Motecuzoma, the Aztec emperor, sent an ambassador to Iximché.

Following the Quiché pattern, the Cakchiquel quickly began their own expansion. A Cakchiquel garrison in the upper Motagua Valley marks an early thrust into Pokom territory. Here environments and natural resources complemented those of the Cakchiquel heartland, providing for greatly increased ecological diversity. The Tzutuhil, with their capital at Atitlán on the lakeshore, closed off Cakchiquel horizons to the west and south. The Tzutuhil felt some pressure from Cakchiquel competition for the cacao-producing piedmont zones, but maintained control of an independent political and economic sphere.

To the east, in Chortí and Pokom territory, the situation was much the same as in the western highlands.[52] Small towns like Mixco Viejo controlled very local spheres of influence. Pokom and Chortí groups mingled with Xinca, Lenca, Paya, Pipil, and other non-Maya peoples along the eastern frontier of the Maya world.[53] Farther east, Maya populations gave way to Maya enclaves, and finally to solid blocks of people who did not share basic Mesoamerican cultural patterns.

Mayapán, Tulum, and other Postclassic cities reflect a clear Classic-period heritage, particularly in architectural styles, but the organization of Postclassic

FIG. 9-10. Ball court, Iximché. The I-shaped playing area, like the one at Zaculeu (cf. Fig. 9-9), is completely enclosed.

states contrasts sharply with that of their Classic forebears. State institutions had undergone sweeping transformations, already under way in the Terminal Classic period.

Kingship was no longer the focus of public affairs and state propaganda. Postclassic sculpture and hieroglyphic texts, like those of Terminal Classic Chichén Itzá, no longer fixate on the persons of individual rulers. To the degree that the legitimation of Classic-period kings depended on genealogical and symbolic connections with deeply rooted local dynasties and traditions, Postclassic kings may have been forced to adopt different symbolic strategies. Several ruling aristocracies not only emphasized their foreign connections, but also alleged foreign origins and even based their claims to political legitimacy on them. The rulers at Naco, Utatlán, and other southern Maya capitals in effect claimed cultural identities and heritages that contrasted with those of their subjects.

Aristocrats and the states they served still maintained—in some cases, expanded—distant connections, especially commercial relationships that provided luxury goods which could be redistributed to bolster state power. But rulers deployed their economic resources differently than their Classic-period ancestors had. The lords of late Maya cities still undertook monumental public building projects, but on a smaller scale and with less exacting standards of craftsmanship. Architecture was evidently far less important as a symbolic manifestation of state power than it had been in earlier times. States themselves operated on a smaller scale in the Postclassic period, both in terms of the size of the territories and with respect to the numbers of people that they controlled.

The Spaniards who invaded the Maya world in the sixteenth century were initially impressed by such cities as Tulum, but their interest quickly shifted to the Aztec empire, which offered far greater concentrations of gold and other materials precious in European eyes. Conquest of the politically fragmented Maya world, with its many autonomous states, represented a very costly undertaking, particularly in relation to immediate rewards in portable material wealth. Invasion and colonization of most of the Maya world came later, when Spanish interest had shifted to land and to the control of Indian labor to work it. For those resources quickly came to be in short supply at the core of Aztec territory, where the first wave of invaders had settled to exploit native populations already decimated by European diseases.

TEN

Perspectives on the Maya

The ancient Maya were the only fully literate Native American people, and the texts they produced offer the possibility of direct access to Maya perspectives on their own history, philosophy, and institutions. They were the greatest scientists in the New World. Without the aid of the simplest optical instrument, Maya astronomers and chronologists created an astonishingly sophisticated calendar system. Maya peoples have produced some of the world's finest architecture, sculpture, painting, poetry, and literature. Maya societies grew and flourished in the seemingly inhospitable tropical forest. By most measures, ancient Maya societies were the most complex in the Americas, but such aspects of technology as metallurgy and wheels were undeveloped, cities were not very densely populated, and states were quite restricted geographically. Maya archaeologists have been far more interested in working out the details of Maya history and elaborating reconstructions of individual Maya societies than in comparing Maya societies with other archaic states and examining Maya history in the context of broader anthropological perspectives on the issues and processes noted above. The potential contribution of Maya culture history to anthropological theory is great but almost untapped.

Unanswered questions about the Maya and their history abound. Information on the Preclassic Maya world is naturally sketchy, but surprising gaps also mar reconstructions of later Maya societies. In some parts of the Maya world, the archaeological record is still entirely blank. Along with archaeology, Maya histories and early Spanish descriptions provide unusually full pictures of a few Maya societies at the period of the conquest. Even in these instances, available information is not uniform. The sources generally reflect politics and economics in detail, other aristocratic concerns less well, and many aspects of culture not at all.

Even basic aspects of Maya civilization are puzzling. What were subsistence systems at the heart of the Maya economies really like? Milpa farming, featuring maize, beans, and squash, was fundamental, but it was not standardized. What were the varied blends of accessory crops? How important were manioc and other root crops? What differences resulted from regional variations in soils, climates, scheduling, and the use of such techniques as terracing? Milpa farming was never the sole agricultural system. How important was wetland cultivation and other methods of intensive farming? Wetland farming began in some regions during the Late Preclassic period, but how early was it a major component of subsistence economies? To what extent did Maya farmers cultivate ramón, chicosapote, and other tree crops? What was the dietary importance of noncrop plants, fish, shellfish, and other wild foods? Evidence of climatic change—including a drought in the Terminal Classic period—is mounting. What effects did climatic variability have on Maya subsistence systems? Did shifts in climatic conditions play a significant role in the developmental history of Maya societies, especially with respect to the Terminal Classic transformation of the political and economic landscape of the Maya world?

Trade networks were vital to Maya societies, distributing great quantities of raw materials and finished products. What perishable goods moved along these networks? How important was the exchange of foods between communities and regions? By what social mechanisms did exchange operate? What balances of market and redistributive patterns characterized Maya economic life? What roles did political leaders play in administering subsistence activities and commerce?

Extreme differences in wealth and social status developed within Maya societies during the Preclassic period. How sharply defined were social groups? How extensive was occupational specialization? To what extent did it coincide with social ranking? What mechanisms of social mobility were available to common folk?

Maya cities boasted impressive concentrations of monumental art and architecture. They were seats of great political and economic power. To what extent were they urban? Tikal, Caracol, Calakmul, Dzibilchaltún, and Chichén Itzá were among the cities with populations that numbered in the tens of thousands. At Mayapán and a few other cities, dense concentrations of dwellings clustered behind community walls. Maya centers certainly embodied many of the economic and political functions of true cities, but none had the urban form of Teotihuacán, with a huge dense population concentrated within a community laid out according to a rigid grid. Did the smaller and more dispersed populations of Maya centers enjoy different patterns of social relations? All of these questions, and many others, can be asked of every part of the Maya world in every period of its precolumbian history.

In part, these gaps in understanding reflect an incomplete archaeological record, although the accelerating pace of archaeological investigation constantly augments available data. Improved archaeological techniques are contributing partial answers to some questions. Flotation techniques that can recover surprising quantities of plant remains, even in the tropics, are becoming standard in Maya excavations. Archaeologists are asking new questions of Maya remains as they broaden their interests beyond the traditional preoccupation with temples, palaces, and monumental art.

The most noteworthy development in Maya studies in recent years has been intensified investigation of Maya hieroglyphic writing and imagery. A flood of new readings of texts and new interpretations of iconography has produced fascinatingly detailed reconstructions of many episodes of Maya history. The potential for new insights into the nature of ancient Maya societies—especially the dynastic history of the Classic period, the subject of most surviving texts—is immense and still largely unrealized. The astonishing pace of advances in epigraphy has outstripped the ability of Maya studies to digest the results. Epigraphy has become an even more esoteric calling than ever, and Mayanists with other specialties have found it difficult to evaluate proposed decipherments and the interpretations based on them. European and North American intellectual traditions are predisposed to privilege written texts over material remains in reconstructing history. Texts often record the kinds of specifics thought to be the essence of history: personal names, place names, calendar dates. Texts often seem to be unambiguous in their recording of events, especially in comparison with material remains. In fact, of course, texts are never unambiguous; they can only be understood in the context of the perspectives and agendas of their authors. In the case of Maya hieroglyphic texts, these perspectives include a concept of history quite unlike our own, in which the cyclical relationship of past, present, and future may demand that history be rewritten to conform more closely with the present. Classic-period Maya texts may seem to record straightforward dynastic history, but they do not. An important challenge confronting the field of Maya archaeology is to develop methods that allow for using textual information and data from material remains to cross-check one another, rather than privileging either.

Perhaps the thorniest problem facing Maya archaeology is that of the ethical issues involved in the use of unprovenienced material. One consideration is that forgers are so skilled that it is impossible to be certain of the authenticity of objects without the assurance of a pedigree provided by properly recorded scientific excavation. Many archaeologists feel that objects without carefully recorded provenience information—whether authentic or not—have virtually nothing to contribute to the reconstruction of ancient societies. Other Mayanists are confident that connoisseurs can distinguish fakes from real pieces, and some argue that texts and imagery can provide useful information even when provenience is lacking. The critical consideration is that most unprovenienced objects in private and museum collections are the product of the looting of sites, which is so intense in many parts of the Maya world that it is rapidly destroying that part of the archaeological record which is not erased by construction and large-scale modern agriculture. Even when the objects have been in collections for many years—something that is very difficult to ascertain, for pedigrees can be forged—using them for scholarly purposes lends a cachet of respectability to collecting and thereby contributes to the continuing destruction of the very contextual information that is so essential. Publishing objects in private collections certainly encourages the antiquities market by increasing their resale value. For many Mayanists, therefore, the cost of using unprovenienced pieces is terribly high and the resulting contribution to our understanding of the past is virtually nil.

As archaeologists and historians fill in more and more of the historical outline of the Maya cultural tradition, they can make better use of the more complete information about late Maya societies to understand earlier periods of Maya history. No culture is static and no group is a fossilized image of its ancestors, but societies are products of their histories. Every contribution to Maya culture history makes possible a better assessment of continuities in the Maya cultural tradition. Improved understanding of these continuities permits a more informed use of analogy based on ethnographic, historical, and archaeological information.

Ethnographic analogy is the most obvious case. Today's Maya groups are functioning, integrated societies, not partial cultures reflecting an incomplete Maya pattern. Modern institutions must be understood in terms of their place in the contemporary social and environmental milieu *and* as historical products of nearly five centuries of interaction between European and Maya cultural traditions. It is impossible to evaluate hypotheses about precolumbian equivalents of such modern institutions as the cargo system without this historical and functional context.

The same is true of analogies based on historical information from the time of the Spanish invasion. The rich documentation of sixteenth-century Quiché mythology, especially in the Popol Vuh, has become a popular source of analogies for interpreting imagery from other parts of the Maya world and from much earlier periods. Appropriate use of this kind of information requires a specific model of historical relationships; simple projection of Quiché names and concepts onto the past is not productive. In the same way, the interplay of political institutions, lineage organizations, social hierarchies, and religion in the operation of the Quiché state provides an apt general model for Classic Maya political organization. Full use of the Quiché pattern to create detailed, testable hypotheses about earlier Maya societies requires a detailed historical framework. What roles did Toltecs, Mexican-influenced northern Maya groups, and local highland societies play in the formation of the Quiché institutions that were functioning at the time of the conquest? What is the relation of each of these traditions to societies of the Classic period? In the same way, it is potentially misleading to base analogies on late Yucatecan societies without an understanding of the Mexican impact on northern Yucatan. In order to use data from the Classic period to help reconstruct Preclassic societies, it is crucial to assess the impact of Teotihuacán on the Classic Maya as well as to understand the basic historical relations among the several regional traditions of development within the Maya world.

The fullest possible reconstruction of Maya culture history, region by region, is the essential framework for understanding the development of the Maya cultural tradition. Explanation—identifying and characterizing processes of culture change—is inseparable from historical reconstruction. Process *is* history. In the Maya world, history is also a catalog of variation on common themes. A regional perspective is essential.

The problem of explaining the transformation that affected most of the Maya world at the end of the Classic period is a perfect example. Almost every conceivable factor has been advanced as the root cause: foreign invasion, peasant revolt, population decline, excessive population growth, limited environmental potential, agricultural failure resulting from the exhaustion or erosion of the soil or from the invasion of grasses, climate change, earthquakes, hurricanes, disease.[1] Progressive improvement in the historical framework of the period has shown that the decline was not uniform and not even universal. It was not an "event," but a series of processes that followed various courses, with the timing and outcome varying from region to region. No explanation that relies on a single cause can possibly account for such varied phenomena. The best interpretation points to internal stresses, complicated by foreign penetration and perhaps by climatic change, as leading factors in a very complex set of chain reactions that eventually affected many related societies. In any case, an obvious lesson to be learned from this aspect of Maya history is that there are limits to growth. Unsustainable growth—expansion beyond the point at which resources and demands remain in equilibrium—inevitably brings about major transformation.

The rise of Maya civilization is an even more complex issue, embracing related developments throughout the Maya world during a period of many centuries. Single-cause explanations have the virtue of focusing attention on processes that may have been important in one or another region at some period, and they sometimes produce insights by presenting familiar information in new frames of reference, but no one factor alone can account for the emergence of Maya civilization.

Demographic factors loom large in explanations of prehistoric developments, and the rise of Maya civilization is no exception.[2] The problems inherent in arriving at reliable estimates of prehistoric populations make it difficult to verify or refute demographic hypotheses. Population profiles of early Maya communities are particularly impressionistic, but available data do suggest basic demographic trends. Not surprisingly, these data indicate considerable variation from region to region. There is a definite pattern of overall growth, but it was neither uniform nor continuous. The timing of population increases varies considerably in relation to the appearance of the various aspects of complexity in the several parts of the Maya world. Population growth certainly accompanied the emergence of Maya civilization, but the relationship is not necessarily direct. It may have been partial cause, effect, or a blend of the two.

The rise of Maya civilization has also been attributed to warfare, itself usually explained as a result of increasing populations.[3] Here, too, the archaeological evidence presents difficulties: to distinguish weapons from hunting implements, and fortifications from constructions having other functions, is not a straightforward task. A regional perspective weakens the warfare hypothesis. The Preclassic ditch-and-embankment system at Becán was probably defensive, but there are very few indications of early conflict elsewhere. Tikal's earthworks may have been fortifications too, but there is no evidence that they were constructed in an early period.

Trade is a third popular causal factor. Maya commerce, involving durable goods easily recognized as imports, did leave clear archaeological traces. Exchange networks covered the Preclassic Maya world. One influential hypothesis attributes the initial development of key features of Maya civilization to an urgent and continuing need to procure vital resources.[4] Societies in the heart of the southern lowlands, lacking natural resources of obvious commercial value, supposedly developed a specialized political leadership to procure salt, obsidian, and hard stone. These are valuable commodities, but the exotic stones were not essential to life. Local chert and limestone are inferior but adequate. The southern lowland core was not really without resources. Dozens of local tropical-forest products are potential trade goods, as are agricultural crops and manufactured commodities. Commerce need not be based on unique or even scarce commodities.[5] The ethnographic literature abounds with descriptions of societies that import items which could be procured or manufactured locally. There is no convincing evidence to show that any sector of the Maya world had a significantly greater need for special procurement institutions than any other. Exchange surely did have an important role in the evolution of Maya social and political institutions, but exchange alone can account neither for the form of those institutions nor for the chronological order in which they appeared in different regions.

Population growth, conflict, and especially exchange did contribute to the development of Maya civilization, but none is the sole or even the primary cause. A full understanding of the emergence of complex organization and institutions in Maya societies requires a multifaceted perspective on the interaction of many factors: population growth, agricultural intensification, mechanisms of resource exploitation and control, urbanization, economic differentiation and the proliferation of specialists, centralization of political power and the proliferation of political offices and institutions, elaboration of ideologies of kingship, and elaboration of writing, mathematics, calendars, and related symbol systems, to name only the most obvious.

A regional perspective on Maya culture history suggests that interaction among communities and regions was more important than any individual factor. Exchange is one straightforward facet of interaction, but residential enclaves, marriage alliances, pilgrimages, and attendance at special ceremonial events also linked Maya communities. At roughly the same time, the several regions of the Maya world experienced varied but comparable processes of development that led from small, homogeneous villages to regional states dominated by cities which were seats of powerful aristocracies. Many causal factors contributed to the rise of Maya civilization, but all did not operate everywhere or even in any one region. Interaction among regions allowed local developments to spread widely, often far beyond the areas immediately affected by the factors that stimulated them. An institution developed in one region as a response to population growth and conflict might be adopted elsewhere, in zones of low population density, because it facilitated the acquisition of needed raw materials. Links among communities and regions are at least as important in explaining the rise of Maya civilization as are the immediate stimuli involved in the varied local developments.

Maya patterns of territorial organization fostered interaction. The cultural and linguistic landscape of the Maya world was not one of neatly bounded neighboring groups. As in the rest of Mesoamerica, people of contrasting cultural identity and linguistic affiliation mingled in complex mosaic arrangements. Enclaves—groups of people who lived and worked away from their own core territories, among people with different cultural traditions—were prominent everywhere.

Modern Maya communities commonly hold outlying pockets of farmland surrounded by fields that belong to neighboring communities. Many Maya farmers spend part of the year far from their home communities, working distant milpas in foreign territory. Outlying farm plots can form the nuclei of new communities. Chan Kom, in northern Yucatan, began as a cluster of houses and milpas that were once an outlying part of the community of Ebtún, 50 kilometers away.[6] At first, most people returned to Ebtún when agricultural activities were completed. Even the few people who lived at Chan Kom year round recognized the authority of Ebtún and retained their rights and obligations as members of that community. Gradually Chan Kom attracted more and more permanent residents, and eventually it became a community in its own right, with an independent political organization. Kinship links, common historical roots, and a host of social ties still marked Chan Kom as an enclave with ethnic ties to Ebtún.

Comparable enclaves dotted the precolumbian Maya world, along with others maintained to serve state political and economic ends.[7] Canek, ruler of Tayasal, told Cortés of his vassals on the coast who raised cacao. This enclave, probably located in the Nito region on the Gulf of Honduras, was far beyond Tayasal's sphere of political control. The brother of Paxbolonacha, ruler of Acalán, governed a Chontal commercial enclave in the distant Chol trading port of Nito. Chetumal and other Yucatecan commercial centers maintained outposts in the lower Ulúa Valley, at the base of the Gulf of Honduras. Xicalango, the great trading port on the Laguna de Términos, was a cosmopolitan community where Chontal, Yucatec, and other Maya traders mingled with Gulf Coast Mexicans. Even Aztec merchants from central Mexico maintained an enclave there.

The most obvious functions of enclaves are economic: they secure access to exotic raw materials, to environmental conditions needed to raise desired crops, to distant markets. The enclave pattern was a strategy of ecological diversification. Enclaves also fostered many kinds of interaction. Maya aristocracies depended on ties with other ruling groups—for formal confirmation of authority and sovereignty and the transfer of their symbols, for exchange of esoteric religious and scientific information, for marriage alliances. Enclaves were vital instruments of state activity. Maya merchants, like their Aztec counterparts, were probably prime sources of military intelligence. Political territories themselves probably often took the form of archipelagoes, with many outlying parcels interspersed among islands of foreign territory. The Aztec empire, Mesoamerica's greatest political entity, tolerated a hostile Tlaxcalan state within the heart of its central Mexican dominions.[8] Mesoamerican notions of normal territorial behavior did not emphasize exclusiveness. Block distributions of people of a single linguistic, cultural, or political affiliation were not the norm.

Cultural and linguistic contrasts are most extreme in frontier zones: between groups within the Maya world, between Maya and Mexican groups, and particularly between Maya and Central American peoples. The eastern frontier of the Maya world (and of Mesoamerica) was a mélange of enclaves, ranging from individual households to neighborhoods to entire communities. Foreign penetration of the Maya world involved the same territorial pattern. The enclave of colonial Teotihuacanos at Kaminaljuyú is the clearest example; Tikal probably housed a similar group from Kaminaljuyú. Recognizing concentrations of foreign elements as reflections of enclaves helps put the issue of foreign impact on Maya societies in perspective. Teotihuacán maintained only a very limited presence in the Maya world. Most communities, especially in the lowlands, had only very indirect connections with Teotihuacán, through a few enclaves at such centers as Tikal and Kaminaljuyú. Even Kaminaljuyú's resident Mexicans may have had indirect ties with the central Mexican metropolis through a subsidiary province of Teotihuacán in the Intermediate Zone. Later Mexican enclaves in the north probably had a much greater impact on the Maya world.

Understanding the relationships between the Maya world and the rest of Mesoamerica is not only the critical factor in working out an array of particular problems in Maya history, but it is also essential to developing an appropriate overall framework for interpreting the Maya cultural tradition. Partly in response to suggestions that Maya civilization was derivative, with a complex organization emerging only under the influence of central Mexican states, Maya archaeology turned inward, seeking to understand the development of Maya societies in their own terms. External relationships came to be thought of in terms of discrete episodes of interaction between particular societies. Now Maya archaeologists must reexamine Maya history to see which trajectories of development can be understood as aspects of processes operating on the broader Mesoamerican stage.

In what ways were Maya societies linked to the Olmec world? Does the near absence of Olmec-style material from the Maya lowlands reflect real historical patterns or is it a function of an incomplete archaeological record? How did patterns of interaction in the highly diverse sociopolitical landscape of the Izapan world contribute to the emergence of distinctively Maya states? What relationships conditioned the simultaneous emergence of Maya and Zoque writing and calendar systems? In what way did lowland Maya societies participate in the development of the stela complex and the associated political art, hieroglyphic texts, and Long Count calendar? Why did aristocrats in the Maya highlands, in the adjacent piedmont and coast, and in the Intermediate Zone cease to use these features after the second century A.D., just as they became the hallmarks of lowland kingdoms? What was the nature of the Teotihuacán presence in the Maya highlands and in lowland cities? To what degree was the transformation of the Maya world in the Terminal Classic period part of a larger process involving the collapse of Teotihuacán and the momentous sociopolitical and demographic dislocations that came in its wake. What social, economic, and political mechanisms conditioned interactions among Gulf Coast Mexicans and Mexicanized Maya peoples and the societies of the rest of the Maya world? Did central Mexican cities maintain direct interactions with parts of the Maya world in the Postclassic period?

Ascertaining the nature of Maya frontiers and assessing the impact of Mexican peoples on the Maya world involve a larger issue: the relation between material culture and basic cultural identity. Language differences do not prevent interaction. Cultural frontiers are not barriers to the spread of objects, ideas, styles, or institutions. Intense interaction among the enclaves that comprise frontier zones actually fosters communication and the sharing of cultural patterns. Maya hieroglyphic inscriptions certainly indicate Mayan speech, and the combination of styles of architecture, art, and crafts that are often associated with Maya texts surely marks Maya communities even when texts are absent, but greater precision is elusive. Ambiguity is acute near the limits of distribution of the hieroglyphic texts. In the lower Ulúa region, for example, basic developmental trajectories are the same as in the southern Maya lowlands, and local societies maintained close ties with their western neighbors, with whom they shared styles of architecture and craft production. The complex iconography of Ulúa polychrome pottery shares many design elements and structural patterns with the art of the southern lowlands. Hieroglyphic texts, however, are absent, as are most of the features of lowland Maya political art, and colonial-period information suggests that the people of the area probably did not speak a Mayan language at the time of the Spanish invasion (nor, presumably, in earlier epochs). Highland communities, almost certainly Mayan-speaking, also did not carve stelae with portraits of lords and texts celebrating their achievements after the Late Preclassic period. Because the most obvious functions of this complex of features are in the limited sphere of maintaining royal power, such features are not suitable markers of the cultural identity of a community or region. Cultural patterns that characterize broad segments of the population—basic settlement patterns and the organization of space at the community and household level; common iconographic conventions that may reflect widely shared aspects of belief—are better indicators of cultural identity. Since these kinds of cultural patterns can be shared across linguistic boundaries, and since the archaeological record only rarely reflects language, it is not very useful to define the Maya world in terms of language. Understanding the internal diversity of the Maya world in terms of cultural identities is an equally complex undertaking. Mexican traits sometimes mark foreign enclaves, but in other instances they reflect imported goods or foreign styles adopted by local craftsmen. Even with rich historical data, it is impossible to separate Yucatec, Itzá, and Mexican components in the archaeological record of the northern lowlands.

Patterns of archaeological evidence in the Maya world—styles of architecture, arts, and crafts; funerary customs; settlement systems and community layouts; traces of social, political, and economic institutions—must embody reflections of Maya identity. Understanding the relations between these patterns and the ethnic and linguistic variety which has always characterized the Maya world is the greatest challenge facing Maya archaeology today.

Notes

Introduction

1. Stephens 1841:1:123–24.
2. Stephens 1841:1:103.
3. Childe 1951, 1954; Sanders and Price 1968.
4. Wittfogel 1957.
5. Sometimes called "Oriental despotism."
6. Sanders and Price 1968; Wittfogel 1972.
7. Quoted in Daniel 1968:142–43.
8. Carmack et al. 1996; Helms 1975; Vogt 1969b; Wolf 1959.
9. Medrano 1992.
10. "Mayan" is the proper way to refer to the family of related languages spoken by the Maya. In all other contexts, the proper form of the adjective is "Maya."
11. Bricker 1981; Sullivan 1989.

Chapter 1. The Discovery of the Maya

1. Morison 1971–74; Sauer 1968.
2. Morison 1971–74; Sale 1990; Sauer 1966; Stannard 1992.
3. MacNutt 1912:317; Sauer 1966:128–30.
4. Sauer 1966:166–68.
5. Tozzer 1941:236.
6. Crosby 1972:35–63; Stewart 1973:35–38.
7. Chamberlain 1953:53–57; Tozzer 1941:8–9, 233–39.
8. Closs 1976.
9. Chamberlain 1948:11–12.
10. Tozzer 1941:12.
11. Chamberlain 1948:13–14.
12. Quoted in Roys 1957:147.
13. Pagden 1971.
14. Pagden 1971:359–61.
15. Pagden 1971:377, 519; Villagutierre Soto-Mayor 1983.
16. Carmack 1981; J. E. Kelly 1932; MacLeod 1973.
17. Recinos and Goetz 1953:119–25.
18. Tozzer 1941:169.
19. Three Maya books—the Dresden, Madrid, and

Paris codices—have been known for more than a century. The fourth, the Grolier Codex, appeared in the 1970s in the hands of a private collector who reported being told that it had been found in a dry cave in the state of Chiapas. With only an anecdotal pedigree provided by looters, the authenticity of this book is open to serious question, although its content—a schematic reckoning of the motions of Venus in relation to the 260-day Ritual Almanac—would imply a very knowledgeable forger.

20. Pagden 1975; Tozzer 1941.

21. Brunhouse 1973.

22. Stephens 1841, 1843; Von Hagen 1948, 1950.

23. Brunhouse 1975.

24. Wauchope 1962:20.

25. Desmond and Messenger 1987.

26. Gordon 1896.

27. Brunhouse 1971; Houston and Fowler 1990; J. E. S. Thompson 1994; Willey and Sabloff 1993.

28. D. Kelley 1962, 1976:3–7.

29. These figures surely represent the supernatural, but they may not be proper deities; see discussion in Chapter 3.

30. D. Kelley 1962.

31. Aveni 1980; Bricker and Bricker 1989; Love 1995.

32. Students of ancient writing.

33. J. E. S. Thompson 1960, 1965.

34. W. Fash 1994; Marcus 1995; Weeks 1993.

35. Originally the "New Archaeology" (Willey and Sabloff 1993).

36. De Montmollin 1989a; Sabloff 1990.

37. Proskouriakoff 1960, 1961a.

38. Knorozov 1967.

39. Bricker 1986, 1992; Houston 1989a, 1989b; Justeson and Campbell 1984; D. Kelley 1962; Knorozov 1967; Schele 1982; D. Stuart 1987.

40. Durbin 1969; D. Kelley 1976:178–80.

41. Landa's original manuscript is lost; his representations of the glyphs may have been less crude than those in the surviving copy.

42. Houston 1989a, 1989b; D. Kelley 1976.

43. Berlin 1958; D. Kelley 1976:213–19; Marcus 1976a; Mathews 1991; D. Stuart 1985; Stuart and Houston 1994.

44. Proskouriakoff 1960, 1961a.

45. Culbert 1991; Proskouriakoff 1963b, 1964, 1993.

46. Proskouriakoff 1961b.

47. D. Kelley 1965; Kubler 1974; Lounsbury 1976; Schele 1986.

48. For example: Culbert 1991; Houston 1993; Houston and Stuart 1989; Marcus 1987; Robertson 1974, 1976, 1980; Robertson and Benson 1985; Robertson and Fields 1985, 1991, 1994; Robertson and Jeffers 1979; Robertson et al. 1996; Schele and Freidel 1990; Schele and Miller 1986; D. Stuart 1987, 1988. Michael Coe (1992) gives an interesting account of the history of the decipherment of Maya writing, but one that is badly flawed by his partisan approach, particularly his hostility to the notion that readings of Maya texts and the interpretations based on them require critical assessment just like other archaeological analyses. Houston (1989a, 1989b) provides a briefer, less personal, and far more balanced account.

49. Nor are they all equally persuasive. A critical assessment of the current state of decipherment—especially in terms of sorting out those readings which are well established from those which are very tentative, and those which are still current from those which have been superseded by more recent readings—is badly needed.

50. Joyce 1993b; Marcus 1992.

51. Bricker 1981; Carmack et al. 1996; Sullivan 1989.

52. Carmack and Morales Santos 1983; Carmack et al. 1996; Freidel et al. 1993:12; Gossen 1994.

Chapter 2. The Maya World

1. Vogt 1969b.

2. Carmack et al. 1996; Helms 1975; Kirchhoff 1943; Wolf 1959.

3. Leyenaar 1978; Scarborough and Wilcox 1991; Stern 1949; Bussel et al. 1991.

4. Henderson 1977, 1978, 1992b.

5. L. Parsons 1978.

6. A. Collier 1964; Gómez Pompa et al. 1990; D. Rice 1993; Stevens 1964; L. Stuart 1964; Tamayo and West 1964; Vivó Escoto 1964; Wagner 1964; West 1964a, 1964b.

7. Thurston 1994.

8. Cancian 1972; G. Collier 1975; Vogt 1969c, 1970.

9. Nations and Nigh 1980; Tozzer 1907:19–22.

10. Campbell 1976, 1977; Campbell and Kaufman 1985; Justeson et al. 1985; Kaufman 1976.

11. Clendinnen 1987; Farriss 1984; G. Jones 1977, 1989; Redfield 1941, 1950; Redfield and Villa Rojas 1934; Sullivan 1989; Villa Rojas 1945, 1969b.

12. Villa Rojas 1969a; Wisdom 1940.

13. Laughlin 1969a.

14. This lack of evidence is probably a function of an incomplete archaeological record. Community location in the Maya lowlands has been stable for the most part, with more recent constructions covering earlier remains; this is especially true of monumental architectural zones. Early and Middle Preclassic monumental architecture and sculpture probably exist in other communities, but buried beneath Classic-period buildings.

15. Unprepossessing remains of villages have not been as appealing to archaeologists as those of great cities, and they are harder to locate in the tropical-forest environment, so the apparent general population decline may be partly a function of an archaeological record heavily biased toward the urban segments of these societies.

16. These societies have held less interest for most archaeologists than their splendid predecessors of the Classic period, and the archaeological record for late prehispanic times is correspondingly sketchy.

17. Duby and Blom 1969; Tozzer 1907.

18. Carter 1969; Wilk 1991.

19. Cancian 1965, 1972, 1992; G. Collier 1975; J. Collier 1973; Fabrega and Silver 1973; Gossen 1974; Guiteras-Holmes 1961; Hunt 1977; Laughlin 1969b; Villa Rojas 1969c; Vogt 1969a, 1969c, 1970, 1976.

20. Montagu 1969; Nash 1969; Wagley 1969.

21. Colby and Colby 1981; Colby and van den Burghe 1969; Nash 1969; Wagley 1969.

22. Bunzel 1952; Carmack 1973, 1988; Hill 1992; Hill and Monaghan 1987; Hinshaw 1975; Nash 1958, 1969; Tax 1953; Tax and Hinshaw 1969; B. Tedlock 1992.

23. Carter 1969; Nash 1969; Reina 1966, 1969; Villa Rojas 1969a; Wilk 1991.

24. Nash 1969; Reina 1969; Wisdom 1940.

Chapter 3. The Maya World on the Eve of the Spanish Conquest

1. A. Andrews 1981; Edmonson 1982, 1986; G. Jones 1989; Roys 1957, 1965, 1967, 1972; Tozzer 1941.

2. E. Graham et al. 1985; G. Jones 1989, 1992b; Pendergast 1985, 1986.

3. Bricker and Bricker 1988.

4. Freidel and Sabloff 1984; Pagden 1971; Roys et al. 1940; Sabloff and Freidel 1975; Sabloff and Rathje 1975a, 1975b; Sabloff et al. 1974.

5. There is no single Maya world view, any more than there is one Maya group that can be made to stand for the entire Maya cultural tradition. As in all facets of Maya culture, beliefs vary from region to region, and they have changed through time. Yet the several Maya cosmologies and symbol systems are quite coherent; in this sphere, Maya cultures share many elements and most major themes. Indeed, it is in this realm, more than any other, that the Maya resemble other Mesoamerican peoples. In a broad sense, then, there is one Maya (even one Mesoamerican) conception of the universe. Names, details, and minor elaborations vary from group to group, and much has changed during the course of Maya culture history; but the basic patterns are remarkably stable. In fact, possession of a variant of this cosmology may be the best criterion for defining the Maya and Mesoamerican cultural traditions. Thus, information from modern Maya ethnography and occasionally from observation of other Mesoamerican peoples can be used sparingly to clarify or expand certain points. The Aztecs are particularly illuminating, for early Spanish churchmen scrutinized Aztec belief systems intensively and recorded their observations in great detail.

The following account of the Maya universe is based on documents of the early colonial period from northern Yucatan, but it matches closely the belief system reflected in the Postclassic native books. Archaeological evidence, moreover, particularly from the Classic period in the southern lowlands, confirms and extends this reconstruction further into the past. Not every Maya group possessed every element described here. Some elaborations of the calendar system did not survive the Classic period. Some features of the pantheon reconstructed from later prehispanic sources no doubt represent a considerable change from the situation in the Classic period. This cosmology is not an exhaustive catalog of Maya beliefs about the universe. Still, it is distinctively Maya. Every well-documented prehispanic Maya group possessed some recognizable variant of it.

6. Gossen 1974; Gossen and Leventhal 1993; Hunt 1977; León-Portilla 1973; A. Stone 1995; B. Tedlock 1992.

7. Reduced to these bald abstractions, the Maya concept of the universe may sound like simplistic mysticism. It is difficult for an outsider to appreciate these seemingly bizarre notions as a coherent, functional system of integrated beliefs. Every society believes that its own version of reality is "real" and classes other realities as fantasy—charming, perhaps, but surely distorted. To escape this trap, one must suspend disbelief to a degree that strains the rationalist mind. Yet only then is it possible to begin to develop the empathy necessary to enter at least a little way into the Maya universe.

Mathematical and calendrical notation is the most straightforward aspect of Maya symbol systems. It is not difficult to work out the mechanics of the time references that fill preconquest hieroglyphic texts. An outsider can easily comprehend the basic structure of the Maya calendar and can even begin to understand the larger principles governing its operation. The subtleties of the Maya philosophy of time, the nuances that lend real meaning to the whole, are elusive. Still, a full understanding of the mechanics of Maya time is the best approach to the conceptual world that lies behind it.

8. Aveni 1980; Bricker 1981; León-Portilla 1973; Sullivan 1989; J. E. S. Thompson 1960.

9. In some Classic-period inscriptions, both the numbers and the units of time may be represented by glyphs that are portraits of deities. They are personified, not inanimate parts of a mechanical device. In a few Initial Series dates, the numbers appear as full figures of deities, each bearing the sign for the corresponding unit of the Long Count on his back. In metaphorical terms, at least, time is not so much a force in its own right as a series of burdens moved through the universe by the gods.

10. Broda de Casas 1969; Caso 1967; Edmonson 1988, 1992; Harris and Stearns 1992; D. Kelley 1976; Lounsbury 1978; Satterthwaite 1965; J. E. S. Thompson 1960.

11. An alternate designation bestowed by modern scholars is *tzolkin*, literally "count of the days" in Yucatec Maya; the actual Maya name is not known. Mayanists conventionally use Yucatec labels in discussing the Maya calendar. Most of these words were part of the late prehispanic Yucatec calendar vocabulary, although *tzolkin* and a few others have been invented. Terms used in other parts of the Maya world and in earlier periods were not necessarily the same.

12. Aveni 1980; Henderson 1974; B. Tedlock 1992:93.

13. The Ritual Almanac is among the most basic items in the Mesoamerican cultural inventory. Every Mesoamerican people possessed a variant of it, and the correspondence among those variants with respect to the meanings of the names assigned to the days is remarkably close. The Ritual Almanac is the oldest attested component of the Mesoamerican calendar, having come into use before 500 B.C., at least in the Valley of Oaxaca (Caso 1965; Marcus 1976b, 1992). It is also the most tenacious. Although almost every other part of the Maya calendar has been lost, the Ritual Almanac survives today among several highland Maya groups in the face of heavy competition from the Christian calendar (LaFarge and Byers 1931; J. S. Lincoln 1942; Miles 1952; B. Tedlock 1992).

14. Like the Ritual Almanac, the 365-day cycle is a basic feature of Mesoamerican cultures. It may be equally ancient, although its first documented appearance, also in the Valley of Oaxaca, is slightly later (Marcus 1976b, 1992). All precolumbian Mesoamerican groups used some version of the 365-day cycle, but there is not nearly the same degree of correspondence in the month names as there is with day names in the Ritual Almanac. The Maya 365-day cycle, confronted with direct competition from the solar year of the Christian calendar, survives today only among a few groups.

15. Naturally, the Calendar Round has the same Pan-Mesoamerican distribution as its constituent cycles. The earliest known Calendar Round date is also the first evidence for the Solar Year system. For most Mesoamerican peoples, the Calendar Round offered sufficient precision

in specifying a day's position in time. For modern interpreters, though, the repetition of the same Calendar Round position every fifty-two years leaves considerable ambiguity in some traditional native histories. Only the Maya calendar includes a more precise mechanism for fixing events in the stream of time.

16. It is also called the "Short Count." Katuns were units of the older Long Count calendar as well (see Chapter 5), and so the system is essentially a shorthand version of the Long Count. The constituent units of the katun—the *tun* (360 days), the *uinal* (20 days), and of course the day itself—also remained in use for tabulating shorter periods, although the carving of fully elaborated Long Count dates came to an end with the decline of Classic Maya civilization.

17. Hunt 1977; D. Kelley 1976:53–59; J. E. S. Thompson 1934, 1960; Vogt 1992.

18. Gossen and Leventhal 1993; D. Kelley 1976:61–105; Schellhas 1904; Taube 1992; J. E. S. Thompson 1960, 1970:197–329.

19. This hypothesis would explain the many images and textual references that seem to blend the names, titles, emblems, and other characteristics of different deities.

20. Carrasco 1982; Davies 1977; Gillespie 1989.

21. The difficulty of separating earlier ideas about the feathered serpent from later beliefs that grew up in the wake of this historical episode illustrate the problems of using information recorded at the time of the Spanish invasion to reconstruct beliefs of the Classic period.

22. Even today, in parts of the Maya world, calendar priests use the traditional calendar to divine the future and to diagnose and cure illness. To judge by ethnographic descriptions of their practice (B. Tedlock 1992), precolumbian divination and curing would have involved a far more personal and subjective use of the Ritual Almanac than my mechanical description of its structure might suggest.

23. Presumably, at least in the thought of the Classic Maya, at the completion of the current Great Cycle of the Long Count—a round of 13 baktuns of 20 katuns each (see Chapter 5)—on 21 December 2012.

24. It is not certain whether they actually planned to submit because the katun cycle made it appropriate or whether the prognostications of the katun were simply part of a subtle political discourse, but the importance of the cyclical conception of time for current affairs is clear (G. Jones 1989, 1992b; Means 1917:72; Puleston 1979; Villagutierre Soto-Mayor 1983).

25. Chapman 1957; Jiménez Valdéz 1987; Matheny 1970; Ochoa and Vargas Pacheco 1987.

26. Andrews IV 1943; Díaz del Castillo 1912–16:vol. 5; Ochoa and Vargas Pacheco 1985; Pagden 1971; Piña Chan and Pavón Abreu 1961; Pincemín 1989; Scholes and Roys 1968.

27. Simpson 1964:354.

28. Hellmuth 1977; G. Jones 1989, 1992a, 1992b; Pagden 1971; Pendergast and Jones 1992; D. Rice et al. 1993; J. E. S. Thompson 1951.

29. Henderson 1977, 1984, 1988, 1992a, 1992b; Joyce 1986, 1991; Robinson 1989; Wonderley 1981, 1985, 1986a, 1986b, 1987.

30. R. M. Adams 1961:359; Díaz del Castillo 1912: 4:305; Vogt 1969a:141–43.

31. Carmack 1973, 1981; Edmonson 1971; J. W. Fox 1978, 1987, 1989; Goetz and Morley 1950; Hill and Monaghan 1987; Orellana 1993; D. Tedlock 1985; Wallace and Carmack 1977; Weeks 1983.

32. Carmack 1981; J. W. Fox 1987.

33. Also written Gumarcaah or K'umarcaaj.

34. J. W. Fox 1978; Guillemin 1967, 1977; Hill 1992; Hill and Monaghan 1987; Recinos and Goetz 1953; Robinson 1994.

35. Miles 1965b.

36. Miles 1957, 1965b.

37. Sharer 1974, 1978b.

Chapter 4. Roots of Mesoamerican Civilization

1. Historical linguists suggest that all later Mayan tongues are descended from a single Proto-Mayan language that existed before 2000 B.C. (Kaufman 1976), but it is not certain how much earlier than this date Mayan would have been recognizably distinct from some even more generalized ancestral stock.

2. Aveleyra Arroyo de Anda 1964; Fagan 1987; Stark 1981; Willey 1971.

3. Dillehay and Collins 1991; Dillehay et al. 1992;

Gruhn and Bryan 1991; Lynch 1990, 1991; Whitley and Dorn 1993.

4. Brown 1980; Gruhn and Bryan 1977.

5. MacNeish et al. 1980; Velázquez Valadez 1980.

6. A system of land reclamation involving the conversion of swampy areas to highly productive garden plots. See Armillas 1971; M. Coe 1964; Denevan 1970; C. González 1992; and Rojas Rabiela 1995.

7. M. Coe and Flannery 1964, 1967; Michaels and Voorhies 1989; Moseley 1975; Voorhies et al. 1991; Wilkerson 1973, 1975.

8. E.g., Holmberg 1950.

9. Bray 1976; Flannery 1973; McClung de Tapia 1992; Stark 1981.

10. Flannery 1968; Parsons and Parsons 1990.

11. The Archaic period is often conceptualized as a stage of "incipient agriculture" in Mesoamerica, characterized by (1) a progressive increase in the importance of plants in the diet, with a corresponding decrease in the contribution of animal foods; (2) the appearance of domesticated plants and a continuous increase in their relative importance; (3) accelerating population growth; and (4) attendant changes in technology, settlement patterns, and other aspects of the overall way of life. By the end of the Archaic period, incipient agriculture had supposedly given way to true settled agriculture in much of Mesoamerica. The Archaic/Preclassic boundary has been set at many dates, mostly falling between 2500 and 1000 B.C. This standard characterization of the Archaic period is arbitrary and potentially very misleading, although it does have some valid dimensions. It is convenient to retain an Archaic period, redefined in strictly chronological terms: the time between the end of the Pleistocene glacial period, about 7000 B.C., and the first appearance of pottery in eastern Mesoamerica, not long after 2000 B.C. Eliminating the implication that the Archaic period represents a subsistence stage on the evolutionary route from hunting to farming contributes to a more realistic understanding of the ways of life followed by Mesoamerican peoples during these millennia.

12. Byers 1967; MacNeish 1972; MacNeish et al. 1972.

13. Bray 1976; Flannery 1968; McClung de Tapia 1992; Stark 1981.

14. MacNeish and Peterson 1962.

15. Brown 1980; MacNeish et al. 1980; Zeitlin 1984.

16. Hammond et al. 1995; Rue 1987. Pollen cores sometimes produce evidence of burning as well as replacement of forest species by secondary growth and cultivated plants, suggesting slash-and-burn farming systems. Slash-mulch farming would be reflected by forest clearance alone.

17. Blake et al. 1995; Michaels and Voorhies 1989; Voorhies 1976; Voorhies et al. 1991.

18. Kaufman 1976.

19. The appearance and rapid spread of a settled-farming way of life, featuring permanent villages and pottery in eastern Mesoamerica not long after 2000 B.C., marks the beginning of the Preclassic period. By A.D. 250, Maya societies had developed the basic institutions of a great civilization. These are logical points at which to divide the continuum of Mesoamerican culture history into manageable segments, but the Preclassic period is still an arbitrary construct. No doubt, new discoveries will soon reveal earlier pottery, calling for a revision of the chronological boundaries.

20. MacNeish 1972; MacNeish et al. 1972:341–504.

21. Brush 1965.

22. Blake et al. 1995.

23. Mokaya refers to an early Pacific Coast pottery stylistic tradition that appeared in the Barra phase and evolved through the subsequent Locona, Ocós, Cherla, Cuadros, and succeeding phases of the Early and early Middle Preclassic periods. The label "Mokaya," used for the overall cultural tradition of the region as well as the pottery, is derived from the word for "corn people" in the Mixe and Zoque languages, the modern descendants of Proto-Zoquean, the language probably spoken by the creators of the tradition.

24. Davis 1975; Green and Lowe 1967; Lowe 1975.

25. Blake 1991.

26. M. Coe 1981; M. Coe and Diehl 1980.

27. M. Coe 1968; Grove 1981; Henderson 1979; Sharer and Grove 1989.

28. M. Coe 1981; M. Coe and Diehl 1980.

29. Grove 1989; Henderson 1979

30. M. Coe 1968; Drucker et al. 1959; Sharer and Grove 1989.

31. Henderson 1979; Sharer and Grove 1989.

32. Ekholm 1973; Henderson 1979; Joesink-Mandeville and Meluzin 1976; Lowe 1977; Sharer and Grove 1989.

33. Rands 1969, 1977.

34. Sedat and Sharer 1972; Sharer and Sedat 1973, 1987; Willey 1977a.

35. Sharer 1978b.

36. Borhegyi 1965a, 1965b; Michels 1979a, 1979b; Rands and Smith 1965; Sanders and Michels 1969; Sharer and Grove 1989.

37. Looters have recovered Olmec celts, serpentine figurines, and jade jewelry in the region.

38. Baudez and Becquelin 1973.

39. These communities were not necessarily initial, pioneering settlements in their respective regions, for increases in the number and size of villages brought a corresponding improvement in the archaeological record.

40. Willey et al. 1967.

41. R. E. W. Adams 1971; A. L. Smith 1972; Willey 1973a; Willey and Smith 1969.

42. A type of wall construction involving a clay or mud coating over a framework of poles.

43. This is the Xe tradition, or ceramic sphere (J. Graham et al. 1972; Sabloff 1975; Willey 1970; Willey et al. 1975).

44. W. Coe 1965; Culbert 1977.

45. Until 1990, radiocarbon dates from Cuello were often cited as evidence that a village had grown up there by 2500 B.C., if not before. It is now clear that the occupation at Cuello began a millennium later, roughly at the same time that settled, pottery-making communities appeared in other regions of Mesomerica (Andrews V and Hammond 1990; Hammond 1991; Hammond et al. 1995).

46. Three varieties were grown, one of which was very much like early South American maize (Hammond 1991; Miksicek et al. 1981).

47. D. R. Potter 1991.

48. Awe and Healy 1994; Gifford 1976; Willey et al. 1965.

49. Hammond 1977a; Hammond et al. 1979; Kosakowsky 1987.

50. R. E. W. Adams 1971; Ball 1977a, 1977b; W. Coe 1965; Culbert 19[illegible]; Gifford 1976; Kosakowsky 1987; Lowe 1977; Lowe and Mason 1965; Rands and Smith 1965; Sabloff 1975; Sharer 1978b; Willey et al. 1967.

51. Ball 1977b; Hammond 1977b; Jackson and Love 1991; Willey 1977a; Willey et al. 1965, 1975.

52. This Mirador group is quite separate from the very large Late Preclassic site with the same name in northern Guatemala.

53. Andrews IV and Andrews V 1980; Andrews V 1981.

54. Willey 1973a, 1977a; Willey et al. 1975.

55. Hansen 1991b.

56. W. Coe and M. Coe 1956.

57. Hammond 1991; Hammond et al. 1995.

58. Borhegyi 1965a, 1965b; Michels 1979a, 1979b; Sanders and Michels 1977.

59. M. Coe 1977.

60. Quirarte 1976, 1977.

61. M. Coe 1968.

62. Campbell and Kaufman 1976; N. Thomas 1974.

63. Some linguists have postulated a close relationship between the two language families. If this hypothesis is correct, linguistic differences between speakers of Zoquean and Mayan would not have been as extreme in the Middle Preclassic period as they were in later times.

64. Lowe 1977.

Chapter 5. Foundations of Maya Civilization

1. This fact may be, at least in part, a function of the limited representation of the Late Preclassic period in the lowland archaeological record. The "Hauberg stela," which bears a date that would correspond to A.D. 199, is allegedly from the lowlands, but its provenience is not documented and, like all such pieces, its authenticity is suspect.

2. Some chronologies still recognize a Protoclassic period between the advent of the Floral Park pottery style in the southern Maya lowlands (ca. 50 B.C.) and the beginning of the Classic period (ca. A.D. 250). Because this style is now recognized as a regional phenomenon—not a reflection of cultural change throughout the Maya world or even of a newly developed local cultural complexity—the Late Preclassic period is extended until A.D. 250.

3. R. E. W. Adams 1971; Ball 1977a, 1977b; W. Coe

1965; Gifford 1976; Hammond 1977b; Kosakowsky 1987; Lowe 1977; Lowe and Mason 1965; Rands and Smith 1965; Sabloff 1975; Sharer 1978b; Willey et al. 1967.

4. Agrinier 1975; Lowe 1962; Lowe and Agrinier 1960.

5. Wetland cultivation systems certainly came into use in several regions during the Late Preclassic period, and some evidence suggests that they became a major component of farming systems during this early period as well (Pohl 1990; Pope and Dahlin 1989; Puleston 1977; Rice 1993; Scarborough 1986; Scarborough et al. 1995).

6. Andrews IV 1965; Andrews IV and Andrews V 1980; Ball 1977b; W. Coe 1965; Hammond 1977a, 1977b, 1991; Lowe 1977; Lowe and Mason 1965; Ringle and Andrews V 1988; Sharer 1978b.

7. Andrews V 1977a, 1977b; Borhegyi 1965a; Lowe and Mason 1965; Miles 1965a; Norman 1973–76.

8. Norman 1973–76; Quirarte 1976, 1977.

9. M. Coe 1957, 1976; J. Graham et al. 1978; Marcus 1976b; Miles 1965a; L. Parsons 1973; Sharer 1978b; Sharer and Sedat 1973, 1987.

10. M. Coe 1957, 1976; Justeson 1986; Justeson and Kaufman 1993; Marcus 1976b, 1992.

11. In later Classic-period inscriptions, the numbers and the units of the Long Count may both be represented by glyphs that are portraits of deities. They are personified, not inanimate parts of a mechanical device. In a few Initial Series dates, the numbers appear as full figures of deities, each bearing the sign for the corresponding unit of the Long Count on his back (Fig. 7-17). See Fig. 6-5 for a later, more elaborated Long Count date.

12. Correlating Long Count dates with the Gregorian calendar assumes that all the dates represent a single system counted from the same zero point. Of that, we cannot be absolutely certain, but it is very likely. In addition to the extraordinary degree of correspondence in the structure of the system itself, the Ritual Almanac and Solar Year positions that accompany so many Long Count dates provide a partial check, since they are counted independently from the zero point. There is a bit more uncertainty with respect to early Long Count dates, since early versions of the day and month signs can be hard to match with later lowland variants, but the numbers are perfectly straightforward. The number associated with the Ritual Almanac position alone provides strong evidence in that there are 13 possibilities, so that the chance of two Long Count dates calculated from different bases corresponding by chance to Ritual Almanac positions with the same day-number is only 7.7 percent (1 in 13).

The actual correlation with the Gregorian calendar is a separate problem. Had the Long Count remained in general use until the Spanish invasion, correlation would be a simple matter. Unfortunately it was not used for formal inscriptions after the tenth century, although time reckoning still made use of some of the *units* of the Long Count. The correlation problem is extremely complex (D. Kelley 1976; Marcus 1992; J. E. S. Thompson 1960). Many lines of evidence are relevant; all are indirect and some are mutually inconsistent. No correlation can accommodate every scrap of data. One key piece of evidence is a statement in a Yucatec document from the seventeenth century that a tun ended on 13 Ahau 8 Xul. Now, 13 Ahau 8 Xul recurs every 52 years, but corresponds to the end of a tun only every 936 years, so the possible Long Count positions are quite limited. The most satisfactory solution places the Spanish invasion of Yucatan at about 11.16.0.0.0 in the Long Count. The 11.16 correlation, sometimes called the Goodman-Martínez-Thompson correlation after its principal exponents, fits best with archaeological data from the southern lowlands, where most Long Count dates have been found. This solution is consistent both with Bishop Landa's statement that 16 July 1553 corresponded to 12 Kan 2 Pop in the Yucatec calendar and with the katun histories that place the events of the Spanish invasion and its aftermath in katuns 13 Ahau and 11 Ahau. It is also reasonably consistent with astronomical events dated in the Long Count, although the majority of these were calculations of canonical positions rather than records of observed events. The 11.16 correlation does create some apparent anomalies, particularly in the chronology of events in northern Yucatan. For this reason, until very recently some specialists preferred an alternative correlation (the Spinden, or 12.9, correlation) which places all Long Count dates 256 years earlier in the Gregorian calendar.

The 11.16 correlation, followed here, places the beginning of the current Great Cycle in the year 3114 B.C. This date is more than three thousand years earlier than the earliest contemporary Long Count record. It must have been determined in later centuries by calculation backward into the time range of creations and mythical events. Texts at Palenque seem to place the births of gods near the beginning of the current Great Cycle (D. Kelley 1965; Lounsbury 1976).

13. A few Long Count dates of the Classic period have been found beyond the Maya frontiers as well, although they may have been produced under Maya influence. The vast majority of Long Count dates are from Classic Maya centers. In the strictest sense, the Long Count may not be peculiarly Maya, but it was certainly of the greatest importance to the Maya of the Classic period.

14. J. Graham et al. 1978; Miles 1965a; L. Parsons 1986.

15. Borhegyi 1965a, 1965b; Kaplan 1995; Michels 1979a, 1979b; Michels and Sanders 1973; Sanders and Michels 1969, 1977; Shook and Kidder 1952.

16. W. Coe 1965; W. Coe and McGinn 1963; Dahlin 1984; Hansen 1991b; Matheny 1980; Valdés 1989; Valdés and Fahsen 1995.

17. Hansen 1991b.

18. Copeland 1989; Dahlin 1984; Demarest et al. 1984; Hansen 1990, 1991a; Howell 1989; Matheny 1980, 1986.

19. These astronomically oriented architectural complexes are called E-groups, after the first such complex to be recognized, in Group E at Uaxactún. Tikal, Yaxhá, Nakum, Caracol, and perhaps a few other cities in the core of the central lowlands also built E-groups during the Classic period.

20. Folan et al. 1995.

21. Pendergast 1981.

22. Freidel 1979; Garber 1989; Robertson and Freidel 1986; Scarborough 1991.

23. A. F. Chase and D. Z. Chase 1981; D. Z. Chase and A. F. Chase 1988.

24. Hammond 1991; Hammond et al. 1995.

25. Pendergast 1969, 1979–90.

26. Mitchum 1991; Moholy-Nagy 1991; Shafer 1991.

27. W. Coe 1990; Culbert 1977; C. Jones 1991; C. Jones et al. 1981; Laporte 1993; Laporte and Fialko 1995.

28. These more elaborate complexes of political buildings to which triadic groups gave rise are called "acropolis" complexes by Valdés and Fahsen (see A. L. Smith 1950; Valdés 1989; Valdés and Fahsen 1995).

29. A. L. Smith 1972; Tourtellot 1988; Willey 1973a; Willey and Smith 1969; Willey et al. 1975.

30. Hammond 1977b; Pring 1977b; Willey et al. 1967.

31. This style, called Floral Park, was formerly thought to reflect an areawide process and was used as the defining feature of a separate "Protoclassic" period. Since the distribution of Floral Park pottery is in fact quite restricted, there is no justification for defining a Protoclassic period.

32. Rands and Smith 1965; Sharer 1978b; Sharer and Gifford 1970.

33. R. E. W. Adams 1971; Gifford 1976; Merwin and Vaillant 1932; Willey et al. 1965.

34. W. Coe 1965; Lowe 1977; Rands 1977; R. E. Smith 1955.

35. R. E. W. Adams 1977b; Ball 1977a, 1977b; Thomas 1981; Webster 1974, 1976.

36. Matheny 1986; Matheny et al. 1980–83.

37. Andrews IV 1965.

38. Andrews IV and Andrews V 1980; Andrews V 1981; Ringle and Andrews V 1988, 1990.

39. Joesink-Mandeville and Meluzin 1976; E. H. Thompson 1897.

40. Hammond 1977b; Pohl 1990; Puleston 1977; Scarborough 1986; Scarborough et al. 1995.

41. Freidel 1979; Rathje 1971, 1977; Sanders 1977; Sharer 1992; Willey 1977b.

Chapter 6. The Crystallization of Maya Civilization

1. Willey and Mathews 1985.

2. The nature and intensity of Teotihuacán's connections with local polities varied widely from region to region, so the process of Teotihuacán interaction is not used to mark a distinct Middle Classic chronological period.

3. W. Coe 1965, 1990; Culbert 1977, 1993; C. Jones 1991; C. Jones et al. 1981; Laporte 1993; Laporte and Fialko 1995; A. L. Smith 1950, 1973; R. E. Smith 1955; Valdés and Fahsen 1995; Willey 1977b.

4. C. Jones and Satterthwaite 1982; Marcus 1992.

5. Schele and Freidel (1990; also Valdés and Fahsen 1995) conclude that Smoking Frog installed himself as the ruler of Uaxactún in the aftermath of a Tikal military victory on 8.17.1.4.12 (16 January 378), a date recorded, at the time and restrospectively, in the texts of both cities. Since Curl Snout, who came to the throne at Tikal shortly thereafter, says that he did so "in the land of Smoking Frog" (whom he mentions on most of his monuments), the relationship may well have been more amicable. The conquest interpretation is consistent with all of the hieroglyphic evidence, with the subsequent developmental trajectories of the two cities, and with an earthwork erected at Tikal that might conceivably be a defensive construction oriented toward Uaxactún; but there is nothing in the material record at Uaxactún that suggests an armed takeover.

6. C. Jones 1991.

7. Stela 31 was relocated from its original position and enshrined in one of the rooms of Temple 33 in the course of a Late Classic remodeling program (C. Jones 1991; C. Jones and Satterthwaite 1982). See Chapter 7.

8. W. Coe 1967; Coggins 1979, 1993; Marcus 1976a; Shook and Kidder 1961.

9. The appearance at Tikal of projectile points in substantial quantities may reflect a sudden popularity of atlatls (Moholy-Nagy 1991).

10. In Structure B-XIII (A. L. Smith 1950).

11. Stormy Sky's later monument, Stela 31, seems to name Curl Snout's father with glyphs for an atlatl and shield, raising the possibility that Curl Snout was in fact the son of a foreigner.

12. These figures, like most goggle-eyed images in Mesoamerica, have usually been identified as Teotihuacán "Tlalocs" on the basis of their resemblance to later Aztec depictions of the rain god, called Tlaloc in Nahuatl. Pasztory's (1974, 1993) analysis of Teotihuacán iconography, however, demonstrates that two distinct rain deities and at least one deity associated with warfare are represented with goggle eyes. The images on Stela 31, along with several related representations at Tikal and elsewhere in the Maya world (J. G. Fox 1993), refer to the war deity, not to a rain god (although a few examples—Stela 11 at Yaxhá, for example—may represent a fusion of the war deity and one of the rain gods). The meanings associated with these images are unlikely to bear very close relationships with Aztec beliefs that crystallized a thousand years later, so the practice of using Aztec names as labels for them is misleading.

13. Borhegyi 1965a; Coggins 1993; Hellmuth 1978; Kidder et al. 1946; Michels 1979a, 1979b; Michels and Sanders 1973; Millon 1973, 1981; Sanders 1978; Sanders and Michels 1969, 1977.

14. Jones 1991; Laporte 1993; Laporte and Fialko 1995; Marcus 1976a; Valdés and Fahsen 1995; Willey 1977b.

15. The hiatus is much more localized and variable than once was thought; it was not a lowland-wide phenomenon (Willey 1974).

16. The evidence consists of depictions of bound and sacrificed individuals and textual references that seem to imply relationships of dominance and subordination and/or conflict between cities. Readings of the relevant hieroglyphic texts are tentative, however, and do not establish the nature of the alleged relationships, let alone the veracity of allegations of subordination or conquest.

17. J. G. Fox 1993; A. Miller 1978; Pendergast 1971; Pring 1977a.

18. E. W. Adams 1990. One of the most fascinating finds at Río Azul is a small jar with a hieroglyphic text that refers to cacao; an actual residue of the cacao was detected in the jar.

19. Folan et al. 1995; Martin and Grube 1995.

20. Hammond 1991; Leventhal 1990; Pendergast 1969, 1979–90, 1981; Willey et al. 1965.

21. Beetz and Satterthwaite 1981; A. Chase and D. Chase 1987; D. Chase and A. Chase 1994; Martin and Grube 1995.

22. These glyphs include an axe and the combined shell and star signs. The shell–star combination clearly refers to conflict between cities, but the nature and scale of the conflict and the implications with respect to the political outcome are unknown. The axe sign is a plausible reference to conflict and/or to the capture and killing of an individual, but its precise connotations remain to be dem-

onstrated. In addition to the suspicions that attach to all such texts which are produced by rulers to serve their own ends, the objectivity of this particular text is doubly dubious because its dates suggest that it was carved several decades after the event. Moreover, the text is so badly eroded that one cannot even be certain that it names Caracol as the "conquering" city. Thus, the archaeological record of subsequent expansion and florescence at Caracol together with the sharply reduced dedication of architectural and sculptural monuments at Tikal is certainly consistent with the hypothesis that Tikal suffered a military defeat at the hands of Caracol, but it does not provide specific confirmation.

23. Pendergast 1981.

24. Carefully flaked stone objects in unusual shapes—geometric, animal, and human figures—that were used for offerings and perhaps in ritual activity rather than having utilitarian functions.

25. Pendergast 1969, 1979–90.

26. Valdez 1987.

27. Hammond and Tourtellot 1993; Schultz et al. 1994; Tourtellot et al. 1993, 1994.

28. Ashmore 1979, 1988, 1990; Baudez 1983; W. Fash 1991; W. Fash and Sharer 1991; Longyear 1952; Sanders 1986–90; Schortman and Urban 1983; Sharer 1978a, 1988; Viel 1993; Willey et al. 1994.

29. R. E. W. Adams 1971; J. Graham 1972; Marcus 1976a; Mathews and Willey 1991; Rands 1977; Sabloff 1975; A. L. Smith 1972; Tourtellot 1988; Willey 1973a, 1977a; Willey and Smith 1969; Willey et al. 1975.

30. Rands 1977.

31. R. E. W. Adams 1977b; Ball 1974b, 1977a; Webster 1974.

32. Andrews IV 1965; Andrews IV and Andrews V 1980; Ball 1977b; Marcus 1976a; Rivera Dorado 1989; Rivera Dorado et al. 1987–89.

33. Stela 1 at Tulum, with a date of 9.6.10.0.0 (A.D. 564), may have been carved elsewhere and moved to Tulum during a much later period, for there is no indication of a contemporary Early Classic occupation there.

34. Andrews V 1977a, 1977b; Borhegyi 1965a, 1965b; Kidder et al. 1946; Michels 1979a, 1979b; Millon 1973, 1981; Rands and Smith 1965; Sanders 1978; Sanders and Michels 1969, 1977; Sharer 1978b; Sheets 1979, 1983; Shook and Kidder 1952.

35. Kievit 1994; Sheets 1983, 1992.

36. Becquelin et al. 1979–91; Lowe 1977; Lowe and Mason 1965; Marcus 1976a; Willey et al. 1967.

Chapter 7. Late Classic Maya Civilization

1. Aveni 1980; Lounsbury 1978; J. E. S. Thompson 1960.

2. Culbert and Rice 1990.

3. Ashmore 1981; Borhegyi 1965b; Bullard 1960; de Montmollin 1989a, 1989b; Fedick 1995; Ford 1986, 1990, 1991; Ford and Fedick 1992; Haviland 1967, 1985; Tourtellot 1988, 1993; Voorhies 1972; Wilk and Ashmore 1988; Willey and Bullard 1965; Willey et al. 1965.

4. R. E. W. Adams 1974; Culbert et al. 1990; Haviland 1969, 1970, 1972a, 1972b; Puleston 1974; J. E. S. Thompson 1971.

5. Webster and Freter 1990a; Webster et al. 1992.

6. Ball and Eaton 1972; Bronson 1966; U. Cowgill 1962; Fedick 1994; Flannery 1982; Folan et al. 1979; Harrison 1977; Harrison and Turner 1978; Lentz 1991; McKillop 1994; Netting 1977; Puleston 1971, 1977; Puleston and Puleston 1971; Reina and Hill 1980; D. Rice 1993; Sanders 1973; Siemens and Puleston 1972; Stark et al. 1976; J. E. S. Thompson 1974; Turner 1974, 1979; Turner and Johnson 1979; Wilken 1971; Zier 1980.

7. Chisholm 1979. How to allow for the length of fallow cycles and for the percentage of farmland given over to other crops is equally difficult. Even with maximum estimates for every factor, potential maize production would still be too low to support the populations of the largest cities.

8. The orthodox view is that most of the known wetland-farming systems were in use during the Late Classic period and represent a response to population growth. In fact, direct indications of the ages of these systems are quite limited, and there is growing evidence that reliance on wetland cultivation not only began much earlier but peaked earlier as well (R. E. W. Adams 1990; Dunning and Beach 1994; Flannery 1982; Harrison 1990; Harrison and Turner 1978; Pohl 1990; D. Rice 1993; Siemens and Puleston 1972; Turner and Harrison 1983).

Investigators have also challenged early reports, based on remote sensing data, of very extensive canal systems (R. E. W. Adams et al. 1981, 1990; Pope and Dahlin 1989).

9. Scarborough and Gallopin 1991; Scarborough, et al. 1994, 1995.

10. Abrams 1994; R. E. W. Adams 1970; A. Andrews 1980; Aoyama 1994, 1995; Asaro et al. 1978; Becker 1973a, 1973b; Braswell et al. 1994; Hammond 1972; Hurtado de Mendoza and Jester 1978; McAnany 1993; McAnany and Isaac 1989; Michels 1975; Moholy-Nagy et al. 1984; Nakamura et al. 1991; Nelson 1985; Nelson et al. 1977; Reents-Budet 1994; P. Rice 1984; P. Rice et al. 1985; Sheets 1975; Sidrys 1976; Sidrys et al. 1975; Stross et al. 1983, Tourtellot and Sabloff 1972; Voorhies 1973.

11. Aldenderfer 1990, 1991a, 1991b; Fedick 1991.

12. R. E. W. Adams 1972; Ball and Taschek 1991; Haviland 1967, 1968, 1971, 1972c, 1977; Marcus 1976a; McAnany 1995; Molloy and Rathje 1974; Sharer 1993; Willey and Shimkin 1973.

13. Vogt 1968.

14. Ball 1993; Fedick 1991; Fry 1980; Fry and Cox 1974; Potter 1993; Potter and King 1995; Rands and Bishop 1980.

15. Ashmore 1991; Lounsbury 1976; Schele 1977.

16. R. E. W. Adams 1971, 1977a; Molloy and Rathje 1974; Schele and Mathews 1991; Yoffee 1991.

17. Culbert 1973a, 1973b, 1988.

18. This Tepeu style was first defined at Uaxactún (R. E. Smith 1955).

19. R. E. W. Adams et al. 1961; Carr and Hazard 1961; W. Coe 1967, 1990; W. Coe and Haviland 1982; C. Jones and Satterthwaite 1982; C. Jones et al. 1981; Maler 1911; Shook et al. 1958; Tozzer 1911.

20. An alternative reading of the name glyph is Hasaw, whose full name is rendered Hasaw Ka'an K'awil (Martin and Grube 1995:45).

21. Martin and Grube 1995.

22. See discussion in Chapter 6.

23. Culbert 1991; Marcus 1976a.

24. Kidder 1947; Ricketson and Ricketson 1937; A. L. Smith 1950, 1973; R. E. Smith 1955; Valdés and Fahsen 1995.

25. D. Stuart 1985.

26. Folan et al. 1995; Marcus 1987; Martin and Grube 1995.

27. Ball and Taschek 1991; Ford 1990, 1991; Ford and Fedick 1992; Healy 1992; Leventhal et al. 1993–96; Martin and Grube 1995.

28. Chase and D. Chase 1987; D. Chase and A. Chase 1994.

29. Pendergast 1981.

30. Pendergast 1969, 1979–90.

31. Aldenderfer 1991a, 1991b; Roemer 1991; Valdez 1987.

32. E. Graham 1994; E. Graham and Pendergast 1989; Guderjan 1993, 1995; Guderjan and Garber 1995; Hammond 1985; Hammond and Tourtellot 1993; McKillop 1995; McKillop and Healy 1989; Schultz et al. 1994; Tourtellot et al. 1993, 1994.

33. Baudez 1983, 1994; W. Fash 1991; Gordon 1896; Longyear 1952; Morley 1920; Sanders 1986–90; Viel 1993; Willey and Leventhal 1979; Willey et al. 1978, 1994.

34. Or possibly Dos Pilas.

35. Fash and Stuart (W. Fash 1991; W. Fash and Sharer 1991; W. Fash and Stuart 1991; D. Stuart 1992) summarize the orthodox view of the history of Copán. Many of the details of the city's dynastic history are susceptible of other interpretations; thus Riese (1992), using the same data, proposes a different reconstruction. For the names of Copán's rulers, I follow Fash.

36. Andrews V and Fash 1992.

37. Cheek and Spink 1986. Such "men's houses"—where adolescents were given instruction in important ritual matters, trained as warriors and perhaps in the ball game, and generally socialized—are described in historical sources of the invasion period. They are comparable in many ways to men's houses in lowland South America.

38. Baudez 1994.

39. This discarded monument, whose surviving glyphs are carved in the style of the Early Classic period, was erected on the first version of the platform, above the burial of a jaguar whose teeth and bones were covered with red pigment (Cheek and Milla Villeda 1983).

40. Early colonial-period Maya documents refer to kings as "nurturers, sucklers" of their people. Maya concepts of gender are complex and not well understood.

41. Baudez 1994; Longyear 1952; Stromsvik 1942.

42. Baudez (1994:28–46), on the basis of the associated death imagery, argues that Stela D was a posthumous monument and suggests that Stela C, which he interprets as very late stylistically, was erected by Yax Pac in honor of his ancestor.

43. One text, associated with the final version of the ball court, contains a Long Count date corresponding to A.D. 738, about a year and a half after the dedication of 18 Rabbit's last stela (W. Fash 1991:125–26). This may be the last contemporary reference to events in 18 Rabbit's lifetime.

44. W. Fash 1991; W. Fash and Stuart 1991; D. Stuart 1992.

45. B. Fash 1992; B. Fash et al. 1992.

46. W. Fash et al. 1992.

47. Some texts do identify Cauac Sky as the fourteenth in a succession. This attribution could refer either to a sequence of Quiriguá rulers (not attested in the inscriptions) or to the position in the dynastic sequence at Copán which Cauac Sky might have claimed as successor to 18 Rabbit, who took the title of thirteenth in a succession (Sharer 1991; Riese 1986).

48. Aoyama 1995; B. Fash 1992; B. Fash et al. 1992. The mat is primarily a royal symbol. The analogy between Structure 22A and the Yucatec Popol Na is plausible, but not compelling, and the building might well have had a different function. In any case, the connection of the glyphs on the façade with powerful families each controlling a sector of the Copán Valley is very tenuous.

49. David Stuart (1992) interprets this text as referring to the name of the monument itself.

50. The text on Stela 63 has been interpreted as including the name of Yax Kuk Mo as well as that of a son who came to the throne early in the fifth century (W. Fash 191:81–84; D. Stuart 1992:172–74).

51. W. Fash and Stuart 1991; Schele 1986, 1992a.

52. It is not certain that there were fifteen or sixteen jaguars—one for each of the rulers in the dynasty—although the symbolism presumably does involve a connection between jaguars and kingship.

53. Sanders 1986–90; Sheehy 1991; Webster 1989.

54. Part of the complex has been washed away by the river.

55. Evidence for the interpretation that Patio D was occupied by foreigners from the Ulúa sphere (Gerstle 1987) is not strong; the proportion of imported material is not significantly higher here than in other patios (Hendon 1987; Sanders 1986–90).

56. Ashmore 1979, 1984, 1988, 1990; Morley 1935; Schortman and Urban 1983; Sharer 1978a, 1988, 1991.

57. Hammond 1975; Leventhal 1990.

58. Henderson 1978; Henderson and Beaudry-Corbett 1993; Robinson 1987; Schortman and Nakamura 1991; Sharer 1978b; D. Stone 1941; Strong et al. 1938; Urban and Schortman 1986.

59. Ashmore et al. 1987; Henderson et al. 1979; Nakamura et al. 1991; Schortman et al. 1986; Urban and Schortman 1988.

60. Baudez and Becquelin 1973; Dixon 1992; Joyce 1993a, 1993c; D. Stone 1957.

61. Beaudry-Corbett et al. 1993; Henderson 1984, 1988, 1992a, 1992b; Joyce 1991.

62. R. E. W. Adams 1971, 1977a; Demarest and Valdés 1993, 1994; Demarest et al. 1995; J. Graham 1972, 1973, 1990; Houston 1992, 1993; Inomata and Stiver 1994; Inomata et al. 1993; Mathews and Willey 1991; Sabloff 1975; A. L. Smith 1972, 1982; Tourtellot 1988, 1990; Willey 1972, 1973a, 1978, 1990; Willey and Smith 1969; Willey et al. 1975.

63. Carnegie Institution 1955; W. Coe 1959; Maler 1901–3; Marcus 1976a; M. Miller 1986, 1993; Proskouriakoff 1950, 1960, 1963b, 1964; Rands 1977; Satterthwaite 1944–54; Schele 1991; Tate 1992.

64. Adopting the name of an earlier ruler (whether real or mythical), was presumably part of a strategy for enhancing power or legitimacy by emphasizing (or fictively creating) a connection with an eminent predecessor. Kings of several other cities followed the same practice, notably at Palenque where several lords named Pacal, Chan Bahlum, Chaacal, Kan Xul, and Kuk appear in dynastic texts. Similar or identical names sometimes appear in the dynastic sequences of different cities as well, as in the case of Jaguar Paw (at Tikal and Calakmul) and 18 Rabbit (at Copán and Naranjo). This pattern of name du-

plication creates considerable potential for confusion when attempting to unravel the dynastic history and political relationships of Classic-period cities.

65. The depiction of his wife with the bundle motif, which is widely associated in Mesoamerica with legitimate authority (especially its supernatural underpinnings), may indicate that Bird Jaguar's marriage brought legitimacy as well as powerful allies.

66. Satterthwaite 1944–54.

67. G. Andrews 1967; Becquelin et al. 1979–91; Carlson 1976; Lounsbury 1974, 1976; Marcus 1976a; Mathews and Schele 1974; Mejía Pérez Campo and Mirambell Silva 1992; Rands 1969, 1973, 1974, 1977; Romano Pacheco 1989; Ruz Lhuiller 1952–58, 1973; Schele 1976, 1977, 1979, 1991, 1992b.

68. According to the texts, Pacal, born in A.D. 603, would have been more than eighty years old at the time of his death. The original analysis of the bones in the sarcophagus, however, indicated that the occupant died in early middle age, probably not much beyond age forty. The inconsistency may be only apparent, stemming from misinterpretation of the age indicators (which are not precise) on the bones. It might also be real, if Pacal adopted fictive birth and accession dates (the texts have him take power in A.D. 615, at age twelve) in order to smooth over some irregularity in his succession. There are other indications in the texts that Pacal's claim to the throne, through his mother, may have been problematic. In any event, a thorough reanalysis of the skeletal remains is needed if we are to resolve the issue.

69. This text may be part of Pacal's strategy of legitimation in the face of a problematic succession from his mother rather than in the male line.

70. This calendrical manipulation is consistent with the possibility that Pacal backdated his birth for political reasons.

71. Becquelin et al. 1979–91; Lowe and Mason 1965; Schele 1991.

72. Andrews IV and Andrews V 1980; Andrews V 1981; Coggins 1984; Kurjack 1974; Robles Castellanos and Andrews 1986; G. Stuart et al. 1979; Taschek 1994.

73. Andrews IV 1965; Ball 1977b; Corson 1976; Matheny et al. 1980–83; Pollock 1980; Rivera Dorado 1989; Rivera Dorado et al. 1987–89; Robles Castellanos and Andrews 1986.

74. Construction of hydraulic facilities at Edzná began in the Late Preclassic period.

75. R. E. W. Adams 1977b; Andrews IV 1965; Ball 1977a; Potter 1977; Thomas 1981.

76. This architectural style may reflect beliefs similar to those of some modern Maya peoples, who conceptualize houses, like virtually every other feature of their environment, as animate. In Zinacantán, in the highlands of Chiapas, a house dedication ritual brings the building to life (J. G. Fox 1996; Vogt 1969c).

77. Folan et al. 1983; Marcus 1976a; J. E. S. Thompson et al. 1932.

78. Arnauld 1986, 1990; Borhegyi 1965a, 1965b; Dillon 1977; Ichon et al. 1979; Rands and Smith 1965; Sharer 1978b.

Chapter 8. Transformations

1. This transformation was formerly referred to as the Classic Maya "collapse." It is now clear that processes varied regionally in character, intensity, and timing and did not amount to a total societal collapse in most of the Maya world.

2. For this reason, and because the processes of transformation are, at least in part, outcomes of the growth processes that produced the Classic florescence, these developments are best treated as part of the Classic period. The differences between Classic and Postclassic Maya societies are sharp, but not total. Viewed in large part as the consequence of internal developmental processes, they no longer seem to define two separate Maya cultural traditions, and the relatively well documented institutions of Maya societies during the invasion period now become potential models for interpreting earlier Maya states (Henderson and Sabloff 1993; Marcus 1993, 1995; Robles Castellanos and Andrews 1986; Sharer 1991).

3. This is not the orthodox view, which is based heavily on overly simplified interpretations of colonial-period historical documents. Archaeological evidence does not resolve the issue beyond dispute, but most of it is consistent with the hypothesis that Chichén Itzá achieved its greatest power and prosperity in the Terminal Classic

period. Chichén continued to be occupied into the Early Postclassic period, but the monumental public buildings would all have been in use at essentially the same time. Jades thrown into the main cenote as offerings date mainly to the Classic period, but the ceramics are mainly Postclassic, and there is no doubt that Chichén's cenote continued to be the focus of pilgrimage (Coggins 1992; Coggins and Shane 1984; Lothrop 1952; Proskouriakoff 1974; Sheets 1991). In this model, there would be no chronological distinction between the so-called Puuc and Toltec buildings, and their style differences would presumably reflect differences in function or in the cultural affiliations of those who commissioned and built them.

4. Edmonson 1971, 1982, 1986; Recinos and Goetz 1953; Roys 1967; Tozzer 1941. Many of these histories are seemingly quite precise in their references to particular places, individuals, events, and dates. It is tempting to make inappropriate use of them to flesh out the archaeological record with circumstantial detail, but this would be a false precision based on a misunderstanding of the nature of Maya and Mesoamerican views of history.

5. Scholars have labored to identify the Kukulcán who figures so prominently in native histories with one or more particular individuals. In fact, the name Kukulcán is used in the documents symbolically or metaphorically to refer to groups of people, to deities or mythic culture heroes, even to abstract qualities—but not to historical individuals. Kukulcán is the Yucatec equivalent of Quetzalcoatl ("quetzal bird–snake"), the Nahuatl name for the "feathered serpent," the great central Mexican deity and culture hero. The Aztec Quetzalcoatl, patron of priests and priestly knowledge, inventor of agriculture, writing, and the calendar, was the conquest-period descendant of an ancient Mesoamerican god. A feathered-serpent deity was certainly known to the lords of Teotihuacán, and perhaps to the Olmecs. Quetzalcoatl was the protagonist of Aztec accounts of Toltec history which describe the end of the great Toltec empire in terms of an epic metaphorical conflict between priestly elements associated with the devout Quetzalcoatl and the warlike forces of Tezcatlipoca, devotees of human sacrifice. In the denouement, Quetzalcoatl and a small band of loyal retainers left Tula, the Toltec capital, to undertake an eastward journey attended by mythical events.

Only the most thoroughly literal interpretation of the documents would envision a deposed king of Tula arriving in Yucatan, but such a view was in vogue until quite recently (Davies 1977; Jiménez Moreno 1941, 1966). In fact, Aztec history is a blend of descriptions of events and interpretations of them, with a liberal dose of myth, all cast in strongly didactic and symbolic terms (Carrasco 1982; Gillespie 1989). The Aztecs rewrote central Mexican history as a great allegory to illustrate and reinforce their own understanding of the underlying meaning of the past. Aztec accounts of the deeds of Quetzalcoatl must not be understood as straightforward factual reports of events. Kukulcán-Quetzalcoatl in Maya histories is more a general designation or title than it is a personal name, and it refers to more than one Mexican group and their leaders. Tula (or Tollan) designated the Toltec capital in central Mexico, but (like the label "Toltec") it also came to have a much broader significance and could refer to other cities that might be considered metaphorical equivalents of Tollan, as centers of cultural sophistication or fonts of political legitimacy. Chichén itself may have been just such a metaphorical Tollan.

6. Tozzer 1941:20–23.

7. Roys 1967:164, 178. Munro Edmonson (1986) argues that these disparaging Xiu comments about the Itzá were politically motivated and not an accurate representation of their identity.

8. Ball 1974a; Ball and Taschek 1989; Davies 1977; Miller 1977; Proskouriakoff 1965:494–95; J. E. S. Thompson 1970:3–47; Tozzer 1957:110–11.

9. The Long Count went out of general use after the Classic period. Late Maya histories date events according to the Short Count, a repeating sequence of thirteen katuns forming a cycle of about 256 years. The Maya concept of time, a blend of history and prophecy, made it appropriate to mention an event in connection with any katun of the correct name, not just at a single point in an elapsed time sequence.

10. An older orthodoxy envisions Toltec overlords and their Itzá allies arriving in northern Yucatan at about A.D. 1000—A.D. 987 in one influential interpretation which

makes very literal use of calendar dates in native histories—led by Kukulcán. In this reconstruction, the Toltec-Itzá allies ruled from their capital at the newly transformed Chichén Itzá until after 1200.

11. Dunning 1992; Dunning and Kowalski 1994; Kowalski 1986a, 1986b, 1987, 1990.

12. Carmean 1991; Dunning 1989, 1992; Sabloff and Tourtellot 1991; Smyth et al. 1995; Tourtellot et al. 1989.

13. Sotuta pottery, associated in the orthodox view with the Postclassic "Toltec" occupation of Chichén Itzá.

14. Andrews IV and Andrews V 1980; Andrews V 1981; Kurjack 1974; Robles Castellanos and Andrews 1986; G. Stuart et al. 1979; Taschek 1994.

15. The remains of Tiho are now covered by the city of Mérida, but early accounts indicate a large city with massive public architecture (Andrews V 1981).

16. A. Andrews 1990a; Bolles 1977; Coggins 1992; Coggins and Shane 1984; C. Lincoln 1986; Morris et al. 1931; Proskouriakoff 1974; Ringle 1990; Ruppert 1935, 1943; Sievert 1990; E. Thompson 1938; Tozzer 1957; Wagner 1995; Wren and Schmidt 1991.

17. More orthodox interpretations envision two styles associated with successive periods at Chichén: (1) an earlier, Late to Terminal Classic (Florescent) occupation featuring Cehpech pottery and Puuc-style architecture; and (2) a later, Early Postclassic (Modified Florescent) Toltec-Itzá period in which new Sotuta pottery styles came into vogue and a cluster of new buildings with Mexican features defined a grand new civic center to the north of the older city core. More recent thinking has tended to favor the notion of at least some chronological overlap between these styles.

18. Coggins and Shane 1984:162–63; Morris et al. 1931:311–13; Tozzer 1957:151; Wren 1984:17–19; Wren et al. 1989.

19. References to *mul tepal*, or "joint rule," in the ethnohistorical sources may refer both to this broad sharing of power within polities and to confederations of at least partly autonomous polities (Marcus 1993; Roys 1957; Tozzer 1941).

20. A. Andrews 1990a. Orthodox interpretations of Maya historical tradition as recorded in the colonial period attribute the end of the Chichén state to a revolt of subject towns, and place its downfall in the thirteenth century. There is no clear sign of this process in the available archaeological evidence.

21. Tozzer 1941:179.

22. Tozzer 1941:158.

23. Tozzer 1941:179–82.

24. Coggins 1992; Coggins and Shane 1984; Lothrop 1952; Proskouriakoff 1974; Sheets 1991.

25. Tozzer 1941:181.

26. Tozzer 1941:109, 183.

27. Hooton 1940:273.

28. The resemblances between these two building complexes are real, but the degree of similarity has been exaggerated. Reconstructed buildings at Tula which are often cited as counterparts of structures at Chichén Itzá were reconstructed on the basis of an assumed relationship with Chichén (Diehl 1981; Kubler 1961; Molina-Montes 1982).

29. Aveni et al. 1975.

30. Kepecs et al. 1994; Robles Castellanos and Andrews 1986.

31. Robles Castellanos and Andrews 1986. Teotihuacán, the great city in highland central Mexico, also grew in this way; as its population increased, that of much of the rest of the Valley of Mexico declined.

32. A. Andrews 1990a, 1990b, 1993; A. Andrews et al. 1988, 1989; Henderson 1977; Wonderley 1981, 1985, 1986b.

33. In general, the passage of so many centuries and the metaphorical quality of these documents makes them poor guides to historical specifics, but archaeological evidence certainly confirms Chichén's commercial ties with the south. Even specific references to another port facility near Ascención Bay where the lords of Chichén Itzá launched trading ventures to Honduras, are plausible, although they might equally refer to Mayapán or later cities (Henderson 1977).

34. A. Andrews and Robles Castellanos 1985, 1986; Robles Castellanos and Andrews 1986.

35. Robles Castellanos and Andrews 1986; Webster 1993.

36. Culbert 1973a; D. Stuart 1993.

37. Coe 1967, 1990; Culbert 1973b; Jones 1991; Jones et al. 1981; Shook et al. 1958.

38. Trik and Kampen 1983. Haviland and Haviland (1995) interpret many of the graffiti as reflections of altered states of consciousness achieved during ritual activity.

39. Marcus 1976a; Proskouriakoff 1950; Rands 1973.

40. Becquelin et al. 1979–91; Schele 1991, 1992b.

41. E. W. Adams 1971, 1973; J. Graham 1972; A. L. Smith 1972; Willey 1972, 1973a; Willey and Smith 1969.

42. Demarest and Valdés 1993, 1994; Demarest et al. 1995; Inomata and Stiver 1994; Inomata et al. 1993.

43. Ball 1974a; J. Graham 1973, 1990; A. Miller 1977; Sabloff 1973, 1975; Sabloff et al. 1982; A. L. Smith 1982; Tourtellot 1988, 1990; Willey et al. 1975, 1978, 1990.

44. These features do not correlate with one another perfectly, and the burial population presumably includes foreigners as well as locals who adopted new trappings to varying degrees (Tourtellot 1990).

45. Ball 1974a; Ball and Taschek 1989; A. Miller 1977; J. E. S. Thompson 1970:3–47.

46. Caso 1967:166–86; Foncerrada de Molina 1993; González Crespo et al. 1995; Vergara Berdejo et al. 1990.

47. Plumbate pottery, manufactured in the Pacific piedmont and coastal region along the southern fringe of the Maya world during the Terminal Classic and Early Postclassic, embodies both a unique technology which produced a vitrified or glazed surface effect and a very distinctive style (Shepard 1948).

48. These murals were found in the Upper Temple of the Jaguars in the ball-court complex (Coggins and Shane 1984; A. Miller 1977).

49. Culbert 1973b; C. Jones 1991; C. Jones et al. 1981.

50. Folan et al. 1995.

51. E. W. Adams 1977b; Andrews IV 1973; Ball 1977a; Thomas 1981.

52. Ball and Taschek 1991; A. Chase and D. Chase 1987; A. Chase et al. 1991; D. Chase and A. Chase 1994; Hammond 1975; Leventhal et al. 1993–96; Willey 1973b.

53. Hester and Shafer 1991; Valdez 1987.

54. Ford 1990, 1991; Ford and Fedick 1992; Pendergast 1969, 1979–90; Willey 1973b; Willey et al. 1965.

55. Pendergast 1985, 1986; Hammond 1985; Tourtellot et al. 1994.

56. Ashmore 1979, 1984, 1988, 1990; Schortman and Urban 1983; Sharer 1978a, 1985, 1988, 1991.

57. Andrews V and Fash 1992; Baudez 1983, 1994; W. Fash 1991; W. Fash and Sharer 1991; W. Fash and Stuart 1991; Sanders 1986–90; Viel 1993; Webster and Freter 1990a; Webster et al. 1992; Willey and Leventhal 1979; Willey et al. 1978, 1994. The argument for a long-term persistence of the basic farming population in the valley after the collapse of the Copán state is based on obsidian hydration dating, a technique whose accuracy is still debated (Braswell 1992; Webster and Freter 1990b; Webster et al. 1993).

58. Lowe and Mason 1965.

59. Borhegyi 1965a; Campbell 1977; Davies 1977; Diehl and Berlo 1989.

60. W. Fox 1978, 1987; Wallace and Carmack 1977.

61. Bruhns 1980; J. Kelley 1988.

62. Cowgill 1979; Hamblin and Pitcher 1980; Henderson and Sabloff 1993; Hosler et al. 1977; Sharer 1977; Willey and Shimkin 1973.

63. Culbert and Rice 1990; Webster et al. 1992.

64. Jacobs and Hallmark 1996; D. Rice 1993.

65. Curtis et al. 1996; Hodell et al. 1995; Sabloff 1995.

66. Dunning and Beach 1994.

67. Graham 1994; E. Graham and Pendergast 1989; Guderjan 1993, 1995; Guderjan and Garber 1995; McKillop 1995; McKillop and Healy 1989; Pendergast 1990.

68. A. Andrews 1993; Andrews IV 1973; Robles Castellanos and Andrews 1986.

69. A. Andrews 1990a; Curtis et al. 1996; Hodell et al. 1995; Sabloff 1995.

Chapter 9. New Orientations

1. The Postclassic period was originally conceptualized as a time of widespread new cultural orientations throughout Mesoamerica, involving some degree of decadence after the aesthetic achievements of the Classic period (Davies 1977). In the traditional view, Classic societies were peace-loving, theocratic, and introverted, preoccupied with farming, arts, crafts, religion, and other domestic concerns. They gave way, sometimes in violent

episodes of destruction and conquest, to new societies that had a thoroughly secular and militaristic cast. The advent of these warlike and expansionist societies brought a general upsurge in international trade, warfare, and conquest. The Classic Maya decline, then, once thought to involve the sudden, spectacular collapse of all the great cities in the face of foreign military intervention, seemed to epitomize the nature of the transition from Classic to Postclassic society. Current interpretations of the Terminal Classic period envision varied processes of transformation, rather than a sudden unitary collapse. Newer views of the Classic Maya acknowledge the Classic-period roots of such Postclassic institutions as sacrifice and warfare. The Classic-to-Postclassic transition no longer seems to be a stark watershed (Marcus 1993; Robles Castellanos and Andrews 1986).

2. Redating Chichén Itzá to the Terminal Classic period reduces the apparent contrast, especially with respect to the prominence of warfare and sacrifice.

3. A. Andrews 1993; D. Chase 1990; Hammond, Housley, and Law 1991.

4. Edmonson 1971, 1982, 1986; Marcus 1993; Recinos and Goetz 1953; Roys 1967; Tozzer 1941.

5. Baudez and Mathews 1979; Carnegie Institution 1955; Coggins and Shane 1984; Demarest et al. 1995; A. Miller 1977; Webster 1993.

6. Orthodox interpretations of Maya dates given in Yucatec histories place the rise of Mayapán in the thirteenth century. Archaeological evidence—Early Postclassic buildings and especially the pottery at Lamanai (Pendergast 1981) and the architectural decoration at Cerro Palenque (Joyce 1986, 1991), bearing strong similarities to Mayapán—suggests that Mayapán styles, and presumably the city itself, became influential rather earlier, perhaps as early as the eleventh century (see also A. Andrews 1990a, 1993).

7. Coggins 1992; Coggins and Shane 1984; Lothrop 1952; Sheets 1991.

8. Edmonson 1986; Pollock et al. 1962; Roys 1967; Tozzer 1941. Details vary considerably in the several documents that recount the fall of Chichén Itzá and in scholars' interpretations of them. Some versions identify Hunac Ceel as the Xiu lord of Uxmal, for example. The common theme in all sources is that Hunac Ceel's plots involving Izamal brought about the fall of Chichén.

9. Edmonson 1986:178.

10. Tozzer 1941:26.

11. A. Andrews 1993; Pollock et al. 1962; Proskouriakoff 1955.

12. Tozzer 1941:25–27.

13. A. Andrews 1993; Andrews IV 1965; Robles Castellanos and Andrews 1986.

14. Tozzer 1941:32, 216.

15. Tozzer 1941:36–37, 39.

16. Henderson 1977, 1984, 1988, 1992b; Wonderley 1985, 1986b.

17. Archaeological data do not yield a precise date for the end of Mayapán's dominance. Orthodox interpretations of the colonial-period histories place the fall of Mayapán in the mid fifteenth century, but an earlier date seems likely.

18. Tozzer 1941:36–37.

19. Tozzer 1941:vii, 44–46.

20. A. Andrews 1981; Roys 1957, 1965, 1972.

21. Tozzer 1941:39.

22. Freidel and Sabloff 1984; Hamblin 1983; Roys et al. 1940; Sabloff and Freidel 1975; Sabloff and Rathje 1975b; Sabloff et al. 1974; Sierra Sosa 1994.

23. A. Andrews 1993.

24. Lothrop 1924; A. Miller 1982, 1985.

25. Karl Taube (1992) connects them with the maize god.

26. Farriss et al. 1975; Fettweis 1988; Gann 1900; A. Miller 1982; Sanders 1960.

27. The archaeological site of Santa Rita, in modern Corozal, probably corresponds to part of the historical Chetumal (D. Chase 1985; D. Chase and A. Chase 1988).

28. Cortés's horse, abandoned at Tayasal, was deified as Tizimin Chac, god of thunder and lightning. In Zinacantán, the Earth Owner (Chac's modern equivalent) rides a deer (Pagden 1971:377, 519; Villagutierre Soto-Mayor 1983; Vogt 1969b, 1970).

29. D. Chase 1985; D. Chase and A. Chase 1988.

30. E. Graham 1994; E. Graham and Pendergast 1989;

Guderjan 1993, 1995; Guderjan and Garber 1995; Hester and Shafer 1991; McKillop 1995; Pendergast 1990; Valdez 1987.

31. Pendergast 1969, 1979–90.

32. Loten 1985; Pendergast 1981, 1985, 1986, 1990.

33. These Mayapán connections were established by at least the mid twelfth century; they are part of the evidence suggesting that Mayapán flourished earlier than the orthodox view allows.

34. A. Andrews 1993; E. Graham et al. 1985, 1989; G. Jones 1989; Lambert 1994; Pendergast 1985, 1986; Pendergast et al. 1993; Simmons 1995.

35. Díaz del Castillo 1912–16:vol. 5; Pagden 1971; Scholes and Roys 1968.

36. A. Andrews 1990b, 1993; Bullard 1970, 1973; Hellmuth 1977; Johnson 1985; D. Rice et al. 1993; P. Rice and D. Rice 1985.

37. G. Jones 1989; D. Rice et al. 1993.

38. G. Jones 1989, 1992a; Pagden 1971; Pendergast and Jones 1992; J. E. S. Thompson 1951.

39. Díaz del Castillo 1912–16:vol. 5; Henderson 1977, 1978, 1984, 1988, 1992a, 1992b; Henderson et al. 1979; Pagden 1971; Simpson 1964; Wonderley 1981, 1985, 1986a, 1986b, 1987.

40. Borhegyi 1965a, 1965b; Campbell 1977; Carmack 1968; Davies 1977; Diehl et al. 1974; J. W. Fox 1980, 1987, 1989; Rands and Smith 1965; Shepard 1948.

41. J. W. Fox 1987; Wallace and Carmack 1977.

42. R. M. Adams 1961; Lowe and Mason 1965; Navarrete 1966.

43. Borhegyi 1965a, 1965b; J. W. Fox 1978; Woodbury and Trik 1953.

44. Campbell 1977; Campbell and Kaufman 1985; Kaufman 1976.

45. Recinos and Goetz 1953:64–65. The rulers' noses were pierced so that jewels could be worn in them as symbols of authority.

46. Edmonson 1971:215–18.

47. Davies 1977; Roys 1967:83, 169; Tozzer 1941:23, 33–34.

48. Carmack 1968; J. W. Fox 1980, 1987, 1989.

49. J. W. Fox 1978; Orellana 1993.

50. Carmack 1973, 1981; Edmonson 1971; J. W. Fox 1978; Orellana 1993; Wallace and Carmack 1977; Weeks 1983.

51. J. W. Fox 1978; Guillemin 1967, 1977.

52. Lehmann 1968; Miles 1957, 1965b; Sharer 1974, 1978b.

53. Fowler 1989.

Chapter 10. Perspectives on the Maya

1. G. Cowgill 1979; Culbert 1973a, 1973b; Hamblin and Pitcher 1980; Henderson and Sabloff 1993; Hosler et al. 1977; Sharer 1977; Willey and Shimkin 1973.

2. Culbert and Rice 1990; Sanders 1977.

3. Carneiro 1967, 1970, 1988; Webster 1977, 1993.

4. Rathje 1971, 1977.

5. Voorhies 1973.

6. Redfield 1950; Redfield and Villa Rojas 1934.

7. Henderson 1977, 1978, 1992a. John Murra (1968, 1971) has described the enclave, or cultural "archipelago," as a fundamental pattern of territorial organization in the Andes (see also Aldenderfer 1993).

8. Berdan 1994; Gibson 1952; Pagden 1971.

Bibliography

Abrams, Elliot M. 1994. *How the Maya Built Their World: Energetics and Ancient Architecture.* Austin: University of Texas Press.

Adams, Richard E. W. 1970. Suggested Classic period occupational specialization in the southern Maya lowlands. In William R. Bullard, ed., *Monographs and Papers in Maya Archaeology,* 487–98. Cambridge: Harvard University, Peabody Museum Papers, vol. 61.

———. 1971. *The Ceramics of Altar de Sacrificios.* Cambridge: Harvard University, Peabody Museum Papers, vol. 63, no. 1.

———. 1972. Reply to Haviland. *American Antiquity* 37: 140.

———. 1973. Maya collapse: transformation and termination in the ceramic sequence at Altar de Sacrificios. In T. Patrick Culbert, ed., *The Classic Maya Collapse,* 133–63. Albuquerque: University of New Mexico Press.

———. 1974. A trial estimation of Classic Maya palace populations at Uaxactún. In Norman Hammond, ed., *Mesoamerican Archaeology: New Approaches,* 285–96. Austin: University of Texas Press.

———. 1977a. Comments on the glyphic texts of the "Altar Vase." In Norman Hammond, ed., *Social Process in Maya Prehistory: Studies in Honour of Sir Eric Thompson,* 409–20. New York: Academic Press.

———. 1977b. Rio Bec archaeology and the rise of Maya civilization. In Richard E. W. Adams, ed., *The Origins of Maya Civilization,* 77–99. Albuquerque: University of New Mexico Press.

———. 1990. Archaeological research at the lowland Maya city of Río Azul. *Latin American Antiquity* 1(1): 23–41.

Adams, Richard E. W., Walter E. Brown, and T. Patrick Culbert. 1981. Radar mapping, archaeology, and ancient Maya land use. *Science* 213:1457–63.

Adams, Richard E. W., et al. 1961. *Tikal Reports,* nos. 5–10. Philadelphia: University of Pennsylvania, University Museum.

———. 1990. Rebuttal to Pope and Dahlin. *Journal of Field Archaeology* 17:241–44.

Adams, Robert M. 1961. Changing patterns of territorial organization in the central highlands of Chiapas, Mexico. *American Antiquity* 26:341–60.

Agrinier, Pierre. 1975. *Mound 1A, Chiapa de Corzo, Chiapas, Mexico.* Provo: New World Archaeological Foundation Papers, no. 37.

Aldenderfer, Mark S. 1990. Defining lithics-using craft specialties in lowland Maya society through microwear analysis: conceptual problems and issues. In B. Gräsland et al., eds., *The Interpretative Possibilities of Microwear Studies*, 53–70. Uppsala: Societas Archaeologica Upsaliensis.

———. 1991a. Functional evidence for lapidary and carpentry craft specialties in the Late Classic of the central Peten lakes region. *Ancient Mesoamerica* 2(2):205–14.

———. 1991b. The structure of Late Classic lithic assemblages in the central Petén lakes region, Guatemala. In Thomas R. Hester and Harry J. Shafer, eds., *Maya Stone Tools: Selected Papers from the Second Maya Lithic Conference*, 119–41. Madison, Wisc.: Prehistory Press.

———, ed. 1993. *Domestic Architecture, Ethnicity, and Complementarity in the South-Central Andes.* Iowa City: University of Iowa Press.

Andrews, Anthony P. 1980. *Maya Salt Production and Trade.* Tucson: University of Arizona Press.

———. 1981. Historical archaeology in Yucatan: a preliminary framework. *Historical Archaeology* 15(1):1–18.

———. 1990a. The fall of Chichen Itza: a preliminary hypothesis. *Latin American Antiquity* 1(3):258–67.

———. 1990b. The role of trading ports in Maya civilization. In Flora S. Clancy and Peter D. Harrison, eds., *Vision and Revision in Maya Studies*, 159–67. Albuquerque: University of New Mexico Press.

———. 1993. Late Postclassic lowland Maya archaeology. *Journal of World Prehistory* 7(1):35–69.

Andrews, Anthony P., and Fernando Robles Castellanos. 1985. Chichen Itza and Coba: an Itza-Maya standoff in Early Postclassic Yucatan. In Arlen F. Chase and Prudence M. Rice, eds., *The Lowland Maya Postclassic*, 62–72. Austin: University of Texas Press.

———. 1986. *Excavaciones arqueológicas en El Meco, Quintana Roo.* Mexico City: Instituto Nacional de Antropología e Historia.

Andrews, Anthony P., et al. 1988. Isla Cerritos: an Itza trading port on the north coast of Yucatan, Mexico. *National Geographic Research* 4:196–207.

———. 1989. The obsidian trade at Isla Cerritos, Yucatan, Mexico. *Journal of Field Archaeology* 16:355–63.

Andrews, George F. 1967. *Comalcalco, Tabasco, Mexico: An Architectonic Survey of a Maya Ceremonial Center.* Eugene: University of Oregon.

Andrews IV, E. Wyllys. 1943. *The Archaeology of Southwestern Campeche.* Washington, D.C.: Carnegie Institution of Washington, Contributions to American Anthropology and History, no. 40.

———. 1965. Archaeology and pre-history in the northern Maya lowlands: an introduction. *Handbook of Middle American Indians* 2:288–330. Austin: University of Texas Press.

———. 1973. The development of Maya civilization after abandonment of the southern cities. In T. Patrick Culbert, ed., *The Classic Maya Collapse*, 243–65. Albuquerque: University of New Mexico Press.

Andrews IV, E. Wyllys, and E. Wyllys Andrews V. 1980. *Excavations at Dzibilchaltun, Yucatan, Mexico.* New Orleans: Tulane University, Middle American Research Institute, Publication 48.

Andrews V, E. Wyllys. 1977a. *The Archaeology of Quelepa, El Salvador.* New Orleans: Tulane University, Middle American Research Institute, Publication 42.

———. 1977b. The southeastern periphery of Mesoamerica: a view from eastern El Salvador. In Norman Hammond, ed., *Social Process in Maya Prehistory: Studies in Honour of Sir Eric Thompson*, 113–34. New York: Academic Press.

———. 1981. Dzibilchaltun. *Handbook of Middle American Indians*, Supplement 1:313–41. Austin: University of Texas Press.

Andrews, V, E. Wyllys, and Barbara W. Fash. 1992. Continuity and change in a royal Maya residential complex at Copan. *Ancient Mesoamerica* 3(1):63–88.

Andrews V, E. Wyllys, and Norman Hammond. 1990. Redefinition of the Swasey phase at Cuello, Belize. *American Antiquity* 55:570–84.

Aoyama, Kazuo. 1994. Socioeconomic implication of chipped stone from the La Entrada region, western Honduras. *Journal of Field Archaeology* 21(2):133–45.

———. 1995. Microwear analysis in the southeast Maya lowlands: two case studies at Copan, Honduras. *Latin American Antiquity* 6(2):129–44.

Armillas, Pedro. 1971. Gardens on swamps. *Science* 174:653–61.

Arnauld, M. Charlotte. 1986. *Archéologie de l'habitat en Alta Verapaz (Guatemala)*. Mexico City: Centre d'Etudes Mexicaines et Centroamericaines, Etudes Americaines, no. 10.

———. 1990. El comercio clásico de obsidiana: rutas entre tierras altas y tierras bajas en el área maya. *Latin American Antiquity* 1(4):347–67.

Asaro, Frank, et al. 1978. High-precision chemical characterization of major obsidian sources in Guatemala. *American Antiquity* 43:436–43.

Ashmore, Wendy. 1979. *Quirigua Reports*, vol. 1. Philadelphia: University of Pennsylvania, University Museum.

———. 1984. Quirigua archaeology and history revisited. *Journal of Field Archaeology* 11:365–80.

———. 1988. Household and community at Classic Quirigua. In Richard R. Wilk and Wendy Ashmore, eds., *Household and Community in the Mesoamerican Past*, 153–69. Albuquerque: University of New Mexico Press.

———. 1990. Ode to a dragline: demographic reconstructions at Classic Quirigua. In T. Patrick Culbert and Don S. Rice, eds., *Precolumbian Population History in the Maya Lowlands*, 63–82. Albuquerque: University of New Mexico Press.

———. 1991. Site-planning principles and concepts of directionality among the ancient Maya. *Latin American Antiquity* 2(3):199–226.

———. ed. 1981. *Lowland Maya Settlement Patterns*. Albuquerque: University of New Mexico Press.

Ashmore, Wendy, et al. 1987. Ancient society in Santa Barbara, Honduras. *National Geographic Research* 3:232–54.

Austin, Donald M., and Gordon Lothson. 1969. Mound B-II-1 excavation. In William T. Sanders and Joseph W. Michels, eds., *The Pennsylvania State University Kaminaljuyu Project—1968 Season*, pt. 1: *The Excavations*, 99–136. State College: Pennsylvania State University, Department of Anthropology, Occasional Papers in Anthropology, no. 2.

Aveleyra Arroyo de Anda, Luis. 1964. The primitive hunters. *Handbook of Middle American Indians* 1:384–412. Austin: University of Texas Press.

Aveni, Anthony F. 1980. *Skywatchers of Ancient Mexico*. Austin: University of Texas Press.

Aveni, Anthony F., S. L. Gibbs, and H. Hartung. 1975. The Caracol tower at Chichen Itza: an ancient astronomical observatory? *Science* 188(4192):977–85.

Awe, Jaime, and Paul F. Healy. 1994. Flakes to blades? Middle Formative development of obsidian artifacts in the upper Belize River valley. *Latin American Antiquity* 5(3):193–205.

Ball, Joseph W. 1974a. A coordinate approach to northern Maya prehistory. *American Antiquity* 39:85–93.

———. 1974b. A Teotihuacán-style cache from the Maya lowlands. *Archaeology* 27(1):2–9.

———. 1977a. *Archaeological Ceramics of Becán, Campeche, Mexico*. New Orleans: Tulane University, Middle American Research Institute, Publication 43.

———. 1977b. The rise of the northern Maya chiefdoms: a socioprocessual analysis. In Richard E. W. Adams, ed., *The Origins of Maya Civilization*, 101–32. Albuquerque: University of New Mexico Press.

———. 1993. Pottery, potters, palaces, and polities: some socioeconomic and political implications of Late Classic Maya ceramic industries. In Jeremy A. Sabloff and John S. Henderson, eds., *Lowland Maya Civilization in the Eighth Century A.D.*, 243–72. Washington, D.C.: Dumbarton Oaks.

Ball, Joseph W., and Jack D. Eaton. 1972. Marine resources and the prehistoric lowland Maya: a comment. *American Anthropologist* 74:772–76.

Ball, Joseph W., and Jennifer T. Taschek. 1989. Teotihuacan's fall and the rise of the Itza: realignments and role changes in the Terminal Classic Maya lowlands. In Richard A. Diehl and J. C. Berlo, eds., *Mesoamerica after the Decline of Teotihuacan, A.D. 700–900*, 187–200. Washington, D.C.: Dumbarton Oaks.

———. 1991. Late Classic lowland Maya political organization and central-place analysis. *Ancient Mesoamerica* 2(2):149–65.

Barrera Rubio, Alfredo. 1985. Littoral-marine economy at Tulum, Quintana Roo, Mexico. In Arlen F. Chase and Prudence M. Rice, eds., *The Lowland Maya Postclassic*, 50–61. Austin: University of Texas Press.

Baudez, Claude F. 1983. *Introducción a la arqueología de Copán, Honduras.* Tegucigalpa: Instituto Hondureño de Antropología e Historia.

———. 1994. *Maya Sculpture of Copan: The Iconography.* Norman: University of Oklahoma Press.

Baudez, Claude F., and Pierre Becquelin. 1973. *Archéologie de Los Naranjos, Honduras.* Mexico City: Mission Archéologique et Ethnologique Française au Méxique.

Baudez, Claude F., and Peter Mathews. 1979. Capture and sacrifice at Palenque. In Merle Greene Robertson and Donnan Call Jeffers, eds., *Tercera Mesa Redonda de Palenque*, 31–40. Monterey, Calif.: Pre-Columbian Art Research Center.

Beaudry-Corbett, Marilyn P., et al. 1993. Lower Ulúa region. In John S. Henderson and Marilyn P. Beaudry-Corbett, eds., *Pottery of Prehistoric Honduras: Regional Classification and Analysis*, 64–135. Los Angeles: UCLA Institute of Archaeology, Monograph no. 35.

Becker, Marshall J. 1973a. Archaeological evidence for occupational specialization among the Classic period Maya at Tikal, Guatemala. *American Antiquity* 38:396–406.

———. 1973b. The evidence for complex exchange systems among the ancient Maya. *Amerian Antiquity* 38:222–23.

Becquelin, Pierre, Claude F. Baudez, and Eric Taladoire. 1979–91. *Toniná: Une cité Maya du Chiapas (Méxique).* 4 vols. Mexico City: Mission Archéologique et Ethnologique Française au Méxique.

Beetz, Carl P., and Linton Satterthwaite. 1981. *The Monuments and Inscriptions of Caracol, Belize.* Philadelphia: University of Pennsylvania, University Museum.

Berdan, Frances F. 1994. Economic alternatives under imperial rule. In Mary G. Hodge and Michael E. Smith, eds., *Economies and Polities in the Aztec Realm*, 291–312. Albany: State University of New York, Institute for Mesoamerican Studies.

Berlin, Heinrich. 1958. El glifo "emblema" en las inscripciones mayas. *Journal de la Société des Américanistes* 47:111–19.

Blake, Michael. 1991. An emerging Early Formative chiefdom at Paso de la Amada, Chiapas, Mexico. In William R. Fowler, ed., *The Formation of Complex Society in Southeastern Mesoamerica*, Boca Raton, Fla.: CRC Press.

Blake, Michael, et al. 1995. Radiocarbon chronology for the Late Archaic and Formative periods on the Pacific coast of southeastern Mesoamerica. *Ancient Mesoamerica* 6(2):161–83.

Bolles, John S. 1977. *Las Monjas: A Major Pre-Mexican Architectural Complex at Chichén Itzá.* Norman: University of Oklahoma Press.

Borhegyi, Stephan F. 1965a. Archaeological synthesis of the Guatemalan highlands. *Handbook of Middle American Indians* 2:3–58. Austin: University of Texas Press.

———. 1965b. Settlement patterns of the Guatemalan highlands. *Handbook of Middle American Indians* 2:59–75. Austin: University of Texas Press.

Braswell, Geoffrey E. 1992. Obsidian-hydration dating, the Coner phase, and revisionist chronology at Copan, Honduras. *Latin American Antiquity* 3(2):130–47.

Braswell, Geoffrey E., E. Wyllys Andrews V, and Michael D. Glascock. 1994. The obsidian artifacts of Quelepa, El Salvador. *Ancient Mesoamerica* 5(2):173–92.

Bray, Warwick. 1976. From predation to production: the nature of agricultural evolution in Mexico and Peru. In G. de G. Sieveking, T. H. Longworth, and K. E. Wilson, eds., *Problems in Economic and Social Archaeology*, 73–95. London: Gerald Duckworth.

Bricker, Victoria R. 1981. *The Indian Christ, the Indian*

King: The Historical Substrate of Maya Myth and Ritual. Austin: University of Texas Press.
———. 1986. *A Grammar of Mayan Hieroglyphs.* New Orleans: Tulane University, Middle American Research Institute, Publication 56.
———. 1992. Noun and verb morphology in the Maya script. *Handbook of Middle American Indians,* Supplement 5:70–81. Austin: University of Texas Press.
Bricker, Victoria R., and Harvey M. Bricker. 1988. The seasonal table in the Dresden Codex and related almanacs. *Journal for the History of Astronomy* 19, suppl. (Archaeoastronomy 12):S1–S62.
———. 1989. Astronomical references in the table on pages 61–9 of the Dresden Codex. In Anthony F. Aveni, ed., *World Archaeoastronomy,* 232–45. Cambridge: Cambridge University Press.
Broda de Casas, Johanna. 1969. *The Mexican Calendar as Compared to Other Mesoamerican Systems.* Vienna: Institut für Völkerkunde, Universität Wien, Acta Ethnologica et Linguistica, no. 15.
Bronson, Bennet. 1966. Roots and the subsistence of the ancient Maya. *Southwestern Journal of Anthropology* 22:251–79.
Brown, Kenneth L. 1980. A brief report on Paleoindian-Archaic occupation in the Quiché Basin, Guatemala. *American Antiquity* 45:313–24.
Bruhns, Karen O. 1980. *Cihuatan: An Early Postclassic Town of El Salvador.* Columbia: University of Missouri–Columbia, Museum of Anthropology, Monographs in Anthropology, no. 5.
Brunhouse, Robert L. 1971. *Sylvanus G. Morley and the World of the Ancient Mayas,* Norman: University of Oklahoma Press.
———. 1973. *In Search of the Maya: The First Archaeologists.* Albuquerque: University of New Mexico Press.
———. 1975. *Pursuit of the Ancient Maya: Some Archaeologists of Yesterday.* Albuquerque: University of New Mexico Press.
Brush, Charles. 1965. Pox pottery: earliest identified Mexican ceramic. *Science* 149:194–95.
Bullard, William R. 1960. Maya settlement pattern in northeastern Petén, Guatemala. *American Antiquity* 25:355–72.
———. 1970. Topoxté: a Postclassic Maya site in Petén, Guatemala. In William R. Bullard, ed., *Monographs and Papers in Maya Archaeology,* 245–307. Cambridge: Harvard University, Peabody Museum Papers, vol. 61.
———. 1973. Postclassic culture in central Petén and adjacent British Honduras. In T. Patrick Culbert, ed., *The Classic Maya Collapse,* 221–41. Albuquerque: University of New Mexico Press.
Bunzel, Ruth. 1952. *Chichicastenango.* Washington, D.C.: American Ethnological Society, Publication 22.
Bussel, Gerard W. van, Paul L. F. van Dongen, and Ted J. J. Leyenaar. 1991. *The Mesoamerian Ballgame.* Leiden: Rijksmuseum voor Volkenkunde.
Byers, Douglas S. 1967. *The Prehistory of the Tehuacán Valley.* Austin: University of Texas Press.
Campbell, Lyle R. 1976. The linguistic prehistory of the southern Mesoamerican periphery. In *XIV Mesa Redonda,* 157–83. Mexico City: Sociedad Mexicana de Antropología.
———. 1977. *Quichean Linguistic Prehistory.* Berkeley: University of California, Publications in Linguistics, no. 8.
Campbell, Lyle R., and Terrence Kaufman. 1976. A linguistic look at the Olmecs. *American Antiquity* 41:80–89.
———. 1985. Mayan linguistics: where are we now? *Annual Review of Anthropology* 14:187–98.
Cancian, Frank. 1965. *Economics and Prestige in a Maya Community.* Stanford: Stanford University Press.
———. 1972. *Change and Uncertainty in a Peasant Economy: The Maya Corn Farmers of Zinacantán.* Stanford: Stanford University Press.
———. 1992. *The Decline of Community in Zinacantán.* Stanford: Stanford University Press.
Carlson, John B. 1976. Astronomical investigations and site orientation influences at Palenque. In Merle Greene Robertson, ed., *The Art, Iconography and Dynastic History of Palenque, Part III,* 107–22. Pebble Beach, Calif.: Robert Louis Stevenson School.
Carmack, Robert M. 1968. Toltec influence on the Postclassic culture history of highland Guatemala. In *Archaeological Studies of Middle America,* 42–92. New

Orleans: Tulane University, Middle American Research Institute, Publication 26.

———. 1973. *Quichean Civilization: The Ethnohistoric, Ethnographic, and Archaeological Sources*. Berkeley: University of California press.

———. 1981. *The Quiché Mayas of Utatlán: The Evolution of a Highland Guatemalan Kingdom*. Norman: University of Oklahoma Press.

———. 1988. *Harvest of Violence: The Maya Indians and the Guatemalan Crisis*. Norman: University of Oklahoma Press.

Carmack, Robert M., Janine Gasco, and Gary H. Gossen. 1996. *The Legacy of Mesoamerica: History and Culture of a Native American Civilization*. Upper Saddle River, N.J.: Prentice Hall.

Carmack, Robert M., and Francisco Morales Santos, eds. 1983. *Nuevas perspectivas sobre el Popol Vuh*. Guatemala City: Editorial Piedra Santa.

Carmean, Kelli. 1991. Architectural labor investment and social stratification at Sayil, Yucatan, Mexico. *Latin American Antiquity* 2(2):151–65.

Carnegie Institution of Washington. 1955. *Ancient Maya Paintings of Bonampak, Mexico*. Supplementary Publication 46.

Carneiro, Robert L. 1967. On the relationships between size of population and complexity of social organization. *Southwestern Journal of Anthropology* 23:234–43.

———. 1970. A theory of the origin of the state. *Science* 169:733–38.

———. 1988. The circumscription theory. *American Behavioral Scientist* 31:497–511.

Carr, Robert F., and James E. Hazard. 1961. Map of the ruins of Tikal, El Petén, Guatemala. *Tikal Report* no. 11. Philadelphia: University of Pennsylvania, University Museum.

Carrasco, David. 1982. *Quetzalcoatl and the Irony of Empire: Myths and Prophecies in the Aztec Tradition*. Chicago: University of Chicago Press.

Carter, William E. 1969. *New Lands and Old Traditions: Kekchi Cultivators in the Guatemalan Lowlands*. Gainesville: University of Florida Press.

Caso, Alfonso. 1965. Zapotec writing and calendar. *Handbook of Middle American Indians* 3:931–47. Austin: University of Texas Press.

———. 1967. *Los calendarios prehispánicos*. Mexico City: Universidad Nacional Autónoma de México, Instituto de Investigaciones Históricas, Serie Cultura Nahuatl, Monografías, no. 6.

Chamberlain, Robert S. 1948. *The Conquest and Colonization of Yucatan: 1517–1550*. Washington, D.C.: Carnegie Institution of Washington, Publication 582.

———. 1953. *The Conquest and Colonization of Honduras: 1502–1550*. Washington, D.C.: Carnegie Institution of Washington, Publication 598.

Chapman, Anne M. 1957. Port of trade enclaves in Aztec and Maya civilizations. In Karl Polanyi, Conrad M. Arensberg, and Harry W. Pearson, eds., *Trade and Market in the Early Empires*, 114–53. Glencoe, Ill.: Free Press.

Chase, Arlen F., and Diane Z. Chase. 1981. Archaeological investigations at Nohmul and Santa Rita, Belize: 1979–1980. *Mexicon* 3(3):42–44.

———, eds. 1987. *Investigations at the Classic Maya City of Caracol, Belize: 1985–1987*. San Francisco: Pre-Columbian Art Research Institute, Monograph no. 3.

Chase, Arlen F., Nikolai Grube, and Diane Z. Chase. 1991. *Three Terminal Classic Monuments from Caracol, Belize*. Washington, D.C.: Center for Maya Research, Research Reports on Ancient Maya Writing, no. 36.

Chase, Diane Z. 1985. Ganned but not forgotten: Late Postclassic archaeology and ritual at Santa Rita Corozal, Belize. In Arlen F. Chase and Prudence M. Rice, eds., *The Lowland Maya Postclassic*, 104–25. Austin: University of Texas Press.

———. 1990. The invisible Maya: population history and archeology at Santa Rita Corozal. In T. Patrick Culbert and Don S. Rice, eds., *Precolumbian Population History in the Maya Lowlands*, 199–213. Albuquerque: University of New Mexico Press.

Chase, Diane Z., and Arlen F. Chase. 1988. *A Postclassic Perspective: Excavations at the Maya Site of Santa Rita Corozal, Belize*. San Francisco: Pre-Columbian Art Research Institute, Monograph no. 4.

———, eds. 1994. *Studies in the Archaeology of Caracol,*

Belize. San Francisco: Pre-Columbian Art Research Institute, Monograph no. 7.

Cheek, Charles D., and Daniel E. Milla Villeda. 1983. La Estructura 10L–4. In Claude F. Baudez, ed., *Introducción a la arqueología de Copán, Honduras,* 37–91. Tegucigalpa: Instituto Hondureño de Antropología e Historia.

Cheek, Charles D., and Mary Spink. 1986. Excavaciones en el Grupo 3, Estructura 223 (Operación VII). In William T. Sanders, ed., *Excavaciones en al área urbana de Copán,* 27–154. Tegucigalpa: Instituto Hondureño de Antropología e Historia.

Childe, V. Gordon. 1951. *Man Makes Himself.* New York: New American Library.

———. 1954. *What Happened in History.* Rev. ed. Baltimore: Penguin Books.

Chisholm, Michael. 1979. *Rural Settlement and Land Use.* 3d ed. London: Hutchinson.

Clendinnen, Inga. 1987. *Ambivalent Conquests: Maya and Spaniard in Yucatan, 1517–1570.* Cambridge: Cambridge University Press.

Closs, Michael P. 1976. New Information on the European discovery of Yucatan and the correlation of the Maya and Christian calendars. *American Antiquity* 41:192–95.

Codex Dresdensis. 1975. Graz: Akademische Druck-u. Verlagsanstalt.

Codex Tro-Cortesianus (Codex Madrid). 1967. Graz: Akademische Druck-u. Verlagsanstalt.

Coe, Michael D. 1957. Cycle 7 monuments in Middle America: a reconsideration. *American Anthropologist* 59:597–611.

———. 1964. The chinampas of Mexico. *Scientific American* 211(1):90–98.

———. 1968. *America's First Civilization.* New York: American Heritage Publishing Co.

———. 1976. Early steps in the evolution of Maya writing. In H. B. Nicholson, ed., *Origins of Religious Art and Iconography in Preclassic Mesoamerica,* 107–22. Los Angeles: UCLA Latin American Center.

———. 1977. Olmec and Maya: a study in relationships. In Richard E. W. Adams, ed., *The Origins of Maya Civilization,* 183–95. Albuquerque: University of New Mexico Press.

———. 1981. San Lorenzo Tenochtitlan. *Handbook of Middle American Indians,* Supplement 1:117–46. Austin: University of Texas Press.

———. 1992. *Breaking the Maya Code.* New York: Thames and Hudson.

Coe, Michael D., and Richard A. Diehl. 1980. *In the Land of the Olmec.* Austin: University of Texas Press.

Coe, Michael D., and Kent V. Flannery. 1964. Microenvironments and Mesoamerican prehistory. *Science* 143:650–54.

———. 1967. *Early Cultures and Human Ecology in South Coastal Guatemala.* Washington, D.C.: Smithsonian Institution, Contributions to Anthropology, no. 3.

Coe, William R. 1959. *Piedras Negras Archaeology: Artifacts, Caches, and Burials.* Philadelphia: University of Pennsylvania, University Museum Monograph.

———. 1965. Tikal, Guatemala, and emergent Maya civilization. *Science* 147:1401–19.

———. 1967. *Tikal: A Handbook of the Ancient Maya Ruins.* Philadelphia: University of Pennsylvania, University Museum.

———. 1990. Excavations in the Great Plaza, North Terrace and North Acropolis of Tikal. *Tikal Report* no. 14. Philadelphia: University of Pennsylvania, University Museum.

Coe, William R., and Michael D. Coe. 1956. Excavations at Nohoch Ek, British Honduras. *American Antiquity* 21:370–82.

Coe, William R., and William A. Haviland. 1982. Introduction to the archaeology of Tikal, Guatemala. *Tikal Report* no. 12. Philadelphia: University of Pennsylvania, University Museum.

Coe, William R., and John J. McGinn. 1963. Tikal: The North Acropolis and an early tomb. *Expedition* 5(2):25–32.

Coggins, Clemency C. 1979. A new order and the role of the calendar: some characteristics of the Middle Classic period at Tikal. In Norman Hammond and Gordon R. Willey, eds., *Maya Archaeology and Ethnohistory,* 38–50. Austin: University of Texas Press.

———. 1984. *The Stucco Decoration and Architectural Assemblage of Structure 1-Sub, Dzibilchaltun, Yucatan, Mexico.* New Orleans: Tulane University, Middle American Research Institute, Publication 49.

———. 1992. *Artifacts from the Cenote of Sacrifice, Chichen Itza, Yucatan.* Cambridge: Harvard University, Peabody Museum Memoirs, vol. 10, no. 3.

———. 1993. The age of Teotihuacan and its mission abroad. In Kathleen Berrin and Esther Pasztory, eds., *Teotihuacan: Art from the City of the Gods,* 140–55. New York: Thames and Hudson.

Coggins, Clemency C., and Orrin C. Shane. 1984. *Cenote of Sacrifice: Maya Treasures from the Sacred Well at Chichén Itzá.* Austin: University of Texas Press.

Colby, Benjamin N., and Lore M. Colby. 1981. *The Daykeeper: The Life and Discourse of an Ixil Diviner.* Cambridge: Harvard University Press.

Colby, Benjamin N., and Pierre L. van den Burghe. 1969. *Ixil Country: A Plural Society in Highland Guatemala.* Berkeley: University of California Press.

Collier, Albert. 1964. The American Mediterranean. *Handbook of Middle American Indians.* 1:122–42. Austin: University of Texas Press.

Collier, George A. 1975. *Fields of the Tzotzil: The Ecological Bases for Tradition in Highland Chiapas.* Austin: University of Texas Press.

Collier, J. 1973. *Law and Social Change in Zinacantan.* Stanford: Stanford University Press.

Copeland, Denis R. E. 1989. *Excavations in the Mono Group, El Mirador, Petén, Guatemala.* Provo: New World Archaeological Foundation, Papers, no. 61.

Corson, Christopher. 1976. *Maya Anthropomorphic Figurines from Jaina Island, Campeche.* Ramona, Calif.: Ballena Press, Studies in Mesoamerican Art, Archaeology, and Ethnohistory, no. 1.

Cowgill, George L. 1979. Teotihuacán, internal militaristic competition, and the fall of the Classic Maya. In Norman Hammond and Gordon R. Willey, eds., *Maya Archaeology and Ethnohistory,* 51–62. Austin: University of Texas Press.

Cowgill, Ursula. 1961. An agricultural study of the southern Maya lowlands. *American Anthropologist* 64:273–86.

Crosby, Alfred W. 1972. *The Columbian Exchange: Biological and Cultural Consequences of 1492.* Westport, Conn.: Greenwood Press.

Culbert, T. Patrick, ed. 1973a. *The Classic Maya Collapse.* Albuquerque: University of New Mexico Press.

———. 1973b. The Maya downfall at Tikal. In T. Patrick Culbert, ed., *The Classic Maya Collapse,* 63–92. Albuquerque: University of New Mexico Press.

———. 1977. Early Maya development at Tikal, Guatemala. In Richard E. W. Adams, ed., *The Origins of Maya Civilization,* 27–43. Albuquerque: University of New Mexico Press.

———. 1988. The collapse of Classic Maya civilization. In Norman Yoffee and George L. Cowgill, eds., *The Collapse of Ancient States and Civilizations,* 69–101. Tucson: University of Arizona Press.

———, 1993. The ceramics of Tikal: vessels from the burials, caches and problematical deposits. *Tikal Report* no. 25, pt. A. Philadelphia: University of Pennsylvania, University Museum.

———, ed. 1991. *Classic Maya Political History: Hieroglyphic and Archaeological Evidence.* Cambridge: Cambridge University Press.

Culbert, T. Patrick, and Don S. Rice, eds. 1990. *Precolumbian Population History in the Maya Lowlands.* Albuquerque: University of New Mexico Press.

Culbert, T. Patrick, et al. 1990. The population of Tikal, Guatemala. In T. Patrick Culbert and Don S. Rice, eds., *Precolumbian Population History in the Maya Lowlands,* 103–21. Albuquerque: University of New Mexico Press.

Curtis, Jason H., David A. Hodell, and Mark Brenner. 1996. Climate variability on the Yucatan peninsula (Mexico) during the past 3500 years, and implications for Maya cultural evolution. *Quaternary Research* 46:37–47.

Dahlin, Bruce H. 1984. A colossus in Guatemala: the Preclassic city of El Mirador. *Archaeology* 37:18–25.

Daniel, Glyn. 1968. *The First Civilizations: The Archaeology of Their Origins.* New York: Thomas Y. Crowell.

Davies, Nigel. 1977. *The Toltecs: Until the Fall of Tula.* Norman: University of Oklahoma Press.

David, Dave D. 1975. Patterns of Early Formative subsistence in southern Mesoamerica. *Man* 10:41–59.

de Montmollin, Olivier. 1989a. *The Archaeology of Political Structure: Settlement Analysis in a Classic Maya Polity*. Cambridge: Cambridge University Press.

———. 1989b. Land tenure and politics in the Late/Terminal Classic Rosario Valley, Chiapas, Mexico. *Journal of Anthropological Research* 45(3):293–314.

Demarest, Arthur A., and Juan Antonio Valdés. 1993. Proyecto Arqueológico Regional Petexbatún: resultados y perspectivas de la cuarta temporada. In Juan Pedro Laporte, Héctor L. Escobedo, and Sandra Villagrán de Brady, eds., *VI Simposio de Investigaciones Arqueológicas en Guatemala, 1992*, 155–58. Guatemala City: Instituto de Antropología e Historia/Asociación Tikal.

———. 1994. Proyecto Arqueológico Regional Petexbatún: temporada 1993. In Juan Pedro Laporte and Héctor L. Escobedo, eds., *VII Simposio de Investigaciones Arqueológicas en Guatemala, 1993*, 507–12. Guatemala City: Instituto de Antropología e Historia/Asociación Tikal.

Demarest, Arthur A., et al. 1984. Proyecto El Mirador de la Harvard University, 1982–1983. *Mesoamérica* 7:1–160.

———. 1995. Reconocimientos en sistemas defensivos de Petexbatún: la evidencia material de la guerra. In Juan Pedro Laporte and Héctor L. Escobedo, eds., *VIII Simposio de Investigaciones Arqueológicas en Guatemala, 1994*, 517–21. Guatemala City: Instituto de Antropología e Historia/Asociación Tikal.

Denevan, William M. 1970. Aboriginal drained-field cultivation in the Americas. *Science* 169:647–54.

Desmond, Lawrence G., and Phyllis M. Messenger. 1987. *A Dream of Maya: Augustus and Alice Le Plongeon in Nineteenth-Century Yucatan*. Aubuquerque: University of New Mexico Press.

Díaz del Castillo, Bernal. 1912–16. *The True History of the Conquest of New Spain*. Vols. 4 and 5. Trans. Alfred P. Maudslay. London: Hakluyt Society.

Diehl, Richard A. 1981. Tula. *Handbook of Middle American Indians*, Supplement 1:277–95. Austin: University of Texas Press.

Diehl, Richard A., and J. C. Berlo, eds. 1989. *Mesoamerica after the Decline of Teotihuacan, A.D. 700–900*. Washington, D.C.: Dumbarton Oaks.

Diehl, Richard A., R. Lomas, and J. T. Wynn. 1974. Toltec trade with Central America: new light and evidence. *Archaeology* 27:182–87.

Dillehay, Tom D., and Michael B. Collins. 1991. Monte Verde, Chile: a comment on Lynch. *American Antiquity* 56(2):33–41.

Dillehay, Tom D., et al. 1991. Earliest hunters and gatherers of South America. *Journal of World Prehistory* 6:145–204.

Dillon, Brian D. 1977. *Salinas de los Nueve Cerros, Guatemala: Preliminary Archaeological Investigations*. Ramona, Calif.: Ballena Press, Studies in Mesoamerican Art, Archaeology, and Ethnohistory, no. 2.

Dixon, Boyd. 1992. Prehistoric political change on the southeast Mesoamerican periphery. *Ancient Mesoamerica* 3(1):11–25.

Dreiss, Meredith L., et al. 1993. Expanding the role of trace-element studies: obsidian use in the Late and Terminal Classic periods at the lowland Maya site of Colha, Belize. *Ancient Mesoamerica* 4(2):271–83.

Drucker, Philip, Robert F. Heizer, and Robert J. Squier. 1959. *Excavations at La Venta, Tabasco, 1955*. Washington, D.C.: Smithsonian Institution, Bureau of American Ethnology, Bulletin 170.

Duby, Gertrude, and Frans Blom. 1969. The Lacandón. *Handbook of Middle American Indians* 7:276–97. Austin: University of Texas Press.

Dunning, Nicholas P. 1989. *Archaeological Investigations at Sayil, Yucatan, Mexico: Intersite Reconnaissance and Soil Studies during the 1987 Field Season*. Pittsburgh: University of Pittsburgh, Anthropological Papers, no. 2.

———. 1992. *Lords of the Hills: Ancient Maya Settlement in the Puuc Region, Yucatán, Mexico*. Madison, Wisc.: Prehistory Press.

Dunning, Nicholas P., and Timothy Beach. 1994. Soil erosion, slope management, and ancient terracing in the Maya lowlands. *Latin American Antiquity* 5(1):51–69.

Dunning, Nicholas P., and Jeff Karl Kowalski. 1994.

Lords of the hills: Classic Maya settlement patterns and political iconography in the Puuc region, Mexico. *Ancient Mesoamerica* 5(1):63–95.

Durbin, Marshall. 1969. *An Interpretation of Bishop Diego de Landa's Maya Alphabet.* New Orleans: Tulane University, Middle American Research Institute, Philological and Documentary Studies, vol. 2, no. 4.

Edmonson, Munro S., trans. and ed. 1971. *The Book of Counsel: The Popol Vuh of the Quiché Maya of Guatemala.* New Orleans: Tulane University, Middle American Research Institute, Publication 35.

———. 1982. *The Ancient Future of the Itza: The Book of Chilam Balam of Tizimin.* Austin: University of Texas Press.

———. 1986. *Heaven Born Merida and Its Destiny: The Book of Chilam Balam of Chumayel.* Austin: University of Texas Press.

———. 1988. *The Book of the Year: Middle American Calendrical Systems.* Salt Lake City: University of Utah Press.

———. 1992. The Middle American Calendar Round. *Handbook of Middle American Indians*, Supplement 5:154–67. Austin: University of Texas Press.

Ekholm, Susanna M. 1973. *The Olmec Rock Carving at Xoc, Chiapas, Mexico.* Provo: New World Archaeological Foundation, Papers, no. 32.

Fabrega, H., and D. B. Silver. 1973. *Illness and Shamanistic Curing in Zinacantan.* Stanford: Stanford University Press.

Fagan, Brian M. 1987. *The Great Journey: The Peopling of Ancient America.* New York: Thames and Hudson.

Farriss, Nancy M. 1984. *Maya Society under Colonial Rule: The Collective Enterprise of Survival.* Princeton: Princeton University Press.

Farriss, Nancy M., Arthur G. Miller, and Arlen F. Chase. 1975. Late Maya rural paintings from Quintana Roo, Mexico. *Journal of Field Archaeology* 2(1):5–10.

Fash, Barbara W. 1992. Late Classic architectural sculpture themes in Copan. *Ancient Mesoamerica* 3(1):89–104.

Fash, Barbara W., et al. 1992. Investigations of a Classic Maya council house at Copán, Honduras. *Journal of Field Archaeology* 19(4):419–42.

Fash, William L. 1991. *Scribes, Warriors, and Kings: The City of Copán and the Ancient Maya.* New York: Thames and Hudson.

———. 1994. Changing perspectives on Maya civilization. *Annual Review of Anthropology* 23:181–208.

Fash, William L., and Robert J. Sharer. 1991. Sociopolitical developments and methodological issues at Copan, Honduras: a conjunctive perspective. *Latin American Antiquity* 2(2):166–87.

Fash, William L., and David S. Stuart. 1991. Dynastic history and cultural evolution at Copan, Honduras. In T. Patrick Culbert, ed., *Classic Maya Political History: Hieroglyphic and Archaeological Evidence*, 147–79. Cambridge: Cambridge University Press.

Fash, William L., et al. 1991. The Hieroglyphic Stairway and its ancestors: investigations of Copan Structure 10L–26. *Ancient Mesoamerica* 3(1):105–15.

Fedick, Scott L. 1991. Chert tool production and consumption among Classic period Maya households. In Thomas R. Hester and Harry J. Shafer, eds., *Maya Stone Tools: Selected Papers from the Second Maya Lithic Conference*, 103–18. Madison, Wisc.: Prehistory Press.

———. 1994. Ancient Maya agricultural terracing in the upper Belize River area. *Ancient Mesoamerica* 5(1):107–27.

———. 1995. Land evaluation and ancient Maya land use in the upper Belize River area, Belize, Central America. *Latin American Antiquity* 6(1):16–34.

Fettweis, Martine. 1988. *Cobá et Xelha: Peintures murales mayas.* Paris: Institut d'Ethnologie, Memoires.

Flannery, Kent V. 1968. Archaeological systems theory and early Mesoamerica. In Betty J. Meggers, ed., *Anthropological Archaeology in the Americas*, 67–87. Washington, D.C.: Anthropological Society of Washington.

———. 1973. The origins of agriculture. *Annual Review of Anthropology* 2:271–310.

———, ed. 1982. *Maya Subsistence: Studies in Memory of Dennis E. Puleston.* New York: Academic Press.

Folan, William J., Laraine A. Fletcher, and Ellen R.

Kintz. 1979. Fruit, fiber, bark, and resin: social organization of a Maya urban center. *Science* 204:697–701.

Folan, William J., Ellen R. Kintz, and Laraine Fletcher. 1983. *Cobá: A Classic Maya Metropolis*. New York: Academic Press.

Folan, William J., et al. 1995. Calakmul: new data from an ancient Maya capital in Campeche, Mexico. *Latin American Antiquity* 6(4):310–34.

Foncerrada de Molina, Marta. 1979. La pintura mural de Cacaxtla. *Actes du XLIIe Congrès International des Américanistes* 7:321–35.

———. 1993. *Cacaxtla: La iconografia de los Olmeca-Xicalanca*. Mexico City: Universidad Nacional Autónoma de México, Instituto de Investigaciones Estéticas.

Ford, Anabel. 1986. *Population Growth and Social Complexity: An Examination of Settlement and Environment in the Central Maya Lowlands*. Tempe: Arizona State University, Anthropological Research Papers, no. 35.

———. 1990. Maya settlement in the Belize River area: variations in residence patterns of the central Maya lowlands. In T. Patrick Culbert and Don S. Rice, eds., *Precolumbian Population History in the Maya Lowlands*, 167–81. Albuquerque: University of New Mexico Press.

———. 1991. Economic variation of ancient Maya residential settlement in the upper Belize River area. *Ancient Mesoamerica* 2(1):35–46.

Ford, Anabel, and Scott L. Fedick. 1992. Prehistoric Maya settlement patterns in the upper Belize River area: initial results of the Belize River Archaeological Settlement Survey, *Journal of Field Archaeology* 19(1):35–49.

Fowler, William R. 1989. *The Cultural Evolution of Ancient Nahua Civilization: The Pipil-Nicarao of Central America*. Norman: University of Oklahoma Press.

Fox, James A., and John S. Justeson. 1986. Classic Maya dynastic alliance and succession. *Handbook of Middle American Indians*, Supplement 4:7–34. Austin: University of Texas Press.

Fox, John G. 1993. The ballcourt markers of Tenam Rosario, Chiapas, Mexico. *Ancient Mesoamerica* 4(1):55–64.

———. 1996. Playing with power: ballcourts and political ritual in southern Mesoamerica. *Current Anthropology* 37(3):483–509.

Fox, John W. 1978. *Quiche Conquest: Centralism and Regionalism in Highland Guatemalan State Development*. Albuquerque: University of New Mexico Press.

———. 1980. Lowland to highland Mexicanization processes in southern Mesoamerica. *American Antiquity* 45:43–54.

———. 1987. *Maya Postclassic State Formation: Segmentary Lineage Migration in Advancing Frontiers*. Cambridge: Cambridge University Press.

———. 1989. On the rise and fall of Tuláns and Maya segmentary states. *American Anthropologist* 91:656–81.

Freidel, David A. 1979. Culture areas and interaction spheres: contrasting approaches to the emergence of civilization in the Maya lowlands. *American Antiquity* 44:36–54.

Freidel, David A., and Jeremy A. Sabloff. 1984. *Cozumel: Late Maya Settlement Patterns*. New York: Academic Press.

Freidel, David A., Linda Schele, and Joy Parker. 1993. *Maya Cosmos: Three Thousand Years on the Shaman's Path*. New York: Morrow.

Freter, AnnCorinne. 1993. Obsidian-hydration dating: its past, present, and future application in Mesoamerica. *Ancient Mesoamerica* 4(2):285–303.

Fry, Robert E. 1980. Models of exchange for major shape classes of lowland Maya pottery. In Robert E. Fry, ed., *Models and Methods in Regional Exchange*, Washington, D.C.: Society for American Archaeology, Papers, no. 1.

Fry, Robert E., and S. C. Cox. 1974. The structure of ceramic exchange at Tikal, Guatemala. *World Archaeology* 6(2):209–25.

Gann, Thomas. 1900. *Mounds in Northern Honduras*. Washington, D.C.: Smithsonian Institution, Nineteenth Annual Report, pt. 2, pp. 655–92.

Garber, James F. 1989. *Archaeology at Cerros, Belize, Central America*. Dallas: Southern Methodist University Press.

Gerstle, Andrea. 1987. Ethnic diversity and interaction at Copan, Honduras. In Eugenia J. Robinson, ed.,

Interaction on the Southeast Mesoamerican Frontier: Prehistoric and Historic Honduras and El Salvador, 328–56. Oxford: British Archaeological Reports, International Series, no. 327.

Gibson, Charles. 1952. *Tlaxcala in the Sixteenth Century.* New Haven: Yale University Press.

Gifford, James C. 1976. *Prehistoric Pottery Analysis and the Ceramics of Barton Ramie in the Belize Valley.* Cambridge: Harvard University, Peabody Museum Memoirs, vol. 18.

Gillepsie, Susan D. 1989. *The Aztec Kings: The Construction of Rulership in Mexica History.* Tucson: University of Arizona Press.

Goetz, Delia, and Sylvanus G. Morley. 1950. *Popol Vuh: The Sacred Book of the Ancient Quiché Maya.* Norman: University of Oklahoma Press.

Gómez Pompa, Arturo, José Salvador Flores, and Mario Aliphat Fernández. 1990. The sacred cacao groves of the Maya. *Latin American Antiquity* 1(3):247–57.

González, Carlos Javier. 1992. *Chinampas prehispánicas.* Mexico City: Instituto Nacional de Antropología e Historia.

González Crespo, Norberto, et al. 1995. Archaeological investigations at Xochicalco, Morelos: 1984 and 1986. *Ancient Mesoameria* 6(2):223–36.

Gordon, G. B. 1896. *Prehistoric Ruins of Copán, Honduras.* Cambridge: Harvard University, Peabody Museum Memoirs, vol. 1, no. 1.

Gossen, Gary H. 1974. *Chamulas in the World of the Sun.* Cambridge: Harvard University Press.

———. 1994. From Olmecs to Zapatistas: a once and future history of souls. *American Anthropologist* 96(3):553–70.

Gossen, Gary H., and Richard M. Leventhal. 1993. The topography of ancient Maya religious pluralism: a dialogue with the present. In Jeremy A. Sabloff and John S. Henderson, eds., *Lowland Maya Civilization in the Eighth Century A.D.*, 185–217. Washington, D.C.: Dumbarton Oaks.

Graham, Elizabeth. 1994. *The Highlands of the Lowlands: Environment and Archaeology in the Stann Creek District, Belize, Central America.* Madison, Wisc.: Prehistory Press.

Graham, Elizabeth, Grant D. Jones, and Robert R. Kautz. 1985. Archaeology and ethnohistory on a Spanish colonial frontier: an interim report on the Macal-Tipu Project in western Belize. In Arlen F. Chase and Prudence M. Rice, eds., *The Lowland Maya Postclassic*, 206–14. Austin: University of Texas Press.

Graham, Elizabeth, and David M. Pendergast. 1989. Excavations at the Marco González site, Ambergris Cay, Belize. *Journal of Field Archaeology* 16(1):1–16.

Graham, Elizabeth, David M. Pendergast, and Grant D. Jones. 1989. On the fringes of conquest: Maya-Spanish contact in colonial Belize. *Science* 246:1254–59.

Graham, Ian, and Eric Von Euw. 1977. *Corpus of Maya Hieroglyphic Inscriptions.* Vol. 3, pt. 1. Cambridge: Harvard University, Peabody Museum.

———. 1979. *Corpus of Maya Hieroglyphic Inscriptions.* Vol. 3, pt. 2. Cambridge: Harvard University, Peabody Museum.

Graham, John A. 1972. *The Hieroglyphic Inscriptions and Monumental Art of Altar de Sacrificios.* Cambridge: Harvard University, Peabody Museum Papers, vol. 64, no. 2.

———. 1973. Aspects of non-Classic presences in the inscriptions and sculptural art of Seibal. In T. Patrick Culbert, ed., *The Classic Maya Collapse*, 207–19. Albuquerque: University of New Mexico Press.

———. 1990. Monumental sculpture and hieroglyphic inscriptions. In *Excavations at Seibal, Department of Peten, Guatemala.* Cambridge: Harvard University, Peabody Museum Memoirs, vol. 17, no. 1.

Graham, John A., Robert F. Heizer, and Edwin M. Shook. 1978. Abaj Takalik 1976: exploratory investigations. *Contributions* 36: 85–109. Berkeley: University of California, Archaeological Research Facility.

Graham, John A., Thomas R. Hester, and Robert N. Jack. 1972. Sources for the obsidian at the ruins of Seibal, Petén, Guatmala. *Contributions* 16:111–16. Berkeley: University of California, Archaeological Research Facility.

Green, Dee F., and Gareth W. Lowe. 1967. *Altamira and Padre Piedra: Early Preclassic Sites in Chiapas, Mexico.*

Provo: New World Archaeological Foundation, Papers, no. 20.

Grove, David C. 1981. The Formative period and the evolution of complex culture. *Handbook of Middle American Indians*, Supplement 1:373–91. Austin: University of Texas Press.

———. 1989. Olmec: what's in a name? In Robert J. Sharer and David C. Grove, eds., *Regional Perspectives on the Olmec*, 8–14. Cambridge: Cambridge University Press.

Gruhn, Ruth, and Alan L. Bryan. 1977. Los Tapiales: A Paleoindian campsite in the Guatemala highlands. *American Philosophical Society, Proceedings* 121(3):235–73.

———. 1991. A review of Lynch's descriptions of South American Pleistocene sites. *American Antiquity* 56(2):342–48.

Guderjan, Thomas H. 1993. *Ancient Maya Traders of Ambergris Caye.* Benque Viejo, Belize: Cubola Productions.

———. 1995. Maya settlement and trade on Ambergris Caye, Belize. *Ancient Mesoamerica* 6(2):147–59.

Guderjan, Thomas H., and James F. Garber. 1995. *Maya Maritime Trade, Settlement, and Populations on Ambergris Caye, Belize.* Culver City, Calif.: Labyrinthos.

Guillemin, Georges F. 1967. The ancient Cakchiquel capital of Iximché. *Expedition* 9(2):22–35.

———. 1977. Urbanism and hierarchy at Iximché. In Norman Hammond, ed., *Social Process in Maya Prehistory: Studies in Honour of Sir Eric Thompson*, 227–64. New York: Academic Press.

Guiteras-Holmes, C. 1961. *Perils of the Soul: The World View of a Tzotzil Indian.* New York: Free Press.

Hamblin, Nancy L. 1983. *Animal Use by the Cozumel Maya.* Tucson: University of Arizona Press.

Hamblin, Robert L., and Brian L. Pitcher. 1980. The Classic Maya collapse: testing class conflict hypotheses. *American Antiquity* 45:246–67.

Hammond, Norman. 1972. Obsidian trade routes in the Maya area. *Science* 178:1092–93.

———. 1975. *Lubaantún: A Classic Maya Realm.* Cambridge: Harvard University, Peabody Museum Monograph no. 2.

———. 1977a. The Early Formative in the Maya lowlands. In Norman Hammond, ed., *Social Process in Maya Prehistory: Studies in Honour of Sir Eric Thompson*, 77–101. New York: Academic Press.

———. 1977b. Ex oriente lux: a view from Belize. In Richard E. W. Adams, ed., *The Origins of Maya Civilization*, 45–76. Albuquerque: University of New Mexico Press.

———, ed. 1985. *Nohmul: A Prehistoric Maya Community in Belize.* Oxford: British Archaeological Reports, International Series, no. 250.

———. 1991. *Cuello: An Early Maya Community in Belize.* Cambridge: Cambridge University Press.

Hammond, Norman, Amanda Clarke, and Sara Donaghy. 1995. The long goodbye: Middle Preclassic Maya archaeology at Cuello, Belize. *Latin American Antiquity* 6(2):120–28.

Hammond, Norman, Rupert A. Housley, and Ian A. Law. 1991. The Postclassic at Cuello, Belize. *Ancient Mesoamerica* 2(1):71–4.

Hammond, Norman, and Gair Tourtellot. 1993. Survey and excavation at La Milpa, Belize, 1992. *Mexicon* 15:71–5.

Hammond, Norman, et al. 1979. The earliest lowland Maya: definition of the Swasey phase. *American Antiquity* 44:92–110.

Hansen, Richard D. 1990. *Excavations in the Tigre Complex, El Mirador, Petén, Guatemala.* Provo: New World Archaeological Foundation, Papers, no. 62.

———. 1991a. *An Early Maya Text from El Mirador, Guatemala.* Washington, D.C.: Center for Maya Research, Research Reports on Ancient Maya Writing, no. 37.

———. 1991b. The road to Nakbe. *Natural History*, May: 8–14.

Harris, John F., and Stephen K. Stearns. 1992. *Understanding Maya Inscriptions: A Hieroglyph Handbook.* Philadelphia: University of Pennsylvania, University Museum.

Harrison, Peter D. 1977. The rise of the *bajos* and the fall of the Maya. In Norman Hammond, ed., *Social Process in Maya Prehistory: Studies in Honour of Sir Eric Thompson*, 469–508. New York: Academic Press.

———. 1990. The revolution in ancient Maya subsistence. In Flora S. Clancy and Peter D. Harrison, eds., *Vision and Revision in Maya Studies*, 99–113. Albuquerque: University of New Mexico Press.

Harrison, Peter D., and B. L. Turner II. 1978. *Pre-Hispanic Maya Agriculture.* Albuquerque: University of New Mexico Press.

Haviland, William A. 1967. Stature at Tikal, Guatemala: implications for ancient Maya demography and social organization. *American Antiquity* 32:316–25.

———. 1968. Ancient lowland Maya social organization. In *Archaeological Studies in Middle America*, 93–117. New Orleans: Tulane University, Middle American Research Institute, Publication 26.

———. 1969. A new population estimate for Tikal, Guatemala. *American Antiquity* 34:429–33.

———. 1970. Tikal, Guatemala, and Mesoamerican urbanism. *World Archaeology* 2:186–97.

———. 1971. Entombment, authority, and descent at Altar de Sacrificios, Guatemala. *American Antiquity* 36:102–5.

———. 1972a. Estimates of Maya population: comments on Thompson's comments. *American Antiquity* 37:261–62.

———. 1972b. Family size, prehistoric population estimates, and the ancient Maya. *American Antiquity* 37:135–39.

———. 1972c. A new look at Classic Maya social organization at Tikal. *Cerámica de Cultura Maya et al.* 8:1–16.

———. 1977. Dynastic genealogies from Tikal, Guatemala: implications for descent and political organization. *American Antiquity* 42:61–7.

———. 1985. Excavations in small residential groups of Tikal: Groups 4F-1 and 4F-2. *Tikal Report* no. 19. Philadelphia: University of Pennsylvania, University Museum.

Haviland, William A., and Anita de Laguna Haviland. 1995. Glimpses of the supernatural: altered states of consciousness and the graffiti of Tikal. *Latin American Antiquity* 6(4):295–309.

Healy, Paul F. 1992. The ancient Maya ball court at Pacbitun, Belize. *Ancient Mesoamerica* 3(2):229–39.

Hellmuth, Nichola. 1977. Cholti-Lacandón (Chiapas) and Petén-Ytzá agriculture, settlement pattern and population. In Norman Hammond, ed., *Social Process in Maya Prehistory: Studies in Honour of Sir Eric Thompson*, 421–28. New York: Academic Press.

———. 1978. Teotihuacán art in the Escuintla, Guatemala region. In Esther Pasztory, ed., *Middle Classic Mesoamerica: A.D. 400–700*, 71–85. New York: Columbia University Press.

Helms, Mary. 1975. *Middle America: A Culture History of Heartland and Frontiers.* Englewood Cliffs, N.J.: Prentice-Hall.

Henderson, John S. 1974. Origin of the 260-day cycle in Mesoamerica. *Science* 185:542.

———. 1977. The Valle de Naco: ethnohistory and archaeology in northwestern Honduras. *Ethnohistory* 24:363–77.

———. 1978. El noroeste de Honduras y la frontera oriental maya. *Yaxkin* 2(4):241–53.

———. 1979. *Atopula, Guerrero, and Olmec Horizons in Mesoamerica.* New Haven: Yale University, Publications in Anthropology, no. 77.

———, 1988. Investigaciones arqueológicas en el valle de Sula. *Yaxkin* 11(1):5–30.

———. 1992a. Elites and ethnicity along the southeastern fringe of Mesoamerica. In Diane Z. Chase and Arlen F. Chase, eds., *Mesoamerican Elites: An Archaeological Assessment*, 157–68. Norman: University of Oklahoma Press.

———. 1992b. Variations on a theme: a frontier view of Maya civilization. In Elin C. Danien and Robert J. Sharer, eds., *New Theories on the Ancient Maya*, 161–71. Philadelphia: University of Pennsylvania, University Museum.

———, ed. 1984. *Archaeology in Northwestern Honduras: Interim Reports of the Proyecto Arqueológico Sula.* Ithaca: Cornell University, Latin American Studies Program.

Henderson, John S., and Marilyn P. Beaudry-Corbett, eds. 1993. *Pottery of Prehistoric Honduras: Regional Classification and Analysis.* Los Angeles: UCLA Institute of Archaeology, Monograph no. 35.

Henderson, John S., and Jeremy A. Sabloff. 1993. Reconceptualizing the Maya cultural tradition: programmatic comments. In Jeremy A. Sabloff and John S. Henderson, eds., *Lowland Maya Civilization in the Eighth Century A.D.*, 445–75. Washington, D.C.: Dumbarton Oaks.

Henderson, John S., et al. 1979. Archaeological investigations in the Valle de Naco, northwestern Honduras: a preliminary report. *Journal of Field Archaeology* 6:169–92.

Hendon, Julia A. 1987. The Uses of Maya Structures: A Study of Architecture and Artifact Distribution at Sepulturas, Copan, Honduras. Ph.D. dissertation, Harvard University.

———. 1991. Status and power in Classic Maya society: an archaeological study. *American Anthropologist* 93(4):894–918.

Hester, Thomas R., and Harry J. Schafer. 1991. Lithics of the Early Postclassic at Colha, Belize. In Thomas R. Hester and Harry J. Shafer, eds., *Maya Stone Tools: Selected Papers from the Second Maya Lithic Conference*, 155–61. Madison, Wisc.: Prehistory Press.

Hill, Robert M. 1992. *Colonial Cakchiquels: Highland Maya Adaptations to Spanish Rule, 1600–1700*. New York: Harcourt Brace Jovanovich.

Hill, Robert M., and John Monaghan. 1987. *Continuities in Highland Maya Social Organization: Ethnohistory in Sacapulas, Guatemala*. Philadelphia: University of Pennsylvania Press.

Hinshaw, Robert E. 1975. *Panajachel: A Guatemalan Town in Thirty-Year Perspective*. Pittsburgh: University of Pittsburgh Press.

Hodell, David A., Jason H. Curtis, and Mark Brenner. 1995. Possible role of climate in the collapse of Classic Maya civilization. *Nature* 375(6530):391–94.

Holmberg, Alan R. 1950. *Nomads of the Long Bow: The Sirionó of Eastern Bolivia*. Washington, D.C.: Smithsonian Institution, Institute of Social Anthropology, Publication 10.

Hooton, Earnest A. 1940. Skeletons from the Cenote of Sacrifice at Chichén Itzá. In *The Maya and Their Neighbors*, 272–80. New York: D. Appleton-Century.

Hosler, Dorothy, Jeremy A. Sabloff, and Dale Runge. 1977. Simulation model development: a case study of the Classic Maya collapse. In Norman Hammond, ed., *Social Process in Maya Prehistory: Studies in Honour of Sir Eric Thompson*, 553–90. New York: Academic Press.

Houston, Stephen D. 1989a. Archaeology and Maya writing. *Journal of World Prehistory* 3:1–32.

———. 1989b. *Maya Glyphs*. Berkeley: University of California Press.

———. 1992. Classic Maya history and politics at Dos Pilas, Guatemala. *Handbook of Middle American Indians*, Supplement 5:110–27. Austin: University of Texas Press.

———. 1993. *Hieroglyphs and History at Dos Pilas*. Austin: University of Texas Press.

Houston, Stephen D., and William R. Fowler, eds. 1990. Remembering Carnegie Archaeology. *Ancient Mesoamerica* 1:245–76.

Houston, Stephen D., and David S. Stuart. 1989. *The Way Glyph: Evidence for 'Co-Essences' among the Classic Maya*. Washington, D.C.: Center for Maya Research, Research Reports on Ancient Maya Writing, no. 30.

Howell, Wayne K. 1989. *Excavations in the Danta Complex at El Mirador, Petén, Guatemala*. Provo: New World Archaeological Foundation, Papers, no. 60.

Hunt, Eva. 1977. *The Transformation of the Hummingbird: Cultural Roots of a Zinacantecan Mythical Poem*. Ithaca: Cornell University Press.

Hurtado de Mendoza, Luis, and William A. Jester. 1978. Obsidian sources in Guatemala: a regional approach. *American Antiquity* 43:424–35.

Ichon, Alain, et al. 1979. *Rabinal et la vallée moyenne du Río Chixoy, Baja Verapaz Guatemala*. Paris: Centre National de la Recherche Scientifique.

Inomata, Takeshi, and Laura R. Stiver. 1994. Investigaciones arqueológicas en Aguateca: la temporada de 1993. In Juan Pedro Laporte and Héctor L. Escobedo, eds., 453–70. *VII Simposio de Investigaciones Arqueológicas en Guatemala, 1993*, 453–70. Guatemala City: Instituto de Antropología e Historia/Asociación Tikal.

Inomata, Takeshi, Daniela Triadan, and Claudia Wolley. 1993. Investigaciones arqueológicas en Aguateca, departamento de Petén. In Juan Pedro Laporte, Héctor L. Escobedo, and Sandra Villagrán de Brady, eds., *VI Simposio de Investigaciones Arqueológicas en Guatemala, 1992*, 185–99. Guatemala City: Instituto de Antropología e Historia/Asociación Tikal.

Jackson, Thomas L., and Michael W. Love. 1991. Blade running: Middle Preclassic obsidian exchange and the introduction of prismatic blades at La Blanca, Guatemala. *Ancient Mesoamerica* 2(1):47–59.

Jacobs, J. S., and C. T. Hallmark. 1996. Holocene stratigraphy of Cobweb Swamp, a Maya wetland in northern Belize. *Geological Society of American Bulletin* 108(7):883–91.

Jiménez Moreno, Wigberto. 1941. Tula y los toltecas según las fuentes históricas. *Revista Mexicana de Estudios Antropológicos* 5:79–83.

———. 1966. Los imperios prehispánicos de Mesoamérica. *Revista Mexicana de Estudios Antropológicos* 20:179–95.

Jiménez Valdéz, G. M. 1987. Algunas consideraciones arqueológicas sobre la península de Xicalango, Campeche. *Anales de Antropología* 24:115–26.

Joesink-Mandeville, L. R. V., and Sylvia Meluzin. 1976. Olmec-Maya relationships: Olmec influence in Yucatan. In H. B. Nicholson, ed., *Origins of Religious Art and Iconography in Preclassic Mesoamerica*, 87–105. Los Angeles: UCLA Latin American Center.

Johnson, Jay K. 1985. Postclassic Maya site structure at Topoxte, El Peten, Guatemala. In Arlen F. Chase and Prudence M. Rice, eds., *The Lowland Maya Postclassic*, 151–65. Austin: University of Texas Press.

Jones, Christopher. 1991. Cycles of growth at Tikal. In T. Patrick Culbert, ed., *Classic Maya Political History: Hieroglyphic and Archaeological Evidence*, 102–27. Cambridge: Cambridge University Press.

Jones, Christopher, William R. Coe, and William A. Haviland. 1981. Tikal: an outline of its field study (1956–1970) and a project bibliography. *Handbook of Middle American Indians*, Supplement 1:296–312. Austin: University of Texas Press.

Jones, Christopher, and Linton Satterthwaite. 1982. The monuments and inscriptions of Tikal: the carved monuments. *Tikal Report* no. 33. Philadelphia: University of Pennsylvania, University Museum.

Jones, Grant D. 1989. *Maya Resistance to Spanish Rule: Time and History on a Colonial Frontier.* Albuquerque: University of New Mexico Press.

———. 1992a. The Canek manuscript in ethnohistorical perspective. *Ancient Mesoamerica* 3(2):243–68.

———. 1992b. Rebellious prophets. In Robert J. Sharer and Elin C. Danien, eds., *New Theories on the Ancient Maya*, 197–204. Philadelphia: University of Pennsylvania, University Museum.

———, ed. 1977. *Anthropology and History in Yucatan.* Austin: University of Texas Press.

Joyce, Rosemary A. 1986. Terminal Classic interaction on the southeastern Maya periphery. *American Antiquity* 51(2):313–29.

———. 1991. *Cerro Palenque: Power and Identity on the Maya Periphery.* Austin: University of Texas Press.

———. 1993a. The construction of the Maya periphery and the Mayoid image of Honduran polychromes. In Mark Miller Graham, ed., *Reinterpreting Prehistory of Central America*, 51–101. Niwot: University Press of Colorado.

———, 1993b. Review of *Classic Maya Political History* by T. P. Culbert and *Scribes, Warriors and Kings* by W. L. Fash. *Journal of Field Archaeology* 20(1):114–16.

———. 1993c. A key to Ulua polychromes. In John S. Henderson and Marilyn P. Beaudry-Corbett, eds., *Pottery of Prehistoric Honduras: Regional Classification and Analysis*, 257–79. Los Angeles: UCLA Institute of Archaeology, Monograph no. 35.

Justeson, John S. 1986. The origin of writing systems: Preclassic Mesoamerica. *World Archaeology* 17:437–58.

Justeson, John S., and Lyle R. Campbell. 1984. *Phoneticism in Mayan Hieroglyphic Writing.* Albany: State University of New York, Institute for Mesoamerican Studies, Publication 9.

Justeson, John S., and Terrence Kaufman. 1993. A decipherment of epi-Olemic hieroglyphic writing. *Science* 259:1665–79.

Justeson, John S., et al. 1985. *The Foreign Impact on Lowland Mayan Language and Script.* New Orleans: Tulane University, Middle American Research Institute, Publication 53.

Kaplan, Jonathon. 1995. The Incienso throne and other thrones from Kaminaljuyu, Guatemala: Late Preclassic examples of a Mesoamerican throne tradition. *Ancient Mesoamerica* 6(2):185–96.

Kaufman, Terrence. 1976. Archaeological and linguistic correlations in Mayaland and associated areas of Meso-America. *World Archaeology* 8(1):101–18.

Kelley, David H. 1962. A history of the decipherment of the Maya script. *Anthropological Linguistics* 4(8):1–48.

———. 1965. The birth of the gods at Palenque. *Estudios de Cultura Maya* 5:93–134.

———. 1976. *Deciphering the Maya Script.* Austin: University of Texas Press.

Kelley, Jane H. 1988. *Cihuatán, El Salvador: A Study in Intrasite Variability.* Nashville: Vanderbilt University, Publications in Anthropology, no. 35.

Kelly, John E. 1932. *Pedro de Alvarado: Conquistador.* Port Washington, N.Y.: Kennikat Press.

Kelly, Thomas C. 1993. Preceramic projectile-point typology in Belize. *Ancient Mesoamerica* 4(2):205–27.

Kepecs, Susan, Gary Feinman, and Sylviane Boucher. 1994. Chichen Itza and its hinterland: a world-systems perspective. *Ancient Mesoamerica* 5(2):141–58.

Kidder, Alfred V. 1947. *The Artifacts of Uaxactún, Guatemala.* Washington, D.C.: Carnegie Institution of Washington, Publication 576.

Kidder, Alfred V., Jesse D. Jennings, and Edwin M. Shook. 1946. *Excavations at Kaminaljuyú, Guatemala.* Washington, D.C.: Carnegie Institution of Washington, Publication 561.

Kievit, Karen A. 1994. Jewels of Cerén: form and function comparisons for the earthen structures of Joya de Cerén, El Salvador. *Ancient Mesoamerica* 5(2):193–208.

Kirchhoff, Paul. 1943. Mesoamerica. *Acta Americana* 1:92–107.

Knorozov, Yurii V. 1967. *Selected Chapters from the Writing of the Maya Indians.* Trans. Sophie Coe. Cambridge: Harvard University, Peabody Museum, Russian Translation Series, no. 4.

Kosakowsky, Laura J. 1987. *Preclassic Maya Pottery at Cuello, Belize.* Tucson: University of Arizona, Anthropological Papers, no. 47.

Kowalski, Jeff Karl. 1986a. Some comments on Uxmal inscriptions. *Mexicon* 8:93–95.

———. 1986b. Uxmal: a Terminal Classic Maya capital in northern Yucatan. In Elizabeth P. Benson, ed., *City-States of the Maya: Art and Architecture,* 138–71. Denver: Rocky Mountain Institute for Pre-Columbian Studies.

———. 1987. *The House of the Governor: A Maya Palace at Uxmal, Yucatan, Mexico.* Norman: University of Oklahoma Press.

———. 1990. *Guide to Uxmal and the Puuc Region.* Mexico: Editorial Dante.

Kubler, George. 1961. Chichén Itzá y Tula. *Estudios de Cultura Maya* 1:47–79.

———. 1974. Mythological ancestries in Classic Maya inscriptions. In Merle Greene Robertson, ed., *Primera Mesa Redonda de Palenque, Part II,* 23–43. Pebble Beach, Calif.: Robert Louis Stevenson School.

Kurjack, Edward B. 1974. *Prehistoric Lowland Maya Community and Social Organization: A Case Study at Dzibilchaltún, Yucatan, Mexico.* New Orleans: Tulane University, Middle American Research Institute, Publication 38.

LaFarge, Oliver, and Douglas S. Byers. 1931. *The Year Bearer's People.* New Orleans: Tulane University, Middle American Research Institute, Publication 3.

Lambert, Joseph B., et al. 1994. Amber and jet from Tipu, Belize. *Ancient Mesoamerica* 5(1):55–60.

Laporte, Juan Pedro. 1989. El Grupo B, Uaxactún: arquitectura y relaciones sociopolíticas durante el Clásico Temprano. In Mercedes de la Garza et al., eds., *II Coloquio Internacional de Mayistas, Memorias,* 625–46. Mexico City: Universidad Nacional Autónoma de México.

———. 1993. Architecture and social change in Late Classic Maya society: the evidence from Mundo Perdido, Tikal. In Jeremy A. Sabloff and John S. Henderson, eds., *Lowland Maya Civilization in the Eighth Century A.D.,* 299–320. Washington, D.C.: Dumbarton Oaks.

Laporte, Juan Pedro, and Vilma Fialko. 1995. Un reencuentro con Mundo Perdido, Tikal, Guatemala. *Ancient Mesoamerica* 6(1):41–94.

Laughlin, Robert M. 1969a. The Huastec. *Handbook of Middle American Indians* 7:298–311. Austin: University of Texas Press.

———. 1969b. The Tzotzil. *Handbook of Middle Ameri-*

can Indians 7:152–94. Austin: University of Texas Press.

Lehmann, Henri. 1968. *Mixco Viejo: Guía de las ruinas de la plaza fuerte Pocomam.* Guatemala City: Tipografía Nacional.

Lentz, David. 1991. Maya diets of the rich and poor: paleoethnobotanical evidence from Copan. *Latin American Antiquity* 2(3):269–87.

León-Portilla, Miguel. 1973. *Time and Reality in the Thought of the Maya.* Boston: Beacon Press.

Leventhal, Richard M. 1990. Southern Belize: an ancient Maya region. In Flora S. Clancy and Peter D. Harrison, eds., *Vision and Revision in Maya Studies,* 125–41. Albuquerque: University of New Mexico Press.

Leventhal, Richard M., et al. 1993–96. Xunatunich Archaeological Project: 1992–1995 Field Seasons. Manuscript.

Leyenaar, Ted J. J. 1978. *Ulama: The Perpetuation in Mexico of the Pre-Spanish Ball Game Ullamaliztli.* Leiden: Brill.

Lincoln, Charles E. 1986. The chronology of Chichen Itza: a review of the literature. In Jeremy A. Sabloff and E. Wyllys Andrews V., eds., *Late Lowland Maya Civilization: Classic to Postclassic,* 141–96. Albuquerque: University of New Mexico Press.

Lincoln, J. Stewart. 1942. *The Maya Calendar of the Ixil of Guatemala.* Washington, D.C.: Carnegie Institution of Washington, Contributions to American Anthropology and History, no. 38.

Longyear, John M. 1952. *Copán Ceramics: A Study of Southeastern Maya Pottery.* Washington, D.C.: Carnegie Institution of Washington, Publication 597.

López, Diana, and Daniel Molina. 1976. Los murales de Cacaxtla. *Instituto Nacional de Antropología e Historia, Boletín* 16:3–8.

Loten, H. Stanley. 1985. Lamanai Postclassic. In Arlen F. Chase and Prudence M. Rice, eds., *The Lowland Maya Postclassic,* 85–90. Austin: University of Texas Press.

Lothrop, Samuel K. 1924. *Tulum: An Archaeological Study of the East Coast of Yucatan.* Washington, D.C.: Carnegie Institution of Washington, Publication 335.

———. 1952. *Metals from the Cenote of Sacrifice, Chichen Itza, Yucatan.* Cambridge: Harvard University, Peabody Museum Memoirs, vol. 10, no. 2.

Lounsbury, Floyd G. 1974. The inscription of the sarcophagus lid at Palenque. In Merle Greene Robertson, ed., *Primera Mesa Redonda de Palenque, Part II,* 5–19. Pebble Beach, Calif.: Robert Louis Stevenson School.

———. 1976. A rationale for the initial date of the Temple of the Cross at Palenque. In Merle Greene Robertson, ed., *The Art, Iconography and Dynastic History of Palenque, Part III,* 211–24. Pebble Beach, Calif: Robert Louis Stevenson School.

———. 1978. Maya numeration, computation, and calendrical astronomy. *Dictionary of Scientific Biography,* vol. 15, suppl. 1:759–818.

Love, Bruce. 1995. A Dresden Codex Mars table? *Latin American Antiquity* 6(4):350–61.

Lowe, Gareth W. 1962. *Mound 5 and Minor Excavations, Chiapa de Corzo, Chiapas, Mexico.* Provo: New World Archaeological Foundation, Papers, no. 12.

———. 1975. *The Early Preclassic Barra Phase of Altamira, Chiapas: A Review with New Data.* Provo: New World Archaeological Foundation, Papers, no. 38.

———. 1977. The Mixe-Zoque as competing neighbors of the early lowland Maya. In Richard E. W. Adams, ed., *The Origins of Maya Civilization,* 197–248. Albuquerque: University of New Mexico Press.

Lowe, Gareth W., and Pierre Agrinier. 1960. *Mound 1, Chiapa de Corzo, Chiapas, Mexico.* Provo: New World Archaeological Foundation, Papers, no. 8.

Lowe, Gareth W., and J. Alden Mason. 1965. Archaeological survey of the Chiapas coast, highlands, and upper Grijalva basin. *Handbook of Middle American Indians* 2:95–236. Austin: University of Texas Press.

Lynch, Thomas F. 1990. Glacial-age man in South America? A critical review. *American Antiquity* 55(1):12–36.

———. 1991. Lack of evidence for glacial-age settlement of South America: reply to Dillehay and Collins and to Gruhn and Bryan. *American Antiquity* 56(2):348–55.

MacLeod, Murdo. 1973. *Spanish Central America: A*

Socioeconomic History, 1520–1720. Berkeley: University of California Press.

MacNeish, Richard S. 1972. The evolution of community patterns in the Tehuacán Valley of Mexico and speculations about the cultural processes. In Peter J. Ucko, Ruth Tringham, and G. W. Dimbleby, eds., *Man, Settlement and Urbanism*, 67–93. London: Gerald Duckworth.

MacNeish, Richard S., and Frederick A. Peterson. 1962. *The Santa Marta Rock Shelter, Ocozocoautla, Chiapas, Mexico.* Provo: New World Archaeological Foundation, Papers, no. 14.

MacNeish, Richard S., S. Jeffrey K. Wilkerson, and Antoinette Nelken-Terner. 1980. *First Annual Report of the Belize Archaic Archaeological Reconnaissance.* Andover, Mass.: Robert S. Peabody Foundation for Archaeology.

MacNeish, Richard S., et al. 1972. *The Prehistory of the Tehuacán Valley*, vol. 5: *Excavations and Reconnaissance.* Austin: University of Texas Press.

MacNutt, Francis A. 1912. *De Orbe Novo: The Eight Decades of Peter Martyr d'Anghiera.* New York: G. P. Putnam's Sons.

Maler, Teobert. 1901–3. *Researches in the Central Portion of the Usumacintla Valley.* Cambridge: Harvard University, Peabody Museum Memoirs, vol. 2, nos. 1–2.

———. 1911. *Explorations in the Department of Peten, Guatemala: Tikal.* Cambridge: Harvard University, Peabody Museum Memoirs, vol. 5, no. 1.

Manzanilla, Linda, and Luis Barba. 1990. The study of activities in Classic households: two case studies from Coba and Teotihuacan. *Ancient Mesoamerica* 1(1):41–49.

Marcus, Joyce. 1976a. *Emblem and State in the Classic Maya Lowlands: An Epigraphic Approach to Territorial Organization.* Washington, D.C.: Dumbarton Oaks.

———. 1976b. The origins of Mesoamerican writing. *Annual Review of Anthropology* 5:35–67.

———. 1987. *The Inscriptions of Calakmul: Royal Marriage at a Maya City in Campeche, Mexico.* Ann Arbor: University of Michigan, Museum of Anthropology, Technical Reports, no. 21.

———. 1992. *Mesoamerican Writing Systems: Propaganda, Myth, and History in Four Ancient Civilizations.* Princeton: Princeton University Press.

———. 1993. Ancient Maya political organization. In Jeremy A. Sabloff and John S. Henderson, eds., *Lowland Maya Civilization in the Eighth Century A.D.*, 111–83. Washington, D.C.: Dumbarton Oaks.

———. 1995. Where is lowland Maya archaeology headed? *Journal of Archaeological Research* 3(1):3–53.

Martin, Simon, and Nikolai Grube. 1995. Maya superstates. *Archaeology* 48(6):41–46.

Matheny, Ray T. 1970. *The Ceramics of Aguacatal, Campeche, Mexico.* Provo: New World Archaeological Foundation, Papers, no. 27.

———. 1980. *El Mirador, Petén, Guatemala: An Interim Report.* Provo: New World Archaeological Foundation, Papers, no. 45.

———. 1986. Early states in the Maya lowlands during the Late Preclassic period: Edzna and El Mirador. In Elizabeth P. Benson, ed., *City-States of the Maya: Art and Architecture*, 1–44. Denver: Rocky Mountain Institute for Pre-Columbian Studies.

Matheny, Ray T., et al. 1980–83. *Investigations at Edzná, Campeche, Mexico.* 3 vols. Provo: New World Archaeological Foundation, Papers, no. 46.

Mathews, Peter. 1991. Classic Maya emblem glyphs. In T. Patrick Culbert, ed., *Classic Maya Political History: Hieroglyphic and Archaeological Evidence*, 19–29. Cambridge: Cambridge University Press.

Mathews, Peter, and Linda Schele. 1974. Lords of Palenque—the glyphic evidence. In Merle Greene Robertson, ed., *Primera Mesa Redonda de Palenque, Part I*, 63–76. Pebble Beach, Calif.: Robert Louis Stevenson School.

Mathews, Peter, and Gordon R. Willey. 1991. Prehistoric polities of the Pasion region: hieroglyphic texts and their archaeological settings. In T. Patrick Culbert, ed., *Classic Maya Political History: Hieroglyphic and Archaeological Evidence*, 30–71. Cambridge: Cambridge University Press.

McAnany, Patricia A. 1993. The economics of social power and wealth among eighth-century Maya households. In Jeremy A. Sabloff and John S. Henderson, eds., *Lowland Maya Civilization in the Eighth Cen-*

tury A.D., 65–89. Washington, D.C.: Dumbarton Oaks.

———. 1995. *Living with the Ancestors: Kinship and Kinship in Ancient Maya Society.* Austin: University of Texas Press.

McAnany, Patricia A., and Barry L. Isaac. 1989. *Prehistoric Maya Economies of Belize.* Greenwich, Conn.: JAI Press, Research in Economic Anthropology, suppl. 4.

McClung de Tapia, Emily. 1992. The origins of agriculture in Mesoamerica and Central America. In C. Wesley Cowan and Patty Jo Watson, eds., *The Origins of Agriculture: An International Perspective*, 143–71. Washington, D.C.: Smithsonian Institution Press.

McKillop, Heather. 1994. Ancient Maya tree cropping: a viable subsistence adaptation for the island Maya. *Ancient Mesoamerica* 5(1):129–40.

———. 1995. Underwater archaeology, salt production, and coastal Maya trade at Stingray Lagoon, Belize. *Latin American Antiquity* 6(3):214–28.

McKillop, Heather, and Paul F. Healy. 1989. *Coastal Maya Trade.* Peterborough: Trent University, Occasional Papers in Anthropology, no. 8.

Means, Phillip A. 1917. *History of the Spanish Conquest of Yucatan and of the Itzas.* Cambridge: Harvard University, Peabody Museum Papers, no. 7.

Medrano, Sonia. 1992. Culto al Dios Mundo de Santa Lucía Cotzumalguapa, Escuintla, Guatemala. *Trace* 21:3–8.

Mejía Pérez Campo, Elizabeth, and Lorena Mirambell Silva, eds. 1992. *Comalcalco.* Mexico City: Instituto Nacional de Antropología e Historia.

Merwin, Raymond E., and George C. Vaillant. 1932. *The Ruins of Holmul, Guatemala.* Cambridge: Harvard University, Peabody Museum Memoirs, vol. 8, no. 2.

Messenger, Lewis C. 1990. Ancient winds of change: climatic settings and prehistoric social complexity in Mesoamerica. *Ancient Mesoamerica* 1(1):21–40.

Michaels, Geroge H., and Barbara Voorhies. 1989. Late Archaic period coastal collectors in southern Mesoamerica: the Chantuto people revisited. Paper presented at the Circum-Pacific Prehistory Conference, Seattle.

Michels, Joseph W. 1975. El Chayal, Guatemala: a chronological and behavioral reassessment. *American Antiquity* 40:103–6.

———. 1979a. *The Kaminaljuyú Chiefdom.* State College: Pennsylvania State University Press.

———. 1979b. *Settlement Pattern Excavations at Kaminaljuyú, Guatemala.* State College: Pennsylvania State University Press.

Michels, Joseph W., and William T. Sanders. 1973. *The Pennsylvania State University Kaminaljuyu Project: 1969, 1970 Seasons*, pt. 1: *Mound Excavations.* University Park: Pennsylvania State University, Occasional Papers in Anthropology, no. 9.

Miksicek, C. H., et al. 1981. Rethinking *ramón*: a comment on Reina and Hill's "Lowland Maya subsistence." *American Antiquity* 46:916–19.

Miles, S. W. 1952. An analysis of modern Middle American calendars. In Sol Tax, ed., *Acculturation in the Americas: Proceedings and Selected Papers of the 29th International Congress of Americanists*, 273–84. Chicago: University of Chicago Press.

———. 1957. *The Sixteenth-Century Pokom-Maya: A Documentary Analysis of Social Structure and Archaeological Setting.* Philadelphia: American Philosophical Society, Transactions (n.s.), no. 47, pt. 4.

———. 1965a. Sculpture of the Guatemala-Chiapas highlands and Pacific slopes and associated hieroglyphs. *Handbook of Middle American Indians* 2:237–75. Austin: University of Texas Press.

———. 1965b. Summary of preconquest ethnology of the Guatemala-Chiapas highlands and Pacific slopes. *Handbook of Middle American Indians* 2:276–87. Austin: University of Texas Press.

Miller, Arthur G. 1977. Captains of the Itzá: unpublished mural evidence from Chichén Itzá. In Norman Hammond, ed., *Social Process in Maya Prehistory: Studies in Honour of Sir Eric Thompson*, 197–225. New York: Academic Press.

———. 1978. A brief outline of the artistic evidence for Classic period cultural contact between Maya lowlands and central Mexican highlands. In Esther Pasztory, ed., *Middle Classic Mesoamerica: A.D. 400–700*, 63–70. New York: Columbia University Press.

———. 1982. *On the Edge of the Sea: Mural Painting at*

Tancah-Tulum, Quintana Roo, Mexico. Washington, D.C.: Dumbarton Oaks.

———. 1985. The Postclassic sequence at Tancah and Tulum, Quintana Roo, Mexico. In Arlen F. Chase and Prudence M. Rice, eds., *The Lowland Maya Postclassic,* 31–49. Austin: University of Texas Press.

Miller, Mary E. 1986. *The Murals of Bonampak.* Princeton: Princeton University Press.

———. 1993. On the eve of the collapse: Maya art of the eighth century. In Jeremy A. Sabloff and John S. Henderson, eds., *Lowland Maya Civilization in the Eighth Century A.D.,* 355–413. Washington, D.C.: Dumbarton Oaks.

Millon, René. 1973. *Urbanization at Teotihuacán, Mexico.* Austin: University of Texas Press.

———. 1981. Teotihuacan: city, state, and civilization. *Handbook of Middle American Indians,* Supplement 1:198–243. Austin: University of Texas Press.

Mitchum, Beverly. 1991. Lithic artifacts from Cerros, Belize: production, consumption, and trade. In Thomas R. Hester and Harry J. Shafer, eds., *Maya Stone Tools: Selected Papers from the Second Maya Lithic Conference,* 45–53. Madison, Wisc.: Prehistory Press.

Moholy-Nagy, Hattula. 1991. The flaked chert industry of Tikal, Guatemala. In Thomas R. Hester and Harry J. Shafer, eds., *Maya Stone Tools: Selected Papers from the Second Maya Lithic Conference,* 189–202. Madison, Wisc.: Prehistory Press.

Moholy-Nagy, Hattula, Frank Asaro, and Fred Stross. 1984. Tikal obsidian: sources and typology. *American Antiquity* 49:104–17.

Moholy-Nagy, Hattula, and Fred W. Nelson. 1990. New data on sources of obsidian artifacts from Tikal, Guatemala. *Ancient Mesoamerica* 1(1):71–80.

Molina-Montes, Augusto. 1982. Archaeological buildings: restoration or misrepresentation. In Elizabeth H. Boone, ed., *Falsifications and Misreconstructions of Pre-Columbian Art,* 125–41. Washington, D.C.: Dumbarton Oaks.

Molloy, John P., and William L. Rathje. 1974. Sexploitation among the Late Classic Maya. In Norman Hammond, ed., *Mesoamerican Archaeology: New Approaches,* 431–44. Austin: University of Texas Press.

Montagu, Roberta. 1969. The Tojolabal. *Handbook of Middle American Indians* 7:226–29. Austin: University of Texas Press.

Morison, Samuel Eliot. 1971–74. *The European Discovery of America.* 2 vols. New York: Oxford University Press.

Morley, Sylvanus G. 1920. *The Inscriptions at Copán.* Washington, D.C.: Carnegie Institution of Washington, Publication 219.

———. 1935. *Guide Book to the Ruins of Quiriguá.* Washington, D.C.: Carnegie Institution of Washington.

Morris, Earl H., Jean Charlot, and Ann Axtell Morris. 1931. *The Temple of the Warriors at Chichén Itzá, Yucatán.* Washington, D.C.: Carnegie Institution of Washington, Publication 406.

Moseley, Michael E. 1975. *The Maritime Foundations of Andean Civilization.* Menlo Park, Calif.: Cummings.

Murra, John V. 1968. An Aymara kingdom in 1567. *Ethnohistory* 15:115–51.

———. 1971. El "control vertical" de un máximo de pisos ecológicos en la economía de las sociedades andinas. In *Visita de la provincia de León de Huanuco (1562),* 429–76. Huanuco: Universidad Hermilio Valdizan.

Nakamura, Seiichi, Kazuo Aoyama, and Eiji Uratsuji. 1991. *Investigaciones arqueológicas en la región de La Entrada.* 3 vols. San Pedro Sula: Instituto Hondureño de Antropología e Historia.

Nash, Manning. 1958. *Machine Age Maya: The Industrialization of a Guatemalan Community.* Washington, D.C.: American Anthropological Association, Memoir no. 87.

———. 1969. Guatemalan highlands. *Handbook of Middle American Indians* 7:30–45. Austin: University of Texas Press.

Nations, J. D., and R. B. Nigh. 1980. The evolutionary potential of Lacandon Maya sustained-yield tropical forest agriculture. *Journal of Anthropological Research* 83:28–56.

Navarrete, Carlos. 1966. *The Chiapanec History and Culture.* Provo: New World Archaeological Foundation, Papers, no. 21.

Nelson, Fred W. 1985. Summary of the results of analysis of obsidian artifacts from the Maya lowlands. *Scanning Electron Microscopy* 2:631–49.

Nelson, Fred W., et al. 1977. Preliminary studies of the

trace element composition of obsidian artifacts from northern Campeche, Mexico. *American Antiquity* 42:209–25.

Netting, Robert McC. 1977. Maya subsistence: mythologies, analogies, possibilities. In Richard E. W. Adams, ed., *The Origins of Maya Civilization*, 299–333. Albuquerque: University of New Mexico Press.

Norman, V. Garth. 1973–76. *Izapa Sculpture*. 2 pts. Provo: New World Archaeological Foundation, Papers, no. 30.

Ochoa, L., and E. Vargas Pacheco. 1985. Informe del reconocimiento arqueológico realizado en la cuenca del río Candelaria, Campeche. *Estudios de Cultura Maya* 16:325–76.

———. 1987. Xicalango, puerto Chontal de intercambio: mito y realidad. *Anales de Antropología* 24:95–114.

Orellana, Sandra L. 1993. Estrategias k'iche's de conquista en la costa sur de Guatemala, 1375–1524. *Mesoamérica* 25:27–38.

Pagden, A. R., trans. and ed., 1971. *Hernán Cortés: Letters from Mexico*. New York: Grossman.

———, trans. 1975. *The Maya: Diego de Landa's Account of the Affairs of Yucatan*. Chicago: J. Philip O'Hara.

Parsons, Jeffrey R., and Mary H. Parsons. 1990. *Maguey Utilization in Highland Central Mexico: An Archaeological Ethnography*. Ann Arbor: University of Michigan, Museum of Anthropology, Anthropological Papers, no. 82.

Parsons, Lee A. 1973. Iconographic notes on a new Izapan stela from Abaj Takalik, Guatemala. In *Atti del XL Congresso Internazionale degli Americanisti*, 203–12. Genoa: Casa Editrice Tilgher.

———. 1978. The peripheral coastal lowlands and the Middle Classic period. In Esther Pasztory, ed., *Middle Classic Mesoamerica: A.D. 400–700*, 25–34. New York: Columbia University Press.

———. 1986. *The Origins of Maya Art: Monumental Stone Sculpture of Kaminaljuyú, Guatemala, and the Southern Pacific Coast*. Washington, D.C.: Dumbarton Oaks, Studies in Pre-Columbian Art and Archaeology, no. 28.

Pasztory, Esther. 1974. *The Iconography of the Teotihuacan Tlaloc*. Washington, D.C.: Dumbarton Oaks, Studies in Pre-Columbian Art and Archaeology, no. 15.

———. 1993. Teotihuacan unmasked: a view through art. In Kathleen Berrin and Esther Pasztory, eds., *Teotihuacan: Art from the City of the Gods*, 44–63. New York: Thames and Hudson.

Pendergast, David M. 1969. *Altun Ha: A Guidebook to the Ancient Maya Ruins*. Belmopan: Government of British Honduras.

———. 1971. Evidence of early Teotihuacán–lowland Maya contact at Altun Ha. *American Antiquity* 36:455–60.

———. 1979–90. *Excavations at Altun Ha, Belize, 1964–1970*. 3 vols. Toronto: Royal Ontario Museum.

———. 1981. Lamanai, Belize: summary of excavation results, 1974–1980. *Journal of Field Archaeology* 8:29–53.

———. 1985. Lamanai, Belize: an updated view. In Arlen F. Chase and Prudence M. Rice, eds., *The Lowland Maya Postclassic*, 91–103. Austin: University of Texas Press.

———. 1986. Stability through change: Lamanai, Belize, from the ninth to the seventeenth century. In Jeremy A. Sabloff and E. Wyllys Andrews V, eds., *Late Lowland Maya Civilization: Classic to Postclassic*, 223–49. Albuquerque: University of New Mexico Press.

———. 1990. Up from the dust: the central lowlands Postclassic as seen from Lamanai and Marco González. In Flora S. Clancy and Peter D. Harrison, eds., *Vision and Revision in Maya Studies*, 169–77. Albuquerque: University of New Mexico Press.

Pendergast, David M., and Grant D. Jones. 1992. Poor beds of sticks and rings of pure gold. *Ancient Mesoamerica* 3(2):281–90.

Pendergast, David M., Grant D. Jones, and Elizabeth Graham. 1993. Locating Maya lowlands Spanish colonial towns: a case study from Belize. *Latin American Antiquity* 4(1)59–73.

Piña Chan, Román, and R. Pavón Abreu. 1961. ¿Fueron las ruinas El Tigre, Itzamkanac? *El México Antiguo* 9:473–91.

Pincemín, S. 1989. Patrón de asentamientos en la cuenca del río Candelaria, Campeche: estudio preliminar. In Mercedes de la Garza et al., eds., *Memorias del Segundo Coloquio Internacional de Mayistas*, 531–54. Mexico City: Universidad Nacional Autónoma de México, Centro de Estudios Mayas.

Pohl, Mary DeLand. 1990. *Ancient Maya Wetland Agriculture: Excavations on Albion Island, Northern Belize.* Boulder: Westview Press.

Pollock, Harry E. D. 1980. *The Puuc: An Architectural Survey of the Hill Country of Yucatan and Northern Campeche, Mexico.* Cambridge: Harvard University, Peabody Museum Memoirs, vol. 19.

Pollock, Harry E. D., Tatiana Proskouriakoff, and A. Ledyard Smith. 1962. *Mayapán, Yucatán, Mexico.* Washington, D.C.: Carnegie Institution of Washington, Publication 619.

Pope, Kevin O., and Bruce Dahlin. 1989. Ancient Maya wetland agriculture: new insights from ecological and remote sensing research. *Journal of Field Archaeology* 16:87–106.

Potter, Daniel R. 1991. A descriptive taxonomy of Middle Preclassic chert tools at Colha, Belize. In Thomas R. Hester and Harry J. Shafer, eds., *Maya Stone Tools: Selected Papers from the Second Maya Lithic Conference,* 21–29. Madison, Wisc.: Prehistory Press.

———. 1993. Analytical approaches to Late Classic Maya lithic industries. In Jeremy A. Sabloff and John S. Henderson, eds., *Lowland Maya Civilization in the Eighth Century A.D.*, 243–72. Washington, D.C.: Dumbarton Oaks.

Potter, Daniel R., and Eleanor M. King. 1995. A heterarchical approach to lowland Maya socioeconomies. In Robert M. Ehrenreich, Carole L. Crumley, and Janet E. Levy, eds., *Heterarchy and the Analysis of Complex Societies.* Arlington, Va.: American Anthropological Association, Archaeological Papers, no. 6.

Potter, David F. 1977. *Maya Architecture of the Central Yucatan Peninsula, Mexico.* New Orleans: Tulane University, Middle American Research Institute, Publication 44.

Pring, Duncan C. 1977a. The dating of Teotihuacán contact at Altún Ha: the new evidence. *American Antiquity* 42:626–28.

———. 1977b. Influence or intrusion? The "Protoclassic" in the Maya lowlands. In Norman Hammond, ed., *Social Process in Maya Prehistory: Studies in Honour of Sir Eric Thompson,* 135–65. New York: Academic Press.

Proskouriakoff, Tatiana. 1950. *A Study of Classic Maya Sculpture.* Washington, D.C.: Carnegie Institution of Washington, Publication 593.

———. 1955. The death of a civilization. *Scientific American* 192(5):82–88.

———. 1960. Historical implications of a pattern of dates at Piedras Negras, Guatemala. *American Antiquity* 25:454–75.

———. 1961a. The lords of the Maya realm. *Expedition* 4(1):14–21.

———. 1961b. Portraits of women in Maya art. In Samuel K. Lothrop et al., eds., *Essays in Pre-Columbian Art and Archaeology,* 81–99. Cambridge: Harvard University Press.

———. 1963a. *An Album of Maya Architecture.* Norman: University of Oklahoma Press.

———. 1963b. Historical data in the inscriptions of Yaxchilán, pt. 1. *Estudios de Cultura Maya* 3:149–67.

———. 1964. Historical data in the inscriptions of Yaxchilán, pt. 2. *Estudios de Cultura Maya* 4:177–201.

———. 1965. Sculpture and major arts of the Maya lowlands. *Handbook of Middle American Indians* 2:469–97. Austin: University of Texas Press.

———. 1974. *Jades from the Cenote of Sacrifice, Chichen Itza, Mexico.* Cambridge: Harvard University, Peabody Museum Memoirs, vol. 10, no. 1.

———. 1993. *Maya History.* Edited by Rosemary A. Joyce. Austin: University of Texas Press.

Puleston, Dennis E. 1971. An experimental approach to the function of Classic Maya chultuns. *American Antiquity* 36:322–35.

———. 1974. Intersite areas in the vicinity of Tikal and Uaxactún. In Norman Hammond, ed., *Mesoamerican Archaeology: New Approaches,* 303–11. Austin: University of Texas Press.

———. 1977. The art and archaeology of hydraulic agriculture in the Maya lowlands. In Norman Hammond, ed., *Social Process in Maya Prehistory: Essays in Honour of Sir Eric Thompson,* 449–67. New York: Academic Press.

———. 1979. An epistemological pathology and the collapse; or, Why the Maya kept the Short Count. In Norman Hammond and Gordon R. Willey, eds., *Maya Archaeology and Ethnohistory,* 63–71. Austin: University of Texas Press.

Puleston, Dennis E., and Olga S. Puleston. 1971. An ecological approach to the origins of Maya civilization. *Archaeology* 24:330–37.

Quirarte, Jacinto. 1976. The relationship of Izapan-style art to Olmec and Maya art: a review. In H. B. Nicholson, ed., *Origins of Religious Art and Iconography in Preclassic Mesoamerica*, 73–86. Los Angeles: UCLA Latin American Center.

———. 1977. Early art styles of Mesoamerica and Early Classic Maya art. In Richard E. W. Adams, ed., *The Origins of Maya Civilization*, 249–83. Albuquerque: University of New Mexico Press.

———. 1982. The Santa Rita murals: a review. In Jennifer S. H. Brown and E. Wyllys Andrews V, eds., *Aspects of the Mixteca-Puebla Style and Mixtec and Central American Culture in Southern Mesoamerica*, 43–59. New Orleans: Tulane University, Middle American Research Institute, Occasional Paper no. 4.

Rands, Robert L. 1969. *Mayan Ecology and Trade: 1967–1968*. Carbondale: Southern Illinois University, University Museum Research Records, Mesoamerican Studies, no. 2.

———. 1973. The Classic Maya collapse: Usumacinta zone and the northwestern periphery. In T. Patrick Culbert, ed., *The Classic Maya Collapse*, 165–205. Albuquerque: University of New Mexico Press.

———. 1974. A chronological framework for Palenque. In Merle Greene Robertson, ed., *Primera Mesa Redonda de Palenque, Part I*, 35–9. Pebble Beach, Calif.: Robert Louis Stevenson School.

———. 1977. The rise of Classic Maya civilization in the northwestern zone: isolation and integration. In Richard E. W. Adams, ed., *The Origins of Maya Civilization*, 159–80. Albuquerque: University of New Mexico Press.

Rands, Robert L., and Ronald L. Bishop. 1980. Resource procurement zones and patterns of ceramic exchange in the Palenque region, Mexico. In Robert E. Fry, ed., *Models and Methods in Regional Exchange*, Washington, D.C.: Society for American Archaeology, Papers, no. 1.

Rands, Robert L., and Robert E. Smith. 1965. Pottery of the Guatemalan highlands. *Handbook of Middle American Indians* 2:95–145. Austin: University of Texas Press.

Rathje, William L. 1971. The origin and development of lowland Classic Maya civilization. *American Antiquity* 36:275–85.

———. 1977. The Tikal connection. In Richard E. W. Adams, ed., *The Origins of Maya Civilization*, 373–82. Albuquerque: University of New Mexico Press.

Recinos, Adrian, and Delia Goetz, trans. 1953. *The Annals of the Cakchiquels*. Norman: University of Oklahoma Press.

Redfield, Robert. 1941. *The Folk Culture of Yucatan*. Chicago: University of Chicago Press.

———. 1950. *A Village That Chose Progress: Chan Kom Revisited*. Chicago: University of Chicago Press.

Redfield, Robert, and Alfonso Villa Rojas. 1934. *Chan Kom: A Maya Village*. Washington, D.C.: Carnegie Institution of Washington, Publication 448.

Reents-Budet, Dorie. 1994. *Painting the Maya Universe: Royal Ceramics of the Classic Period*. Durham: Duke University Press.

Reina, Ruben E. 1966. *The Law of the Saints*. New York: Bobbs-Merrill.

———. 1969. Eastern Guatemalan highlands: the Pokomames and Chorti. *Handbook of Middle American Indians* 7:101–32. Austin: University of Texas Press.

Reina, Ruben E., and Robert M. Hill. 1980. Lowland Maya subsistence: notes from ethnohistory and ethnography. *American Antiquity* 45:74–9.

Rice, Don S. 1993. Eighth-century physical geography, environment, and natural resources in the Maya lowlands. In Jeremy A. Sabloff and John S. Henderson, eds., *Lowland Maya Civilization in the Eighth Century A.D.*, 11–63. Washington, D.C.: Dumbarton Oaks.

Rice, Don S., Prudence M. Rice, and Grant D. Jones. 1993. Geografía política del Petén central en el siglo XVII: la arqueología de las capitales mayas. *Mesoamérica* 26:281–318.

Rice, Prudence M. 1984. Obsidian procurement in the central Peten lakes region, Guatemala. *Journal of Field Archaeology* 11:181–94.

Rice Prudence M., and Don S. Rice. 1985. Topoxte, Macanche and the central Peten Postclassic. In Arlen

F. Chase and Prudence M. Rice, eds., *The Lowland Maya Postclassic*, 166–83. Austin: University of Texas Press.

Rice, Prudence M., et al. 1985. Provenience analysis of obsidians from the central Peten lakes region, Guatemala. *American Antiquity* 50:591–604.

Ricketson, Oliver G., and Edith B. Ricketson. 1937. *Uaxactún, Guatemala: Group E, 1926–1931*. Washington, D.C.: Carnegie Institution of Washington, Publication 477.

Riese, Berthold. 1986. Late Classic relationship between Copan and Quirigua: some epigraphic evidence. In Patricia A. Urban and Edward M. Schortman, eds., *The Southeast Maya Periphery*, 94–101. Austin: University of Texas Press.

———. 1992. The Copan dynasty. *Handbook of Middle American Indians*, Supplement 5:128–53. Austin: University of Texas Press.

Ringle, William M. 1990. Who was who in ninth-century Chichen Itza. *Ancient Mesoamerica* 1:233–43.

Ringle, William M., and E. Wyllys Andrews V. 1988. Formative residences at Komchen, Yucatan, Mexico. In Richard R. Wilk and Wendy Ashmore, eds., *Household and Community in the Mesoamerican Past*, 171–97. Albuquerque: University of New Mexico Press.

———. 1990. The demography of Komchen, an early Maya town in northern Yucatan. In T. Patrick Culbert and Don S. Rice, eds., *Precolumbian Population History in the Maya Lowlands*, 215–43. Albuquerque: University of New Mexico Press.

Rivera Dorado, Miguel. 1989. Tres temporadas en Oxkintok, Yucatán. *Revista Española de Antropología Americana* 19:49–89.

Rivera Dorado, Miguel, et al. 1987–89. *Oxkintok*. 2 vols. Madrid: Misión Arqueológica de España en México.

Robertson, Merle Greene, ed. 1974. *Primera Mesa Redonda de Palenque.* Pebble Beach, Calif.: Robert Louis Stevenson School.

———. 1976. *The Art, Iconography and Dynastic History of Palenque, Part III.* Pebble Beach, Calif.: Robert Louis Stevenson School.

———. 1980. *Third Palenque Round Table, 1978*. Austin: University of Texas Press.

Robertson, Merle Greene, and Elizabeth P. Benson, eds. 1985. *Fourth Palenque Round Table, 1980*. San Francisco: Pre-Columbian Art Research Institute.

Robertson, Merle Greene, and Virginia M. Fields, eds. 1985. *Fifth Palenque Round Table, 1983*. San Francisco: Pre-Columbian Art Research Institute.

———. 1991. *Sixth Palenque Round Table, 1986*. Norman: University of Oklahoma Press.

———. 1994. *Seventh Palenque Round Table, 1989*. San Francisco: Pre-Columbian Art Research Institute.

Robertson, Merle Greene, and Donnan Call Jeffers, eds. 1979. *Tercera Mesa Redonda de Palenque.* Monterey, Calif.: Pre-Columbian Art Research Center.

Robertson, Merle Greene, Martha J. Macri, and Jan McHargue, eds. 1996. *Eighth Palenque Round Table, 1993*. San Francisco: Pre-Columbian Art Research Institute.

Robertson, Merle Greene, Robert L. Rands, and John A. Graham. 1972. *Maya Sculpture from the Southern Lowlands, the Highlands and the Pacific Piedmont.* Berkeley: Lederer, Street, and Zeus.

Robertson, Robin A., and David A. Freidel, eds. 1986. *Archaeology at Cerros, Belize, Central America*, vol. 1: *An Interim Report.* Dallas: Southern Methodist University.

Robinson, Eugenia J. 1989. The Prehistoric Communities of the Sula Valley, Honduras: Regional Interaction in the Southeast Mesoamerican Frontier. Ph.D. dissertation, Tulane University.

———. 1994. Chitak Tzak: un centro regional Postclásico Tardío de los Mayas Kaqchikel. In Juan Pedro Laporte and Héctor L. Escobedo, eds., *VII Simposio de Investigaciones Arqueológicas en Guatemala, 1993*, 175–84. Guatemala City: Instituto de Antropología e Historia/Asociación Tikal.

———, ed. 1987. *Interaction on the Southeast Mesoamerican Frontier: Prehistoric and Historic Honduras and El Salvador.* Oxford: British Archaeological Reports, International Series, no. 327.

Robles Castellanos, Fernando, and Anthony P. Andrews. 1986. A review and synthesis of recent Postclassic archeology in northern Yucatan. In Jeremy A.

Sabloff and E. Wyllys Andrews V, eds., *Late Lowland Maya Civilization: Classic to Postclassic*, 53–98. Albuquerque: University of New Mexico Press.

Roemer, Erwin. 1991. A Late Classic workshop at Colha, Belize. In Thomas R. Hester and Harry J. Shafer, eds., *Maya Stone Tools: Selected Papers from the Second Maya Lithic Conference*, 55–66. Madison, Wisc.: Prehistory Press.

Rojas Rabiela, Teresa, ed. 1995. *Pasado y futuro de las chinampas.* Mexico: Centro de Investigaciones y Estudios en Antropología Social.

Romano Pacheco, Arturo, 1989. El entierro del Templo de las Inscripciones en Palenque. In Mercedes de la Garza et al., eds., *Memorias del Segundo Coloquio Internacional de Mayistas*, 1413–74. Mexico City: Universidad Nacional Autónoma de México.

Roys, Ralph L. 1957. *The Political Geography of the Yucatan Maya.* Washington, D.C.: Carnegie Institution of Washington, Publication 613.

———. 1965. Lowland Maya native society at Spanish contact. *Handbook of Middle American Indians* 3:659–78. Austin: University of Texas Press.

———. 1972. *The Indian Background of Colonial Yucatan.* New ed. Norman: University of Oklahoma Press.

———, trans. and ed. 1967. *The Book of Chilam Balam of Chumayel.* New ed. Norman: University of Oklahoma Press.

Roys, Ralph L., France V. Scholes, and E. B. Adams. 1940. *Report and Census of the Indians of Cozumel, 1570.* Washington, D.C.: Carnegie Institution of Washington, Contributions to American Anthropology and History, no. 30.

Rue, David J. 1987. Early agriculture and Early Postclassic occupation in western Honduras. *Nature* 326(6110):285–86.

Ruppert, Karl. 1935. *The Caracol at Chichén Itzá, Yucatán, Mexico.* Washington, D.C.: Carnegie Institution of Washington, Publication 454.

———. 1943. *The Mercado, Chichén Itzá, Yucatán.* Washington, D.C.: Carnegie Institution of Washington, Contributions to American Anthropology and History, no. 43.

Ruz Lhuiller, Alberto. 1952–58. Exploraciones arqueológicas en Palenque: 1949–1956. *Instituto nacional de Antropología e Historia, Anales* 4(32):49–60; 5(33):25–65; 6(34):79–110; and 10(39):62–299.

———. 1973. *El Templo de las Inscripciones.* Mexico City: Instituto Nacional de Antropología e Historia.

Sabloff, Jeremy A. 1973. Continuity and disruption during Terminal Late Classic times at Seibal: ceramic and other evidence. In T. Patrick Culbert, ed., *The Classic Maya Collapse*, 107–31. Albuquerque: University of New Mexico Press.

———. 1975. *Excavations at Seibal, Department of Peten, Guatemala: Ceramics.* Cambridge: Harvard University, Peabody Museum Memoirs, vol. 13, no. 2.

———. 1990. *The New Archaeology and the Ancient Maya.* New York: W. H. Freeman.

———. 1995. Drought and decline. *Nature* 375(6530):357.

Sabloff, Jeremy A., and David A. Freidel. 1975. A model of a pre-Columbian trading center. In Jeremy A. Sabloff and C. C. Lamberg-Karlovsky, eds., *Ancient Civilization and Trade*, 369–408. Albuquerque: University of New Mexico Press.

Sabloff, Jeremy A., and William L. Rathje. 1975a. The rise of a Maya merchant class. *Scientific American* 223(4):72–82.

———. 1975b. *A Study of Changing Pre-Columbian Commercial Systems: The 1972–1973 Seasons at Cozumel, Mexico.* Harvard University, Peabody Museum Monographs, no. 3.

Sabloff, Jeremy A., and Gair Tourtellot. 1991. *The Ancient Maya City of Sayil: The Mapping of a Puuc Region Center.* New Orleans: Tulane University, Middle American Research Institute, Publication 60.

Sabloff, Jeremy A., et al. 1974. Trade and power in Postclassic Yucatan: initial observations. In Norman Hammond, ed., *Mesoamerican Archaeology: New Approaches*, 397–416. Austin: University of Texas Press.

———. 1982. *Excavations at Seibal, Department of Peten, Guatemala: Analyses of Fine Paste Ceramics.* Cambridge: Harvard University, Peabody Museum Memoirs, vol. 15, no. 2.

Sale, Kirkpatrick. 1990. *The Conquest of Paradise: Christopher Columbus and the Columbian Legacy.* New York: Knopf.

Sanders, William T. 1960. *Prehistoric Ceramics and Settlement Patterns in Quintana Roo, Mexico.* Washington, D.C.: Carnegie Institution of Washington, Contributions to American Anthropology and History, no. 60.

———. 1973. The cultural ecology of the lowland Maya: a reevaluation. In T. Patrick Culbert, ed., *The Classic Maya Collapse,* 325–65. Albuquerque: University of New Mexico Press.

———. 1977. Environmental heterogeneity and the evolution of lowland Maya civilization. In Richard E. W. Adams, ed., *The Origins of Maya Civilization,* 287–97. Albuquerque: University of New Mexico Press.

———. 1978. Ethnographic analogy and the Teotihuacán horizon style. In Esther Pasztory, ed., *Middle Classic Mesoamerica: A.D. 400–700,* 35–44. New York: Columbia University Press.

———, ed. 1986–90. *Excavationes en el área urbana de Copán.* 3 vols. Tegucigalpa: Instituto Hondureño de Antropología e Historia.

Sanders, William T., and Joseph W. Michels. 1969. *The Pennsylvania State University Kaminaljuyú Project—1968 Season,* pt. 1: *The Excavations.* State College: Pennsylvania State University, Occasional Papers in Anthropology, no. 2.

———. 1977. *Teotihuacán and Kaminaljuyá: A Study in Prehistoric Culture Contact.* State College: Pennsylvania State University Press.

Sanders, William T., and Barbara J. Price. 1968: *Mesoamerica: The Evolution of a Civilization.* New York: Random House.

Satterthwaite, Linton. 1944–54. *Piedras Negras Archaeology: Architecture.* 3 vols. Philadelphia: University of Pennsylvania, University Museum Monograph.

———. 1965. Calendrics of the Maya lowlands. *Handbook of Middle American Indians* 3:603–31. Austin: University of Texas Press.

Sauer, Carl O. 1966. *The Early Spanish Main.* Berkeley: University of California Press.

———. 1968. *The Northern Mists.* Berkeley: University of California Press.

Scarborough, Vernon L. 1986. Drainage canal and raised field excavations. In Robin A. Robertson and David A. Freidel, eds., *Archaeology at Cerros, Belize, Central America,* vol. 1: *An Interim Report,* 75–87. Dallas: Southern Methodist University.

———. 1991. *Archaeology at Cerros Belize, Central America,* vol. 3: *The Settlement System in a Late Preclassic Maya Community.* Dallas: Southern Methodist University Press.

Scarborough, Vernon L., Robert P. Connolly, and Steven P. Ross. 1994. The pre-Hispanic Maya reservoir system at Kinal, Peten, Guatemala. *Ancient Mesoamerica* 5(1):97–106.

Scarborough, Vernon L., and G. G. Gallopin. 1991. A water storage adaptation in the Maya lowlands. *Science* 261: 658–62.

Scarborough, Vernon L., and David R. Wilcox, eds. 1991. *The Mesoamerican Ball Game.* Tucson: University of Arizona Press.

Scarborough, Vernon L., et al. 1995. Water and land at the ancient Maya community of La Milpa. *Latin American Antiquity* 6(2):98–119.

Schele, Linda. 1976. Accession iconography of Chan-Bahlum in the Group of the Cross at Palenque. In Merle Greene Robertson, ed., *The Art, Iconography and Dynastic History of Palenque, Part III,* 9–34. Pebble Beach, Calif.: Robert Louis Stevenson School.

———. 1977. Palenque: the house of the dying sun. In Anthony F. Aveni, ed., *Native American Astronomy,* 42–56. Austin: University of Texas Press.

———. 1979. Genealogical documentation on the tri-figure panels at Palenque. In Merle Greene Robertson and Donnan Call Jeffers, eds., *Tercera Mesa Redonda de Palenque,* 41–70. Monterey, Calif.: Pre-Columbian Art Research Center.

———. 1982. *Maya Glyphs: The Verbs.* Austin: University of Texas Press.

———. 1986. The founders of lineages at Copán and other Maya sites. *Copán Notes,* no. 8.

———. 1991. An epigraphic history of the western

Maya region. In T. Patrick Culbert, ed., *Classic Maya Political History: Hieroglyphic and Archaeological Evidence*, 72–101. Cambridge: Cambridge University Press.

———. 1992a. The founders of lineages at Copan and other Maya sites. *Ancient Mesoamerica* 3(1):135–44.

———. 1992b. A new look at the dynastic history of Palenque. *Handbook of Middle American Indians*, Supplement 5:82–109. Austin: University of Texas Press.

Schele, Linda, and David A. Freidel. 1990. *A Forest of Kings: The Untold Story of the Ancient Maya*. New York: Morrow.

Schele, Linda, and Peter Mathews. 1991. Royal visits and other intersite relationships among the Classic Maya. In T. Patrick Culbert, ed., *Classic Maya Political History: Hieroglyphic and Archaeological Evidence*, 226–52. Cambridge: Cambridge University Press.

Schele, Linda, and Mary E. Miller. 1986. *The Blood of Kings: Dynasty and Ritual in Maya Art*. Fort Worth: Kimbell Art Museum.

Schellhas, Paul. 1904. *Representation of Deities of the Maya Manuscripts*. Cambridge: Harvard University, Peabody Museum Papers, vol. 4, no. 1.

Scholes, France V., and Ralph L. Roys. 1968. *The Maya Chontal Indians of Acalán-Tixchel: A Contribution to the History and Ethnography of the Yucatan Peninsula*. New ed. Norman: University of Oklahoma Press.

Schortman, Edward M., and Seiichi Nakamura. 1991. A crisis of identity and interaction: Late Classic competition and interaction on the southeast Maya periphery. *Latin American Antiquity* 2(4):311–36.

Schortman, Edward M., and Patricia A. Urban, eds., 1983. *Quirigua Reports*. Vol. 2. Philadelphia: University of Pennsylvania, University Museum.

Schortman, Edward M., et al. 1986. Interregional interaction in the southeast Maya periphery: the Santa Barbara Archaeological Project, 1983–1984 seasons. *Journal of Field Archaeology* 13:259–72.

Schultz, Kevan C., Jason J. Gonzalez, and Norman Hammond. 1994. Classic Maya ball courts at La Milpa, Belize. *Ancient Mesoamerica* 5(1):45–53.

Sedat, David W., and Robert J. Sharer. 1972. Archaeological investigations in the northern Maya highlands: new data on the Maya Preclassic. *Contributions* 16:23–35. Berkeley: University of California, Archaeological Research Facility.

Shafer, Harry J. 1991. Late Preclassic formal stone tool production at Colha, Belize. In Thomas R. Hester and Harry J. Shafer, eds., *Maya Stone Tools: Selected Papers from the Second Maya Lithic Conference*, 31–44. Madison, Wisc.: Prehistory Press.

Sharer, Robert J. 1974. The prehistory of the southeastern Maya periphery. *Current Anthropology* 15:165–87.

———. 1977. The Maya collapse revisited: internal and external perspectives. In Norman Hammond, ed., *Social Process in Maya Prehistory: Studies in Honour of Sir Eric Thompson*, 532–52. New York: Academic Press.

———. 1978a. Archaeology and history at Quiriguá, Guatemala. *Journal of Field Archaeology* 5:51–70.

———. 1978b. *The Prehistory of Chalchuapa, El Salvador*. 3 vols. Philadelphia: University of Pennsylvania Press.

———. 1985. Terminal events in the southeastern lowlands: a view from Quirigua. In Arlen F. Chase and Prudence M. Rice, eds., *The Lowland Maya Postclassic*, 245–53. Austin: University of Texas Press.

———. 1988. *Quirigua: A Classic Maya Center and Its Sculptures*. Durham: Carolina Academic Press.

———. 1991. Diversity and continuity in Maya civilization: Quirigua as a case study. In T. Patrick Culbert, ed., *Classic Maya Political History: Hieroglyphic and Archaeological Evidence*, 180–98. Cambridge: Cambridge University Press.

———. 1992. The Preclassic origin of lowland Maya states. In Elin C. Danien and Robert J. Sharer, eds., *New Theories on the Ancient Maya*, 131–36. Philadelphia: University of Pennsylvania, University Museum.

———. 1993. The social organization of the Late Classic Maya: problems of definition and approaches. In Jeremy A. Sabloff and John S. Henderson, eds., *Lowland Maya Civilization in the Eighth Century A.D.*, 11–63. Washington, D.C.: Dumbarton Oaks.

Sharer, Robert J., and James C. Gifford. 1970. Preclassic ceramics from Chalchuapa, El Salvador, and their relationships with the Maya lowlands. *American Antiquity* 35:441–62.

Sharer, Robert J., and David C. Grove, eds. 1989. *Regional Perspectives on the Olmec.* Cambridge: Cambridge University Press.

Sharer, Robert J., and David W. Sedat. 1973. Monument 1, El Portón, Guatemala, and the development of Maya calendrical and writing systems. *Contributions* 18:177–94. Berkeley: University of California, Archaeological Research Facility.

———. 1987. *Archaeological Investigations in the Northern Maya Highlands, Guatemala: Interaction and the Development of Maya Civilization.* Philadelphia: University of Pennsylvania, University Museum Monographs, no. 59.

Sheehy, James J. 1991. Structure and change in a Late Classic Maya domestic group at Copan, Honduras. *Ancient Mesoamerica* 2(1):1–19.

Sheets, Payson D. 1975. A reassessment of the precolumbian obsidian industry of El Chayal, Guatemala. *American Antiquity* 40:98–103.

———. 1979. Maya recovery from volcanic disasters: Ilopango and Cerén. *Archaeology* 32(3):32–42.

———. 1991. Flaked lithics from the cenote of sacrifice, Chichén Itzá, Yucatan. In Thomas R. Hester and Harry J. Shafer, eds., *Maya Stone Tools: Selected Papers from the Second Maya Lithic Conference,* 163–87. Madison, Wisc.: Prehistory Press.

———. 1992. *The Ceren Site: A Prehistoric Village Buried by Volcanic Ash in Central America.* New York: Harcourt Brace Jovanovich.

———, ed. 1983. *Archaeology and Volcanism in Central America: The Zapotitlan Valley of El Salvador.* Austin: University of Texas Press.

Sheets, Payson D., et al. 1990. Household archaeology at Cerén, El Salvador. *Ancient Mesoamerica* 1(1):81–90.

Shepard, Anna O. 1948. *Plumbate: A Mesoamerican Trade Ware.* Washington, D.C.: Carnegie Institution of Washington, Publication 573.

Shook, Edwin M., and Alfred V. Kidder. 1952. *Mound E-III-3, Kaminaljuyu, Guatemala.* Washington, D.C.: Carnegie Institution of Washington, Contributions to American Anthropology and History, no. 53.

———. 1961. The painted tomb at Tikal. *Expedition* 4(1):2–7.

Shook, Edwin M., et al. 1958. *Tikal Reports,* nos. 1–4. Philadelphia: University of Pennsylvania, University Museum.

Sidrys, Raymond V. 1976. Classic Maya obsidian trade. *American Antiquity* 41:449–64.

Sdirys, Raymond V., John Andresen, and Derek Marcucci. 1975. Obsidian sources in the Maya area. *Journal of New World Archaeology* 5(1):1–13.

Siemens, Alfred H., and Dennis E. Puleston. 1972. Ridged fields and associated features in southern Campeche: new perspectives on the lowland Maya. *American Antiquity* 37:228–39.

Sierra Sosa, Thelma Noemí. 1994. *Contribución al estudio de los asentamientos de San Gervasio, Isla de Cozumel.* Mexico City: Instituto Nacional de Antropología e Historia.

Sievert, April K. 1990. Postclassic Maya ritual behavior: microwear analysis of stone tools from ceremonial contexts. In B. Gräslund et al., eds., *The Interpretative Possibilities of Microwear Studies,* 147–57. Uppsala: Societas Archaeologica Upsaliensis.

Simmons, Scott E. 1995. Maya resistance, Maya resolve: the tools of autonomy from Tipu, Belize. *Ancient Mesoamerica* 6(2):135–46.

Simpson, Lesley Byrd, trans. and ed. 1964. *Cortés: The Life of the Conquerer by His Secretary, Francisco López de Gómara.* Berkeley: University of California Press.

Smith, A. Ledyard. 1950. *Uaxactún, Guatemala: Excavations of 1931–1937.* Washington, D.C.: Carnegie Institution of Washington, Publication 588.

———. 1972. *Excavations at Altar de Sacrificios: Architecture, Settlement, Burials, and Caches.* Cambridge: Harvard University, Peabody Museum Papers, vol. 62, no. 2.

———. 1973. *Uaxactún: A Pioneering Excavation in Guatemala.* Reading, Mass.: Addison-Wesley, Module in Anthropology no. 40.

———. 1982. *Excavations at Seibal, Department of Peten, Guatemala: Major Architecture and Caches.* Cambridge: Harvard University, Peabody Museum Memoirs, vol. 15, no. 1.

Smith, Robert E. 1955. *Ceramic Sequence at Uaxactún,*

Guatemala. New Orleans: Tulane University, Middle American Research Institute, Publication 20.

Smyth, Michael P. 1990. Maize storage among the Puuc Maya: the development of an archeological method. *Ancient Mesoamerica* 1(1):51–69.

Smyth, Michael P., and Christopher D. Dore. 1992. Large-site archeological methods at Sayil, Yucatán, Mexico. *Latin American Antiquity* 3(1):3–21.

Smyth, Michael P., et al. 1995. The origin of Puuc slate ware: new data from Sayil, Yucatan, Mexico. *Ancient Mesoamerica* 6(2):119–34.

Stannard, David E. 1992. *American Holocaust: Columbus and the Conquest of the New World.* New York: Oxford University Press.

Stark, Barbara L. 1981. The rise of sedentary life. *Handbook of Middle American Indians*, Supplement 1:345–72. Austin: University of Texas Press.

Stark, Barbara L., Alfred H. Siemens, and Dennis E. Puleston. 1976. Comments on southern Campeche Maya canals. *American Antiquity* 41:381–84.

Stephens, John Lloyd. 1841. *Incidents of Travel in Central America, Chiapas, and Yucatan.* 2 vols. Reprint 1949. New Brunswick: Rutgers University Press.

———. 1843. *Incidents of Travel in Yucatan.* 2 vols. Reprint 1963. New York: Dover.

Stern, Theodore. 1949. *The Rubber-Ball Games of the Americas.* Washington, D.C.: American Ethnological Society, Monograph no. 17.

Stevens, Rayfred L. 1964. The soils of Middle America and their relation to Indian peoples and cultures. *Handbook of Middle American Indians* 1:265–315. Austin: University of Texas Press.

Stewart, T. Dale. 1973. *The People of America.* New York: Charles Scribner's Sons.

Stone, Andrea J. 1995. *Images from the Underworld: Naj Tunich and the Tradition of Maya Cave Painting.* Austin: University of Texas Press.

Stone, Doris Z. 1941. *Archaeology of the North Coast of Honduras.* Cambridge: Harvard University, Peabody Museum Memoirs, vol. 9, no. 1.

———. 1957. *The Archaeology of Central and Southern Honduras.* Cambridge: Harvard University, Peabody Museum Papers, vol. 49, no. 3.

Stromsvik, Gustav. 1942. *Substela Caches and Stela Foundations at Copan and Quirigua.* Washington, D.C.: Carnegie Institution of Washington, Contributions to American Anthropology and History, no. 37.

Strong, William Duncan, Alfred V. Kidder, and A. J. Drexel Paul. 1938. *Preliminary Report on the Smithsonian Institution–Harvard University Archeological Expedition to Northwestern Honduras, 1936.* Washington, D.C.: Smithsonian Institution, Miscellaneous Collections, vol. 97, no. 1.

Stross, Fred H., et al. 1983. Precise characterization of Guatemalan obsidian sources and source determination of artifacts from Quirigua. *American Antiquity* 48:323–46.

Stuart, David S. 1985. *The Yaxha Emblem Glyph as "Yaxha."* Washington, D.C.: Center for Maya Research, Research Reports on Ancient Maya Writing, no. 1.

———. 1987. *Ten Phonetic Syllables.* Washington, D.C.: Center for Maya Research, Research Reports on Ancient Maya Writing, no. 14.

———. 1988. Blood symbolism in Maya iconography. In Elizabeth P. Benson and Gillette G. Griffin, eds., *Maya Iconography*, 175–221. Princeton: Princeton University Press.

———. 1992. Hieroglyphs and archaeology at Copan. *Ancient Mesoamerica* 3(1):169–84.

———. 1993. Historical inscriptions and the Maya collapse. In Jeremy A. Sabloff and John S. Henderson, eds., *Lowland Maya Civilization in the Eighth Century A.D.*, 321–54. Washington, D.C.: Dumbarton Oaks.

Stuart, David S., and Stephen D. Houston. 1994. *Classic Maya Place Names.* Washington, D.C.: Dumbarton Oaks, Studies in Pre-Columbian Art and Archaeology, no. 33.

Stuart, George E. 1975. The Maya: riddle of the glyphs. *National Geographic* 148:768–91.

Stuart, George E., et al. 1979. *Map of the Ruins of Dzibilchaltun, Yucatan, Mexico.* New Orleans: Tulane University, Middle American Research Institute, Publication 47.

Stuart, L. C. 1964. Fauna of Middle America. *Handbook of Middle American Indians* 1:316–62. Austin: University of Texas Press.

Stuiver, M., and P. J. Reimer. 1993. Extended ^{14}C database and revised CALIB radiocarbon calibration program. *Radiocarbon* 35:215–30.

Sullivan, Paul. 1989. *Unfinished Conversations: Mayas and Foreigners between Two Wars.* New York: Knopf.

Tamayo, Jorge L., and Robert C. West. 1964. The hydrography of Middle America. *Handbook of Middle American Indians* 1:84–121. Austin: University of Texas Press.

Taschek, Jennifer T. 1994. *The Artifacts of Dzibilchaltun, Yucatan, Mexico: Shell, Polished Stone, Bone, Wood, and Ceramics.* New Orleans: Tulane University, Middle American Research Institute, Publication 50.

Tate, Carolyn E. 1992. *Yaxchilán: The Design of a Maya Ceremonial City.* Austin: University of Texas Press.

Taube, Karl A. 1992. *The Major Gods of Ancient Yucatan.* Washington, D.C.: Dumbarton Oaks, Studies in Pre-Columbian Art and Archaeology, no. 32.

Tax, Sol. 1953. *Penny Capitalism: A Guatemalan Indian Economy.* Washington, D.C.: Smithsonian Institution, Institute of Social Anthropology, Publication 16.

Tax, Sol, and Robert E. Hinshaw. 1969. The Maya of the midwestern highlands. *Handbook of Middle American Indians* 7:69–100. Austin: University of Texas Press.

Tedlock, Barbara. 1992. *Time and the Highland Maya.* Albuquerque: University of New Mexico Press.

Tedlock, Dennis, trans. and ed. 1985. *Popol Vuh: The Mayan Book of the Dawn of Life.* New York: Simon and Schuster.

Thomas, Cyrus. 1904. *Mayan calendar systems, II.* Washington, D.C.: Smithsonian Institution, Bureau of American Ethnology, Twenty-second Annual Report, 1900–1901, pt. 1, pp. 197–305.

Thomas, Norman D. 1974. *The Linguistic, Geographic, and Demographic Position of the Zoque of Southern Mexico.* Provo: New World Archaeological Foundation, Papers, no. 36.

Thomas, Prentice M. 1981. *Prehistoric Maya Settlement Patterns at Becán, Campeche, Mexico.* New Orleans: Tulane University, Middle American Research Institute, Publication 45.

Thompson, Edward H. 1897. *Cave of Loltún, Yucatan.* Cambridge: Harvard University, Peabody Museum Memoirs, vol. 1, no. 2.

———. 1938. *The High Priest's Grave, Chichén Itzá, Yucatán, Mexico.* Edited by J. Eric S. Thompson. Chicago: Field Museum of Natural History, Anthropology Series, vol. 27, no. 1.

Thompson, J. Eric S. 1934. *Sky Bearers, Colors and Directions in Maya and Mexican Religion.* Washington, D.C.: Carnegie Institution of Washington, Contributions to American Anthropology and History, no. 10.

———. 1951. The Itzá of Tayasal, Petén. In *Homenaje al Dr. Alfonso Caso*, 389–400. Mexico City: Nuevo Mundo.

———. 1960. *Maya Hieroglyphic Writing: An Introduction.* New ed. Norman: University of Oklahoma Press.

———. 1965. Maya hieroglyphic writing. *Handbook of Middle American Indians* 3:632–58. Austin: University of Texas Press.

———. 1970. *Maya History and Religion.* Norman: University of Oklahoma Press.

———. 1971. Estimates of Maya population: deranging factors. *American Antiquity* 36:214–16.

———. 1974. "Canals" of the Río Candelaria basin, Campeche, Mexico. In Norman Hammond, ed., *Mesoamerican Archaeology: New Approaches*, 297–302. Austin: University of Texas Press.

———. 1994. *Maya Archaeologist.* Foreword by Norman Hammond. Norman: University of Oklahoma Press.

Thompson, J. Eric S., Harry E. D. Pollock, and Jean Charlot. 1932. *A Preliminary Study of the Ruins of Cobá, Quintana Roo, Mexico.* Washington, D.C.: Carnegie Institution of Washington, Publication 424.

Thurston, H. David 1994. *Tapado: Slash/Mulch.* Ithaca: Cornell International Institute for Food, Agriculture, and Development.

Tourtellot, Gair. 1988. *Excavations at Seibal, Department of Peten, Guatemala. Peripheral Survey and Excavations: Settlement and Community Patterns.* Cambridge: Harvard University, Peabody Museum Memoirs, vol. 16.

———. 1990. *Excavations at Seibal, Department of Peten, Guatemala. Burials: A Cultural Analysis.* Cambridge:

Harvard University, Peabody Museum Memoirs, vol. 17, no. 2.

———. 1993. A view of ancient Maya settlements in the eighth century. In Jeremy A. Sabloff and John S. Henderson, eds., *Lowland Maya Civilization in the Eighth Century A.D.*, 219–41. Washington, D.C.: Dumbarton Oaks.

Tourtellot, Gair, Amanda Clarke, and Norman Hammond. 1993. Mapping La Milpa: a Maya city in northwestern Belize. *Antiquity* 67:96–108.

Tourtellot, Gair, and Jeremy A. Sabloff. 1972. Exchange systems among the ancient Maya. *American Antiquity* 37:126–35.

Tourtellot, Gair, et al. 1989. *Archaeological Investigations at Sayil, Yucatan, Mexico. Phase II: The 1987 Field Season.* Pittsburgh: University of Pittsburgh, Anthropological Papers, no. 1.

———. 1994. More light on La Milpa: Maya settlement archaeology in northwestern Belize. *Mexicon* 16:119–24.

Tozzer, Alfred M. 1907. *A Comparative Study of the Mayas and the Lacandones.* New York: Archaeological Institute of America.

———. 1911. *A Preliminary Study of the Prehistoric Ruins of Tikal, Guatemala.* Cambridge: Harvard University, Peabody Museum Memoirs, vol. 5, no. 1.

———. 1957. *Chichén Itzá and Its Cenote of Sacrifice: A Comparative Study of Contemporaneous Maya and Toltec.* Cambridge: Harvard University, Peabody Museum Memoirs, vols. 11 and 12.

———, ed. 1941. *Landa's "Relación de las Cosas de Yucatán."* Cambridge: Harvard University, Peabody Museum Papers, vol. 18.

Trik, Helen, and Michael E. Kampen. 1983. The graffiti of Tikal. *Tikal Report* no. 33. Philadelphia: University of Pennsylvania, University Museum.

Turner II, B. L., 1974. Prehistoric intensive agriculture in the Maya lowlands. *Science* 185:118–24.

———. 1979. Prehispanic terracing in the central Maya lowlands: problems of agricultural intensification. In Norman Hammond and Gordon R. Willey, eds., *Maya Archaeology and Ethnohistory*, 103–15. Austin: University of Texas Press.

Turner II, B. L., and Peter D. Harrison. 1983. *Pulltrouser Swamp: Ancient Maya Habitat, Agriculture, and Settlement in Northern Belize.* Austin: University of Texas Press.

Turner II, B. L., and William C. Johnson. 1979. A Maya dam in the Copán valley, Honduras. *American Antiquity* 44:299–305.

Urban, Patricia A., and Edward M. Schortman. 1988. The southeastern zone viewed from the east: lower Motagua-Naco valleys. In Elizabeth Boone and Gordon R. Willey, eds., *The Southeast Classic Maya Zone*, 223–67. Washington, D.C.: Dumbarton Oaks.

———, eds. 1986. *The Southeast Maya Periphery.* Austin: University of Texas Press.

Valdés, Juan Antonio. 1989. El Grupo H de Uaxactún: evidencias de un centro de poder durante el Preclásico. In Mercedes de la Garza et al., eds., *Memorias del Segundo Coloquio Internacional de Mayistas*, 603–24. Mexico City: Universidad Nacional Autónoma de México.

Valdés, Juan Antonio, and Frederico Fahsen. 1995. The reigning dynasty of Uaxactun during the Early Classic: the rulers and the ruled. *Ancient Mesoamerica* 6(2):197–219.

Valdez, Fred. 1987. The Prehistoric Ceramics of Colha, Northern Belize. Ph.D. dissertation, Harvard University.

Velázquez Valadez, R. 1980. Recent discoveries in the caves of Loltun, Yucatan, Mexico. *Mexicon* 2:53–55.

Vergara Berdejo, Sergio, et al. 1990. *Cacaxtla: Proyecto de investigación y conservación.* Mexico City: Instituto Nacional de Antropología e Historia.

Viel, René. 1993. *Evolución de la cerámica de Copán, Honduras.* Tegucigalpa: Instituto Hondureño de Antropología e Historia.

Villa Rojas, Alfonso. 1945. *The Maya of East Central Quintana Roo.* Washington, D.C.: Carnegie Institution of Washington, Publication 559.

———. 1969a. Maya lowlands: the Chontal, Chol, and Kekchi. *Handbook of Middle American Indians* 7:230–43. Austin: University of Texas Press.

———. 1969b. The Maya of Yucatan. *Handbook of Middle American Indians* 7:244–75. Austin: University of Texas Press.

———. 1969c. The Tzeltal. *Handbook of Middle American Indians* 7:195–225. Austin: University of Texas Press.

Villagutierre Soto-Mayor, Juan de. 1983. *History of the Conquest of the Province of the Itza.* Translated by Robert D. Wood. Culver City, Calif.: Labyrinthos.

Vivó Escoto, Jorge A. 1964. Weather and climate of Mexico and Central America. *Handbook of Middle American Indians* 1:187–215. Austin: University of Texas Press.

Vogt, Evon Z. 1968. Some aspects of Zinacantan settlement patterns and ceremonial organization. In K. C. Chang, ed., *Settlement Archaeology,* 154–73. Palo Alto, Calif.: National Press Books.

———. 1969a. Chiapas highlands. *Handbook of Middle American Indians* 7:133–51. Austin: University of Texas Press.

———, ed. 1969b. *Ethnology, Part 1.* Vol. 7 of *Handbook of Middle American Indians.* Austin: University of Texas Press.

———. 1969c. *Zinacantan: A Maya Community in the Highlands of Chiapas.* Cambridge: Harvard University Press.

———. 1970. *The Zinacantecos of Mexico: A Modern Maya Way of Life.* New York: Holt, Rinehart, and Winston.

———. 1975. *Tortillas for the Gods: A Symbolic Analysis of Zinacanteco Rituals.* Cambridge: Harvard University Press.

———. 1992. Cardinal directions in Mayan and southwestern Indian cosmology. In Victor Manuel Esponda Jimeno, Sophia Pincemín Deliberos, and Mauricio Rosas Kifuri, eds., *Antropología mesoamericana: Homenaje a Alfonso Villa Rojas,* 105–27. Tuxtla Gutiérrez: Gobierno del Estado de Chiapas.

Von Hagen, Victor W. 1948. *Maya Explorer: John Lloyd Stephens and the Lost Cities of Central America and Yucatan.* Norman: University of Oklahoma Press.

———. 1950. *Frederick Catherwood, Archt.* New York: Oxford University Press.

Voorhies, Barbara. 1972. Settlement patterns in two regions of the southern Maya lowlands. *American Antiquity* 37:115–26.

———. 1973. Possible social factors in the exchange system of the prehistoric Maya. *American Antiquity* 38:486–89.

———. 1976. *The Chantuto People: An Archaic Period Society of the Chiapas Littoral, Mexico.* Provo: New World Archaeological Foundation, Papers, no. 41.

Voorhies, Barbara, George H. Michaels, and George M. Riser. 1991. Ancient shrimp fishery. *National Geographic Research and Exploration* 7(1):20–35.

Wagley, Charles. 1969. The Maya of northwestern Guatamala. *Handbook of Middle American Indians* 7:46–68. Austin: University of Texas Press.

Wagner, Elisabeth. 1995. The dates of the High Priest Grave ("Osario") inscription, Chichén Itzá, Yucatán. *Mexicon* 17:10–13.

Wagner, Philip L. 1964. Natural vegetation of Middle America. *Handbook of Middle American Indians* 1:216–64. Austin: University of Texas Press.

Wallace, Dwight T., and Robert M. Carmack. 1977. *Archaeology and Ethnohistory of the Central Quiche.* Albany: State University of New York, Institute for Mesoamerican Studies, Publication 1.

Wauchope, Robert. 1962. *Lost Tribes and Sunken Continents: Myth and Method in the Study of American Indians.* Chicago: University of Chicago Press.

Webster, David L. 1974. The fortifications of Becán, Campeche, Mexico. In *Archaeological Investigations on the Yucatan Peninsula,* 123–27. New Orleans: Tulane University, Middle American Research Institute, Publication 31.

———. 1976. *Defensive Earthworks at Becán, Campeche, Mexico: Implications for Maya Warfare.* New Orleans: Tulane University, Middle American Research Institute, Publication 41.

———. 1977. Warfare and the evolution of Maya civilization. In Richard E. W. Adams, ed., *The Origins of Maya Civilization,* 335–72. Albuquerque: University of New Mexico Press.

———. 1989. *The House of the Bacabs, Copan, Honduras.* Washington, D.C.: Dumbarton Oaks, Studies in Pre-Columbian Art and Archaeology, no. 29.

———. 1993. The study of Maya warfare: what it tells us about the Maya and what it tells us about Maya archaeology. In Jeremy A. Sabloff and John S. Henderson, eds., *Lowland Maya Civilization in the Eighth Century A.D.*, 415–44. Washington, D.C.: Dumbarton Oaks.

Webster, David, and AnnCorinne Freter. 1990a. The demography of Late Classic Copan. In T. Patrick Culbert and Don S. Rice, eds., *Precolumbian Population History in the Maya Lowlands*, 37–61. Albuquerque: University of New Mexico Press.

———. 1990b. Settlement history and the Classic collapse at Copan: a redefined chronological perspective. *Latin American Antiquity* 1(1):66–85.

Webster, David L., AnnCorinne Freter, and David Rue. 1993. The obsidian hydration dating project at Copan: a regional approach and why it works. *Latin American Antiquity* 4(4):303–24.

Webster, David L., William T. Sanders, and Peter van Rossum. 1992. A simulation of Copan population history and its implications. *Ancient Mesoamerica* 3(1):185–97.

Weeks, John M. 1983. *Chisalin: A Late Postclassic Maya Settlement in Highland Guatemala.* Oxford: British Archaeological Reports, International Series, no. 169.

———. 1993. *Maya Civilization*. New York: Garland.

West, Robert C. 1964a. The natural regions of Middle America. *Handbook of Middle American Indians* 1:363–83. Austin: University of Texas Press.

———. 1964b. Surface configuration and associated geology of Middle America. *Handbook of Middle American Indians* 1:33–83. Austin: University of Texas Press.

Whitley, David S., and Ronald I. Dorn. 1993. New perspectives on the Clovis vs. pre-Clovis controversy. *American Antiquity* 58:626–47.

Wilk, Richard R. 1991. *Household Ecology: Economic Change and Domestic Life among the Kekchi Maya in Belize.* Tucson: University of Arizona Press.

Wilk, Richard R., and Wendy Ashmore, eds. 1988. *Household and Community in the Mesoamerican Past.* Albuquerque: University of New Mexico Press.

Wilken, Gene C. 1971. Food-producing systems available to the ancient Maya. *American Antiquity* 36:432–48.

Wilkerson, S. Jeffrey K. 1973. An archaeological sequence from Santa Luisa, Veracruz, Mexico. *Contributions* 18:37–50. Berkeley: University of California, Archaeological Research Facility.

———. 1975. Pre-agricultural village life: the Late Preceramic period in Veracruz. *Contributions* 27:111–22. Berkeley: University of California, Archaeological Research Facility.

Willey, Gordon R. 1970. Type descriptions of the ceramics of the Real Xe complex, Seibal, Petén, Guatemala. In William R. Bullard, ed., *Monographs and Papers in Maya Archaeology*, 313–55. Cambridge: Harvard University, Peabody Museum Papers, vol. 61.

———. 1971. *An Introduction to American Archaeology.* Englewood Cliffs, N.J.: Prentice-Hall.

———. 1972. *The Artifacts of Altar de Sacrificios.* Cambridge: Harvard University, Peabody Museum Papers, vol. 64, no. 1.

———. 1973a. *The Altar de Sacrificios Excavations: General Summary and Conclusions.* Cambridge: Harvard University, Peabody Museum Papers, vol. 64, no. 3.

———. 1973b. Certain aspects of the Late Classic to Postclassic periods in the Belize Valley. In T. Patrick Culbert, ed., *The Classic Maya Collapse*, 93–106. Albuquerque: University of New Mexico Press.

———. 1974. The Classic Maya hiatus: a "rehearsal" for the collapse? In Norman Hammond, ed., *Mesoamerican Archaeology: New Approaches*, 417–30. Austin: University of Texas Press.

———. 1977a. The rise of Classic Maya civilization: a Pasión Valley perspective. In Richard E. W. Adams, ed., *The Origins of Maya Civilization*, 133–57. Albuquerque: University of New Mexico Press.

———. 1977b. The rise of Maya civilization: a summary view. In Richard E. W. Adams, ed., *The Origins of Maya Civilization*, 383–423. Albuquerque: University of New Mexico Press.

———. 1978. *Excavations at Seibal, Department of Peten, Guatemala: Artifacts.* Cambridge: Harvard University, Peabody Museum Memoirs, vol. 14, no. 1.

———. 1990. *Excavations at Seibal, Department of Peten, Guatemala: General Summary and Conclusions.* Cambridge: Harvard University, Peabody Museum Memoirs, vol. 17, no. 4.

Willey, Gordon R., and William R. Bullard. 1965. Prehistoric settlement patterns in the Maya lowlands. *Handbook of Middle American Indians* 2:360–77. Austin: University of Texas Press.

Willey, Gordon R., T. Patrick Culbert, and Richard E. W. Adams. 1967. Maya lowland ceramics: a report from the 1965 Guatemala City conference. *American Antiquity* 32:289–315.

Willey, Gordon R., John B. Glass, and James C. Gifford. 1965. *Prehistoric Maya Settlements in the Belize Valley.* Cambridge: Harvard University, Peabody Museum Papers, vol. 54.

Willey, Gordon R., and Richard M. Leventhal. 1979. Prehistoric settlement at Copán. In Norman Hammond and Gordon R. Willey, eds., *Maya Archaeology and Ethnohistory,* 75–102. Austin: University of Texas Press.

Willey, Gordon R., Richard M. Leventhal, and William L. Fash. 1978. Maya settlement in the Copán Valley. *Archaeology* 31(4):32–43.

Willey, Gordon R., and Peter Mathews, eds. 1985. *A Consideration of the Early Classic Period in the Maya Lowlands.* Albany: State University of New York, Institute for Mesoamerican Studies, Publication 10.

Willey, Gordon R., and Jeremy A. Sabloff. 1993. *A History of American Archaeology.* 3d ed. San Francisco: W. H. Freeman.

Willey, Gordon R., and Demitri B. Shimkin. 1973. The Maya collapse: a summary view. In T. Patrick Culbert, ed., *The Classic Maya Collapse,* 457–501. Albuquerque: University of New Mexico Press.

Willey, Gordon R., and A. Ledyard Smith. 1969. *The Ruins of Altar de Sacrificios, Department of Petén, Guatemala: An Introduction.* Cambridge: Harvard University, Peabody Museum Papers, vol. 62, no. 1.

Willey, Gordon R., et al. 1975. *Excavations at Seibal, Department of Petén, Guatemala. Introduction: The Site and its Setting.* Cambridge: Harvard University, Peabody Museum Memoirs, vol. 13, no. 1.

———. 1994. *Ceramics and Artifacts from Excavations in the Copan Residential Zone.* Cambridge: Harvard University, Peabody Museum Papers, vol. 80.

Wisdom, Charles. 1940. *The Chorti Indians of Guatemala.* Chicago: University of Chicago Press.

Wittfogel, Karl. 1957. *Oriental Despotism: A Comparative Study of Total Power.* New Haven: Yale University Press.

———. 1972. The hydraulic approach to pre-Spanish Mesoamerica. In Frederick Johnson, ed., *The Prehistory of the Tehuacán Valley,* vol. 4: *Chronology and Irrigation,* 59–80. Austin: University of Texas Press.

Wolf, Eric R. 1959. *Sons of the Shaking Earth.* Chicago: University of Chicago Press.

Wonderley, Anthony W. 1981. Late Postclassic Excavations at Naco, Honduras. Ph.D. dissertation, Cornell University.

———. 1985. The land of Ulua: research in the Naco and Sula Valleys, Honduras. In Arlen F. Chase and Prudence M. Rice, eds., *The Lowland Maya Postclassic,* 245–69. Austin: University of Texas Press.

———. 1986a. Material symbolics in pre-Columbian households: the painted pottery of Naco, Honduras. *Journal of Anthropological Research* 42(4):497–534.

———. 1986b. Naco, Honduras: some aspects of a late pre-Columbian community on the eastern Maya frontier. In Patricia A. Urban and Edward M. Schortman, eds., 313–32. Austin: University of Texas Press.

———. 1987. Imagery in household pottery from 'La Gran Provincia de Naco.' In Eugenia J. Robinson, ed., *Interaction on the Southeast Mesoamerican Frontier: Prehistoric and Historic Honduras and El Salvador,* 304–27. Oxford: British Archaeological Reports, International Series, no. 327.

Woodbury, Richard B., and Aubrey Trik. 1953. *The Ruins of Zaculeu, Guatemala.* Richmond: William Byrd Press.

Wren, Linnea H. 1984. Chichén Itzá: the site and its people. In Clemency C. Coggins and Orrin C. Shane, eds., *Cenote of Sacrifice: Maya Treasures from the Sacred Well at Chichén Itzá,* 13–21. Austin: University of Texas Press.

Wren, Linnea H., and Peter Schmidt. 1991. Elite interaction during the Terminal Classic period: new evidence from Chichen Itza. In T. Patrick Culbert, ed., *Classic Maya Political History: Hieroglyphic and Archaeological Evidence,* 199–225. Cambridge: Cambridge University Press.

Wren, Linnea H., Peter Schmidt, and Ruth Krochock. 1989. *The Great Ball Court Stone of Chichén Itzá*. Washington, D.C.: Center for Maya Research, Research Reports on Ancient Maya Writing, no. 30.

Yoffee, Norman. 1991. Maya elite interaction: through a glass, sideways. In T. Patrick Culbert, ed., *Classic Maya Political History: Hieroglyphic and Archaeological Evidence*, 285–310. Cambridge: Cambridge University Press.

Zeitlin, Robert N. 1984. A summary report on three seasons of field investigations into the Archaic period prehistory of lowland Belize. *American Anthropologist* 86:358–69.

Zier, Christian J. 1980. A Classic-period Maya agricultural field in western El Salvador. *Journal of Field Archaeology* 7(1):65–74.

Index